NYSTCE CST
MULTI-SUBJECT 002
TEACHER CERTIFICATION EXAM

By: Sharon Wynne, M.S.

XAMonline, INC.
Boston

MW00760861

To obtain permission(s) to use the material from this work for any purpose including workshops or seminars, please submit a written request to:

XAMonline, Inc.
25 First Street, Suite 106
Cambridge, MA 02141
Toll Free 1-800-509-4128
Email: info@xamonline.com
Web: www.xamonline.com
Fax: 1-617-583-5552

Library of Congress Cataloging-in-Publication Data

Wynne, Sharon A.
    NYSTCE CST Multi-Subject 002 / Sharon A. Wynne. 3rd ed
    ISBN 978-1-60787-156-9
    1. CST Multi-Subject 002
    2. Study Guides
    3. NYSTCE
    4. Teachers' Certification & Licensure
    5. Careers

Disclaimer:

The opinions expressed in this publication are the sole works of XAMonline and were created independently from the National Education Association, Educational Testing Service, or any State Department of Education, National Evaluation Systems or other testing affiliates.

Between the time of publication and printing, state specific standards as well as testing formats and Web site information may change and therefore would not be included in part or in whole within this product. Sample test questions are developed by XAMonline and reflect content similar to that on real tests; however, they are not former test questions. XAMonline assembles content that aligns with state standards but makes no claims nor guarantees teacher candidates a passing score. Numerical scores are determined by testing companies such as NES or ETS and then are compared with individual state standards. A passing score varies from state to state.

Printed in the United States of America   œ-1

NYSTCE CST Multi-Subject 002
ISBN: 978-1-60787-156-9

Table of Contents

COMPETENCY 2
UNDERSTAND SKILLS AND STRATEGIES INVOLVED IN READING COMPREHENSION

COMPETENCY 3
UNDERSTAND AND APPLY READING SKILLS AND STRATEGIES FOR VARIOUS PURPOSES (INCLUDING INFORMATION AND UNDERSTANDING, CRITICAL ANALYSIS AND EVALUATION, LITERARY RESPONSE, AND SOCIAL INTERACTION)

COMPETENCY 4
UNDERSTAND PROCESSES FOR GENERATING, DEVELOPING, REVISING, EDITING, AND PRESENTING/PUBLISHING WRITTEN TEXTS

DOMAIN II
MATHEMATICS 101

COMPETENCY 9
UNDERSTAND FORMAL AND INFORMAL REASONING PROCESSES, INCLUDING LOGIC AND SIMPLE PROOFS, AND APPLY PROBLEM-SOLVING TECHNIQUES AND STRATEGIES IN A VARIETY OF CONTEXTS 105

COMPETENCY 10

COMPETENCY 11

COMPETENCY 12

COMPETENCY 13

DOMAIN III
SCIENCE AND TECHNOLOGY

COMPETENCY 16
UNDERSTAND AND APPLY THE PRINCIPLES AND PROCESSES OF SCIENTIFIC INQUIRY AND INVESTIGATION

COMPETENCY 17
UNDERSTAND AND APPLY CONCEPTS, PRINCIPLES, AND THEORIES PERTAINING TO THE PHYSICAL SETTING (INCLUDING EARTH SCIENCE, CHEMISTRY, AND PHYSICS)

COMPETENCY 18
UNDERSTAND AND APPLY CONCEPTS, PRINCIPLES, AND THEORIES PERTAINING TO THE LIVING ENVIRONMENT

COMPETENCY 19
APPLY KNOWLEDGE OF TECHNOLOGY AND THE PRINCIPLES OF ENGINEERING DESIGN

COMPETENCY 20
UNDERSTAND THE RELATIONSHIPS AMONG AND COMMON THEMES
THAT CONNECT MATHEMATICS, SCIENCE, AND TECHNOLOGY, AND THE
APPLICATION OF KNOWLEDGE AND SKILLS IN THESE DISCIPLINES TO

DOMAIN IV
SOCIAL STUDIES

COMPETENCY 21
UNDERSTAND MAJOR IDEAS, ERAS, THEMES, DEVELOPMENTS, AND TURNING POINTS IN THE HISTORY OF NEW YORK STATE, THE UNITED STATES, AND THE WORLD

COMPETENCY 22
UNDERSTAND GEOGRAPHIC CONCEPTS AND PHENOMENA AND ANALYZE THE INTERRELATIONSHIPS OF GEOGRAPHY, SOCIETY, AND CULTURE IN THE DEVELOPMENT OF NEW YORK STATE, THE UNITED STATES, AND THE WORLD

COMPETENCY 23
UNDERSTAND CONCEPTS AND PHENOMENA RELATED TO HUMAN
DEVELOPMENT AND INTERACTIONS

COMPETENCY 24
UNDERSTAND ECONOMIC AND POLITICAL PRINCIPLES, CONCEPTS,
AND SYSTEMS, AND RELATE THIS KNOWLEDGE TO HISTORICAL AND
CONTEMPORARY DEVELOPMENTS IN NEW YORK STATE, THE UNITED
STATES, AND THE WORLD

COMPETENCY 25

COMPETENCY 26

DOMAIN V
THE FINE ARTS

COMPETENCY 27
UNDERSTAND THE CONCEPTS, TECHNIQUES, AND MATERIALS OF THE VISUAL ARTS; ANALYZE WORKS OF VISUAL ART; AND UNDERSTAND THE CULTURAL DIMENSIONS AND CONTRIBUTIONS OF THE VISUAL ARTS

NYSTCE
CST MULTI-SUBJECT 002

SECTION 1
ABOUT XAMONLINE

XAMonline—A Specialty Teacher Certification Company

Created in 1996, XAMonline was the first company to publish study guides for state-specific teacher certification examinations. Founder Sharon Wynne found it frustrating that materials were not available for teacher certification preparation and decided to create the first single, state-specific guide. XAMonline has grown into a company of over 1,800 contributors and writers and offers over 300 titles for the entire PRAXIS series and every state examination. No matter what state you plan on teaching in, XAMonline has a unique teacher certification study guide just for you.

Putting the ONLINE in XAMonline

In the beginning, our guides were spiral-bound pamphlets. Now fifteen years later, they are in full color and available online. ONLINE features include electronic sticky notes, electronic flashcards, and much more. As a technology-driven company, we remain committed to bringing new and innovative ways of studying and learning to the teaching profession.

SMART Content is Custom Content.

Please visit *www.XAMonline.com* for information about the Intelliguide technology companion to this book. This is a free, Web-hosted platform that increases and enhances the functionality of this book. You'll be able to personalize your study guide with your own electronic sticky-notes, highlight important sections, and quiz yourself. Why get writer's cramp when there is a digital solution? By making your study tools portable, we hope to give you multiple opportunities to expand learning: study during a commute, your lunch hours, or in between other life commitments. Be sure to visit our Web site regularly to take advantage of additional features and applications as they are added.

XAMonline—Value and Innovation

We are committed to providing value and innovation. Our print-on-demand technology allows us to be the first in the market to reflect changes in test standards and user feedback as they occur. Our guides are written by experienced teachers who are experts in their fields. And our content reflects the highest standards of quality. Comprehensive practice tests with varied levels of rigor mean that your study experience will closely match the actual in-test experience.

To date, XAMonline has helped nearly 600,000 teachers pass their certification or licensing exams. Our commitment to preparation exceeds simply providing the proper material for study—it extends to helping teachers **gain mastery** of the subject matter, giving them the **tools** to become the most effective classroom leaders possible, and ushering today's students toward a **successful future**.

SECTION 2
ABOUT THIS STUDY GUIDE

Purpose of this Guide

Is there a little voice inside of you saying, "Am I ready?" Our goal is to replace that little voice and remove all doubt with a new voice that says, "I AM READY. **Bring it on!**" by offering the highest quality of teacher certification study guides.

Our PROMISE to you is that you will have:

1. The detailed content you need to prepare successfully

2. The ability to modify the content with your personalized notes and enhanced online features

3. Hundreds of sample test questions as assessment tools

4. The benefit of technology to identify your strengths and weakness

5. The tools you need to use your time most effectively

Organization of Content

After passing the battery of exams, LAST, ATS-W, ATS-P and your NY Multi-Subject Exam, you will be licensed in New York. Should you wish to teach in another U.S. state, you will see that while every test may start with overlapping general topics, each is very unique in the skills it is meant to test. Only XAMonline presents custom content that analyzes deeper than a title, a subarea, or an objective. Only XAMonline presents content and sample test assessments along with **focus statements**, the deepest-level rationale and interpretation of the skills that are unique to the New York Multi-Subject Exam.

New York Multi- Subject (002)

Each exam has its own name and number. XAMonline's guides are written to give you the content you need to know for the specific exam you are taking. You can be confident when you buy our guide that it contains the information you need to study for the specific test you are taking.

Subareas

These are the major content categories found on the exam. XAMonline's guides are written to cover all of the subareas found in the test frameworks developed for the exam.

Objectives

These are standards that are unique to the exam and represent the main sub categories of the subareas/content categories. XAMonline's guides are written to address every specific objective required to pass the exam.

Focus statements

These are examples and interpretations of the objectives. You find them in parenthesis directly following the objective. They provide detailed examples of the range, type, and level of content that appear on the test questions. **Only XAMonline's guides drill down to this level.**

How do We Compare with Our Competitors?

XAMonline—drills down to the focus statement level.
CliffsNotes and REA—organized at the objective level
Kaplan—provides only links to content
MoMedia—content not specific to the state test

Each subarea is divided into manageable sections that cover the specific skill areas. Explanations are easy-to-understand and thorough. If you are using the online resources, you'll find that every test answer contains a rejoinder so if you need a refresher or further review after taking the test, you'll know exactly to which section you must return.

How to Use This Book

Our informal polls show that most people begin studying up to eight weeks prior to the test date, so start early. Then ask yourself some questions: How much do you really know? Are you coming to the test straight from your teacher-education program or are you having to review subjects you haven't considered in ten years? Either way, take a **diagnostic or assessment test** first. Also, spend time on sample tests so that you become accustomed to the way the actual test will appear.

This guide comes with an online diagnostic test of thirty questions found online at *www.XAMonline.com*. It is a little boot camp to get you up for the task and reveal things about your compendium of knowledge in general. Although this guide is structured to follow the order of the test, you are not required to study in that order. By finding a time-management and study plan that fits your life you will be more effective. The results of your diagnostic or self-assessment test can be a guide for how to manage your time and point you toward an area that needs more attention.

After taking the diagnostic exam, fill out the **Personalized Study Plan** page at the beginning of each chapter. Review the competencies and skills covered in that chapter and check the boxes that apply to your study needs. If there are sections you already know you can skip, check the "skip it" box. If there are sections you want to study using eflashcards, check the "eflashcards" box. Taking this step will give you a study plan for each chapter.

Week	Activity
8 weeks prior to test	Take a diagnostic test found at www.XAMonline.com
7 weeks prior to test	Build your Personalized Study Plan for each chapter. Check the "skip it" box for sections you feel you are already strong in. ✗ SKIP IT ☐
6-3 weeks prior to test	For each of these 4 weeks, choose a content area to study. You don't have to go in the order of the book. It may be that you start with the content that needs the most review. Alternately, you may want to ease yourself into plan by starting with the most familiar material.
2 weeks prior to test	Take the sample test, score it, and create a review plan for the final week before the test.
1 week prior to test	Following your plan (which will likely be aligned with the areas that need the most review) go back and study the sections that align with the questions you may have gotten wrong. Then go back and study the sections related to the questions you answered correctly. If need be, create flashcards and drill yourself on any area that you makes you anxious.

SECTION 3
ABOUT THE NY MULTI-SUBJECT EXAM

General Information about the NYSTCE

The New York State Teacher Certification Examinations are **criterion referenced** and objective-based. Your answer will be compared to the standard established by New York rather than in comparison to other candidates in your field. You will also note that passing scores vary from discipline to discipline. A passing score indicates that a candidate meets the knowledge components that are important for an **initial teacher** to work in the public schools in New York. NYSTCE exams measure the knowledge of specific content areas used in public schools. The test is a way of ensuring that educators are prepared to not only teach in a particular subject area, but that they also have the necessary teaching skills to be effective.

The State of New York at its sole discretion determines whether or not you should take any particular test. The most reliable source of information regarding this is the New York Department of Education, which should have a complete list of testing centers and dates. Test dates vary by subject area and not all test dates necessarily include your particular test, so be sure to check carefully.

If you are in a teacher-education program, check with the Education Department or the Certification Officer for specific information for testing and testing time-lines. The Certification Office should have most of the information you need.

If you choose an alternative route to certification you can either rely on our Web site at *www.XAMonline.com* or on the resources provided by an alternative certi-fication program. Many states now have specific agencies devoted to alternative certification and there are some national organizations as well:

National Center for Education Information
http://www.ncei.com/Alt-Teacher-Cert.htm

National Associate for Alternative Certification
http://www.alt-teachercert.org/index.asp

Interpreting Test Results

Contrary to what you may have heard, the results of a NYSTCE test are not based on time. More accurately, you will be scored on the raw number of points you earn in relation to the raw number of points available. Each question is worth one raw point. It is likely to be to your benefit to complete as many questions as you can in the time allotted, but it will not necessarily work to your advantage if you hurry through the test.

Follow the guidelines provided by Pearson for interpreting your score. The Web site offers a sample test score sheet and clearly explains how the scores are scaled and what to expect if you have an essay portion on your test.

What's on the Test?

For the CST: Multiple Subjects (002), the test lasts for four hours and consists of approximately ninety multiple-choice questions and one constructed response assignment.

You can skip a section and move on to the next one and then come back to the skipped material so that you have more time to spend on it. At the end of the four hour session, you do have to pass in all the test material.

A breakdown on the question categories of the test is as follows:

Subarea	Approximate Number of Questions	Approximate Percentage of the test
1: English Language Arts	21	21%
II: Mathematics	18	18%
III: Science and Technology	13	13%
IV: Social Studies	15	15%
V: The Fine Arts	8	8%
VI: Health and Fitness	8	8%
VII: Family and Consumer Science and Career Development	7	7%
VIII: Foundations of Reading: Constructed Response Assignment	1	10%

This chart can be used to build a study plan. Twenty-one percent may seem like a lot of time to spend on English Language Arts, but when you consider that amounts to about 1 out of 5 multiple choice questions, it might change your perspective.

Question Types

You're probably thinking, enough already, I want to study! Indulge us a little longer while we explain that there is actually more than one type of multiple-choice question. You can thank us later after you realize how well prepared you are for your exam.

1. Complete the Statement. The name says it all. In this question type you'll be asked to choose the correct completion of a given statement. For example:

> **The Dolch Basic Sight Words consist of a relatively short list of words that children should be able to:**
>
> A. Sound out
>
> B. Know the meaning of
>
> C. Recognize on sight
>
> D. Use in a sentence

The correct answer is A. In order to check your answer, test out the statement by adding the choices to the end of it.

2. Which of the Following. One way to test your answer choice for this type of question is to replace the phrase "which of the following" with your selection. Use this example:

> **Which of the following words is one of the twelve most frequently used in children's reading texts:**
>
> A. There
>
> B. This
>
> C. The
>
> D. An

Don't look! Test your answer. _____ is one of the twelve most frequently used in children's reading texts. Did you guess C? Then you guessed correctly,

3. Roman Numeral Choices. This question type is used when there is more than one possible correct answer. For example:

> **Which of the following two arguments accurately supports the use of cooperative learning as an effective method of instruction?**
> I. Cooperative learning groups facilitate healthy competition between individuals in the group.
> II. Cooperative learning groups allow academic achievers to carry or cover for academic underachievers.
> III. Cooperative learning groups make each student in the group accountable for the success of the group.
> IV. Cooperative learning groups make it possible for students to reward other group members for achieving.
>
> A. I and II
> B. II and III
> C. I and III
> D. III and IV

Notice that the question states there are **two** possible answers. It's best to read all the possibilities first before looking at the answer choices. In this case, the correct answer is D. Notice that the question states there are two possible answers. It's best to read all the possibilities first before looking at the answer choices. In this case, the correct answer is D.

4. Negative Questions. This type of question contains words such as "not," "least," and "except." Each correct answer will be the statement that does **not** fit the situation described in the question. Such as:

> **Multicultural education is not**
> A. An idea or concept
> B. A "tack-on" to the school curriculum
> C. An educational reform movement
> D. A process

Think to yourself that the statement could be anything but the correct answer. This question form is more open to interpretation than other types, so read carefully and don't forget that you're answering a negative statement.

5. Questions That Include Graphs, Tables, or Reading Passages. As always, read the question carefully. It likely asks for a very specific answer and not a broad interpretation of the visual. Here is a simple (though not statistically accurate) example of a graph question:

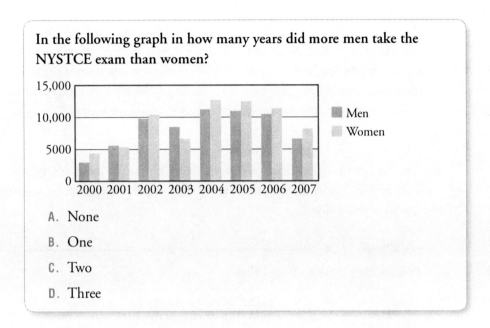

In the following graph in how many years did more men take the NYSTCE exam than women?

A. None

B. One

C. Two

D. Three

It may help you to simply circle the two years that answer the question. Make sure you've read the question thoroughly and once you've made your determination, double check your work. The correct answer is C.

SECTION 4
HELPFUL HINTS

Study Tips

1. You are what you eat. Certain foods aid the learning process by releasing natural memory enhancers called CCKs (cholecystokinin) composed of tryptophan, choline, and phenylalanine. All of these chemicals enhance the neurotransmitters associated with memory and certain foods release memory enhancing chemicals. A light meal or snacks of one of the following foods fall into this category:

- Milk
- Rice
- Eggs
- Fish
- Nuts and seeds
- Oats
- Turkey

The better the connections, the more you comprehend!

2. The pen is mightier than the sword. Learn to take great notes. A by-product of our modern culture is that we have grown accustomed to getting our information in short doses. We've subconsciously trained ourselves to assimilate information into neat little packages. Messy notes fragment the flow of information. Your notes can be much clearer with proper formatting. *The Cornell Method* is one such format. This method was popularized in *How to Study in College*, Ninth Edition, by Walter Pauk. You can benefit from the method without purchasing an additional book by simply looking up the method online. Below is a sample of how *The Cornell Method* can be adapted for use with this guide.

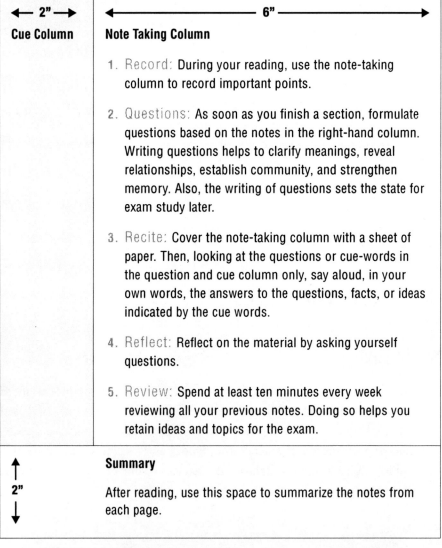

← 2" → Cue Column	←————— 6" —————→ Note Taking Column
	1. Record: During your reading, use the note-taking column to record important points.
	2. Questions: As soon as you finish a section, formulate questions based on the notes in the right-hand column. Writing questions helps to clarify meanings, reveal relationships, establish community, and strengthen memory. Also, the writing of questions sets the state for exam study later.
	3. Recite: Cover the note-taking column with a sheet of paper. Then, looking at the questions or cue-words in the question and cue column only, say aloud, in your own words, the answers to the questions, facts, or ideas indicated by the cue words.
	4. Reflect: Reflect on the material by asking yourself questions.
	5. Review: Spend at least ten minutes every week reviewing all your previous notes. Doing so helps you retain ideas and topics for the exam.
↑ 2" ↓	**Summary** After reading, use this space to summarize the notes from each page.

*Adapted from How to Study in College, Ninth Edition, by Walter Pauk, ©2008 Wadsworth

3. See the forest for the trees. In other words, get the concept before you look at the details. One way to do this is to take notes as you read, paraphrasing or summarizing in your own words. Putting the concept in terms that are comfortable and familiar may increase retention.

4. Question authority. Ask why, why, why? Pull apart written material paragraph by paragraph and don't forget the captions under the illustrations. For example, if a heading reads *Stream Erosion*, put it in the form of a question (Why do streams erode? or What is stream erosion?) then find the answer within the material. If you train your mind to think in this manner, you will learn more and prepare yourself for answering test questions.

5. Play mind games. Using your brain for reading or puzzles keeps it flexible. Even with a limited amount of time your brain can take in data (much like a computer) and store it for later use. In ten minutes you can: read two paragraphs (at least), quiz yourself with flash cards, or review notes. Even if you don't fully understand something on the first pass, your mind stores it for recall, which is why frequent reading or review increases chances of retention and comprehension.

6. Place yourself in exile and set the mood. Set aside a particular place and time to study that best suits your personal needs and biorhythms. If you're a night person, burn the midnight oil. If you're a morning person set yourself up with some coffee and get to it. Make your study time and place as free from distraction as possible and surround yourself with what you need, be it silence or music. Studies have shown that music can aid in concentration, absorption, and retrieval of information. Not all music, though. Classical music is said to work best.

7. Get pointed in the right direction. Use arrows to point to important passages or pieces of information. It's easier to read than a page full of yellow highlights. Highlighting can be used sparingly, but add an arrow to the margin to call attention to it.

8. Check your budget. You should at least review all the content material before your test, but allocate the most amount of time to the areas that need the most refreshing. It sounds obvious, but it's easy to forget. You can use the study rubric above to balance your study budget.

The proctor will write the start time where it can be seen and then, later, provide the time remaining, typically fifteen minutes before the end of the test.

Testing Tips

1. **Get smart, play dumb.** Sometimes a question is just a question. No one is out to trick you, so don't assume that the test writer is looking for something other than what was asked. Stick to the question as written and don't overanalyze.

2. **Do a double take.** Read test questions and answer choices at least twice because it's easy to miss something, to transpose a word or some letters. If you have no idea what the correct answer is, skip it and come back later if there's time. If you're still clueless, it's okay to guess. Remember, you're scored on the number of questions you answer correctly and you're not penalized for wrong answers. The worst case scenario is that you miss a point from a good guess.

3. **Turn it on its ear.** The syntax of a question can often provide a clue, so make things interesting and turn the question into a statement to see if it changes the meaning or relates better (or worse) to the answer choices.

4. **Get out your magnifying glass.** Look for hidden clues in the questions because it's difficult to write a multiple-choice question without giving away part of the answer in the options presented. In most questions you can readily eliminate one or two potential answers, increasing your chances of answering correctly to 50/50, which will help out if you've skipped a question and gone back to it (see tip #2).

5. **Call it intuition.** Often your first instinct is correct. If you've been studying the content you've likely absorbed something and have subconsciously retained the knowledge. On questions you're not sure about trust your instincts because a first impression is usually correct.

6. **Graffiti.** Sometimes it's a good idea to mark your answers directly on the test booklet and go back to fill in the optical scan sheet later. You don't get extra points for perfectly blackened ovals. If you choose to manage your test this way, be sure not to mismark your answers when you transcribe to the scan sheet.

7. **Become a clock-watcher.** You have a set amount of time to answer the questions. Don't get bogged down laboring over a question you're not sure about when there are ten others you could answer more readily. If you choose to follow the advice of tip #6, be sure you leave time near the end to go back and fill in the scan sheet.

Do the Drill

No matter how prepared you feel it's sometimes a good idea to apply Murphy's Law. So the following tips might seem silly, mundane, or obvious, but we're including them anyway.

1. **Remember, you are what you eat, so bring a snack.** Choose from the list of energizing foods that appear earlier in the introduction.

2. **You're not too sexy for your test.** Wear comfortable clothes. You'll be distracted if your belt is too tight or if you're too cold or too hot.

3. **Lie to yourself.** Even if you think you're a prompt person, pretend you're not and leave plenty of time to get to the testing center. Map it out ahead of time and do a dry run if you have to. There's no need to add road rage to your list of anxieties.

4. **Bring sharp number 2 pencils.** It may seem impossible to forget this need from your school days, but you might. And make sure the erasers are intact, too.

5. **No ticket, no test.** Bring your admission ticket as well as **two** forms of identification, including one with a picture and signature. You will not be admitted to the test without these things.

6. **You can't take it with you.** Leave any study aids, dictionaries, note-books, computers, and the like at home. Certain tests **do** allow a scientific or four-function calculator, so check ahead of time to see if your test does.

7. **Prepare for the desert.** Any time spent on a bathroom break **cannot** be made up later, so use your judgment on the amount you eat or drink.

8. **Quiet, Please!** Keeping your own time is a good idea, but not with a timepiece that has a loud ticker. If you use a watch, take it off and place it nearby but not so that it distracts you. And **silence your cell phone**.

To the best of our ability, we have compiled the content you need to know in this book and in the accompanying online resources. The rest is up to you. You can use the study and testing tips or you can follow your own methods. Either way, you can be confident that there aren't any missing pieces of information and there shouldn't be any surprises in the content on the test.

If you have questions about test fees, registration, electronic testing, or other content verification issues please visit *www.nystce.nesinc.com*.

Good luck!

Sharon Wynne
Founder, XAMonline

IntelliGuide by XAMonline

Same comprehensive content, new interactive study tools.

XAMonline's new platform transforms the traditional eBook experience into an enhanced study and test practice session through innovative tools such as sticky notes and flashcards. The IntelliGuide™ technology companion is FREE with the purchase of this NYSTCE Multi-Subject 002 study guide and features:

Easy Navigation: Previously viewed content can be quickly recalled using the "History" tab. This saves time and prevents frustration as you can easily flip back and reference a previous page or topic you recently viewed.

eStickynotes: Allows you to write digital notes anywhere in the study guide, then combine and print out all your notes for easy, "on-the-go" studying.

In-text Search: Where was that topic mentioned? This feature enables you to quickly locate the content you need. Simply type in the search term and the IntelliGuide™ lists the page numbers and highlights where in the page the reference occurs.

eFlashcards: A digital flashcard featuring any combination of words, numbers or symbols provides a learning drill. XAMonline's eFlashcards enable you to study pre-made cards or create your own. The "Hide" function allows you to skip cards you already know, creating a customized study experience. Use them digitally or print them out and study on-the-go.

More Sample Tests: Additional practice tests assess how much you know and help identify the areas you need to focus on. With up to 125 questions, these exams can be timed to provide you with an experience that mirrors the real test or you can pause the timer as you flip back and reference specific skills or competencies. You can grade the entire completed test or just a portion of it, then determine which content areas and rigor levels you need improvement in.

Get it now!

To register and access your NYSTCE-002 IntelliGuide™, please visit: XAMonlineIntelliGuide.com/ NYregistration

DOMAIN I
ENGLISH LANGUAGE ARTS

Enhanced features only available in our ebook edition:

 eStickynotes: allows you take digital notes anywhere in the ebook edition. It further allows you to aggregate and print all enotes for easy studying.

 eFlashcards: a digital representation of a card represented with words, numbers or symbols or any combination of each and briefly displayed as part of a learning drill. eFlashcards takes away the burden of carrying around traditional cards that could easily be disarranged, dropped, or soiled.

 More Sample Tests: more ways to assess how much you know and how much further you need to study. Ultimately, makes you more prepared and attain mastery in the skills and techniques of passing the test the FIRST TIME!

Visit www.XAMonline.com
and click on ebook.

PERSONALIZED STUDY PLAN

PAGE	COMPETENCY AND SKILL	KNOWN MATERIAL/ SKIP IT	BRIEFLY REVIEW eSTICKYNOTES	MAKE eFLASHCARDS	TAKE ADDITIONAL SAMPLE TESTS
5	**1: Foundations of Reading Development**	☐	☐	☐	☐
	1.1: Developmental knowledge of literacy	☐	☐	☐	☐
	1.2: Phonological and phonemic awareness	☐	☐	☐	☐
	1.3: Knowledge of print concepts	☐	☐	☐	☐
	1.4: Knowledge and use of alphabetic principles	☐	☐	☐	☐
	1.5: Knowledge of word identification strategies	☐	☐	☐	☐
	1.6: Constructing meaning from texts	☐	☐	☐	☐
21	**2: Reading Comprehension Strategies**	☐	☐	☐	☐
	2.1: Literal comprehension skills	☐	☐	☐	☐
	2.2: Inferential comprehension skills	☐	☐	☐	☐
	2.3: Evaluative comprehension skills	☐	☐	☐	☐
	2.4: Applying knowledge of strategies that enhance comprehension	☐	☐	☐	☐
	2.5: Methods for aiding reader comprehension	☐	☐	☐	☐
	2.6: Methods for assessing reading comprehension	☐	☐	☐	☐
37	**3: Reading Skills for Various Purposes**	☐	☐	☐	☐
	3.1: How to vary reading strategies	☐	☐	☐	☐
	3.2: Gathering, interpreting, and synthesizing reading techniques	☐	☐	☐	☐
	3.3: Analyzing and assessing a writer's credibility or objectivity	☐	☐	☐	☐
	3.4: Analyzing and interpreting visuals	☐	☐	☐	☐
	3.5: Strategies to promote literary response skills	☐	☐	☐	☐
	3.6: Modeling and encouraging independent reading	☐	☐	☐	☐
45	**4: Developing and Publishing Written Texts**	☐	☐	☐	☐
	4.1: Knowledge of prewriting strategies	☐	☐	☐	☐
	4.2: Techniques for note taking, outlining, and drafting	☐	☐	☐	☐
	4.3: Revising written texts	☐	☐	☐	☐
	4.4: Editing written work to ensure conformity to standard English usage	☐	☐	☐	☐
	4.5: Editing and proofreading written work	☐	☐	☐	☐
	4.6: Use of technology to plan and manage written work	☐	☐	☐	☐
61	**5: Writing Skills and Strategies**	☐	☐	☐	☐
	5.1: Writing for a variety of audiences and purposes	☐	☐	☐	☐
	5.2: Incorporating graphic representations	☐	☐	☐	☐
	5.3: Writing a research paper	☐	☐	☐	☐
	5.4: Expressing a point of view and avoiding bias	☐	☐	☐	☐
	5.5: Writing a response to a literary selection	☐	☐	☐	☐
	5.6: Voice in writing	☐	☐	☐	☐

PERSONALIZED STUDY PLAN

PAGE	COMPETENCY AND SKILL	KNOWN MATERIAL/ SKIP IT	BRIEFLY REVIEW eSTICKYNOTES	MAKE eFLASHCARDS	TAKE ADDITIONAL SAMPLE TESTS
69	**6: Listening and Speaking Skills**	☐	☐	☐	☐
	6.1: Listening strategies for contexts and purposes	☐	☐	☐	☐
	6.2: Factors that affect effectively listening	☐	☐	☐	☐
	6.3: Features of spoken language	☐	☐	☐	☐
	6.4: Speaking strategies for different needs	☐	☐	☐	☐
	6.5: Oral language conventions for social situations	☐	☐	☐	☐
76	**7: Literary Analysis**	☐	☐	☐	☐
	7.1: Comparison of fiction and nonfiction	☐	☐	☐	☐
	7.2: Story elements in fiction	☐	☐	☐	☐
	7.3: Analyzing dramatic structure	☐	☐	☐	☐
	7.4: Knowledge of nonfiction types	☐	☐	☐	☐
	7.5: Conveying style, tone, and point of view	☐	☐	☐	☐
	7.6: Formal elements of a poetic text	☐	☐	☐	☐
91	**8: Literature**	☐	☐	☐	☐
	8.1: How literary texts reflect the time and place	☐	☐	☐	☐
	8.2: How literary works reflect cultural values and ideas	☐	☐	☐	☐
	8.3: Themes and characteristics of well-known authors	☐	☐	☐	☐
	8.4: Works of literature for children and adolescents	☐	☐	☐	☐
	8.5: Traditional and contemporary literature	☐	☐	☐	☐

COMPETENCY 1

UNDERSTAND THE FOUNDATIONS OF READING DEVELOPMENT

> SKILL **Demonstrating knowledge of the developmental progression from**
> 1.1 **prereading to conventional literacy, with individual variations,**
> **and analyzing how literacy develops in multiple contexts through**
> **reading, writing, and oral language experiences**

When students practice fluency, they practice by reading connected pieces of text. In other words, instead of looking at a word as just a word, they might read a sentence straight through. Reading fluently is important because it enables students to comprehend what they are reading. Students who are NOT fluent in reading would sound out each letter or word slowly and pay more attention to the phonics of each word. Fluent readers, on the other hand, might read a sentence aloud using appropriate intonations. The best way to test for fluency, in fact, is to have a student read something aloud, preferably a few sentences in a row—or more. Sure, most students just learning to read will probably not be very fluent right away; but with practice, they will increase their fluency. Even though fluency is not the same as comprehension, it is said that fluency is a good predictor of comprehension. Think about it: If you're focusing too much on sounding out each word, you're not going to be paying attention to the meaning.

During the preschool years, children acquire cognitive skills in oral language that they apply later on to reading comprehension. Reading aloud to young children is one of the most important things that an adult can do because they are teaching children how to monitor, question, predict, and confirm what they hear in the stories. Reid (1988, p. 165) describes four metalinguistic abilities that young children acquire through early involvement in reading activities:

1. Word consciousness. Children who have access to books can first tell the story through the pictures. Gradually they begin to realize the connection between the spoken words and the printed words. The beginning of letter and word discrimination begins in the early years.

2. Language and conventions of print. During this stage, children learn how to hold a book, where to begin to read, the left-to-right motion, and how to continue from one line to another.

3. Functions of print. Children discover that print can be used for a variety of purposes and functions, including entertainment and information.

The typical variation in literacy backgrounds that children bring to reading can make teaching more difficult. Often a teacher has to choose between focusing on the learning needs of a few students at the expense of the group, or focusing on the group at the risk of leaving some students behind academically. This situation is particularly critical for children with gaps in their literacy knowledge who may be at risk in subsequent grades for becoming "diverse learners."

Areas of Emerging Evidence

Experiences with print help preschool children develop an understanding of the conventions, purposes, and functions of print. Children learn about print from a variety of sources (through reading and writing) and in the process come to realize that print carries the story. They also learn how text is structured visually (e.g., text begins at the top of the page, moves from left to right, and carries over to the next page when it is turned). While knowledge about the conventions of print enables children to understand the physical structure of language, the conceptual knowledge that printed words convey a message also helps children bridge the gap between oral and written language.

Phonological awareness and letter recognition contribute to initial reading acquisition by helping children develop efficient word-recognition strategies, such as detecting pronunciations and storing associations in memory. Phonological awareness and knowledge of print–speech relations play an important role in facilitating reading acquisition. Therefore, phonological awareness instruction should be an integral component of early reading programs. Within the emergent literacy research, viewpoints diverge on whether acquisition of phonological awareness and letter recognition are preconditions of literacy acquisition or whether they develop interdependently with literacy activities such as story reading and writing.

Storybook reading affects children's knowledge about, strategies for, and attitudes toward reading. Of all the strategies intended to promote growth in literacy acquisition, none is as commonly practiced, nor as strongly supported across the emergent literacy literature, as storybook reading. Children from different social and cultural backgrounds have differing degrees of access to storybook reading. For example, it is not unusual for a teacher to have students who have experienced thousands of hours of story reading time, along with other students who have had little or no such exposure.

It has long been recognized that early language development follows a continuum. This early language development is important to later reading development. Some early theories focus on experience and thought processes in explaining language development, though all theories indicate a progression of development.

Reading activities for emergent readers:

http://www.readingrockets. org/article/392

http://www.leeandlow.com/ images/pdfs/intro.pdf

Learning approach

Early theories of language development were formulated from learning theory research. The assumption was that language development evolved from learning the rules of language structures and applying them through imitation and reinforcement. This approach also assumed that language, cognitive, and social developments were independent of each other. Thus, children were expected to learn language from patterning after adults who spoke and wrote Standard English. No allowance was made for communication through child jargon, idiomatic expressions, or grammatical and mechanical errors resulting from too strict adherence to the rules of inflection (childs instead of children) or conjugation (runned instead of ran). No association was made between physical and operational development and language mastery.

Linguistic approach

Studies spearheaded by Noam Chomsky in the 1950s formulated the theory that language ability is innate and develops through natural human maturation as environmental stimuli trigger acquisition of syntactical structures appropriate to each exposure level. The assumption of a hierarchy of syntax downplayed the significance of semantics. Because of the complexity of syntax and the relative speed with which children acquire language, linguists attributed language development to biological rather than cognitive or social influences.

Cognitive approach

Researchers in the 1970s proposed that language knowledge derives from both syntactic and semantic structures. Drawing on the studies of Piaget and other cognitive learning theorists, supporters of the cognitive approach maintained that children acquire knowledge of linguistic structures after they have acquired the cognitive structures necessary to process language. For example, joining words for specific meaning necessitates sensory motor intelligence. Children must be able to coordinate movement and recognize objects before they can identify words to name the objects or word groups to describe the actions performed with those objects. Children must have developed the mental abilities for organizing concepts as well as concrete operations, predicting outcomes, and theorizing before they can assimilate and verbalize complex sentence structures, choose vocabulary for particular nuances of meaning, and examine semantic structures for tone and manipulative effect.

Sociocognitive approach

Other theorists in the 1970s proposed that language development results from sociolinguistic competence. Language, cognitive, and social competencies are interactive elements of total human development. Emphasis on verbal

For further information on phonological and phonemic awareness:

http://www.indiana.edu/~reading/ieo/digests/d119.html

communication as the medium for language expression resulted in the inclusion of speech activities in most language arts curricula.

Unlike previous approaches, the sociocognitive approach allowed that determining the appropriateness of language in given situations for specific listeners is as important as understanding semantic and syntactic structures. By engaging in conversation, children at all stages of development have opportunities to test their language skills, receive feedback, and make modifications. As a social activity, conversation is as structured by social order as grammar is structured by the rules of syntax. Conversation satisfies the learner's need to be heard and understood and to influence others. Thus, choices of vocabulary, tone, and content are dictated by the ability to assess the language knowledge of listeners. Children are constantly applying cognitive skills to using language in a social interaction. If the capacity to acquire language is inborn, without an environment in which to practice language, a child would not pass beyond grunts and gestures as did primitive man.

Of course, the varying degrees of environmental stimuli to which children are exposed at all age levels creates a slower or faster development of language. Some children are prepared to articulate concepts and recognize symbolism by the time they enter fifth grade because they have been exposed to challenging reading and conversations with well-spoken adults at home or in their social groups. Others are still trying to master the sight recognition skills and are not yet ready to combine words in complex patterns.

Sample Test Questions and Rationale

Average Rigor

1. **Which of the following indicates that a student is a fluent reader?**

   A. reads texts with expression or prosody.

   B. reads word-to-word and haltingly.

   C. must intentionally decode a majority of the words.

   D. in a writing assignment, sentences are poorly-organized structurally.

   Answer: A – reads texts with expression or prosody.

   Rationale: Student reads texts with expression or prosody. The teacher should listen to the children read aloud, but there are also clues to reading levels in their writing.

Easy

2. **All of the following are true about phonological awareness EXCEPT:**

   A. It may involve print.

   B. It is a prerequisite for spelling and phonics.

   C. Activities can be done by the children with their eyes closed.

   D. Starts before letter recognition is taught.

   Answer: A – may not involve print.

   Rationale: The key word here is EXCEPT which will be highlighted in upper case on the test as well. All of the options are correct aspects of phonological awareness except the first one, A, because phonological awareness DOES NOT involve print.

Average Rigor

3. **Which of the following theories was spearheaded by Noam Chomsky in the 1950s?**

   A. Learning approach

   B. Linguistic approach

   C. Cognitive approach

   D. Montessori approach

   Answer: B – Linguistic approach

   Rationale: Studies spearheaded by Noam Chomsky in the 1950s formulated the theory that language ability is innate and develops through natural human maturation as environmental stimuli trigger acquisition of syntactical structures appropriate to each exposure level. The assumption of a hierarchy of syntax downplayed the significance of semantics. Because of the complexity of syntax and the relative speed with which children acquire language, linguists attributed language development to biological rather than cognitive or social influences.

**SKILL Defining phonological awareness and phonemic awareness, and
1.2 analyzing their role in reading development**

Phonological Awareness

PHONOLOGICAL AWARENESS is the ability of the reader to recognize the sounds of spoken language. This recognition includes how these sounds can be blended together, segmented (divided up), and manipulated (switched around). This awareness then leads to phonics, a method for teaching children to read. It helps them "sound out words."

Development of phonological skills may begin during pre-K years. Indeed, by the age of five, a child who has been exposed to rhyme can recognize a rhyme. Such a child can demonstrate phonological awareness by filling in the missing rhyming word in a familiar rhyme or rhymed picture book.

You teach children phonological awareness when you teach them the sounds made by the letters and the sounds made by various combinations of letters, as well as how to recognize individual sounds in words.

Phonemic Awareness

PHONEMIC AWARENESS is understanding that words are composed of sounds. To be phonemically aware means that the reader and the listener can recognize and manipulate specific sounds in spoken words.

Phonemic awareness deals with sounds in words that are spoken. The majority of phonemic awareness tasks, activities, and exercises are **oral**.

Theorist Marilyn Jager Adams, who researches early reading, has outlined five basic types of phonemic awareness tasks.

Task 1: Ability to hear rhymes and alliteration. Children listen to a poem, rhyming picture book, or song and identify the rhyming words heard, which the teacher might then record or list on an experiential chart.

Task 2: Ability to do oddity tasks (recognize the member of a set that is different, or odd, among the group). Children look at the pictures of a blade of grass, a garden, and a rose, and identify which starts with a different sound.

Task 3: Ability to orally blend words and split syllables. Children say the first sound of a word and then the rest of the word and put it together as a single word.

PHONOLOGICAL AWARENESS: the ability of the reader to recognize the soUNDS OF SPOken language

Phonological awareness skills:

- *Rhyming and syllabification*
- *Blending sounds into words—such as pic-tur-bo-k*
- *Identifying the beginning or starting sounds of words and the ending or closing sounds of words*
- *Breaking words down into sounds, also called "segmenting" words*
- *Recognizing other smaller words in the big word, by removing starting sounds—such as hear to ear*

PHONEMIC AWARENESS: understanding that words are composed of sounds

---

Task 4: Ability to orally segment words. The ability to count sounds. Children would be asked as a group to count the sounds in "hamburger."

Task 5: Ability to do phonics manipulation tasks. Children replace the "r" sound in rose with a "p" sound.

Because the ability to distinguish between individual sounds, or phonemes, within words is a prerequisite to association of sounds with letters and manipulating sounds to blend words—a fancy way of saying "reading"—the teaching of phonemic awareness is crucial to emergent literacy (early childhood K-2 reading instruction). Children need a strong background in phonemic awareness in order for phonics instruction (sound-spelling relationship–printed materials) to be effective.

Instructional methods that may be effective for teaching phonemic awareness can include:

- Clapping out syllables in words

- Distinguishing between a word and a sound

- Using visual cues and movements to help children understand when the speaker goes from one sound to another

- Incorporating oral segmentation activities that focus on easily distinguished syllables rather than sounds

- Singing familiar songs (e.g., Happy Birthday, Knick Knack Paddy Wack) and replacing key words in them with words with a different ending or middle sound (oral segmentation)

- Dealing children a deck of picture cards and having them sound out the words for the pictures on their cards or calling for a picture by asking for its first and second sound

---

SKILL 1.3 **Demonstrating knowledge of concepts about print** *(e.g., book-handling skills, awareness that print carries meaning, recognition of directionality, ability to track print, ability to recognize and name letters)*

Understanding that print carries meaning is demonstrated every day in the elementary classroom as the teacher holds up a selected book to read it aloud to the class. The teachers explicitly and deliberately think aloud about how to hold the book, how to focus the class on looking at its cover, where to start reading, and in what direction to begin.

Even in writing the morning message on the board, the teacher targets the children on the placement of the message and its proper place at the top of the board to be followed by additional activities and a schedule for the rest of the day.

When a teacher challenges children to make letter posters of a single letter and the items in the classroom, their home, or their knowledge base that start with that letter, the children are making concrete the understanding that print carries meaning.

Teachers should look for five basic behaviors in students:

1. Do students know how to hold the book?

2. Can students match speech to print?

3. Do students know the difference between letters and words?

4. Do students know that print conveys meaning?

5. Can students track print from left to right?

In order for students to understand concepts of print, they must be able to recognize text and understand the various mechanics that text contains. This includes:

• All text contains a message

• The English language has a specific structure

• In order to decode words and read text, students must be able to understand that structure

The structure of the English language consists of rules of grammar, capitalization, and punctuation. For younger children, this means being able to recognize letters and form words. For older children, it means being able to recognize different types of text, such as lists, stories, and signs, and knowing the purpose of each one.

When reading to children, teachers point to words as they read them. Illustrations and pictures also contribute to being able to understand the meaning of the text. Therefore, teachers should also discuss illustrations related to the text. Teachers also discuss the common characteristics of books, such as the author, title page, and table of contents. Asking students to predict what the story might be about is a good strategy to help teach students about the cover and its importance to the story. Pocket charts, big books, and song charts provide ample opportunity for teachers to point to words as they read.

Instructional Strategies

Using Big Books in the Classroom	Gather the children around you in a group with the big book placed on a stand. This allows all children to see the words and pictures. As you read, point to each word. It is best to use a pointer so that you are not covering any other words or part of the page. When students read from the big book on their own, have them also use the pointer for each word. When students begin reading from smaller books, have them transfer what they have learned about pointing to the words by using their finger to track the reading. Observation is a key point in assessing students' ability to track words and speech.
A Classroom Rich in Print	Having words from a familiar rhyme or poem in a pocket chart lends itself to an activity where the students arrange the words in the correct order and then read the rhyme. This is an instructional strategy that reinforces directionality of print. It also reinforces punctuation, capitalization, and matching print to speech. Using highlighters or sticky tabs to locate upper and lower case letters or specific words can help students isolate words and learn about the structure of language they need to have for reading. There should be plenty of books in the classroom for children to read on their own or in small groups. As you observe each of these groups, take note of how the child holds the book in addition to how he or she tracks and reads the words.
Word Wall	A word wall is a great teaching tool for words in isolation and with writing. Each of the letters of the alphabet is displayed with words that begin with that letter under each one. Students are able to find the letter on the wall and read the words under each one.
Sounds of the Letters	In addition to teaching the letter names, students should learn the corresponding sound of each letter. This is a key feature of decoding when beginning to read. The use of rhyming words is an effective way to teach letter sounds so that children have a solid background.

Students should be exposed to daily opportunities for viewing and reading texts. Teachers can do this by engaging the students in discussions about books during shared, guided, and independent reading times. The teacher should draw the students' attention to the conventions of print and discuss with them the reasons for choosing different books. For example, teachers should let the students know that it is perfectly acceptable to return a book and select another if they think it is too hard for them.

Predictable books help engage the students in reading. Once the students realize what words are repeated in the text, they will eagerly chime in to repeat the words at the appropriate time during the reading. Rereading of texts helps the students learn the words and helps them to read these lines fluently.

Sites with information on using word walls:

http://www.teachingfirst. net/wordwallact.htm

http://www.theschoolbell. com/Links/word_walls/ words.html

Some things for teachers to observe during reading:

- Students' responses during reading conferences, such as pointing to letters or words

- Students' knowledge about where they should begin reading and how to stop or pause depending on the punctuation

- Students' behavior when holding a book (e.g., holding the book right side up or upside down, reading from left to right, stopping to look at the pictures to confirm meaning)

SKILL 1.4 **Demonstrating knowledge of the alphabetic principle and analyzing how emergent readers use this principle to master letter-sound correspondence and to decode simple words**

There are basically two parts to the alphabetic principle:

- *An understanding that words are made up of letters and that each of these letters has a specific sound.*
- *The correspondence between sounds and letters leads to phonological reading. This consists of reading regular and irregular words and doing advanced analysis of words.*

The alphabetic principle is sometimes called graphophonemic awareness. This multisyllabic technical reading foundation term details the theory that written words are composed of patterns of letters that represent the sounds of spoken words.

Because the English language is dependent on the alphabet, being able to recognize and sound out letters is the first step for beginning readers. Relying simply on memorization of words is just not feasible as a way for children to learn to recognize words. Therefore, decoding is essential. The most important goal of beginning reading teachers is to teach students to decode text so that they can read fluently and with understanding.

There are four basic features of the alphabetic principle:

1. Students need to be able to take spoken words apart and blend different sounds together to make new words

2. Students need to apply letter sounds to all their reading

3. Teachers need to use a systematic effective program in order to teach children to read

4. The teaching of the alphabetic principle usually begins in kindergarten

Critical skills that students need to learn are:

- *Letter–sound correspondence*
- *How to sound out words*
- *How to decode text to make meaning*

It is important to keep in mind that some children already know the letters and sounds before they come to school. Others may catch on to this quickly and still others need to have one-on-one instruction in order to learn to read.

> **SKILL 1.5** Demonstrating knowledge of a variety of word identification strategies, including use of phonics, use of semantic and syntactic cues, context clues, syllabication, analysis of word structure *(e.g., roots, prefixes, suffixes)*, **and sight-word recognition**

The Structure of Language

MORPHOLOGY is the study of word structure. When readers develop morphemic skills, they are developing an understanding of patterns they see in words. For example, English speakers realize that cat, cats, and caterpillar share some similarities in structure. This understanding helps readers to recognize words at a faster and easier rate, because each word doesn't need individual decoding.

MORPHOLOGY: the study of word structure

Syntax refers to the rules or patterned relationships that correctly create phrases and sentences from words. When readers develop an understanding of syntax, they begin to understand the structure of how sentences are built, and eventually the beginning of grammar.

> *Example: "I am going to the movies."*

This statement is syntactically and grammatically correct.

> *Example: "They am going to the movies."*

This statement is syntactically correct since all the words are in their correct place, but it is grammatically incorrect with the use of the word "They" rather than "I."

Semantics refers to the meaning expressed when words are arranged in a specific way. This is where connotation and denotation of words eventually will have a role with readers.

All of these skill sets are important to eventually developing effective word recognition skills, which help emerging readers develop fluency.

Phonics

Unlike phonemic awareness, the study of phonics must be done with the eyes open. It's the connection between the sounds and letters on a page. In other words, students learning phonics might see the word "bad" and sound each letter out slowly until they recognize that they just said the word. *See also Skill 1.2*

Decoding, Word Recognition, and Spelling

WORD ANALYSIS (also called phonics or decoding) is the process readers use to figure out unfamiliar words based on written patterns. WORD RECOGNITION is the process of automatically determining the pronunciation and some degree of the meaning of an unknown word. In other words, fluent readers recognize most written words easily and correctly, without consciously decoding or breaking them down. These elements of literacy are skills readers need for word recognition.

To DECODE means to change communication signals into messages. Reading comprehension requires that the reader learn the code within which a message is written and be able to decode it to get the message. Encoding involves changing a message into symbols. For example, to encode oral language into writing (spelling) or to encode an idea into words or to encode a mathematical or physical idea into appropriate mathematical symbols.

Although effective reading comprehension requires identifying words automatically (Adams, 1990, Perfetti, 1985), children do not have to be able to identify every single word or know the exact meaning of every word in a text to understand it. Indeed, Nagy (1988) says that children can read a work with a high level of comprehension even if they do not fully know as many as fifteen percent of the words within a given text. Children develop the ability to decode and recognize words automatically. They then can extend their ability to decode to multisyllabic words.

Spelling instruction should include practicing words misspelled in daily writing, generalizing spelling knowledge, and mastering objectives in progressive phases of development.

The developmental stages of spelling are:

1. **Prephonemic spelling:** Children know that letters stand for a message, but they do not know the relationship between spelling and pronunciation.

2. **Early phonemic spelling:** Children are beginning to understand spelling. They usually write the beginning letter correctly, followed by consonants or long vowels.

3. **Letter-name spelling:** Some words are consistently spelled correctly. The student is developing a sight vocabulary and a stable understanding of letters as representing sounds. Long vowels are usually used accurately, but silent vowels are omitted. Unknown words are spelled by the child attempting to match the name of the letter to the sound.

WORD ANALYSIS: the process readers use to figure out unfamiliar words based on written patterns

WORD RECOGNITION: the process of automatically determining the pronunciation and some degree of the meaning of an unknown word

DECODE: to change communication signals into messages

---

4. Transitional spelling: This phase is typically entered in late elementary school. Short vowel sounds are mastered and some spelling rules known. They are developing a sense of which spellings are correct and which are not.

5. Derivational spelling: This is usually reached from high school to adulthood. This is the stage where spelling rules are being mastered.

How Words Are Built

Knowledge of how words are built can help students with basic and more advanced decoding. A ROOT WORD is the primary base of a word.
A PREFIX is the affix (a morpheme that attaches to a base word) that is placed at the start of a root word, but can't make a word on its own.

> *Examples of prefixes include re-, pre-, and un-.*

A SUFFIX follows the root word to which it attaches and appears at the end of the word.

> *Examples of suffixes include –s, -es, -ed, -ly, and –tion.*

In the word unlikely, "un" is a prefix, "like" is the root word, and "ly" is a suffix.

ROOT WORD: the primary base of a word

PREFIX: the affix that is placed at the start of a root word, but can't make a word on its own

SUFFIX: follows the root word to which it attaches and appears at the end of the word

Sample Test Questions and Rationale

Average Rigor

1. **The arrangement and relationship of words in sentences or sentence structure best describes:**

   A. style

   B. discourse

   C. thesis

   D. syntax

   Answer: D – syntax

   Rationale: Syntax is the grammatical structure of sentences.

Rigorous

2. **To decode is to:**

   A. Use a special code to decipher a message

   B. Sound out a printed sequence of letters

   C. Change communication signals into messages

   D. Change a message into symbols

   Answer: C – Change communication signals into messages

   Rationale: To decode means to change communication signals into messages. Reading comprehension requires that the reader learn the code within which a message is written and be able to decode it to get the message.

Rigorous

3. **To encode means that you:**

   A. Change a message into symbols

   B. Construct meaning from a code.

   C. Change communication signals into messages

   D. Sound out a printed sequence of letters

   Answer: A – Change a message into symbols

   Rationale: Encoding involves changing a message into symbols. For example to encode oral language into writing (spelling) or to encode an idea into words or to encode a mathematical or physical idea into appropriate mathematical symbols.

SKILL 1.6 Analyzing factors that affect a reader's ability to construct meaning from texts (*e.g., word recognition, reading fluency, vocabulary development, context clues, visual cues, prior knowledge and experience*)

If any two words are synonymous with reading comprehension, as far as the balanced literacy approach is concerned, they would be Constructing Meaning.

Cooper, Taberski, Strickland, and other key theorists and classroom teachers, conceptualize readers as designating a specific meaning to the text using both clues in the text and their own prior knowledge. Comprehension for the balanced literacy theorists is a strategic process.

Readers interact with the text and bring their prior knowledge and experience to it, or their **lack** of prior knowledge and experience. Writing is interlaced with reading and is a mutually integrative and supportive parallel process. Hence the division of literacy learning by the balanced literacy folks into reading workshop and writing workshop, with the same anchor readings, or books, being used for both.

Consider the sentence

> *"The test booklet was white with black print, but very scary looking."*

The ultimate meaning that the reader derives from the sentence is from the reader's own responses and experiences with the ideas the author presents. The reader constructs a meaning that reflects the author's intent and also the reader's response to that intent.

One must also remember that readings are generally fairly lengthy passages, composed of paragraphs, which, in turn, are composed of more than one sentence. With each successive sentence, and every new paragraph, the reader refocuses, the schemata are reconsidered, and a new meaning is constructed.

The purpose of reading is to convert visual images (the letters and words) into a message. Pronouncing the words is not enough; the reader must be able to extract the meaning of the text. When people read, they utilize four sources of background information to comprehend the meaning behind the literal text (Reid, pp.166-171).

1. **Word Knowledge.** Information about words and letters. One's knowledge about word meanings is lexical knowledge—a sort of dictionary. Knowledge about spelling patterns and pronunciation is orthographic knowledge. Poor readers do not develop the level of automatically using orthographic knowledge to identify words and decode unfamiliar words.

2. **Syntax and Contextual Information.** When children encounter unknown words in a sentence, they rely on their background knowledge to choose a word that makes sense. The errors of younger children, therefore, are often substitutions of words in the same syntactic class. Poor readers often fail to make use of context clues to help them identify words or activate the background knowledge that would help them with comprehension. Poor readers also process sentences word by word, instead of "chunking" phrases and clauses, resulting in a slow pace that focuses on the decoding rather than comprehension. They also have problems answering "wh-" questions (who, what, where, when, why) due to these problems with syntax.

3. **Semantic Knowledge.** This includes the reader's background knowledge about a topic, which is combined with the text information as the

reader tries to comprehend the material. New information is compared to the background information and incorporated into the reader's schema. Poor readers have problems using their background knowledge, especially with passages that require inference or cause-and-effect.

4. Text Organization. Good readers are able to differentiate types of text structure, such as story narrative, exposition, compare–contrast, or time sequence. They use knowledge of text to build expectations and construct a framework of ideas on which to build meaning. Poor readers may not be able to differentiate types of text and miss important ideas. They may also miss important ideas and details by concentrating on lesser or irrelevant details.

Research on reading development has yielded information on the behaviors and habits of good readers versus poor readers. Some of the characteristics of good readers are:

- They think about the information that they will read in the text, formulate questions that they predict will be answered in the text, and confirm those predictions from the information in the text

- When faced with unfamiliar words, they attempt to pronounce them using analogies to familiar words

- Before reading, they establish a purpose for reading, select possible text structure, choose a reading strategy, and make predictions about what will be in the reading

- As they read, they continually test and confirm their predictions, go back when something does not make sense, and make new predictions

COMPETENCY 2
UNDERSTAND SKILLS AND STRATEGIES INVOLVED IN READING COMPREHENSION

SKILL 2.1 **Demonstrating knowledge of literal comprehension skills** *(e.g., the ability to identify the sequence of events in a text, the ability to identify explicitly stated main ideas, details, and cause-and-effect patterns in a text)*

Main Idea

The TOPIC of a paragraph or story is what the paragraph or story is about. The MAIN IDEA of a paragraph or story states the important idea(s) that the author wants the reader to know about a topic. The topic and main idea of a paragraph or story are sometimes directly stated. There are times, however, when the topic and main idea are not directly stated, but simply implied.

Look at this paragraph:

> *Henry Ford was an inventor who developed the first affordable automobile. The cars that were being built before Mr. Ford created his Model-T were very expensive. Only rich people could afford to have cars.*

The topic of this paragraph is Henry Ford. The main idea is that Henry Ford built the first affordable automobile.

The TOPIC SENTENCE indicates what the passage is about. It is the subject of that portion of the narrative. The ability to identify the topic sentence in a passage will enable the student to focus on the concept being discussed and better comprehend the information provided.

You can find the main ideas by examining how paragraphs are written. A PARAGRAPH is a group of sentences about one main idea. Paragraphs usually have two types of sentences: a topic sentence, which contains the main idea, and two or more detail sentences which support, prove, provide more information, explain, or give examples. You can only tell if you have a detail or topic sentence by comparing the sentences with each other.

TOPIC: what the paragraph or story is about

MAIN IDEA: states the important idea(s) that the author wants the reader to know about a topic

TOPIC SENTENCE: indicates what the passage is about

PARAGRAPH: a group of sentences about one main idea

Look at this sample paragraph:

> *Fall is the best of the four seasons. The leaves change colors to create a beautiful display of golds, reds, and oranges. The air turns crisp and windy. The scent of pumpkin muffins and apple pies fill the air. Finally, Halloween marks the start of the holiday season. Fall is my favorite time of year!*

Breakdown of sentences:

> *Fall is the best of the four seasons. (TOPIC SENTENCE)*
>
> *The leaves change colors to create a beautiful display of golds, reds, and oranges. (DETAIL)*
>
> *The air turns crisp and windy. (DETAIL)*
>
> *The scent of pumpkin muffins and apple pies fill the air. (DETAIL)*
>
> *Finally, Halloween marks the start of the holiday season. (DETAIL)*
>
> *Fall is my favorite time of year! (CLOSING SENTENCE—Often a restatement of the topic sentence)*

The first sentence introduces the main idea and the other sentences support and provide more detail and information.

Tips for Finding the Topic Sentence

How can you be sure that you have a topic sentence? Try this trick: Switch the sentence you think is the topic sentence into a question. If the other sentences seem to "answer" the question, then you've got it.

- The topic sentence is usually first, but could be in any position in the paragraph.

- A topic sentence is usually more general than the other sentences; that is, it talks about many things and looks at the big picture. Sometimes it refers to more that one thing. Plurals and the words many, numerous, or several often signal a topic sentence.

- Detail sentences are usually more specific than the topic, that is, they usually talk about one single or small part of an idea. The words *for example, i.e., that is, first, second, third, etc.,* and *finally* often signal a detail.

- Most of the detail sentences support, give examples, prove, talk about, or point toward the topic in some way.

For example, reword the topic sentence "Fall is the best of the four seasons" in one of the following ways:

> *"Why is fall the best of the four season?"*
>
> *"Which season is the best season?"*
>
> *"Is fall the best season of the year?"*

Then, as you read the remaining sentences (the ones you didn't pick), you will find that they answer (support) your question. If you attempt this with a sentence other than the topic sentence, it won't work.

For example, in the sample paragraph about fall, suppose you select "Halloween marks the start of the holiday season," and you reword it in the following way:

> *"Which holiday is the start of the holiday season?"*

You will find that the other sentences fail to help you answer (support) your question.

Supporting Details

The SUPPORTING SENTENCES provide more information and details about the topic and the main idea.

For example, the supporting details in the paragraph about Henry Ford would be that he was an inventor and that before he created his Model-T only rich people could afford cars because they were too expensive.

> **SUPPORTING SENTENCES:** provide more information and details about the topic and the main idea

Inferences and Conclusions

In order to draw inferences and make conclusions, a reader must use prior knowledge and apply it to the current situation. A conclusion or inference is never stated. You must rely on your common sense.

Read the following passage.

> *The Smith family waited patiently around carousel number 7 for their luggage to arrive. They were exhausted after their five-hour trip and were eager to get to their hotel. After about an hour, they realized that they no longer recognized any of the other passengers' faces. Mrs. Smith asked the person who appeared to be in charge if they were at the right carousel. The man replied, "Yes, this is it, but we finished unloading that baggage almost half an hour ago."*

From the man's response we can infer that:

1. The Smiths were ready to go to their hotel

2. The Smith's luggage was lost

3. The man had their luggage

4. They were at the wrong carousel

The Smiths were still waiting for their luggage, so we know that they were not yet ready to go to their hotel. From the man's response, we know that they were not at the wrong carousel and that he did not have their luggage. Therefore, though not directly stated, it appears that their luggage was lost. Choice 2. is the correct answer.

Cause and Effect

Linking cause to effect seems to be ingrained in human thinking. We get chilled and then the next day come down with a cold; therefore, we believe that getting chilled caused the cold, even though medical experts tell us that the virus that causes colds must be communicated by another human being. Socrates and the other Greek orators theorized about this way of thinking and developed a system for analyzing the links between causes and their effects and when they are valid— that is, when a specific cause did, in fact, bring about a particular effect. They also spelled out ways to determine whether or not the reasoning is reliable. If the cause and effect reasoning is not reliable, it is called a fallacy.

A common fallacy in reasoning is the *post hoc ergo propter hoc*, which means *after this, therefore because of this*, or the false-cause fallacy. These occur in cause-and-effect reasoning, which may either go from cause to effect or effect to cause. They happen when an inadequate cause is offered for a particular effect; when the possibility of more than one cause is ignored; and when a connection between a particular cause and a particular effect is not made.

An example of a post hoc:

> *Our sales shot up thirty-five percent after we ran that television campaign; therefore, the campaign caused the increase in sales.*

It might have been a cause, of course, but more evidence is needed to prove it.

> *An Iraqi truck driver reported that Saddam Hussein had nuclear weapons; therefore, Saddam Hussein is a threat to world security.*

More causes would have been needed to prove the conclusion.

An example of failing to make a connection between a particular cause and an effect assigned to it:

> *Anna fell into a putrid pond on Saturday; on Monday she came down with polio; therefore, the polio was caused by the water in the pond.*

This, of course, is not a valid conclusion unless the polio virus is found in a sample of water from the pond. A connection must be proven.

SKILL 2.2 Demonstrating knowledge of inferential comprehension skills
(e.g., the ability to draw conclusions or generalizations from a text, the ability to infer ideas, details, and cause-and-effect relationships that are not explicitly stated in a text)

Conclusions are drawn as a result of a line of reasoning. INDUCTIVE REASONING moves from specific to general and is usually based on observations.

INDUCTIVE REASONING: moves from specific to general and is usually based on observations

An example of inductive reasoning would be:

1. *When I was a child, I bit into a green apple from my grandfather's orchard, and it was sour. (SPECIFIC FACT)*
2. *I once bought green apples from a roadside vendor, and when I bit into one, it was sour. (SPECIFIC FACT)*
3. *My grocery store had a sale on green Granny Smith apples last week, and I bought several only to find that they were sour when I bit into one. (SPECIFIC FACT)*

Conclusion: All green apples are sour.

While this is an example of inductive reasoning, it is also an example of the weakness of such reasoning. The speaker has not tasted all the green apples in the world, and there very well may be some apples that are green that are not sour.

DEDUCTIVE REASONING begins with the generalization: "Green apples are sour" and supports that generalization with the specifics.

An inference is drawn from an inductive line of reasoning. The most famous one is

> *All men are mortal*

DEDUCTIVE REASONING: begins with a generalization and supports that generalization with the specifics

which is drawn from the observation that everyone a person knows has died or will die and that everyone else concurs in that judgment. It is assumed to be true and for that reason can be used as proof of another conclusion:

> *Socrates is a man; therefore, he will die.*

Sometimes the inference is assumed to be proven when it is not reliably true in all cases, such as

> *Aging brings physical and mental infirmity.*

Reasoning from that inference, many companies will not hire anyone above a certain age. Actually, being old does not necessarily imply physical and/or mental impairment. There are many instances where elderly people have made important contributions that require exceptional ability.

SKILL 2.3 **Demonstrating knowledge of evaluative comprehension skills** *(e.g., the ability to distinguish between facts and opinions in a text, the ability to detect faulty reasoning in a text, the ability to detect bias and propaganda in a text)*

Fact and Opinion

FACTS: statements that are verifiable

OPINIONS: statements that must be supported in order to be accepted

FACTS are statements that are verifiable. OPINIONS are statements that must be supported in order to be accepted. Facts are used to support opinions. For example, "Jane is a bad girl" is an opinion. However, "Jane hit her sister with a baseball bat" is a fact upon which the opinion is based.

Judgments are opinions—decisions or declarations based on observation or reasoning that express approval or disapproval. Facts report what has happened or exists and come from observation, measurement, or calculation. Facts can be tested and verified whereas opinions and judgments cannot. They can only be supported with facts.

Most statements cannot be so clearly distinguished. "I believe that Jane is a bad girl" is a fact. The speaker knows what he or she believes. However, it obviously includes a judgment that could be disputed by another person who might believe otherwise. Judgments are not usually so firm. They are, rather, plausible opinions that provoke thought or lead to factual development.

Resources for teaching fact/opinion:

http://www.dowlingcentral. com/MrsD/area/ readingcomp/terms/ factfeeling.html

http://www.kidport.com/ Grade5/TAL/G5-TAL- FactOpinion.htm

Author's Purpose

An author may have more than one purpose in writing. An AUTHOR'S PURPOSE may be to entertain, to persuade, to inform, to describe, or to narrate. There are no tricks or rules to follow in attempting to determine an author's purpose. It is up to the reader to use his or her judgment.

Read this paragraph.

> *Charles Lindbergh had no intention of becoming a pilot. He was enrolled in the University of Wisconsin until a flying lesson changed the entire course of his life. He began his career as a pilot by performing daredevil stunts at fairs.*

AUTHOR'S PURPOSE: to entertain, to persuade, to inform, to describe, or to narrate

The author wrote this paragraph primarily to:

1. Describe

2. Inform

3. Entertain

4. Narrate

Since the author is simply telling us or informing us about the life of Charles Lindbergh, the correct answer here is 2. Inform.

Author's Tone and Point of View

The AUTHOR'S TONE is his or her attitude as reflected in the statement or passage. The author's choice of words will help the reader determine the overall tone of that statement or passage. For example, read this paragraph.

AUTHOR'S TONE: his or her attitude as reflected in the statement or passage

> *I was shocked by your article, which said that sitting down to breakfast was a thing of the past. Many families consider breakfast time, family time. Children need to realize the importance of having a good breakfast. It is imperative that they be taught this at a young age. I cannot believe that a writer with your reputation has difficulty comprehending this.*

The author's tone in this passage is one of

1. Concern

2. Anger

3. Excitement

4. Disbelief

Since the author directly states that he "cannot believe" that the writer feels this way, the answer is 4. Disbelief.

Valid and Invalid Arguments

An **ARGUMENT** is a generalization that is proven or supported with facts. If the facts are not accurate, the generalization remains unproven. Using inaccurate "facts" to support an argument is called a fallacy in reasoning. Some factors to consider in judging whether the facts used to support an argument are accurate follow:

- Are the facts current or are they out of date? For example, if the proposition is "birth defects in babies born to drug-using mothers are increasing," then the data must be the most current available.

- Where were the data obtained, and is that source reliable?

- Are the calculations on which the facts are based reliable? It is a good idea to run one's own calculations before using a piece of derived information.

Even facts that are true and have a profound effect on the argument may not be relevant to the case at hand. For example, health statistics from an entire state may have no or little relevance to a particular county or zip code. Statistics from an entire country are not likely to prove very much about a particular state or county.

An analogy can be useful in making a point, but the comparison must match up in all characteristics or it will not be relevant. Analogy should be used very carefully. It is often just as likely to destroy an argument as it is to strengthen it.

The importance or significance of a fact may not be sufficient to strengthen an argument. For example, of the millions of immigrants in the United States, using a single family to support a solution to the immigration problem will not make much difference overall even though those single-example arguments are often used to support one approach or another. They may achieve a positive reaction, but they will not prove that one solution is better than another. If enough cases were cited from a variety of geographical locations, the information might be significant.

Three strong supporting facts are sufficient to establish the thesis of an argument.

How much is enough? Generally speaking, three strong supporting facts are sufficient to establish the thesis of an argument. For example:

Conclusion: Teenagers are bad drivers.

1 *When I was a teenager, I was not a good driver.*

2. *Many teenagers receive speeding tickets.*

3. *Teenagers do not have a lot of experience driving.*

Sometimes more than three arguments are too many. On the other hand, it's not unusual to hear public speakers, particularly politicians, cite a long litany of facts to support their positions.

A very good example of the omission of facts in an argument is the resumé of an applicant for a job. The applicant is arguing that she should be chosen to be awarded a particular job. The application form will ask for information about past employment; the applicant may omit positions that resulted in an unfavorable dismissal. Employers are usually suspicious of periods of time when the applicant has not listed an employer.

A writer makes choices about which facts will be used and which will be discarded in developing an argument. He may exclude anything that is not supportive of the point of view the he is taking. It's always a good idea for the reader to do some research to identify the omissions and to consider whether they affect the point of view presented in the argument.

Judgments are seldom black or white. If the argument seems too neat or too compelling, it is reasonable to assume that relevant facts have not been included.

SKILL 2.4 **Applying knowledge of strategies to use before, during, and after reading to enhance comprehension** *(e.g., developing and activating prior knowledge, connecting texts to personal experience, previewing a text, making predictions about a text, using K-W-L charts and other graphic organizers, taking notes on a text, discussing a text)*

Making Predictions

One theory or approach to the teaching of reading that gained currency in the late 1960s and the early 1970s was the importance of asking inferential and critical thinking questions, which would challenge and engage the children to read text. This approach to reading went beyond the literal level of what was stated in the text to an inferential level of using text clues to make predictions and to a critical level of involving the child in evaluating the text. While asking engaging and thought-provoking questions is still viewed as part of the teaching of reading, it is currently viewed as just one of several components of the teaching of reading.

Sites on teaching reading comprehension:

http://www.readingrockets. org/article/3479

http://web001.greece. k12.ny.us/academics. cfm?subpage=930

Prior Knowledge

PRIOR KNOWLEDGE can be defined as all of an individual's prior experiences, learning, and development that precede his or her entering a specific learning situation or attempting to comprehend a specific text. Sometimes prior knowledge can be erroneous or incomplete. Obviously, if there are misconceptions in a child's prior knowledge, these must be corrected so that the child's overall comprehension skills can progress.

PRIOR KNOWLEDGE: all of an individual's prior experiences, learning, and development that precede entering a specific learning situation or attempting to comprehend a specific text

Even the prior knowledge of kindergarteners includes their accumulated positive and negative experiences both in and out of school. These might range from wonderful family travels, watching television, visiting museums and libraries, to visiting hospitals, prisons, and surviving poverty. Whatever prior knowledge that the child brings to the school setting, the independent reading and writing the child does in school immeasurably expands his prior knowledge and, hence, broadens that child's reading comprehension capabilities.

Literary response skills are dependent on prior knowledge, schemata, and background. SCHEMATA (the plural of schema) are those structures that represent generic concepts stored in our memory. Readers who effectively comprehend text, whether they are adults or children, use both their schemata and prior knowledge plus the ideas from the printed text for reading comprehension. Graphic organizers help organize this information.

> **SCHEMATA:** those structures that represent generic concepts stored in our memory

Graphic Organizers

Graphic organizers solidify in a chart or diagram format a visual relationship among various reading and writing ideas including: sequence, timelines, character traits, fact and opinion, main idea and details, and differences and likenesses (generally done using a Venn diagram of interlocking circles, KWL chart, etc). These charts and diagrams are essential for providing scaffolding for instruction through activating pertinent prior knowledge.

KWL CHARTS aid reading comprehension by outlining what readers *KNOW*, what they *WANT* to know, and what they've *LEARNED* after reading. Students are asked to activate prior knowledge about a topic and further develop their knowledge about a topic using this organizer. Teachers often opt to display and maintain KWL charts throughout the reading of a text to continually record pertinent information about a student's reading.

> **KWL CHARTS:** aid reading comprehension by outlining what readers KNOW, what they WANT to know, and what they've LEARNED after reading

When the teacher first introduces the KWL strategy, the children should be allowed sufficient time to brainstorm in response to the first question, listing what all of them in the class or small group actually know about the topic. The children should have a three-columned KWL worksheet template for their journals and the teacher should use a KWL chart to record the responses from class or group discussion. The children can write under each column in their own journal and should also help the teacher with notations on the chart. This strategy allows the children to gain experience in note taking and in creating a concrete record of new data and information they have gleaned from the passage about the topic.

Depending on the grade level of the participating children, the teacher may also want to ask them to consider categories of information they hope to find out from the expository passage. For instance, they may be reading a book on animals to find out more about the animal's habitats during the winter or about the animal's mating habits.

Use this chart during your study of spiders. First write what you know about spiders. Then write what you would like to know about spiders. At the end of your study write the most important things you learned.

SPIDER KWL		
What I know	**What I want to know**	**What I have learned**
•	•	•
•	•	•
•	•	•
The most interesting fact I learned was:		
_____		
_____		

When children are working on the middle section of their KWL strategy sheet—What I want to know—the teacher may want to give them a chance to share what they would like to learn further about the topic and help them to express it in question format.

KWL is useful and can even be introduced as early as Grade 2 with extensive teacher discussion support. It not only serves to support the child's comprehension of a particular expository text, but also models for children a format for note taking. Beyond note taking, when the teacher wants to introduce report writing, the KWL format provides excellent outlines and question introductions for at least three paragraphs of a report.

Cooper (2004) recommends this strategy for use with thematic units and with reading chapters in required science, social studies, or health text books.

In addition to its usefulness with thematic unit study, KWL is wonderful for providing the teacher with a concrete format to assess how well children have absorbed pertinent new knowledge within the passage by looking at the third section—What I have learned. Ultimately, it is hoped that students will learn to use this strategy, not only under explicit teacher direction with templates of KWL sheets, but also on their own by informally writing questions they want to find out about in their journals and then going back to their own questions and answering them after the reading.

Note Taking

Older children take notes in their reading journals, while younger children and those more in need of explicit teacher support contribute their ideas and responses as part of the discussion in class. Their responses are recorded on the experiential chart. *See also Skill 4.2*

Connecting Texts

The concept of readiness is generally regarded as a developmentally based phenomenon. Various abilities, whether cognitive, affective, or psychomotor, are perceived to be dependent upon the mastery or development of certain prerequisite skills or abilities.

Readiness for subject area learning is dependent not only on prior knowledge, but also on affective factors such as interest, motivation, and attitude. These factors are often more influential on student learning than the preexisting cognitive base.

Discussing the Text

Discussion is an activity in which the children (and this activity works well from grades 3–6 and beyond) consider a particular text. Among the prompts, the teacher–coach might suggest that the children focus on words of interest they encountered in the text. These can also be words that they heard if the text was read aloud. Children can be asked to share something funny or upsetting or unusual about the words they have read. Through this focus on children's response to words as the center of the discussion circle, peers become more interested in word study.

When texts relate to a student's life or other reading materials or areas of study, they become more meaningful and relevant to the student's learning. Students enjoy seeing reading material connect to their lives, other subject areas, and other reading material.

In the current teaching of literacy, reading, writing, thinking, listening, viewing, and discussing, are not viewed as separate activities or components of instruction, but rather as developing and being nurtured simultaneously and interactively.

Sample Test Questions and Rationale

Rigorous

1. Which of the following is NOT a reading comprehension strategy?

   A. K-W-L chart

   B. Note-taking

   C. Standardized test

   D. Venn diagram

Answer: C – Standardized test

Rationale: Graphic organizers solidify in a chart or diagram and format a visual relationship to improve reading comprehension including: sequence, timelines, character traits, fact and opinion, main idea and details, differences and likenesses (generally done using a VENN DIAGRAM of interlocking circles, KWL Chart, etc. KWL charts are exceptionally useful for reading comprehension by outlining what readers KNOW, what they WANT to know, and what they've LEARNED after reading. Standardized tests are not a reading comprehension strategy.

Average Rigor

2. A K-W-L chart is which of the following?

   A. graphic organizer

   B. abbreviations chart

   C. word list

   D. Venn diagram

Answer: A – graphic organizer

Rationale: K-W-L is a graphic organizer strategy which activates children's prior knowledge and also helps them to target their reading of expository texts. This focus is achieved through having the children reflect on three key questions.

Before the child reads the expository passage:

"What do I know?" and "What do I want to find out?"

After the child has read the expository passage:

"What have I learned from the passage?" and "What do I still want to learn?"

Average Rigor

3. K-W-L charts are useful for which of the following?

   A. comprehension of expository text

   B. format for note taking

   C. report writing

   D. all of the above

Answer: D – all of the above

Rationale: K-W-L is useful and can even be introduced as early as grade 2 with extensive teacher discussion support. It not only serves to support the child's comprehension of a particular expository text, but also models for children a format for note taking. Beyond note taking, when the teacher wants to introduce report writing, the K-W-L format provides excellent outlines and question introductions for at least three paragraphs of a report.

SKILL 2.5 Demonstrating knowledge of methods for helping readers monitor their own comprehension as they read *(e.g., think-alouds, self-questioning strategies)*

Reading comprehension is not a passive process. When we read for understanding, we are consciously focused on obtaining meaning through a variety of methods. For instance, we might access background knowledge to help us understand new ideas or we might go back and re-read a few sentences to clarify a confusing concept.

When we apply various strategies to make sense of text, we first have to monitor our levels of comprehension. In other words, we need to know when comprehension is breaking down; we need to notice that we aren't actually understanding something. Furthermore, we need to know what it is that is causing our confusion. By understanding what we do not understand, as well as why we do not understand, we will be in a better position to pick the right strategy to fix our comprehension. There are various ways to teach students how to monitor their comprehension. Below is a brief description of two of the most common methods.

THINK-ALOUDS:
deliberate explanations of comprehension strategies provided to students out-loud by the teacher

THINK-ALOUDS are deliberate explanations of comprehension strategies provided to students out-loud by the teacher. Basically, the teacher models to students his or her own comprehension strategies as he or she reads aloud some text. For example, the teacher might run across a confusing idea and mention to the class that an ideal strategy would be to go back and re-read a section of text. Or, the teacher might come across a difficult word and look at the rest of the sentence to see if meaning can be derived from context. This strategy helps students in a few ways. First, students see that reading is not necessarily a continuous process, but rather one that takes multiple strategies to successfully understand what is written. Second, it actually gives students specific strategies they can use when they come across similar situations.

SELF-QUESTIONING:
reminders to students to keep comprehension visible as they read by asking themselves common questions about their text.

Another way to teach the monitoring of comprehension is by teaching students to use SELF-QUESTIONING strategies. Self-questioning strategies simply are active reading cues—essentially, reminders to students that they can keep comprehension visible as they read by asking themselves common questions about their text. For example, at the end of each section of a long story, students can be trained to self-predict about the next section. They can also ask themselves continuously, "why?" In other words, as events unfold in a story, they can constantly ask themselves, "Why did this occur?" or "Why did the character do this or that?" These types of questions greatly assist in the comprehension of text simply because they force readers to be more aware of what is going on within the text. In essence, they cause readers to be less lazy as they read.

SKILL
2.6
Demonstrating knowledge of various methods for assessing comprehension of a text *(e.g., questioning the reader, having the reader give an oral or written retelling, asking the reader to identify the theme(s) or to paraphrase or summarize the main idea)*

The point of comprehension instruction is not necessarily to focus just on the text(s) students are using at the very moment of instruction, but rather to help them learn the strategies that they can use independently with any other text.

COMMON METHODS OF TEACHING INSTRUCTION	
Summarization	Students go over the main point of the text, either in writing or verbally, along with strategically chosen details that highlight the main point. This is not the same as paraphrasing, which is saying the same thing in different words. Teaching students how to summarize is very important as it will help them look for the most critical areas in a text, and in nonfiction. For example, it will help them distinguish between main arguments and examples. In fiction, it helps students to learn how to focus on the main characters and events and distinguish those from the lesser characters and events.
Question Answering	While this tends to be overused in many classrooms, it is still a valid method of teaching students to comprehend. As the name implies, students answer questions regarding a text, either out loud, in small groups, or individually on paper. The best questions are those that cause students to have to think about the text (rather than just find an answer within the text).
Question Generating	This is the opposite of question answering, although students can then be asked to answer their own questions or the questions of peer students. In general, we want students to constantly question texts as they read. This is important because it causes students to become more critical readers. To teach students to generate questions helps them to learn the types of questions they can ask, and it gets them thinking about how best to be critical of texts.
Graphic Organizers	Graphic organizers are graphical representations of content within a text. For example, Venn Diagrams can be used to highlight the difference between two characters in a novel or two similar political concepts in a social studies textbook. Or, a teacher can use flowcharts with students to talk about the steps in a process such as the steps of setting up a science experiment or the chronological events of a story. Semantic organizers are similar in that they graphically display information. The difference, usually, is that semantic organizers focus on words or concepts. For example, a word web can help students make sense of a word by mapping from the central word all the similar and related concepts to that word.

Table continued on next page

Text Structure	Often in nonfiction, particularly in textbooks, and sometimes in fiction, text structures will give important clues to readers about what to look for. Students may not know how to make sense of all the types of headings in a textbook and do not realize that, for example, the sidebar story about a character in history is not the main text on a particular page in the history textbook. Teaching students how to interpret text structures gives them tools in which to tackle other similar texts.
Monitoring Comprehension	Students need to be aware of their comprehension, or lack of it, in particular texts. So, it is important to teach students what to do when suddenly text stops making sense. For example, students can go back and reread the description of a character. Or, they can go back to the table of contents or the first paragraph of a chapter to see where they are headed.
Textual Marking	This is where students interact with the text as they read. For example, armed with Post-it notes, students can insert questions or comments regarding specific sentences or paragraphs within the text. This helps students focus on the importance of the small things, particularly when they are reading larger works (such as novels in high school). It also gives students a reference point on which to go back into the text when they need to review something.
Discussion	Small group or whole-class discussion stimulates thoughts about texts and gives students a larger picture of the impact of those texts. For example, teachers can strategically encourage students to discuss related concepts to the text. This helps students learn to consider texts within larger societal and social concepts. Or teachers can encourage students to provide personal opinions in discussion. By listening to various students' opinions, all students in a class can see the wide range of possible interpretations and thoughts regarding one text.

Many people mistakenly believe that the terms "research-based" or "research-validated" or "evidence-based" relate mainly to specific programs, such as early reading textbook programs. While research does validate that some of these programs are effective, much research has been conducted regarding the effectiveness of particular instructional strategies. In reading, many of these strategies have been documented in the report from the National Reading Panel (2000).

Just because a strategy has not been validated as effective by research, however, does not necessarily mean that it is not effective with certain students in certain situations. The number of strategies out there far outweighs researchers' ability to test their effectiveness. Some of the strategies listed above have been validated by rigorous research, while others have been shown consistently to help improve students' reading abilities in localized situations. There simply is not enough space to list all the strategies that have been proven effective; just know that the above strategies are very commonly cited as working in a variety of situations.

COMPETENCY 3

UNDERSTAND AND APPLY READING SKILLS AND STRATEGIES FOR VARIOUS PURPOSES (INCLUDING INFORMATION AND UNDERSTANDING, CRITICAL ANALYSIS AND EVALUATION, LITERARY RESPONSE, AND SOCIAL INTERACTION)

SKILL 3.1 **Recognizing how to vary reading strategies for different texts and purposes** (e.g., skimming, scanning, in-depth reading, rereading) **and for different types and genres of written communication** (e.g., fiction, nonfiction, poetry)

One of the common fallacies students have about reading comes from the ways in which students are taught to read. Sure, as students are being taught to read, they must learn the strategies of careful reading, which includes sounding out words, focusing on fluency, obtaining meaning, etc. However, at points in the learning-to-read process, teachers can help students learn that there are various reasons why people read. Sometimes people read for pleasure, in which case they can decide whether to skim through quickly for the content or read slowly to savor ideas and language. Other times, people simply want to find information quickly, in which case they will skim or scan. In some texts, rereading is necessary to fully comprehend information.

READING STRATEGIES	
Skimming	Skimming is when readers read quickly while paying little attention to specific words. This is often done when readers want a full picture of a text but do not want to focus on the details. Skimming can be done as a preview or a review. When done as a preview, often readers will look to see what it is they can expect from the text. When done as a review, readers will hope to be reminded of the main points through the skim.
Scanning	Scanning is a bit different from skimming. In skimming, readers read connected text quickly. In scanning, readers go straight to specific ideas, words, sections, or examples. They pick and choose what they will read within a text. This is done when the reader does not need to know everything from a text.

Table continued on next page

In-Depth Reading	In-depth reading is the reading most people think is the only legitimate type of reading. Strangely, though, all types of reading are done by all types of people—all the time! In-depth reading is done when readers want to enjoy a text or learn from it thoroughly. For the most part, in this type of reading, readers will move forward quickly and not stop to focus on a specific word or idea, although sometimes this is necessary. The main idea of this type of reading, though, is that readers do not skip over or read fast to get information. They read everything carefully and thoroughly.
Rereading	Rereading is the final type of reading, which comes in many forms. Sometimes, whole texts must be reread for the concepts. This is usually the case when the text is difficult. Rereading can also be done as someone is doing regular in-depth reading. For example, a word, concept, or a few ideas may need to be reviewed before the reader can go on. Another method of rereading is rereading a whole text months or years after reading it the first time. This is done when readers realize that through their life experiences since the first reading, they will view the text in a different light.

All these methods are acceptable forms of reading, however, all must be done with specific purposes in mind. Generally, it is not a good idea to skim or scan a class novel, but skimming and scanning through a textbook may be acceptable if only a few ideas are crucial. *See also Skill 7.5*

SKILL 3.2 Applying knowledge of techniques for gathering, interpreting, and synthesizing information when reading a variety of printed texts and electronic sources

Searching for information from printed and electronic sources is a critical literacy-related activity. Increasingly, teachers realize that it is impossible to memorize or even be exposed to the majority of basic facts in our world today. Information is produced so rapidly that knowing **how to access, judge, and synthesize information will help students throughout their lives**.

To understand what this standard means, let's take it apart piece by piece. First, the gathering of information requires that students are competent with everything from a traditional library catalog system to Web-based collections. The best way to get students to feel comfortable with these sources of information is simply to have to search for specific items with proper teacher guidance. It is usually not a good idea to set students out on a journey for information without first explaining the tools and modeling how information can be found from them.

One of the most important parts of gathering information is judging the sources.

One simple cause of the rapid increase in information is that it is easier now than it has ever been for anyone to provide information to the public. For example, anyone can post wikis, blogs, and Web sites. Print material is no safer: more journals and magazines are published today, and many have very uncertain records of reliability. While even the best teacher can fall prey to bad sources of information, generally, experienced adult readers will know when quality is not sufficient. A good way to teach students how to evaluate the quality of an information source is to model how decisions are made in the judging process. For example, a teacher can show students a variety of Web sites on a particular topic. While showing students these sites, the teacher can do a "think aloud," whereby he or she expresses her opinions about the ways in which the information presented demonstrates quality or a lack thereof.

Interpreting information from a variety of sources can be challenging, as well. Many students who have experienced little nonfiction will tend to view information sources in much the same way they view their textbooks: objective and straightforward. Experienced readers will note that information sources are often opinionated, embedded in other ideas or works, part of a greater dialogue, or highly slanted. Often, the sources found are not necessarily meant for extraction of ideas from students; rather, intended audiences vary incredibly for each work. Even though we may have access to quite a bit, we may not be the anticipated audience of the writer. To teach students how to interpret nonfiction sources, have them focus on these components of the work:

- Purpose—the author's intended purpose in writing the piece

- Audience—the author's intended audience (for example, an article about a scientific phenomenon could be written for other scientists, the general public, a source of funding for an experiment, etc.)

- Argument—it is important for students to determine if the author has an argument, and what that argument is; all the information in the piece will make better sense when this is figured out

Finally, synthesizing information is a complex task. When multiple sources regarding the same concept are used, students can outline the main points of each source and look at how the pieces differ. Students can also trace similar ideas through each of the pieces to see how authors treat subjects differently or similarly. Graphic organizers can be very helpful in the synthesis of a variety of sources.

SKILL 3.3 Recognizing how to analyze and assess a writer's credibility or objectivity when reading printed and electronic texts

In analyzing and assessing a writer's credibility and objectivity when reading a printed text, there are a few straightforward methods, as well as some subtle methods.

First, the straightforward methods include investigating the background of the author, looking for the level of details provided, and examining the extent to which various sides of an issue are presented. Investigating the background of an author is fairly simple when such details are available. If so, students should determine whether or not the writer is an expert in the subject. They might also look to see the types of activities the author has done in order to establish him or herself as an expert.

Looking for the level of details provided is another method to establish the writer's credibility, whether or not a biography is provided. If an author, for example, states a proposition and does not follow it up with significant evidence, perhaps this is a text to avoid. Anyone can offer opinions, but experts are better capable of providing plentiful details as support.

It is likewise important to see that, even if an author is arguing one side of an issue, both sides of the argument are presented. If an author does not provide the other side to his or her argument, it is either possible that he or she does not know the other side (and therefore has not fully thought-out the issue) or that the author does not want the reader to know about the other side, for fear that it will make the argument less appealing.

Some more subtle ways of determining whether or not an author has the expertise or is being fair enough to both sides is including the analysis of the author's references and investigating the source of the text. If an author has no references, or only a few references, possibly that are very old, the author may not have kept up-to-date on the topic or there is a significant advancement in the field that the author would rather have readers ignore.

Finally, investigating the source of the text is crucial. Even though it is acceptable—and even encouraged—to use Web sites, students need to remember that anyone can post a Web site. Furthermore, popularized magazines may be less credible than trade or professional journals. While sources from such locations should still be considered, students must realize that their credibility is lessened slightly when published in these forms.

It is important to emphasize that just because a source argues for one side of an issue does not mean it should not be used. Students simply need to realize what the author is arguing (hence, what the author wants the reader to know about the topic)—and then to use this information as simply one source of many sources on the topic.

SKILL 3.4 Analyzing and interpreting information from texts containing tables, charts, graphs, maps, and other illustrations

Quantitative data is often easily presented in graphs and charts in many content areas. However, if students are unable to decipher the graph, its use is limited. Because information can clearly be displayed in a graph or chart form, accurate interpretation of the information is an important skill for students.

For graphs, students should be taught to evaluate all the features of the graph, including main title, what the horizontal axis represents, and what the vertical axis represents. Also, students should locate and evaluate the graph's key (if there is one) in the event there is more than one variable on the graph. For example, line graphs are often used to plot data from a scientific experiment. If more than one variable was used, a key or legend would indicate what each line on the line graph represented. Then, once students have evaluated the axes and titles, they can begin to assess the results of the experiment.

There are two good reasons for using a graph:

- To present a model or theory visually in order to show how two or more variables interrelate,

- To present real world data visually in order to show how two or more variables interrelate

Graphs are most useful when one wishes to demonstrate the sequential increase or decrease of a variable or to show specific correlations between two or more variables in a given circumstance. In all graphs, an upward sloping line represents a direct relationship between the two variables. A downward slope represents an inverse relationship between the two variables. In reading any graph, you must be very careful to understand what is being measured, what can be deduced, and what cannot be deduced from the given graph.

For charts (such as a pie chart), the process is similar to interpreting bar or line graphs. The key which depicts what each section of the pie chart represents is very important to interpreting the pie chart. Be sure to provide students with lots of assistance and practice with reading and interpreting graphs and charts so their experience with, and confidence in, reading them develops.

Information can be gained looking at a map that might take hundreds of words to explain otherwise. To show such a variety of information, maps are made in many different ways. Because of this variety, maps must be understood in order to make the best sense of them. Once they are understood, maps provide a meaningful and useful tool in communicating a particular point of view.

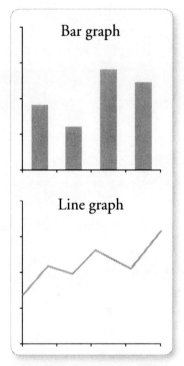

GRAPHS: show specific correlations between two or more variables in a given circumstance.

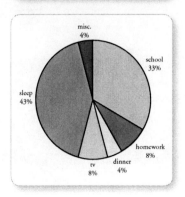

To use charts correctly, you should remember the reasons for using graphs. The general ideas are similar. It is usually a question as to which is more capable of adequately portraying the information you want to illustrate. You can see the difference between them and realize that in many ways graphs and charts are interrelated. One of the most common types, because it is easiest to read and understand, even for the lay person, is the pie chart. Pie charts get a lot of use, especially for illustrating the differences in percentages among various items or when the divisions of a whole are being demonstrated.

To interpret data in tables, we read across rows and down columns. Each item of interest has different data points listed under different column headings.

TABLE 1: SAMPLE PURCHASE ORDER				
Item	Unit	$/Unit	Qty	Tot $
Coffee	lb.	2.79	45	125.55
Milk	gal.	1.05	72	75.60
Sugar	lb.	0.23	150	34.50

In this table the first column on the left contains the items in a purchase order. The other columns contain data about each item labeled with column headings. The second column from the left gives the unit of measurement for each item, the third column gives the price per unit, the fourth column gives the quantity of each item ordered, and the fifth column gives the total cost of each item.

SKILL 3.5 Demonstrating knowledge of strategies to promote literary response skills (e.g., connecting the text to personal experience and prior knowledge, citing evidence from a text to support an interpretation, using reading logs or guided reading techniques)

BEHAVIORAL LEARNING THEORY: suggests that people learn socially or through some sort of stimulation or repetition

First, teachers should realize that historically, there are two broad sides regarding the construction of meaning, the application of strategies, etc. One is BEHAVIORAL LEARNING. Behavioral learning theory suggests that people learn socially or through some sort of stimulation or repetition. For example, when we touch a hot stove, we learn not to do that again. Or when we make a social error, and are made fun of for it, we learn proper social conventions. Or we learn to produce something by watching someone do the same thing.

The other broad theory is COGNITIVE LEARNING. Cognitive learning theories suggest that learning takes place in the mind and that the mind processes ideas through brain mapping and connections with other material and experiences. With cognitive theories, learning is internal. For example, we see something, analyze it in our minds, and make sense of it for ourselves. Then, if we choose to copy it, we do, but we do so having internalized (or thought about) the process.

Today, even though behavioral theories exist, most educators believe that children learn cognitively. So, for example, when teachers introduce new topics by relating those topics to information students are already familiar with or exposed to, they are expecting that students will be able to better integrate new information into their memories by attaching it to something that is already there. Or when teachers apply new learning to real-world situations, they are expecting that the information will make more sense when it is applied to a real situation. In all of the examples given in this standard, the importance is the application of new learning to something concrete. In essence, what is going on with these examples is that the teacher is slowing building on knowledge or adding knowledge to what students already know. Cognitively, this makes a great deal of sense. Think of a file cabinet. When we already have files for certain things, it's easy for us to find a file and throw new information into it. When we're given something that doesn't fit into one of the preexisting files, we struggle to know what to do with it. The same is true with human minds.

> **COGNITIVE LEARNING THEORY:** suggests that learning takes place in the mind and that the mind processes ideas through brain mapping and connections with other material and experiences

> *Today most educators believe that children learn cognitively.*

> *Sites on teaching reading strategies on making connections:*
>
> *TEXT-TO-TEXT:*
> *http://www.learner.org/ channel/workshops/tml/ workshop2/teaching.html*
>
> *TEXT-TO-SELF:*
> *http://www.learner.org/ channel/workshops/tml/ workshop2/teaching.html*
>
> *TEXT-TO-WORLD:*
> *http://www.learner.org/ channel/workshops/tml/ workshop2/teaching.html*

SKILL 3.6 Identifying effective ways of modeling independent reading for enjoyment and encouraging participation in a community of readers *(e.g., book clubs, literature circles)*

As with any learning experience, it is important for students to connect learning with real-world experiences. Therefore with reading, students should be given opportunities to experience reading outside the classroom or traditional classroom methods.

Literature circles involve a group discussion with no more than six children, but usually fewer than four, who have read the same work of literature (narrative or expository text). They talk about key parts of the work, relate it to their own experience, listen to the responses of others, and discuss how parts of the text relate to the whole. Literature circles are excellent for the classroom setting because they mimic book clubs while providing a format for the discussion meeting for students who are learning to discuss literature.

Book clubs are another excellent opportunity for students to discuss reading in an open setting. Whether it be at a local library, school library group, recess group, or parent–child evening reading program, book clubs promote reading in an enjoyable setting not attached to traditional homework assignments and book reports.

Sample Test Questions and Rationale

Rigorous

1. **Behavioral learning theory suggests that people:**

   A. Learn socially

   B. Learn through stimulation

   C. Learn through repetition

   D. All of the above

   Answer: D – All of the above

   Rationale: Behavioral learning theory suggests that people learn socially or through some sort of stimulation or repetition. For example, when we touch a hot stove, we learn not to do that again. Or, when we make a social error, and are made fun of for it, we learn proper social conventions. Or, we learn to produce something by watching someone do the same thing.

Rigorous

2. **Most educators believe that children learn:**

   A. Cognitively

   B. Behaviorally

   C. Physically

   D. Emotionally

   Answer: A – Cognitively

   Rationale: Today, even though behavioral theories exist, most educators believe that children learn cognitively. So, for example, when teachers introduce new topics by relating those topics to information students are already familiar with or exposed to, they are expecting that students will be able to better integrate new information into their memories by attaching it to something that is already there.

COMPETENCY 4
UNDERSTAND PROCESSES FOR GENERATING, DEVELOPING, REVISING, EDITING, AND PRESENTING/ PUBLISHING WRITTEN TEXTS

SKILL 4.1 Applying knowledge of prewriting strategies (e.g., brainstorming, prioritizing and selecting topics including clustering and other graphic organizers)

Students gather ideas before writing. PREWRITING may include clustering, listing, brainstorming, mapping, free writing, and charting.

Remind students that as they prewrite that they need to consider their audience. Prewriting strategies assist students in a variety of ways. Listed below are the most common prewriting strategies students can use to explore, plan, and write on a topic. It is important to remember when teaching these strategies that not all prewriting must eventually produce a finished piece of writing. In fact, in the initial lesson of teaching prewriting strategies, it might be more effective to have students practice prewriting strategies without the pressure of having to write a finished product.

- Keep an idea book so that they can jot down ideas that come to mind

- Write in a daily journal

- Write down whatever comes to mind; this is called free writing. Students do not stop to make corrections or interrupt the flow of ideas.

A variation of this technique is focused FREE WRITING—writing on a specific topic—to prepare for an essay.

- Make a list of all ideas connected with their topic; this is called BRAINSTORMING.

- Make sure students know that this technique works best when they let their mind work freely. After completing the list, students should analyze the list to see if there is a pattern or way to group the ideas.

- Ask the questions Who? What? When? Where? When? and How? Help the writer approach a topic from several perspectives.

- Create a visual map on paper to gather ideas. Cluster circles and lines to show connections between ideas. Students should try to identify the relationship that exists between their ideas. If they cannot see the relationships, have them pair up, exchange papers, and have their partners look for some related ideas.

PREWRITING: gathering ideas before writing

Providing many ways for a student to develop ideas on a topic will increase his or her chances for success.

FREE WRITING: writing on a specific topic

BRAINSTORMING: making a list of all ideas connected with a topic

To learn more about teaching writing:

http://school.discoveryeducation.com/lessonplans/programs/writingStrat/#mat

http://www.gse.buffalo.edu/org/writingstrategies/steps.htm

http://www2.scholastic.com/browse/teach.jsp

- Observe details of sight, hearing, taste, touch, and smell.

- Visualize by making mental images of something and write down the details in a list.

After they have practiced with each of these prewriting strategies, ask them to pick out the ones they prefer and ask them to discuss how they might use the techniques to help them with future writing assignments. It is important to remember that they can use more than one prewriting strategy at a time. Also they may find that different writing situations may suggest certain techniques. *For more information on graphic organizers, see Skill 2.4*

TEACHING-LEARNING STRATEGIES		
Teacher-Guided	**Student Empowerment**	**Specific Strategies**
BEFORE		
• Discovering what to say about a particular topic • Considering the variables of purpose, audience, and form • Planning	• What is my topic? My purpose? • Who is my audience? • What should I say? • What form should I use? • How should I organize my ideas?	• Talking, interviewing, reading, researching • Brainstorming, listing, clustering, mapping, webbing, flowcharting, outlining • Focused free writing • Heuristics (questions/prompts/leads) • Reading and examining models • Viewing, visualization, guided imagery • Journal writing
DURING		
• Saying what is meant as directly and clearly as possible • Finding an appropriate voice and point of view • Telling the reader about the topic	• How can I introduce my topic? • How can I develop each part? • How can I conclude my topic?	• Mapping thoughts • Writing off a lead • Fast or free writing • Personal letter • Conferencing • Reflecting and questioning self

Table continued on next page

REVISING		
• Editing for ideas and organization • Proofreading for conventions other than content	• Have I edited and proofread? • Have I practiced a variety of editing and proofreading methods? Which work best for me?	• Reading aloud to another • Using revision checklists • Check and question marks • Using a "pass" strategy • Self-monitoring • Peer conferencing

Sample Test Questions and Rationale

Easy

1. **Which of the following is not a technique of prewriting?**

   A. Clustering

   B. Listing

   C. Brainstorming

   D. Proofreading

Answer: D – Proofreading

Rationale: Proofreading cannot be a method of prewriting, since it is done on already written texts only.

SKILL 4.2 Identifying effective techniques of note taking, outlining, and drafting

Once information is collected and categorized according to the research design and outline, the user can begin to take notes on the gathered information to create a cut-and-paste format for the final report.

Being an effective note taker requires consistent technique, whether the mode of note taking is on 5x7 note cards; lined notebook; or on a computer. Organizing all collected information according to a research outline will allow the user to take notes on each section and begin the writing process. If the computer is used, then the actual format of the report can be word-processed and information input to speed up the writing process of the final research report. Creating a title page and bibliography page will allow each downloaded report to have its resources cited immediately in that section.

Note taking involves identification of specific resources that include the author's or organization's name, year of publication, title, publisher location, and publisher. When taking notes, whether on the computer or using note cards, use the author's last name and page number on cited information. In citing information for major categories and subcategories on the computer, create a file for notes that includes summaries of information and direct quotes. When direct quotes are put into a word processor file, the cut-and-paste process for incorporation into the report is quick and easy.

In outline information, it is crucial to identify the headings and subheadings for the topic being researched. When researching information, it is easier to cut and paste information under the indicated headings in creating a visual flow of information for the report. In the actual drafting of the report, the writer is able to lift direct quotations and citations from the posted information to incorporate in the writing.

SKILL 4.3 Revising written texts to improve unity and logical organization
(e.g., formulating topic sentences, reordering paragraphs or sentences, adding transition words and phrases, eliminating distracting sentences)

> *Revision is probably the most important step for the writer in the writing process.*

Revise comes from the Latin word *revidere*, meaning, "to see again." Revision is probably the most important step for the writer in the writing process. Here, students examine their work and make changes in wording, details and ideas. So many times, students write a draft and then feel they're done. On the contrary—students must be encouraged to develop, change, and enhance their writing as they go, as well as once they've completed a draft.

Therefore, effective teachers realize that revision and editing go hand-in-hand and that students often move back and forth between these stages during the course of one written work. Also, these stages must be practiced in small groups, pairs, and/ or individually. Students must learn to analyze and improve their own work as well as the works of their peers. Some methods to use include:

> *Teachers who facilitate effective Writer's Workshops are able to meet with students one at a time and can guide that student in their individual writing needs. This approach allows the teacher to differentiate instruction for each student's writing level.*

- Students, working in pairs, analyze sentences for variety

- Students work in pairs or groups to ask questions about unclear areas in the writing or to help students add details, information, etc.

- Students perform final edit

Many teachers introduce Writer's Workshop to their students to maximize learning about the writing process. Writer's Workshops vary across classrooms, but the main idea is for students to become comfortable with the writing process to produce written work. A basic Writer's Workshop will include a block of classroom time committed to writing various projects (i.e., narratives, memoirs, book summaries, fiction, book reports,). Students use this time to write, meet with others to review/edit writing, make comments on writing, revise their own work, proofread, meet with the teacher, and publish their work.

Students need to be trained to become effective at proofreading, revising, and editing strategies. Begin by training them using both desk-side and scheduled conferences. Here are some strategies to use to guide students through the final stages of the writing process (and these can easily be incorporated into a Writer's Workshop).

- Provide some guide sheets or forms for students to use during peer responses.

- Allow students to work in pairs and limit the agenda.

- Model the use of the guide sheet or form for the entire class.

- Give students a time limit or number of written pieces to be completed in a specific amount of time.

- Have the students read their partners' papers and ask at least three who, what, when, why, how questions. The students answer the questions and use them as a place to begin discussing the piece.

- At this point in the writing process a mini-lesson that focuses on some of the problems your students are having would be appropriate.

To help students revise, provide them with a series of questions that will assist them in revising their writing.

- Do the details give a clear picture? Add details that appeal to more than just the sense of sight.

- How effectively are the details organized? Reorder the details if it is needed.

- Are the thoughts and feelings of the writer included? Add personal thoughts and feelings about the subject.

As you discuss revision, begin by discussing the definition of revise. Also, state that all writing must be revised to improve it. After students have revised their writing, it is time for the final editing and proofreading.

Writing Introductions

It is important to remember that in the writing process, the introduction should be written last. Until the body of the paper has been determined—thesis, develop-ment—it's difficult to make strategic decisions regarding the introduction. The Greek rhetoricians called this part of a discourse *exordium*, a "leading into." The basic purpose of the introduction, then, is to lead the audience into the discourse.

In the writing process, the introduction should be written last. It can let the reader know what the purpose of the discourse is and it can condition the audience to be receptive to what the writer wants to say.

It can let the reader know what the purpose of the discourse is and it can condition the audience to be receptive to what the writer wants to say. It can be very brief or it can take up a large percentage of the total word count. Aristotle said that the introduction could be compared to the flourishes that flute players make before their performance—an overture in which the musicians display what they can play best in order to gain the favor and attention of the audience for the main performance.

In order to do this, we must first of all know what we are going to say; who the readership is likely to be; what the social, political, economic, climate is; what preconceived notions the audience is likely to have regarding the subject; and how long the discourse is going to be.

There are many ways to do this:

- Show that the subject is important

- Show that although the points we are presenting may seem improbable, they are true

- Show that the subject has been neglected, misunderstood, or misrepresented

- Explain an unusual mode of development

- Forestall any misconception of the purpose

- Apologize for a deficiency

- Arouse interest in the subject with an anecdotal lead in

- Ingratiate oneself with the readership

- Establish one's own credibility

The introduction often ends with the thesis, the point or purpose of the paper. However, this is not set in stone. The thesis may open the body of the discussion or it may conclude the discourse. The most important thing to remember is that the purpose and structure of the introduction should be deliberate if it is to serve the purpose of "leading the reader into the discussion."

Writing Conclusions

It is easier to write a conclusion after the decisions regarding the introduction have been made. Aristotle taught that the conclusion should strive to do five things:

1. Inspire the reader with a favorable opinion of the writer

2. Amplify the force of the points made in the body of the paper

3. Reinforce the points made in the body

4. Rouse appropriate emotions in the reader

5. Restate in a summary way what has been said

The conclusion may be short or it may be long depending on its purpose in the paper. Recapitulation, a brief restatement of the main points or certainly of the thesis, is the most common form of effective conclusion. A good example is the closing argument in a court trial.

Text Organization

In studies of professional writers and how they produce their successful works, it has been revealed that writing is a process that can be clearly defined although in practice it must have enough flexibility to allow for creativity. The teacher must be able to define the various stages that a successful writer goes through in order to make a statement that has value. There must be a discovery stage when ideas, materials, supporting details, etc., are deliberately collected. These may come from many possible sources: the writer's own experience and observations, deliberate research of written sources, interviews of live people, television presentations, or the Internet.

The next stage is organization, where the purpose, thesis, and supporting points are determined. Most writers will put forth more than one possible thesis and in the next stage—the writing of the paper—settle on one as the result of trial and error. Once the paper is written, the editing stage is necessary and is probably the most important stage. This is not just the polishing stage. At this point, decisions must be made regarding whether the reasoning is cohesive: Does it hold together? Is the arrangement the best possible one or should the points be rearranged? Are there holes that need to be filled in? What form will the introduction take? Does the conclusion lead the reader out of the discourse or is it inadequate or too abrupt?

It's important to remember that the best writers engage in all of these stages recursively. They may go back to discovery at any point in the process. They may go back and rethink the organization. To help students become effective writers, the teacher needs to give them adequate practice in the various stages and encourage them to engage deliberately in the creative thinking that makes writers successful.

> ### SKILL 4.4 Editing written work to ensure conformity to conventions of standard English usage (e.g., eliminating misplaced or dangling modifiers, eliminating sentence fragments, correcting errors in subject-verb agreement and pronoun-antecedent agreement)

Revise Misplaced or Dangling Modifiers

Particular phrases that are not placed near the word they modify often result in misplaced modifiers. Particular phrases that do not relate to the subject being modified result in dangling modifiers.

> *Error:*
>
> *Weighing the options carefully, a decision was made regarding the punishment of the convicted murderer.*

Problem: Who is weighing the options? No one capable of weighing is named in the sentence; thus, the participle phrase *weighing the options carefully* dangles. This problem can be corrected by adding a subject of the sentence capable of doing the action.

> *Correction:*
>
> *Weighing the options carefully, the judge made a decision regarding the punishment of the convicted murderer.*

Sentence Completeness

Avoid fragments and run-on sentences. Recognition of sentence elements necessary to make a complete thought, proper use of independent and dependent clauses (see section titled, "Use correct coordination and subordination"), and proper punctuation will correct such errors.

Recognize simple, compound, complex, and compound-complex sentences. Use dependent (subordinate) and independent clauses correctly to create these sentence structures.

Simple	*Joyce wrote a letter.*
Compound	*Joyce wrote a letter, and Dot drew a picture.*
Complex	*While Joyce wrote a letter, Dot drew a picture.*
Compound/Complex	*When Mother asked the girls to demonstrate their new-found skills, Joyce wrote a letter, and Dot drew a picture.*

Note: Do **not** confuse compound sentence elements with compound sentences.

Simple sentence with compound subject

Joyce and *Dot* wrote letters.

The *girl* in row three and the *boy* next to her were passing notes across the aisle.

Simple sentence with compound predicate

Joyce *wrote letters* and *drew pictures*.

The captain of the high school debate team *graduated with honors* and *studied broadcast journalism in college*.

Subject-Verb Agreement

A verb agrees in number with its subject. Making them agree relies on the ability to properly identify the subject.

One of the boys *was playing* too rough.

No one in the class, not the teacher nor the students, *was listening* to the message from the intercom.

The *candidates*, including a grandmother and a teenager, *are debating* some controversial issues.

If two singular subjects are connected by *and* the verb must be plural.

A *man* and his *dog* were jogging on the beach.

If two singular subjects are connected by *or* or *nor*, a singular verb is required.

Neither Dot nor Joyce has missed a day of school this year.

If one singular subject and one plural subject are connected by *or* or *nor*, the verb agrees with the subject nearest to the verb.

Neither the coach nor the players were able to sleep on the bus.

If the subject is a collective noun, its sense of number in the sentence determines the verb: singular if the noun represents a group or unit and plural if the noun represents individuals.

The **House of Representatives has adjourned** for the holidays.

The **House of Representatives have failed** to reach agreement on the subject of adjournment.

Sample Test Questions and Rationale

Rigorous

1. Which of the following is a complex sentence?

   A. Anna and Margaret read a total of fifty-four books during summer vacation.

   B. The youngest boy on the team had the best earned run average, which mystifies the coaching staff.

   C. Earl decided to attend Princeton; his twin brother Roy, who aced the ASVAB test, will be going to Annapolis.

   D. "Easy come, easy go," Marcia moaned.

Answer: B – The youngest boy on the team had the best earned run average, which mystifies the coaching staff

Rationale: Mother's-in-law frown is the best answer. Mother-in-Law is a compound common noun and the inflection should be at the end of the word, according to the rule.

SKILL 4.5 Editing and proofreading written work to correct misspellings and eliminate errors in punctuation and capitalization

Students should proofread the draft for punctuation and mechanical errors. There are a few key points to remember when helping students learn to edit and proofread their work.

- It is crucial that students are not taught grammar in isolation, but in context of the writing process

- Ask students to read their writing and check for specific errors like using a subordinate clause as a sentence

- Provide students with a proofreading checklist to guide them as they edit their work

Spelling

Concentration in this section will be on spelling plurals and possessives. The multiplicity and complexity of spelling rules based on phonics, letter doubling, and exceptions to rules—not mastered by adulthood—should be replaced by a good dictionary. As spelling mastery is also difficult for adolescents, our recommendation is the same. Learning the use of a dictionary and thesaurus will be a more rewarding use of time.

Most plurals of nouns that end in hard consonants or hard consonant sounds followed by a silent e are made by adding *s*. Some words ending in vowels only add s.

> *fingers, numerals, banks, bugs, riots, homes, gates, radios, bananas*

Nouns that end in soft consonant sounds *s, j, x, z, ch,* and *sh*, add *es*. Some nouns ending in *o* add *es*.

> *dresses, waxes, churches, brushes, tomatoes, potatoes*

Nouns ending in *y* preceded by a vowel just add *s*.

> *boys, alleys*

Nouns ending in *y* preceded by a consonant change the *y* to *i* and add *es*.

> *babies, corollaries, frugalities, poppies*

Some nouns plurals are formed irregularly or remain the same.

> *sheep, deer, children, leaves, oxen*

Capitalization

Capitalize all PROPER NAMES of **people** (including specific organizations or agencies of government); **places** (countries, states, cities, parks, and specific geographical areas); and **things** (political parties, structures, historical and cultural terms, and calendar and time designations); and religious terms (any deity, revered person or group, sacred writings).

PROPER NOUNS: people, places, and things

> *Percy Bysshe Shelley, Argentina, Mount Rainier National Park, Grand Canyon, League of Nations, the Sears Tower, Birmingham, Lyric Theater, Americans, Midwesterners, Democrats, Renaissance, Boy Scouts of America, Easter, God, Bible, Dead Sea Scrolls, Koran*

Capitalize proper adjectives and titles used with proper names.

> *California gold rush, President John Adams, French fries, Homeric epic, Romanesque architecture, Senator John Glenn*

Note: Some words that represent titles and offices are not capitalized unless used with a proper name.

Capitalized	Not Capitalized
Congressman McKay	*the congressman from Florida*
Commander Alger	*commander of the Pacific Fleet*
Queen Elizabeth	*the queen of England*

Capitalize all main words in titles of works of literature, art, and music.

The candidate should be cognizant of proper rules and conventions of punctuation, capitalization, and spelling. Competency exams will generally test the ability to apply the more advanced skills; thus, a limited number of more frustrating rules is presented here. Rules should be applied according to the American style of English, i.e., spelling theater instead of theatre and placing terminal marks of punctuation almost exclusively within other marks of punctuation.

Punctuation

Quotation marks

In a quoted statement that is either declarative or imperative, place the period inside the closing quotation marks.

> *"The airplane crashed on the runway during takeoff."*

If the quotation is followed by other words in the sentence, place a comma inside the closing quotation marks and a period at the end of the sentence.

> *"The airplane crashed on the runway during takeoff," said the announcer.*

In most instances in which a quoted title or expression occurs at the end of a sentence, the period is placed before either the single or double quotation marks.

> *"The middle school readers were unprepared to understand Bryant's poem 'Thanatopsis.'"*
>
> *Early book-length adventure stories like* Don Quixote *and* The Three Musketeers *were known as "picaresque novels."*

In sentences that are interrogatory or exclamatory, the question mark or exclamation point should be positioned outside the closing quotation marks if the quote itself is a statement or command or cited title.

> *Who decided to lead us in the recitation of the "Pledge of Allegiance"?*
>
> *Why was Tillie shaking as she began her recitation, "Once upon a midnight dreary..."?*
>
> *I was embarrassed when Mrs. White said, "Your slip is showing"!*

In sentences that are declarative but the quotation is a question or an exclamation, place the question mark or exclamation point inside the quotation marks.

> *The hall monitor yelled, "Fire! Fire!"*
>
> *Cory shrieked, "Is there a mouse in the room?" (In this instance, the question supersedes the exclamation.)*

Using periods with parentheses

Place the period inside the parentheses or brackets if they enclose a complete sentence that is independent of the other sentences around it.

> *Stephen Crane was a confirmed alcohol and drug addict. (He admitted as much to other journalists in Cuba.)*

If the parenthetical expression is a statement inserted within another statement, the period in the enclosure is omitted.

> *Mark Twain used the character Indian Joe (he also appeared in* The Adventures of Tom Sawyer*) as a foil for Jim in* The Adventures of Huckleberry Finn.

Commas

Separate two or more coordinate adjectives modifying the same word and three or more nouns, phrases, or clauses in a list.

> *Maggie's hair was dull, dirty, and lice-ridden.*
>
> *Dickens portrayed the Artful Dodger as a skillful pickpocket, loyal follower of Fagin, and defendant of Oliver Twist.*
>
> *Ellen daydreamed about getting out of the rain, taking a shower, and eating a hot dinner.*
>
> *In Elizabethan England, Ben Johnson wrote comedy, Christopher Marlowe wrote tragedies, and William Shakespeare composed both.*

Use commas to separate antithetical or complimentary expressions from the rest of the sentence.

> *The veterinarian, not his assistant, would perform the delicate surgery.*
>
> *The more he knew about her, the less he wished he had known.*
>
> *Randy hopes to, and probably will, get an appointment to the Naval Academy.*
>
> *His thorough, though esoteric, scientific research could not easily be understood by high school students.*

Semicolons

Use semicolons to separate independent clauses when the second clause is introduced by a transitional adverb. (These clauses may also be written as separate sentences, preferably by placing the adverb within the second sentence.)

> *The Elizabethans modified the rhyme scheme of the sonnet; thus, it was called the English sonnet.*
>
> *or*
>
> *The Elizabethans modified the rhyme scheme of the sonnet. It thus was called the English sonnet.*

Use semicolons to separate items in a series that are long and complex or have internal punctuation.

> *The Italian Renaissance produced masters in the fine arts: Dante Alighieri, author of the Divine Comedy; Leonardo da Vinci, painter of The Last Supper; and Donatello, sculptor of the Quattro Coronati, the four saints.*
>
> *The leading scorers in the WNBA were Haixia Zheng, averaging 23.9 points per game; Lisa Leslie, 22; and Cynthia Cooper, 19.5.*

Colons

Place a colon at the beginning of a list of items. (Note its use in the sentence about Renaissance Italians on the previous page.)

> *The teacher directed us to compare Faulkner's three symbolic novels:* Absalom, Absalom; As I Lay Dying; *and* Light in August.

Do not use a comma if the list is preceded by a verb.

> *Three of Faulkner's symbolic novels are* Absalom, Absalom; As I Lay Dying, *and* Light in August.

Dashes

Place dashes to denote sudden breaks in thought.

> *Some periods in literature—the Romantic Age, for example—spanned different time periods in different countries.*

Use dashes instead of commas if commas are already used elsewhere in the sentence for amplification or explanation.

> *The Fireside Poets included three Brahmans—James Russell Lowell, Henry David Wadsworth, Oliver Wendell Holmes—and John Greenleaf Whittier.*

Use italics to punctuate the titles of long works of literature, names of periodical publications, musical scores, works of art and motion picture television, and radio programs. (When unable to write in italics, students should be instructed to underline in their own writing where italics would be appropriate.)

> *The Idylls of the King*   *Hiawatha*   *The Sound and the Fury*
> *Mary Poppins*   *Newsweek*   *The Nutcracker Suite*

SKILL 4.6 **Applying knowledge of the uses of technology to plan, create, revise, edit, and present/publish written texts and multimedia works**

Students may have their work displayed on a bulletin board, read aloud in class, or printed in a literary magazine or school anthology. It is important to realize that these steps are recursive; as a student engages in each aspect of the writing process, he or she may begin with prewriting, write, revise, write, revise, edit, and publish. They do not engage in this process in a lockstep manner; it is more circular.

There are many uses of technology for each of the steps of the writing process. When students write in school, they do not get the opportunity to fully express their sense of creativity and talent by simply turning in text for the teacher to read. That is why students gain so much from presenting their writing to other students, as well as mix into their writing multimedia elements. For example, a report on history comes alive when students can develop a multimedia presentation that involves photographs, short video, music, poetry, and narration. Such activity definitely requires good technology; however, when it is available, teachers find that it dramatically enhances students' enjoyment and learning.

Technology is very instrumental in the writing and learning process. Today, there is not a widespread conception that what gets written down is final. Typewriters are no longer the norm. Instead, anything can be cut, moved, deleted, and modified by the movement of the mouse.

Now while it is true that technology has assisted writers in feeling more confident with making spontaneous changes to text, students often still have a strange conception that the first draft is golden. They simply need to learn that typical first drafts look nothing like good final drafts. Students can learn this by understanding the writing process from the perspective of word processing (as we describe the writing process while using technology, we will also make parallels to multimedia work).

First, all forms of technology that allow users to create and revise give us the opportunity to create rough sketches and to constantly monitor and modify those rough sketches. While we create new material, we can and should always go back to the material we have already created to ensure that it fits in with what we are currently creating. Often, writers end up on tangents. By constantly going back to the beginning and rereading what we have written, we ensure that our original intent is still in the forefront of our minds.

Second, because editing is so simple through technology, we can genuinely focus on content for the majority of the time. Editing can be done at the end, once the content is in the order and mode we want it in.

Finally, publishing and sharing work through technology does not have to be an "end-product" activity. Through technology, we can share work with others before we consider it to be in final draft stage. With input from others, we can add and revise based on others' suggestions. Whereas with the typewriter, the "final" typed product would have to be completely retyped if suggestions were given, today, with our wide array of technology, making even the most minor of adjustments does not harm the integrity of the work, nor does it require extensive revision to fix it. *See also Skill 5.2*

COMPETENCY 5

UNDERSTAND AND APPLY WRITING SKILLS AND STRATEGIES FOR VARIOUS PURPOSES (INCLUDING INFORMATION AND UNDERSTANDING, CRITICAL ANALYSIS AND EVALUATION, LITERARY RESPONSE AND PERSONAL EXPRESSION, AND SOCIAL INTERACTION)

> **SKILL** Analyzing factors a writer should consider when writing for
> **5.1** a variety of audiences and purposes *(e.g., informative, persuasive, expressive)*, including factors related to selection of topic and mode of written expression

In the past, teachers have assigned reports, paragraphs, and essays that focused on the teacher as the audience with the purpose of explaining information. However, for students to be meaningfully engaged in their writing, they must write for a variety of reasons. Writing for different audiences and aims allows students to be more involved in their writing. If they write for the same audience and purpose, they will continue to see writing as just another assignment. Listed here are suggestions that give students an opportunity to write in more creative and critical ways.

- Write letters to the editor, to a college, to a friend, to another student who would be sent to the intended audience.

- Write stories that would be read aloud to a group (the class, another group of students, to a group of elementary school students) or published in a literary magazine or class anthology.

- Write plays that would be performed.

- Discuss the parallels between the different speech styles we use and writing styles for different readers or audiences.

- Write a particular piece for different audiences.

- Expose students to writing that is on the same topic but with a different audience and have them identify the variations in sentence structure and style.

• As part of the prewriting have students identify the audience. Make sure students consider these points when analyzing the needs of their audience:

– Why is the audience reading my writing? Do they expect to be informed, amused, or persuaded?

– What does my audience already know about my topic?

– What does the audience want or need to know? What will interest them?

– What type of language suits my readers?

Remind your students that it is not necessary to identify all the specifics of the audience in the initial stage of the writing process but that at some point they must make some determinations about audience.

Sample Test Questions and Rationale

Average Rigor

1. **Which of the following is not an approach to keep students ever conscious of the need to write for audience appeal?**

    A. Pairing students during the writing process

    B. Reading all rough drafts before the students write the final copies

    C. Having students compose stories or articles for publication in school literary magazines or newspapers

    D. Writing letters to friends or relatives

Answer: B – Reading all rough drafts before the students write the final copies

Rationale: Reading all rough drafts will not encourage the students to take control of their text and might even inhibit their creativity. On the contrary, pairing students will foster their sense of responsibility, and having them compose stories for literary magazines will boost their self esteem as well as their organization skills. As far as writing letters is concerned, the work of authors such as Madame de Sevigne in the seventeenth century is a good example of epistolary literary work.

SKILL 5.2 Recognizing how to incorporate graphic representations *(e.g., diagrams, graphs, time lines)* into writing for various purposes

While the teaching of writing undoubtedly involves an enormous amount of work on the composition of text, it also involves the general concept of ideas conveyed in the best possible manner. In other words, the results of a survey could be explained in words, but it might be easier to understand in a graph or chart. If that is the case, why would we want to present it in words? The important point is for the information to be conveyed effectively.

So, as students write reports and respond to ideas in writing, they can learn how to incorporate multiple representations of information, including various graphic representations, into written text. While this is seemingly fairly easy to do considering the word processing technology we have available to us, students struggle with knowing how to appropriately and successfully do this. They can learn to do this in three primary ways: explanation, observation/modeling, and practice.

First, students need to have clear explanations from teachers on appropriate forms of graphical representations in text, as well as the methods in which to include those representations. They need to see plenty of examples of how it is done.

Second, they need to be able to see teacher-modeled examples where text has been replaced or enhanced by graphical representations. The more they see of examples, the clearer the concepts will be to them.

Finally, students need to get a chance to practice incorporating graphical representations in their writing. This, of course, will require technology and plenty of feedback.

Students will most likely appreciate the ability to utilize graphical representations in place of text, but they will soon realize that deciding which type of representation to use and how to actually use it will be very challenging.

> *Generally, graphical representations should be used only if they can convey information better than written text can. This is an important principal that students will need to learn through constant practice.*

SKILL 5.3 Applying knowledge of skills involved in writing a research paper *(e.g., generating ideas and questions, posing problems, evaluating and summarizing data from a variety of print and nonprint sources)*

A research paper begins with an idea. Once the idea or thesis is formulated, the real work begins in collecting data and evaluating that data in connection with the proposed topic. The topic, thesis, or idea becomes the controlling statement that is analyzed throughout the research paper and supported using electronic and print resources. The documentation of data to support the controlling statement provides crucial validity to the research project. In other words, it is not simply the opinion of the writer that a thesis is valid, but it is the documentation of data from valid resources that support that thesis.

Information comes from a variety of sources. There are primary and secondary sources of print and nonprint information. Primary sources are first-person interviews and original resources that can provide direct citations for reports. Secondary sources are writings about primary sources that include reviews and interpretations of events. For a research project, the goal is to include a diversity of sources to provide credibility and validity to the final product. Here is a list of primary and secondary sources:

Primary Sources	Secondary Sources
• Novels, diaries, manuscripts, autobiographies, plays	• Reviews, biographies, articles
• Speeches, government reports	• Reports, magazines
• Survey results, case studies, reports from certified practitioners	• Evaluation of reports, books, articles
• Experiments, scientific findings, observations	• Analysis of test results, reviews
• Films, music	• Business world reviews, documents, journals
• Business research surveys, computer data	• Evaluation of data, books, reports, studies
• Research studies, surveys, statistical results	

SKILL 5.4 Identifying techniques for expressing point of view, using logical organization, and avoiding bias in writing for critical analysis, evaluation, or persuasion

In writing, students can be taught to express their points of view either implicitly or explicitly, depending on the situation, the intended audience, and purpose. Often, in a clear-cut argumentative essay, students should portray their points of view and opinions explicitly. In other words, they should make it very clear what their belief or argument is. However, in persuasive or critical essays that are intended to slowly draw someone from one perspective to the student's perspective, it is often a better idea to hide the argument within the examples and other areas of support. For an audience who may already agree with the writer's perspective, it is useful to clearly state the argument; for an audience who may not agree with the writer's perspective, it is safer to ease the audience into the argument with examples and support first.

Logical organization for a **supportive audience** looks like this:

- Argument

- Weak example

- Adequate example

- Strong example

By organizing in this fashion, the writer clearly states the opinion up front (so to keep the audience interested). Then, the writer arranges the weakest arguments first, so that the strong examples at the end assist in a strong, emphasis-filled conclusion.

Logical organization for a **nonsupportive audience** looks like this:

- Example

- Example

- Example

- Argument

Or

- Argument (stated very lightly)

- Strong example

- Adequate example

- Weak example

The reason for this approach is that we want the audience to be drawn in by the facts of the case first. Then, once they have, in essence, agreed on the facts, the writer can suggest that, "If you believe X, you must also believe Y." And hence, Y is the argument that they first did not accept.

This type of approach works for persuasive writing, argumentation, critical analysis, and evaluation. In each type of writing, we are trying to convince the reader of our thesis. Even with critical analysis, where opinions might not be as heated, if we propose out of the ordinary ideas, we might be better off using the approach for a nonsupportive audience.

Finally, in order to write—either for or against an idea—and not utilize biased language, we need to write as much as possible in an active voice and be concise. If a word is not needed, it should be eliminated. Writers can further remove bias by putting themselves in the frames of mind of various people for or against an issue and rereading the essay. Even if we are arguing for a particular topic, we want to remain bias-free, so that we look like we are simply presenting the best possible solution to any problem, for example. Let's say we are arguing for gun control. We want to write not as if we have always been gun control supporters, but rather as unbiased people who have simply come to the best decision about the topic.

Sample Test Questions and Rationale

Easy

1. **Writing that is intended to change the reader's mind is called:**

   A. Narration

   B. Expository

   C. Persuasion

   D. Description

Answer: C – Persuasion

Rationale: Persuasion is a piece of writing, a poem, a play, or a speech whose purpose is to change the minds of the audience members or to get them to do something. Exposition is discourse whose only purpose is to inform. Narration is discourse that is arranged chronologically: something happened, and then something else happened, and then something else happened. Description is discourse whose purpose is to make an experience available through one of the five senses: seeing, smelling, hearing, feeling (as with the fingers), and tasting

SKILL 5.5 Demonstrating knowledge of strategies for writing a response to a literary selection by referring to the text, to other works, and to personal experience

Writing about literature is a very tough task. It demands that students fully comprehend the text. It demands that they understand unstated elements of the text, such as character motives. It demands that they dig deep into their personal experiences to help make connections to the author's intentions. Finally, it also demands that they consider other works of literature to help explain literary conventions, issues, and other complex components of literature.

Of course, when you incorporate writing into the mix just presented above, you make the task even more difficult! Imagine just for a moment that you, the teacher, have given students the assignment of writing about a novel or story they have just read. Your students must face a blank piece of paper and make sense of a complex piece of literature. They must explain literary conventions, characters, settings, and plot. Most will sit and stare at the blank piece of paper, nervous about how to even begin.

What are some ways to help students get beyond that fear of writing about literature? First, utilizing graphic organizers helps students make visual sense of various literary elements. This often helps them organize their writing. Sometimes, outlining major points is also helpful.

Even more helpful is giving students a more authentic task than simply writing about literature in an abstract sense. Although writing about literature analytically may be the goal in mind, teachers can help students get there by giving them very specific writing tasks. For example, teachers can ask students to write a newspaper story explaining an event in the story. Or they can have students write a letter from one character to another. Once students feel comfortable with these tasks, teachers can move them beyond by having them incorporate knowledge of more than one book—or they can have them involve their own personal experiences into writing about literature. Eventually, with enough practice, students will be so much more facile with writing about literature that an analysis writing task will not be so strenuous. The key, though, is building students up to the task by having them experiment with writing about the literature in fun, authentic, natural ways.

SKILL 5.6 Demonstrating awareness of voice in writing for personal expression and social interaction

Whether teachers use children's literature to introduce literary concepts to students or to give students fun, simple ways to enjoy literature, children's literature is no doubt a great way to get students to feel comfortable with literary analysis.

Let's take a fifth-grade class, for example. The students are about to embark on the study of a complex novel. The teacher knows that students will need to understand the author's style, the theme of the work, and the author's voice. Does the teacher jump right into the novel? Or does the teacher use a simple piece of literature to first teach the concepts so that when they get into the more complex novel, for example, they will already know what the concepts mean?

Consider this: A novel involves a character telling the story of his friend. There is no doubt that if the author had the friend's mother tell the story, the novel would come across quite differently. So, the teacher presents *The Three Bears*. This is a story that is told in third person. The teachers ask students to redesign the story as if Goldilocks had told the story. Then the teacher asks the students to redesign the story once more as if Papa Bear had told the story. Students will quickly see that while the plot does not change, the way the plot is presented changes slightly.

Children's literature can similarly enlighten students on the various aspects of theme and style, as well as many other literary elements.

The more children learn literary elements through simple children's stories, the easier it will be for them to make connections to more complex literature.

Voice includes, besides point of view, originality, authenticity, and individuality. The piece needs to be written in such a way that the individuality of the author shows through. It should be written in a way that only that author would write it. That means not copying the language that another author might use, but using one's own words. Originality is closely related, meaning the ideas belong to the writer and are not borrowed from another writer. Authenticity merely means that the piece sounds like it was written by the author. If the author is a child, then the writing will sound differently from something written by an adult.

COMPETENCY 6

UNDERSTAND SKILLS AND STRATEGIES INVOLVED IN LISTENING AND SPEAKING FOR VARIOUS PURPOSES (INCLUDING INFORMATION AND UNDERSTANDING, CRITICAL ANALYSIS AND EVALUATION, LITERARY RESPONSE AND EXPRESSION, AND SOCIAL INTERACTION)

> SKILL **Recognizing appropriate listening strategies for given contexts and**
> 6.1 **purposes** (e.g., interpreting and analyzing information that is presented orally, appretiating literary texts that are read aloud, understanding small group and large-group discussions)

Listening is not a skill that is talked about much, except when someone clearly does not listen. The truth is, though, that listening is a very specific skill for very specific circumstances. There are two aspects of listening that warrant attention. The first is comprehension. This is simply understanding what someone says, the purposes behind the message, and the contexts in which it is said. The second is purpose. While someone may completely understand a message, what is the listener supposed to do with it? Just nod and smile? Go out and take action? While listening comprehension is indeed a significant skill in itself that deserves a lot of focus in the classroom (much in the same way that reading comprehension does), we will focus on purpose here. Often, when we understand the purpose of listening in various contexts, comprehension will be much easier. Furthermore, when we know the purpose of listening, we can better adjust our comprehension strategies.

First, when complex or new information is provided to us orally, we must analyze and interpret that information. What is the author's most important point? How do the figures of speech impact meaning? How are conclusions arrived at? Often, making sense of this information can be tough when presented orally—first, because we have no place to go back and review material already stated; second, because oral language is so much less predictable and even than written language. However, when we focus on extracting the meaning, message, and speaker's purpose, rather than just "listen" and wait for things to make sense for us—in other words, when we are more "active" in our listening—we have greater success in interpreting speech.

> There are two aspects of listening that warrant attention. The first is comprehension. The second is purpose.

Second, listening is often done for the purpose of enjoyment. We like to listen to stories; we enjoy poetry; we like radio dramas and theater. Listening to literature can also be a great pleasure. The problem today is that students have not learned how to extract great pleasure on a wide-spread scale from listening to literature, poetry, or language read aloud. Perhaps that is because we have not done a good enough job of showing students how listening to literature, for example, can indeed be more interesting than television or video games.

In the classrooms of exceptional teachers, we will often find that students are captivated by the reading aloud of good literature. It is refreshing and enjoyable to just sit and soak in the language, story, and poetry of literature being read aloud. Therefore, we must teach students how to listen and enjoy such work. We do this by making it fun and providing many possibilities and alternatives to capture the wide array of interests in each classroom.

Finally, we will discuss listening in large and small group conversation. The difference here is that conversation requires more than just listening: It involves feedback and active involvement. This can be particularly challenging as, in our culture, we are trained to move conversations along, to discourage silence in a conversation, and to always get the last word in. This poses significant problems for the art of listening. In a discussion, for example, when we are instead preparing our next response—rather than listening to what others are saying—we do a large disservice to the entire discussion. Students need to learn how listening carefully to others in discussions actually promotes better responses on the part of subsequent speakers. One way teachers can encourage this in both large and small group discussions is to expect students to respond directly to the previous student's comments before moving ahead with their new comments. This will encourage them to pose their new comments in light of the comments that came just before them.

> ### SKILL 6.2 Analyzing factors that affect the ability to listen effectively and to construct meaning from oral messages in various listening situations (e.g., using prior knowledge, recognizing transitions, interpreting nonverbal cues, using notetaking and outlining), and applying measures of effective listening (e.g., the ability to repeat instructions, the ability to retell stories)

Oral speech can be very difficult to follow. First, we have no written record in which to "reread" things we didn't hear or understand. Second, oral speech can be much less structured and even than written language. Yet, aside from rereading, many of the skills and strategies that help us in reading comprehension can help us in listening comprehension. For example, as soon as we start listening to something new, we should tap into our prior knowledge in order to attach new information to what we already know. This will not only help us understand the new information more quickly, it will also assist us in remembering the material.

We can also look for transitions between ideas. Sometimes, in oral speech, this is pretty simple when voice tone or body language changes. Of course, we don't have the luxury of looking at paragraphs in oral language, but we do have the animation that comes along with live speech. Human beings have to try very hard to be completely nonexpressive in their speech. Listeners should take advantage of this and notice how the speaker changes character and voice in order to signal a transition of ideas.

Related to animation of voice and body language, listeners can also better comprehend the underlying intents of authors when they notice nonverbal cues. Simply looking to see expression on the face of a speaker can do more to signal irony, for example, than trying to extract irony from actual words. And often in oral speech, unlike written text, elements like irony are not indicated by the actual words, but rather by the tone and nonverbal cues.

One good way to follow oral speech is to take notes and outline major points. Because oral speech can be more circular (as opposed to linear) than written text, it can be of great assistance to keep track of an author's message. Students can learn this strategy in many ways in the classroom: by taking notes of the teacher's oral messages, as well as of other students' presentations and speeches.

One good way to follow oral speech is to take notes and outline major points.

Other classroom methods can help students learn good listening skills. For example, teachers can have students practice following complex directions. They can also have students orally retell stories—or retell (in writing or in oral speech) oral presentations of stories or other materials. These activities give students direct practice in the very important skills of listening. They provide students with outlets in which they can slowly improve their abilities to comprehend oral language and take decisive action based on oral speech.

Sample Test Questions and Rationale

Average Rigor

1. **Which of the following is NOT an effective listening skill for students?**

   A. follows complex directions

   B. orally retells stories

   C. watches body language

   D. takes notes

Answer: C – watches body language

Rationale: Various classroom methods can help students develop good listening skills. For example, teachers can have students practice following complex directions. They can also have students orally retell stories. Another good way to follow oral speech is to take notes and outline major points.

SKILL 6.3 Analyzing how features of spoken language (e.g., word choice, rate, pitch, tone, volume) **and nonverbal cues** (e.g., body language, visual aids, facial expressions) **affect a speaker's ability to communicate effectively in given situations**

Analyzing the speech of others is a very good technique for helping students improve their own public speaking abilities. Because in most circumstances, students cannot view themselves as they give speeches and presentations, when they get the opportunity to critique, question, and analyze others' speeches, they begin to learn what works and what doesn't work in effective public speaking. However, a very important word of warning: DO NOT have students critique each others' public speaking skills. It could be very damaging to a student to have his or her peers point out what did not work in a speech. Instead, video is a great tool teachers can use. Any appropriate source of public speaking can be used in the classroom for students to analyze and critique.

Some of the things students can pay attention to include:

- Volume: A speaker should use an appropriate volume—not too loud to be annoying, but not too soft to be inaudible.
- Pace: The rate at which words are spoken should be appropriate—not too fast to make the speech nonunderstandable, but not too slow so as to put listeners to sleep.
- Pronunciation: A speaker should make sure words are spoken clearly. Listeners do not have a text to go back and reread things they didn't catch.

- **Body language:** While animated body language can help a speech, too much of it can be distracting. Body language should help convey the message, not detract from it.

- **Word choice:** The words speakers choose should be consistent with their intended purpose and the audience.

- **Visual aids:** Visual aids, like body language, should enhance a message. Many visual aids can be distracting, and that detracts from the message.

Overall, instead of telling students to keep these factors in mind when presenting information orally, having them view speakers who do these things well and poorly will help them know and remember the next time they give a speech.

FEATURES OF SPOKEN LANGUAGE	
Voice	Many people fall into one of two traps when speaking: using a monotone or talking too fast. These are both caused by anxiety. A monotone restricts your natural inflection, but can be remedied by releasing tension in upper and lower body muscles. Talking fast, on the other hand, is not necessarily a bad thing if the speaker is exceptionally articulate. If not, or if the speaker is talking about very technical things, it becomes far too easy for the audience to become lost. When you talk too fast and begin tripping over your words, consciously pause after every sentence you say. Don't be afraid of brief silences. The audience needs time to absorb what you are saying.
Volume	Problems with volume, whether too soft or too loud, can usually be combated with practice. If you tend to speak too softly, have someone stand the back of the room and give you a signal when your volume is strong enough. If possible, have someone in the front of the room as well to make sure you're not overcompensating with excessive volume. Conversely, if you have a problem with speaking too loudly, have the person in the front of the room signal you when your voice is soft enough and check with the person in the back to make sure it is still loud enough to be heard. In both cases, note your volume level for future reference. Don't be shy about asking your audience, "Can you hear me in the back?" Suitable volume is beneficial for both you and the audience.
Pitch	Pitch refers to the length, tension, and thickness of a person's vocal bands. As your voice gets higher, the pitch gets higher. In oral performance, pitch reflects upon the emotional arousal level. More variation in pitch typically corresponds to more emotional arousal, but can also be used to convey sarcasm or highlight specific words.
Posture	Maintain a straight, but not stiff posture. Instead of shifting weight from hip to hip, point your feet directly at the audience and distribute your weight evenly. Keep shoulders orientated toward the audience. If you have to turn your body to use a visual aid, turn 45 degrees and continue speaking toward the audience.
Movement	Instead of staying glued to one spot or pacing back and forth, stay within four to eight feet of the front row of your audience, and take maybe a step or half-step to the side every once in a while. If you are using a lectern, feel free to move to the front or side of it to engage your audience more. Avoid distancing yourself from the audience—you want them to feel involved and connected.

Table continued on next page

Gestures	Gestures are a great way to keep a natural atmosphere when speaking publicly. Use them just as you would when speaking to a friend. They shouldn't be exaggerated, but they should be utilized for added emphasis. Avoid keeping your hands in your pockets or locked behind your back, wringing your hands and fidgeting nervously, or keeping your arms crossed.
Eye Contact	Many people are intimidated by using eye contact when speaking to large groups. Interestingly, eye contact usually helps the speaker overcome speech anxiety by connecting with their attentive audience and easing feelings of isolation. Instead of looking at a spot on the back wall or at your notes, scan the room and make eye contact for one to three seconds per person.

SKILL 6.4 Recognizing how to vary speaking strategies for different audiences, purposes, and occasions (e.g., providing instructions, participating in group discussions, persuading or entertaining an audience, giving an oral presentation or Interpretation of a literary work)

In public speaking, not all speeches require the same type of speaking style. For example, when providing a humorous speech, it is important to utilize body language in order to accent humorous moments. However, when giving instructions, it is extremely important to speak clearly and slowly, carefully noting the mood of the audience, so that if there is general confusion on peoples' faces, the speaker can go back and review something.

In group discussions, it is important for speakers to ensure that they are listening to other speakers carefully and tailoring their messages so that the messages fit into the general mood and location of the discussion at hand. When giving an oral presentation, the mood should be both serious and friendly. The speaker should focus on ensuring that the content is covered, while also relating to audience members as much as possible.

The steps of persuasive speaking should be explicitly taught to students. They are:

1. *Expressing an opinion*
2. *Staying focused on topic of discussion*
3. *Supporting opinions with detail*
4. *Using good speaking etiquette in discussions*

As students practice these skills, they can receive guidance and modeling from video of various types of speeches appropriate to the types they are giving themselves. Also, the various attributes of each type of oral speaking strategy should be covered with students so that they clearly hear the differences.

It used to be that we thought of speaking and communication only in terms of effective and noneffective. Today, we realize that there is more to communication than just good and bad. We must take into consideration that we must adjust our communication styles for various audiences. While we should not stereotype audiences, we can still recognize that certain methods of communication are more appropriate with certain people than with others. Age is an easy one to consider: Adults know that when they talk to children, they should come across as pleasant and nonthreatening and they should use vocabulary that is simple for children to understand. On the other hand, teenagers realize that they should not speak to their grandmothers they way the speak with their peers. When dealing with communications between cultures and genders, people must be sensitive, considerate, and appropriate.

Teachers must also consider these aspects as they deal with colleagues, parents, community members, and even students. They must realize that all communication should be tailored so that it conveys appropriate messages and tones to listeners.

> *How do teachers help students understand these "unspoken" rules of communication? Teachers must model these behaviors, and they must have high expectations for students (clearly communicated, of course) inside and outside the classroom walls.*

SKILL 6.5 Applying knowledge of oral language conventions appropriate to a variety of social situations (e.g., informal conversations, job interviews)

Informal and formal language is a distinction made on the basis of the occasion as well as the audience. At a "formal" occasion, for example, a meeting of executives or of government officials, even conversational exchanges are likely to be more formal. A cocktail party or a golf game are examples where the language is likely to be informal. Formal language uses fewer or no contractions, less slang, longer sentences, and more organization in longer segments.

Speeches delivered to executives, college professors, government officials, etc., are likely to be formal. Speeches made to fellow employees are likely to be informal. Sermons tend to be formal; Bible lessons will tend to be informal.

Different from the basic writing forms of discourse is the art of debating, discussion, and conversation. The ability to use language and logic to convince the audience to accept your reasoning and to side with you is an art. This form of writing/speaking is extremely confined/structured and logically sequenced, with supporting reasons and evidence. At its best, it is the highest form of propaganda. A position statement, evidence, reason, evaluation, and refutation are integral parts of this writing schema.

Interviewing provides opportunities for students to apply expository and informative communication. It teaches them how to structure questions to evoke fact-filled responses. Compiling the information from an interview into a biographical essay or speech helps students to list, sort, and arrange details in an orderly fashion.

> *Teaching oral language conventions:*
> http://englishonline/tki.org.nz/

Speeches that encourage students to describe people, places, or events in their own lives or oral interpretations of literature help them sense the creativity and effort used by professional writers.

COMPETENCY 7

UNDERSTAND AND APPLY TECHNIQUES OF LITERARY ANALYSIS TO WORKS OF FICTION, DRAMA, POETRY, AND NONFICTION

SKILL 7.1 Analyzing similarities and differences between fiction and nonfiction

Students often misrepresent the differences between fiction and nonfiction. They mistakenly believe that stories are always examples of fiction. The simple truth is that stories are both fiction and nonfiction. The primary difference is that fiction is made up by the author and nonfiction is generally true (or an opinion). It is harder for students to understand that nonfiction entails an enormous range of material, from textbooks to true stories to newspaper articles to speeches. Fiction, on the other hand, is fairly simple—made up stories, novels, etc. But it is also important for students to understand that most of fiction throughout history has been based on true events. In other words, authors use their own life experiences to help them create works of fiction.

Important in understanding fiction, apart from nonfiction, is the artistry in telling a story to convey a point. When students see that an author's choice in a work of fiction is for the sole purpose of conveying a viewpoint, they can make better sense of the specific details in the work of fiction.

Important in understanding nonfiction, apart from fiction, is realizing what is truth and what is perspective. Often, a nonfiction writer will present an opinion, and that opinion is very different from a truth. Knowing the difference between the two is very crucial.

Overall, students can begin to see patterns that identify fiction apart from nonfiction. Often, the more fanciful or unrealistic a text or story is, the more likely it is fiction.

> In fiction, students can generally expect to see plot, characters, setting, and themes. In nonfiction, students may see a plot, characters, settings, and themes, but they will also experience interpretations, opinions, theories, research, and other elements.

Sample Test Questions and Rationale

Average rigor

1. **The following elements: plot, characters, settings, and themes, interpretations, opinions, theories, and research, can be found in what type of literature?**

   A. nonfiction

   B. fairy tale

   C. fiction

   D. folktales

Answer: A – nonfiction

Rationale: In nonfiction, students may see a plot, characters, settings, and themes, but they will also experience interpretations, opinions, theories, research, and other elements. Overall, students can begin to see patterns that identify fiction apart from nonfiction. Often, the more fanciful or unrealistic a text or story is, the more likely it is fiction.

SKILL 7.2 Demonstrating knowledge of story elements in works of fiction
(e.g., plot, character, setting, theme, mood)

Most works of fiction contain a common set of elements that make them come alive to readers. In a way, even though writers do not consciously think about each of these elements as story elements when they sit down to write, all stories essentially contain these "markers" that make them the stories that they are. But, even though all stories have these elements, they are a lot like fingerprints: Each story's story elements are just a bit different.

Let's look at a few of the most commonly discussed elements. The most commonly discussed story element in fiction is plot. Plot is the series of events in a story. Typically, but not always, plot moves in a predictable fashion:

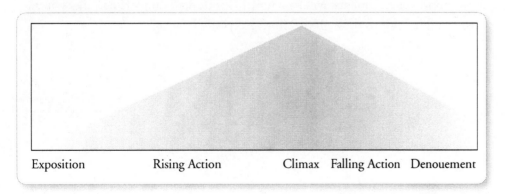

Exposition   Rising Action   Climax   Falling Action   Denouement

Exposition is where characters and their situations are introduced. *Rising action* is the point at which conflict starts to occur. *Climax* is the highest point of conflict, often a turning point. *Falling action* is the result of the climax. *Denouement* is the final resolution of the plot.

Character is another commonly studied story element. We will often find in stories heroes, villains, comedic characters, dark characters, etc. When we examine the characters of a story, we look to see who they are and how their traits contribute to the story. Often, because of their characteristics, plot elements become more interesting. For example, authors will pair unlikely characters together somehow that, in turn, creates specific conflict.

The setting of a story is the place or location where it occurs. Often, the specific place is not as important as some of the specifics about the setting. For example, the setting of *The Great Gatsby*, New York, is not as significant as the fact that it takes place among incredible wealth. Conversely, *The Grapes of Wrath*, although taking place in Oklahoma and California, has a more significant setting of poverty. In fact, as the story takes place around other migrant workers, the setting is even more significant. In a way, the setting serves as a reason for various conflicts to occur.

The theme of a story is the underlying message, above and beyond all plot elements, that writers want to convey. Very rarely will one find that good literature is without a theme—or a lesson, message, or ideal. The best writers in the English language all seem to want to convey something about human nature or the world, and they turn to literature in order to do that. Common themes in literature are jealousy, money, love, human against corporation or government, etc. These themes are never explicitly stated; rather, they are the result of the portrayal of characters, settings, and plots. Readers get the message even if the theme is not directly mentioned.

Finally, the mood of a story is the atmosphere or attitude the writer conveys through descriptive language. Often, mood fits in nicely with theme and setting. For example, in Edgar Allen Poe's stories, we often find a mood of horror and darkness. We get that from the descriptions of characters and the setting, as well as from specific plot elements. Mood simply helps us better understand the writer's theme and intentions through descriptive, stylistic language.

Sample Test Questions and Rationale

Rigorous

1. At what point does exposition occur within a story?

   A. after the rising action

   B. after the denouement

   C. before the rising action

   D. before the setting

   Answer: C – before the rising action

   Rationale: Exposition is where characters and their situations are introduced. *Rising action* is the point at which conflict starts to occur. *Climax* is the highest point of conflict, often a turning point. *Falling action* is the result of the climax. *Denouement* is the final resolution of the plot.

Average Rigor

1. Which is an untrue statement about a theme in literature?

   A. The theme is always stated directly somewhere in the text.

   B. The theme is the central idea in a literary work.

   C. All parts of the work (plot, setting, mood, etc.) should contribute to the theme in some way.

   D. By analyzing the various elements of the work, the reader should be able to arrive at an indirectly stated theme.

   Answer: A – The theme is always stated directly somewhere in the text

   Rationale: The theme is always stated directly somewhere in the text. The theme may be stated directly, but it can also be implicit in various aspects of the work, such as the interaction between characters, symbolism, or description.

SKILL **Applying knowledge of drama to analyze dramatic structure** *(e.g.,*
7.3 *introduction, rising action, climax, falling action, conclusion)* **and identify common dramatic devices** *(e.g., soliloquy, aside)*

In both drama and fiction, various dramatic events occur in a fairly predictable fashion. For example, all dramatic action begins with some sort of introductory scene where characters are introduced, basic premises are covered, and the plot is set so that action can occur. Rising action begins as the plot ramps up. It occurs as elements in the plot move toward some sort of problematic circumstance, whether comedic or tragic. If the plot is tragic, something bad will happen; if the plot is comedic, something good or humorous will happen. Let's take this difference one step further: Classically, a tragedy would end with a funeral and a comedy would end in a wedding. Today, however, there are greater variations, but generally, most works fit into one of those two categories.

As the rising action continues to move toward some ultimate fate, whether comedic or tragic, eventually it will hit a climax. The climax is the major turning point or significant event in the work. Everything that occurs after the climax is considered falling action, and the general idea is that once a work has hit the climax, the work is now moving toward conclusion. Falling action is generally the response to the climax (or the result of it). Often, though, most works of fiction and drama will not provide too much falling action, as that might be considered giving away too much. After the climax, most works like to allow readers/viewers to imagine some of the consequences. Conclusion is the final event or the moment when the work entirely finishes. After that, everything else is left to the readers'/viewers' imagination.

In drama, particularly, certain devices enhance the viewers' understanding of the plot. We will discuss three of these devices:

1. Suspense: Suspense occurs at any moment where the audience knows something that a character on stage does not—and the "thing" the character does not know will cause him or her adverse effects. Now, suspense does not always equal tragedy. Often, the result is comedic. But the point is that the audience will have possibly heard something in a previous scene and a character comes on stage and has no idea that something is going to occur. Or, within a scene, something suspenseful is going to occur, and the audience has a sense that the plot in the scene will not be so docile.

2. Soliloquy: In essence, this is a speech to oneself. This is where a character possibly shares his or her feelings to the audience, almost as if the character is thinking out loud. This gives the audience clues as to what may happen, how the character is handling something, etc.

3. Aside: Usually, soliloquies occur in an aside, but not all asides contain soliloquies. An aside is any time where "real" time in the drama stops for a moment so that a character can address the audience or his/her thoughts so that the audience hears them (and the other characters do not).

Sample Test Questions and Rationale

Rigorous

1. **Plot is the series of events in a story. Typically, plot moves in the following sequence:**

   A. rising action, exposition, climax, denouement, falling action

   B. exposition, rising action, climax, falling action, denouement

   C. denouement, rising action, climax, falling action, exposition

   D. rising action, exposition, denouement, climax, falling action

Answer: B – exposition, rising action, climax, falling action, denouement

Rationale: Exposition is where characters and their situations are introduced. Rising action begins as the plot ramps up. It occurs as elements in the plot move toward some sort of problematic circumstance, whether comedic or tragic. The climax is the major turning point or significant event in the work. Everything that occurs after the climax is considered falling action. After the climax, most works like to allow readers/viewers to imagine some of the consequences. Conclusion is the final event or the moment when the work entirely finishes. Rising action is the point at which conflict starts to occur. Climax is the highest point of conflict, often a turning point. Falling action is the result of the climax. Denouement is the final resolution of the plot.

SKILL **Applying knowledge of various types of nonfiction** (*e.g., informational*
7.4 *texts, newspaper articles, essays, biographies, memoirs, letters, journals*)

Nonfiction comes in a variety of styles. While many students simplify nonfiction as being true (as opposed to fiction, which is make-believe), nonfiction is much deeper than that. Nonfiction can include opinion and perspective. The following are various types of nonfiction, all of which students should be exposed to:

TYPES OF NONFICTION	
Informational Texts	These types of books explain concepts or phenomena. An informational text might explain the history of a state or the idea of photosynthesis. These types of text usually are based on research.
Newspaper Articles	These short texts rely completely on factual information and are presented in a very straightforward, sometimes choppy manner. The purpose of these texts simply is to present information to readers in a quick and efficient manner.
Essays	Usually, essays take an opinion (whether it is about a concept, a work of literature, a person, or an event) and describe how the opinion was arrived at or why the opinion is a good one.
Biographies	These texts explain the lives of individuals. They usually are based on extensive research.
Memoirs	In a way, a memoir is like an autobiography, but usually based on a specific idea, concept, issue, or event in life. For example, most presidents of the United States write memoirs about their time in office.
Letters	When letters are read and analyzed in the classroom, students generally are studying the writer's style or the writer's true, deep-down opinions and feelings about certain events. Often, students will find letters of famous individuals in history reprinted in textbooks.
Journals	Similar to letters, journals present very personal ideas. They give students, when available (as most people never want their journals published), an opportunity to see peoples' thought processes about various events or issues.

The key in teaching students about nonfiction is to expose them to a variety of types of nonfiction and discuss how those types are similar and different from one another. But, again, the key is exposure. How will students ever know about these types of literature in a deep and analytical sense without getting the chance to read them and study them academically in the classroom?

Sample Test Questions and Rationale

Easy

1. Texts that present information to readers in a quick and efficient manner are called:

   A. essays

   B. memoirs

   C. journals

   D. newspaper articles

Answer: D – newspaper articles

Rationale: Nonfiction comes in a variety of styles and can include opinion and perspective. Newspaper articles are short texts which rely completely on factual information and are presented in a very straightforward, sometimes choppy manner. The purpose of these texts simply is to present information to readers in a quick and efficient manner. The key in teaching students about nonfiction is to expose them to a variety of types of nonfiction and discuss how those types are similar and different from one another.

SKILL 7.5 Analyzing the use of language to convey style, tone, and point of view in works of fiction and nonfiction

In both fiction and nonfiction, authors portray ideas in very subtle ways through their skillful use of language. Style, tone, and point of view are the most basic of ways in which authors do this.

WAYS TO CONVEY IDEAS	
Style	Style is the artful adaptation of language to meet various purposes. For example, authors can modify their word choice, sentence structure, and organization in order to convey certain ideas. For example, an author may write on a topic (the environment, for example) in many different styles. In an academic style, the author would use long, complex sentences, advanced vocabulary, and very structured paragraphing. However, in an informal explanation in a popular magazine, the author may use a conversational tone where simple words and simple sentence structures are utilized.

Table continued on next page

Tone	Tone is the attitude an author takes toward his or her subject. That tone is exemplified in the language of the text. For example, consider the environment once again. One author may dismiss the idea of global warming; his tone may be one of derision against environmentalists. A reader might notice this through the style (word choice, for example), the details the author decides to present, and the order in which details are presented. Another author may be angry about global warming and therefore might use harsh words and other tones that indicate anger. Finally, yet another author may not care one bit about the issue of the environment, either way. Let's say this author is a comedian who likes to poke fun at political activists. Her tone is humorous, therefore, she will adjust her language accordingly, as well. All types of tones are about the same subject—they simply reveal, through language, different opinions and attitudes about the subject.
Point of View	Point of view is the perspective through which the story is told. While most of us think of point of view in terms of first or third person (or even the points of view of various characters in stories), point of view also helps explain a lot of language and presentation of ideas in nonfiction and fiction texts. The above environmentalism example proves this. Three points of view are represented, and each creates a different style of language.

Students need to learn that language and text is changed dramatically by tone, style, and point of view. They can practice these concepts by exploring these elements in everything they read. It takes little time for each nonfiction or fiction text they have to read in class, but it goes a long way in helping them comprehend text at a more advanced level.

Sample Test Questions and Rationale

Average Rigor

1. **Which is not a true statement concerning an author's literary tone?**

   A. Tone is partly revealed through the selection of details.

   B. Tone is the expression of the author's attitude toward his/her subject.

   C. Tone in literature is usually satiric or angry.

   D. Tone in literature corresponds to the tone of voice a speaker uses.

Answer: C – Tone in literature is usually satiric or angry

Rationale: Tone in literature is usually satiric or angry. Tone in literature conveys a mood and can be as varied as the tone of voice of a speaker (see D., e.g. sad, nostalgic, whimsical, angry, formal, intimate, satirical, sentimental, etc.).

SKILL 7.6 Recognizing the formal elements of a poetic text (e.g., meter, rhyme scheme, stanza structure, alliteration, assonance, onomatopoeia, figurative language) and analyzing their relationship to the meaning of the text

People read poetry for many reasons, and they are often the very same reasons poets would give for writing it. Just the feel and sounds of the words that are turned by the artistic hands and mind of a poet into a satisfying and sometimes delightful experience is a good reason to read a poem. Good poetry constantly surprises.

However, the major purpose a writer of poetry has for creating his works of art is the sharing of an experience, a feeling, an emotion, and that is also the reason a reader turns to poetry rather than prose in his search for variety, joy, and satisfaction.

There is another important reason that poets create and that readers are drawn to their poems: they are interpreters of life. Poets feel deeply the things that others feel or even things that may be overlooked by others, and they have the skill and inspiration to recreate those feelings and interpret them in such a way that understanding and insight may come from the experience. They often bring understanding to life's big (or even not-so-big) questions.

Children can respond to poetry at very early stages. Elementary students are still at the stage where the sounds of unusual words intrigue them and entertain them. They are also very open to emotional meanings of passages. Teaching poetry to fifth graders can be an important introduction to seeking for meaning in literature. If a fifth grader enjoys reading poetry both silently and aloud, a habit may be formed that will last a lifetime.

When we speak of structure with regard to poetry, we usually mean one of three things.

The Pattern of the Sound and Rhythm

It helps to know the history of this peculiarity of poetry. History was passed down in oral form almost exclusively until the invention of the printing press, and it was often set to music. A rhymed story is much easier to commit to memory. Adding a tune makes it even easier to remember, so it's not a surprise that much of the earliest literature—epics, odes, etc.—are rhymed and were probably sung. When we speak of the pattern of sound and rhythm, we are referring to two things: verse form and stanza form.

VERSE FORM: the rhythmic pattern of a single verse

STANZA: a group of a certain number of verses

The **VERSE FORM** is the rhythmic pattern of a single verse. An example would be any meter: blank verse, for instance, is iambic pentameter. A **STANZA** is a group of a certain number of verses (lines), having a rhyme scheme. If the poem is written, there is usually white space between the verses although a short poem may be only one stanza. If the poem is spoken, there will be a pause between stanzas.

The Visible Shape it Takes

In the seventeenth century, some poets shaped their poems to reflect the theme. A good example is George Herbert's "Easter Wings." Since that time, poets have occasionally played with this device; it is, however, generally viewed as nothing more than a demonstration of ingenuity. The rhythm, effect, and meaning are often sacrificed to the forcing of the shape.

Rhyme and Free Verse

Poets also use devices to establish form that will underscore the meanings of their poems. Following a strict rhyming pattern can add intensity to the meaning of the poem in the hands of a skilled and creative poet. On the other hand, the meaning can be drowned out by the steady beat-beat-beat of it. Shakespeare very skillfully used the regularity of *rhyme* in his poetry, breaking the rhythm at certain points to very effectively underscore a point. For example, in Sonnet #130, "My mistress' eyes are nothing like the sun," the rhythm is primarily iambic pentameter. It lulls the reader (or listener) to accept that this poet is following the standard conventions for love poetry, which in that day reliably used rhyme and, more often than not, iambic pentameter to express feelings of romantic love along conventional lines. However, in Sonnet #130, the last two lines sharply break from the monotonous pattern, forcing reader or speaker to pause:

> *And yet, by heaven, I think my love as rare*
> *As any she belied with false compare*

Shakespeare's purpose is clear: he is not writing a conventional love poem; the object of his love is not the red-and-white conventional woman written about in other poems of the period. This is a good example where a poet uses form to underscore meaning.

Poets eventually began to feel constricted by the rhyming conventions and began to break away and make new rules for poetry. When poetry was only rhymed, it was easy to define it. When *free verse*, or poetry written in a flexible form, came upon the scene in France in the 1880s, it quickly began to influence English-language poets such as T.S. Eliot, whose memorable poem, "The Wasteland," had an alarming but desolate message for the modern world. It's impossible to imagine that it could have been written in the soothing, lulling rhymed verse of previous periods. Those who first began writing in free verse in English were responding to the influence of the French *vers libre*. However, it should be noted that it could be loosely applied to the poetry of Walt Whitman, writing in the mid-nineteenth century, as can be seen in the first stanza of "Song of Myself":

> I celebrate myself, and sing myself,
> And what I assume you shall assume,
> For every atom belonging to me as good belongs to you.

When poetry was no longer defined as a piece of writing arranged in verses that had a rhyme-scheme of some sort, distinguishing poetry from prose became a point of discussion. *Merriam Webster's Encyclopedia of Literature* defines poetry as follows: "Writing that formulates a concentrated imaginative awareness of experience in language chosen and arranged to create a specific emotional response through its meaning, sound and rhythm."

A poet chooses the form of his poetry deliberately, based upon the emotional response he hopes to evoke and the meaning he wishes to convey. Robert Frost, a twentieth-century poet who chose to use conventional rhyming verse to make his point is a memorable and often-quoted modern poet. Who can forget his closing lines in "Stopping by Woods"?

> And miles to go before I sleep,
> And miles to go before I sleep.

Would they be as memorable if the poem had been written in free verse?

FORMS OF POETRY	
Slant Rhyme	Occurs when the final consonant sounds are the same, but the vowels are different. Occurs frequently in Irish, Welsh, and Icelandic verse. Examples include: green and gone, that and hit, ill and shell.
Alliteration	Alliteration occurs when the initial sounds of a word, beginning either with a consonant or a vowel, are repeated in close succession. Examples include: Athena and Apollo, Nate never knows, People who pen poetry. Note that the words only have to be close to one another: Alliteration that repeats and attempts to connect a number of words is little more than a tongue-twister. The function of alliteration, like rhyme, might be to accentuate the beauty of language in a given context, or to unite words or concepts through a kind of repetition. And like rhyme, alliteration can follow specific patterns. Sometimes the consonants aren't always the initial ones, but they are generally the stressed syllables. Alliteration is less common than rhyme, but because it is less common, it can call our attention to a word or line in a poem that might not have the same emphasis otherwise.

Table continued on next page

Assonance	If alliteration occurs at the beginning of a word and rhyme at the end, assonance takes the middle territory. Assonance occurs when the vowel sound within a word matches the same sound in a nearby word, but the surrounding consonant sounds are different. "Tune" and "June" are rhymes; "tune" and "food" are assonant. The function of assonance is frequently the same as end rhyme or alliteration; all serve to give a sense of continuity or fluidity to the verse. Assonance might be especially effective when rhyme is absent: It gives the poet more flexibility, and it is not typically used as part of a predetermined pattern. Like alliteration, it does not so much determine the structure or form of a poem; rather, it is more ornamental.
Onomatopoeia	Word used to evoke the sound in its meaning. The early *Batman* series used pow, zap, whop, zonk, and eek in an onomatopoetic way.

RHYTHM: the recurrence of stresses at equal intervals

METER: the pattern of the rhythm

RHYTHM in poetry refers to the recurrence of stresses at equal intervals. A stress (accent) is a greater amount of force given to one syllable in speaking than is given to another. For example, we put the stress on the first syllable of such words as father, mother, daughter, children. The unstressed or unaccented syllable is sometimes called a slack syllable. All English words carry at least one stress except articles and some prepositions such as by, from, and at. Indicating where stresses occur is to scan; doing this is called *scansion*. Very little is gained in understanding a poem or making a statement about it by merely scanning it. The pattern of the rhythm—the METER—should be analyzed in terms of its overall relationship to the message and impression of the poem.

Slack syllables, when they recur in pairs cause rhythmic trippings and bouncings; on the other hand, recurrent pairs of stresses will create a heavier rocking effect. The rhythm is dependent on words to convey meaning. Alone, they communicate nothing. When examining the rhythm and meaning of a poem, a good question to ask is whether the rhythm is appropriate to the theme. A bouncing rhythm, for example, might be dissonant in a solemn elegy.

Stops are those places in a poem where the punctuation requires a pause. An end-stopped line is one that ends in a pause whereas one that has no punctuation at its end and is, therefore, read with only a slight pause after it is said to be run-on and the running on of its thought into the next line is called *enjambment*. These are used by a poet to underscore, intensify, and communicate meaning.

Rhythm, then, is a pattern of recurrence and in poetry is made up of stressed and relatively unstressed syllables. The poet can manipulate the rhythm by making the intervals between his stresses regular or varied, by making his lines short or long, by end-stopping his lines or running them over, by choosing words that are easier or less easy to say, by choosing polysyllabic words or monosyllables. The most important thing to remember about rhythm is that it conveys meaning.

The basic unit of rhythm is called a *foot* and is usually one stressed syllable with one or two unstressed ones or two stressed syllables with one unstressed one. A foot made up of one unstressed syllable and one stressed one is called an iamb. If a line is made of five *iambs*, it is iambic pentameter. A rhymed poem typically establishes a pattern such as iambic pentameter, and even though there will be syllables that don't fit the pattern, the poem, nevertheless, will be said to be in iambic pentameter. In fact, a poem may be considered weak if the rhythm is too monotonous.

The most common kinds of feet in English poetry:

iamb	anapest	trochee	dactyl	Monosyllabic	Spondee	Pyrrhic foot
_ '	_ _ '	' _	' _ _	'	"	_ _

Iambic and anapestic are said to be rising because the movement is from slack to stressed syllables. Trochaic and dactylic are said to be falling.

Meters are named as follows:

Monometer	a line of one foot	Pentameter	a line of five feet
Dimeter	a line of two feet	Hexameter	a line of six feet
Trimeter	a line of three feet	Heptameter	a line of seven feet
Tetrameter	a line of four feet	Octameter	a line of eight feet

Longer lines are possible, but a reader will tend to break it up into shorter lengths.

A *caesura* is a definite pause within a line, in scansion indicated by a double line: ||

A stanza is a group of a certain number of lines with a rhyme scheme or a particular rhythm or both, typically set off by white space.

Some typical patterns of English poetry:

- Blank verse: unrhymed iambic pentameter.
- Couplet: two-line stanza, usually rhymed and typically not separated by white space.
- Heroic couplet or closed couplet: two rhymed lines of iambic pentameter, the first ending in a light pause, the second more heavily end-stopped.
- Tercet: a three-line stanza, which, if rhymed, usually keeps to one rhyme sound.

- Terza rima: the middle line of the tercet rhymes with the first and third lines of the next tercet.

- The quatrain: four-line stanza, the most popular in English.

- The ballad stanza: four iambic feet in lines one and three, three in lines two and four. Rhyming is abcb.

- The refrain: a line or lines repeated in a ballad as a chorus.

- Terminal refrain: follows a stanza in a ballad.

  - Five-line stanzas occur, but not frequently.

  - Six-line stanzas, more frequent than five-line ones.

- The sestina: six six-line stanzas and a tercet. Repeats in each stanza the same six end-words in a different order.

- Rime royal: seven-line stanza in iambic pentameter with rhyme ababbcc.

- Ottava rima: eight-line stanza of iambic pentameter rhyming abababcc.

- Spenserian stanza: nine lines, rhyming ababbcbcc for eight lines then concludes with an Alexandrine.

- The Alexandrine: a line of iambic hexameter.

- Free verse: no conventional patterns of rhyme, stanza, or meter.

- Sonnet: a fourteen-line poem in iambic pentameter.

  - *English sonnet:* sometimes called a Shakespearean sonnet. Rhymes cohere in four clusters: abab cdcd efef gg

  - *Italian or Petrarchan sonnet:* first eight lines (the octave), abbaabba; then the sestet, the last six lines add new rhyme sounds in almost any variation; does not end in a couplet.

Sample Test Questions and Rationale

Easy

1. The following examples; "Nate never knows" and "People who pen poetry" are representative of what form of poetry?

   A. assonance

   B. slant rhyme

   C. alliteration

   D. onomatopoeia

Answer: C –alliteration

Rationale: Alliteration occurs when the initial sounds of a word, beginning either with a consonant or a vowel are repeated in close succession. The function of alliteration might be to accentuate the beauty of language in a given context, or to unite words or concepts through a kind of repetition. Alliteration, like rhyme, can follow specific patterns. Sometimes the consonants aren't always the initial ones, but they are generally the stressed syllables.

COMPETENCY 8

DEMONSTRATE KNOWLEDGE OF LITERATURE, INCLUDING LITERATURE FROM DIVERSE CULTURES AND LITERATURE FOR CHILDREN/ADOLESCENTS

SKILL 8.1 Demonstrating awareness of ways in which literary texts reflect the time and place in which they were written

J.K. Rowling's *Harry Potter* series is an excellent example of how an author used the genre of fantasy to manipulate and create settings to fit a constructive narrative and storyline. The success of Rowling's books can best be reflected in how her stories combine real world experiences and magical illusions in a way that readers can escape and connect to in individualized ways. Fairy tales, folklore, and myths are literary genres that reflect a historical perspective of tradition and meaning.

Current literature explores current times and is reflective of the historical decades. The authors are able to incorporate the themes of the time into literature work that spans the ages. The works of Shakespeare and other historical writings create a world that is rich in character development and plots. Plots written during those eras mirror the plots of today and the past. A good writer is able to manipulate historical facts into current fiction that engages and transforms the reader.

SKILL 8.2 Demonstrating awareness of the ways in which literary works reflect and express cultural values and ideas

When a writer contextualizes a work of fiction or nonfiction in the cultural realm, there are inherent lessons and issues that move the plot and theme of the work. Cultural values and ideas are actually the point of view of works that focus on a particular cultural theme or resolve.

The characters and protagonist generally reflect the cultural values of the writing or create a plot that is dynamic in the oppositional position of the point of view. Understanding the audience targeted for the writing is important if the writer wants to target a specific age group or gender. Creating a work for a high school audience is quite different from creating a similar theme targeting early readers who may not have the cognizance to understand the response elicited from them.

The point of many cultural pieces is to immerse the reader into a world different from their own worldview. The thought is that if the reader is able to empathize with someone or some issue that is culturally different, then his/her world is broadened and expanded from a cultural sense.

SKILL 8.3 Recognizing major themes and characteristics of works written by well known authors

Young readers respond to themes that reflect their lives. Some simplistic examples are:

- The world is black or white (there are no gray areas)
- Different is fine, but hard
- Good guys always win and bad guys are simply bad
- Body functions are gross, but funny

- Magic and adventure are natural

- Being good is nice

MAJOR LITERARY GENRES	
Science Fiction	Relies on the suspension of disbelief to create worlds beyond today that are sometimes surreal. Sci-fi takes scientific knowledge to the planets and beneath the sea to create imaginary life worlds.
Fantasy	Readers must suspend belief to enter into a world that includes mythical creatures and fairies that are dealing with parallel issues in the current world. The stories have origins and themes from old traditions and stories that have been handed down historically.
Horror and Ghost Stories	Always grounded in reality, these stories and books are developed upon the fears and phobias of the reader. They are designed to make the reader second guess reality and they are created to perpetuate and heighten the things in life that frighten and create physical reactions.
Action and Adventure	Elicit the adventure spirit of the reader with plots that are busy and dangerous. The protagonist is self-reliant and conquers a dangerous situation alone using mental and physical acuity to assess and problem-solve issues. Crime-solving adventures are popular with middle readers and detective novels with younger characters. Using wit and brains to problem-solve is popular with young juvenile readers.
Historical Fiction	Based on real-life events and people who have overcome adversity and left a mark on society in deeds and events. The themes are based in historical events and constructed to engage the reader and also teach the reader something about history.
Biography	Take true-life people who have existed at some point on the planet and create real life drama about their lives or relevant segments of their lives.
Educational Books	Every school has a curriculum of core subject books used in teaching students academic facts and required knowledge.

SKILL 8.4 Demonstrating knowledge of important works and authors of literature for children and adolescents

The social changes of post-World War II significantly affected adolescent literature. Issues such as the Civil Rights movement, feminism, the protest of the Vietnam conflict, issues surrounding homelessness, neglect, teen pregnancy, drugs, and violence have all bred a new vein of contemporary fiction that helps adolescents understand and cope with the world they live in.

Popular books for preadolescents deal more with establishing relationships with members of the opposite sex (*Sweet Valley High* series) and learning to cope with their changing bodies, personalities, or life situations, as in Judy Blume's *Are You There, God? It's Me, Margaret*. Adolescents are still interested in the fantasy and science fiction genres as well as popular juvenile fiction. Middle school students still read the *Little House on the Prairie* series and the mysteries of the Hardy boys and Nancy Drew. Teens value the works of Emily and Charlotte Bronte, Willa Cather, Jack London, William Shakespeare, and Mark Twain as much as those of Piers Anthony, S.E. Hinton, Madeleine L'Engle, Stephen King, and J.R.R. Tolkien, because they're fun to read whatever their underlying worth may be.

FAVORITE AUTHORS BY GENRE	
Fantasy	Piers Anthony, Ursula LeGuin, Ann McCaffrey
Horror	V.C. Andrews, Stephen King
Juvenile Fiction	Judy Blume, Robert Cormier, Rosa Guy, Virginia Hamilton, S.E. Hinton, M.E. Kerr, Harry Mazer, Norma Fox Mazer, Richard Newton Peck, Cynthia Voight, and Paul Zindel
Science Fiction	Isaac Asimov, Ray Bradbury, Arthur C. Clarke, Frank Herbert, Larry Niven, H.G. Wells.

These classic and contemporary works combine the characteristics of multiple theories. Functioning at the concrete operations stage (Piaget), being of the "good person" orientation (Kohlberg), still highly dependent on external rewards (Bandura), and exhibiting all five needs discussed from Maslow's hierarchy, these eleven to twelve year olds should appreciate the following titles, grouped by reading level. These titles are also cited for interest at that grade level and do not reflect high-interest titles for older readers who do not read at grade level. Some high interest titles will be cited later.

READING LEVEL 6.0 TO 6.9	
Barrett, William	*Lilies of the Field*
Cormier, Robert	*Other Bells for Us to Ring*
Dahl, Roald	*Danny, Champion of the World; Charlie and the Chocolate Factory*
Lindgren, Astrid	*Pippi Longstocking*

Table continued on next page

Lindbergh, Anne	*Three Lives to Live*
Lowry, Lois	*Rabble Starkey*
Naylor, Phyllis	*The Year of the Gopher, Reluctantly Alice*
Peck, Robert Newton	*Arly*
Speare, Elizabeth	*The Witch of Blackbird Pond*
Sleator, William	*The Boy Who Reversed Himself*

For Seventh and Eighth Grades

Most seventh and eight grade students, according to learning theory, are still functioning cognitively, psychologically, and morally as sixth graders. As these are not inflexible standards, there are some twelve and thirteen year olds who are much more mature socially, intellectually, and physically than the younger children who share the same school.

They are becoming concerned with establishing individual and peer group identities that presents conflicts with breaking from authority and the rigidity of rules. Some at this age are still tied firmly to the family and its expectations while others identify more with those their own age or older. Enrichment reading for this group must help them cope with life's rapid changes or provide escape and thus must be either realistic or fantastic depending on the child's needs. Adventures and mysteries (the Hardy Boys and Nancy Drew series) are still popular today. These preteens also become more interested in biographies of contemporary figures rather than legendary figures of the past.

READING LEVEL 7.0 TO 7.9	
Armstrong, William	*Sounder*
Bagnold, Enid	*National Velvet*
Barrie, James	*Peter Pan*
London, Jack	*White Fang, Call of the Wild*
Lowry, Lois	*Taking Care of Terrific*
McCaffrey, Anne	*The Dragonsinger* series

Table continued on next page

Montgomery, L. M.	*Anne of Green Gables* and sequels
Steinbeck, John	*The Pearl*
Tolkien, J. R. R.	*The Hobbit*
Zindel, Paul	*The Pigman*

READING LEVEL 8.0 TO 8.9	
Cormier, Robert	*I Am the Cheese*
McCullers, Carson	*The Member of the Wedding*
North, Sterling	*Rascal*
Twain, Mark	*The Adventures of Tom Sawyer*
Zindel, Paul	*My Darling, My Hamburger*

SKILL 8.5 Analyzing themes and elements of traditional and contemporary literature for children and adolescents

Children's literature often contains themes related to moral issues. In a way, children's literature has been a vehicle for various cultures, including our own, to instill proper values in children. Therefore, it is not uncommon to find such themes in children's literature as the nature between good and evil, multiculturalism, sharing, or following advice given by parents or other adults.

Themes in children's literature are not difficult to figure out. Usually, part-way through a story, a character encounters a situation that he or she must make a decision about. Often, that very decision is directly related to the theme. Typically, characters will not choose the most moral of decisions and in the rest of the story they will face various consequences. By the end of the story, there may be some reconciliation and an acknowledgement from the character that the wrong decision has been made.

Of course, not all children's literature follows that pattern; however, when themes are presented in children's literature, typically, they are much easier to pick up on. For example, more and more children's literature is focusing on elements of multiculturalism. The theme is made evident through very explicit characters, plot events, or situations.

In general, children's literature does indeed focus greatly on themes that pertain to choices, morals, and values. They are intended to instruct students through entertaining stories, while also promoting an interest in the very act of reading, itself.

MAJOR LITERARY GENRES	
Allegory	A story in verse or prose with characters representing virtues and vices. There are two meanings, symbolic and literal. John Bunyan's *The Pilgrim's Progress* is the most renowned of this genre.
Ballad	An *in medias res* story, told or sung, usually in verse and accompanied by music. Literary devices found in ballads include the refrain, or repeated section, and incremental repetition, or anaphora, for effect. Earliest forms were anonymous folk ballads. Later forms include Coleridge's Romantic masterpiece, "The Rime of the Ancient Mariner."
Drama	Plays—comedy, modern, or tragedy—typically in five acts. Traditionalists and neoclassicists adhere to Aristotle's unities of time, place, and action. Plot development is advanced via dialogue. Literary devices include asides, soliloquies, and the chorus representing public opinion. Greatest of all dramatists/playwrights is William Shakespeare. Other dramaturges include Ibsen, Williams, Miller, Shaw, Stoppard, Racine, Moliére, Sophocles, Aeschylus, Euripides, and Aristophanes.
Epic	Long poem usually of book length reflecting values inherent in the generative society. Epic devices include an invocation to a Muse for inspiration, purpose for writing, universal setting, protagonist and antagonist who possess supernatural strength and acumen, and interventions of a God or the gods. Understandably, there are very few epics: Homer's *Iliad* and *Odyssey*, Virgil's *Aeneid*, Milton's *Paradise Lost*, Spenser's *The Fairie Queene*, Barrett Browning's "Aurora Leigh," and Pope's mock-epic, *The Rape of the Lock*.
Epistle	A letter that is not always originally intended for public distribution, but due to the fame of the sender and/or recipient, becomes public domain. Paul wrote epistles that were later placed in the Bible.
Essay	Typically a limited length prose work focusing on a topic and propounding a definite point of view and authoritative tone. Great essayists include Carlyle, Lamb, DeQuincy, Emerson, and Montaigne, who is credited with defining this genre.
Fable	Terse tale offering up a moral or exemplum. Chaucer's "The Nun's Priest's Tale" is a fine example of a *bête fabliau* or beast fable in which animals speak and act characteristically human, illustrating human foibles.
Legend	A traditional narrative or collection of related narratives, popularly regarded as historically factual but actually a mixture of fact and fiction.

Table continued on next page

Myth	Stories that are more or less universally shared within a culture to explain its history and traditions.
Novel	The longest form of fictional prose containing a variety of characterizations, settings, local color, and regionalism. Most have complex plots, expanded description, and attention to detail. Some of the great novelists include Austin, the Brontes, Twain, Tolstoy, Hugo, Hardy, Dickens, Hawthorne, Forster, and Flaubert.
Poem	The only requirement is rhythm. Subgenres include fixed types of literature such as the sonnet, elegy, ode, pastoral, and villanelle. Unfixed types of literature include blank verse and dramatic monologue.
Romance	A highly imaginative tale set in a fantastical realm dealing with the conflicts between heroes, villains and/or monsters. "The Knight's Tale" from Chaucer's *Canterbury Tales*, *Sir Gawain and the Green Knight* and Keats' "The Eve of St. Agnes" are prime representatives.
Short Story	Typically a terse narrative, with less developmental background about characters. Short stories may include description, author's point of view, and tone. Poe emphasized that a successful short story should create one focused impact. Considered to be great short story writers are Hemingway, Faulkner, Twain, Joyce, Shirley Jackson, Flannery O'Connor, de Maupassant, Saki, Edgar Allen Poe, and Pushkin.
Children's Literature	A genre of its own and emerged as a distinct and independent form in the second half of the eighteenth century. *The Visible World in Pictures* by John Amos Comenius, a Czech educator, was one of the first printed works and the first picture book. For the first time, educators acknowledged that children are different from adults in many respects. Modern educators acknowledge that introducing elementary students to a wide range of reading experiences plays an important role in their mental/social/psychological development.

LITERATURE SPECIFICALLY FOR CHILDREN	
Traditional Literature	Traditional literature opens up a world where right wins out over wrong, where hard work and perseverance are rewarded, and where helpless victims find vindication—all worthwhile values that children identify with even as early as kindergarten. In traditional literature, children will be introduced to fanciful beings, humans with exaggerated powers, talking animals, and heroes that will inspire them. For younger elementary children, these stories in Big Book format are ideal for providing predictable and repetitive elements that can be grasped by these children.
Folktales/ Fairy Tales	Adventures of animals or humans and the supernatural characterize these stories. The hero is usually on a quest and is aided by other-worldly helpers. More often than not, the story focuses on good and evil and reward and punishment. Some examples: *The Three Bears*, *Little Red Riding Hood*, *Snow White*, *Sleeping Beauty*, *Puss-in-Boots*, *Rapunzel*, and *Rumpelstiltskin*.

Table continued on next page

Fables	Animals that act like humans are featured in these stories and usually reveal human foibles or sometimes teach a lesson. Example: Aesop's *Fables*.
Myths	These stories about events from the earliest times, such as the origin of the world, are considered true in their own societies.
Legends	These are similar to myths except that they tend to deal with events that happened more recently. Example: Arthurian legends.
Tall Tales	These are purposely exaggerated accounts of individuals with superhuman strength. Examples: Paul Bunyan, John Henry, and Pecos Bill.
Modern Fantasy	Many of the themes found in these stories are similar to those in traditional literature. The stories start out based in reality, which makes it easier for the reader to suspend disbelief and enter worlds of unreality. Little people live in the walls in *The Borrowers* and time travel is possible in *The Trolley to Yesterday*. Including some fantasy tales in the curriculum helps elementary-grade children develop their senses of imagination. These often appeal to ideals of justice and issues having to do with good and evil; and because children tend to identify with the characters, the message is more likely to be retained.
Science Fiction	Robots, spacecraft, mystery, and civilizations from other ages often appear in these stories. Most presume advances in science on other planets or in a future time. Most children like these stories because of their interest in space and the "what if" aspect of the stories. Examples: *Outer Space and All That Junk* and *A Wrinkle in Time*.
Modern Realistic Fiction	These stories are about real problems that real children face. By finding that their hopes and fears are shared by others, young children can find insight into their own problems. Young readers also tend to experience a broadening of interests as the result of this kind of reading. It's good for them to know that a child can be brave and intelligent and can solve difficult problems.
Historical Fiction	The stories are presented in a historically accurate setting. One example of this kind of story is *Rifles for Watie*. This story is about a young boy (16 years) who serves in the Union army. He experiences great hardship but discovers that his enemy is an admirable human being. It provides a good opportunity to introduce younger children to history in a beneficial way
Biography	Reading about inventors, explorers, scientists, political and religious leaders, social reformers, artists, sports figures, doctors, teachers, writers, and war heroes help children to see that one person can make a difference. They also open new vistas for children to think about when they choose an occupation to fantasize about.
Informational Books	These are ways to learn more about something you are interested in or something that you know nothing about. Encyclopedias are good resources, of course, but a book like *Polar Wildlife* by Kamini Khanduri shows pictures and facts that will capture the imaginations of young children.

Sample Test Questions and Rationale

Rigorous

1. Which of the following is a ballad?

   A. "The Knight's Tale"

   B. *Julius Caesar*

   C. *Paradise Lost*

   D. "The Rime of the Ancient Mariner"

Answer: D – "The Rime of the Ancient Mariner"

Rationale: The answer is "The Rime of the Ancient Mariner." "The Knight's Tale" is a Romantic poem from the longer *Canterbury Tales* by Chaucer. *Julius Caesar* is a Shakespearian play. *Paradise Lost* is an epic poem in blank verse. A ballad is an *in medias res* story told or sung, usually in verse and accompanied by music, and usually with a refrain—a repeated section. Typically, ballads are based on folk stories

Rigorous

2. Which of the following is an epic?

   A. *On the Choice of Books*

   B. *The Faerie Queene*

   C. *Northanger Abbey*

   D. *A Doll's House*

Answer: B – *The Faerie Queene*

Rationale: The correct answer is *The Faerie Queene*. An epic is a long poem, usually of book length, reflecting the values of the society in which it was produced. *On the Choice of Books* is an essay by Thomas Carlyle. *Northanger Abbey* is a novel written by Jane Austen, and *A Doll's House* is a play written by Henrik Ibsen.

DOMAIN II
MATHEMATICS

Enhanced features only available in our ebook edition:

 eStickynotes: allows you take digital notes anywhere in the ebook edition. It further allows you to aggregate and print all enotes for easy studying.

 eFlashcards: a digital representation of a card represented with words, numbers or symbols or any combination of each and briefly displayed as part of a learning drill. eFlashcards takes away the burden of carrying around traditional cards that could easily be disarranged, dropped, or soiled.

 More Sample Tests: more ways to assess how much you know and how much further you need to study. Ultimately, makes you more prepared and attain mastery in the skills and techniques of passing the test the FIRST TIME!

Visit www.XAMonline.com
and click on ebook.

PERSONALIZED STUDY PLAN

PAGE	COMPETENCY AND SKILL	KNOWN MATERIAL/ SKIP IT	BRIEFLY REVIEW eSTICKYNOTES	MAKE eFLASHCARDS	TAKE ADDITIONAL SAMPLE TESTS
105	**9: Formal and Informal Reasoning**	☐	☐	☐	☐
	9.1: Drawing conclusions about mathematical problems	☐	☐	☐	☐
	9.2: Logic of mathematical arguments	☐	☐	☐	☐
	9.3: Drawing a valid mathematical conclusion	☐	☐	☐	☐
	9.4: Inductive reasoning for mathematical conjectures	☐	☐	☐	☐
	9.5: Problem-solving strategies to model and solve problems	☐	☐	☐	☐
	9.6: Use specific models or mental math procedures	☐	☐	☐	☐
113	**10: Mathematical Terminology and Symbols**	☐	☐	☐	☐
	10.1: Mathematical notation to relationships	☐	☐	☐	☐
	10.2: Models, diagrams, and symbols	☐	☐	☐	☐
	10.3: Vocabulary to express mathematical ideas	☐	☐	☐	☐
	10.4: Ordinary language to express mathematical ideas	☐	☐	☐	☐
	10.5: Different representations of mathematical relationships	☐	☐	☐	☐
	10.6: Modeling and interpreting physical, social, and mathematical phenomena	☐	☐	☐	☐
118	**11: Number Skills and Concepts**	☐	☐	☐	☐
	11.1: Computational and operational methods	☐	☐	☐	☐
	11.2: Commutative, distributive, and associative properties	☐	☐	☐	☐
	11.3: Ratios, proportions, and percents	☐	☐	☐	☐
	11.4: Fractions, decimals, and percents	☐	☐	☐	☐
	11.5: Equivalent numbers	☐	☐	☐	☐
	11.6: Number properties in operational algorithms	☐	☐	☐	☐
	11.7: Number properties in algebraic expressions	☐	☐	☐	☐
128	**12: Linear Algebraic Relations and Functions**	☐	☐	☐	☐
	12.1: Mathematical relationships	☐	☐	☐	☐
	12.2: Representations to recognize and extend patterns	☐	☐	☐	☐
	12.3: Tables, verbal rules, and graphs	☐	☐	☐	☐
	12.4: Algebraic expressions to represent relationships	☐	☐	☐	☐
	12.5: Algebraic functions to describe graphic examples	☐	☐	☐	☐
	12.6: Algebraic operations to solve equations	☐	☐	☐	☐
	12.7: Changing variables in linear and nonlinear functions	☐	☐	☐	☐
144	**13: Geometry and Trigonometry**	☐	☐	☐	☐
	13.1: Two- and three-dimensional geometric shapes	☐	☐	☐	☐
	13.2: Solving real-world problems involving complex patterns	☐	☐	☐	☐
	13.3: Similarity and congruence	☐	☐	☐	☐
	13.4: Inductive and deductive reasoning in geometry	☐	☐	☐	☐
	13.5: Coordinate geometry	☐	☐	☐	☐
	13.6: Transformations and symmetry	☐	☐	☐	☐

PERSONALIZED STUDY PLAN

PAGE	COMPETENCY AND SKILL	KNOWN MATERIAL/ SKIP IT	BRIEFLY REVIEW eSTICKYNOTES	MAKE eFLASHCARDS	TAKE ADDITIONAL SAMPLE TESTS
153	**14: Customary and Metric Measurement**	☐	☐	☐	☐
	14.1: Fundamental units of measurement	☐	☐	☐	☐
	14.2: Appropriate units of measurement	☐	☐	☐	☐
	14.3: Estimating and converting measurements	☐	☐	☐	☐
	14.4: Using formulas to determine perimeter, area, and volume	☐	☐	☐	☐
	14.5: Derived measurement problems	☐	☐	☐	☐
	14.6: Pythagorean theorem and right triangle trigonometry	☐	☐	☐	☐
168	**15: Data Analysis, Probability, and Statistics**	☐	☐	☐	☐
	15.1: Collecting, organizing, and analyzing data	☐	☐	☐	☐
	15.2: Displaying and interpreting data	☐	☐	☐	☐
	15.3: Computing probabilities	☐	☐	☐	☐
	15.4: Estimating probabilities with simulations	☐	☐	☐	☐
	15.5: Measures of central tendency	☐	☐	☐	☐
	15.6: Statistical experiments	☐	☐	☐	☐
	15.7: Patterns and trends in data	☐	☐	☐	☐

COMPETENCY 9

UNDERSTAND FORMAL AND INFORMAL REASONING PROCESSES, INCLUDING LOGIC AND SIMPLE PROOFS, AND APPLY PROBLEM-SOLVING TECHNIQUES AND STRATEGIES IN A VARIETY OF CONTEXTS

SKILL 9.1 Using models, facts, patterns, and relationships to draw conclusions about mathematical problems or situations

Conditional statements are frequently written in **"if-then"** form. The "if" clause of the conditional is known as the **hypothesis**, and the "then" clause is called the **conclusion**. In a proof, the hypothesis is the information that is assumed to be true, while the conclusion is what is to be proven true. A conditional is considered to be of the form:

If p, then q

p is the hypothesis. q is the conclusion.

Conditional statements can be diagrammed using a Venn diagram. A diagram can be drawn with one figure inside another figure. The inner portion represents the hypothesis. The outer portion represents the conclusion. If the hypothesis is taken to be true, then you are located inside the inner circle. If you are located in the inner circle then you are also inside the outer circle, so that proves the conclusion is true.

Example: If an angle has a measure of 90°, then it is a right angle.
In this statement "an angle has a measure of 90°" is the hypothesis.
In this statement "it is a right angle" is the conclusion.

Example: If you are in Pittsburgh, then you are in Pennsylvania.
In this statement "you are in Pittsburgh" is the hypothesis.
In this statement "you are in Pennsylvania" is the conclusion.

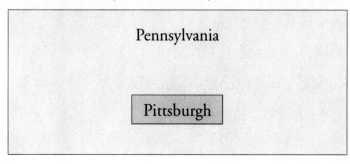

Conditional: If p, then q

p is the hypothesis. q is the conclusion.

Inverse: If ~ p, then ~ q.

Negate both the hypothesis (If not p, then not q) and the conclusion from the original conditional.

Converse: If q, then p.

Reverse the two clauses.

The original hypothesis becomes the conclusion.

The original conclusion then becomes the new hypothesis.

Contrapositive: If ~ q, then ~ p.

Reverse the two clauses. The "If not q, then not p" original hypothesis becomes the conclusion.

The original conclusion then becomes the new hypothesis.

THEN negate both the new hypothesis and the new conclusion.

Example: Given the conditional: If an angle has 60°, then it is an acute angle.

Its **inverse**, in the form "If ~ p, then ~ q," would be:

If an angle doesn't have 60°, then it is not an acute angle.

Notice that the inverse is not true, even though the conditional statement was true.

Tip: If you are asked to pick a statement that is logically equivalent to a given conditional, look for the contrapositive. The inverse and converse are not always logically equivalent to every conditional. The contrapositive is ALWAYS logically equivalent.

Its **converse**, in the form "If q, then p," would be:

If an angle is an acute angle, then it has 60°.

Notice that the converse is not true, even though the conditional statement was true.

Its **contrapositive**, in the form "If ~ q, then ~ p," would be:

If an angle isn't an acute angle, then it doesn't have 60°.

Notice that the contrapositive is true, assuming original conditional statement was true.

Find the inverse, converse, and contrapositive of the following conditional statement. Also determine if each of the four statements is true or false.

Conditional: If $x = 5$, then $x^2 - 25 = 0$. TRUE

Inverse: If $x \neq 5$, then $x^2 - 25 \neq 0$. FALSE, x could be -5

Converse: If $x^2 - 25 = 0$, then $x = 5$. FALSE, x could be -5

Contrapositive: If $x^2 - 25 \neq 0$, then $x \neq 5$. TRUE

Conditional: If $x = 5$, then $6x = 30$. TRUE

Inverse: If $x \neq 5$, then $6x \neq 30$. TRUE

Converse: If $6x = 30$, then $x = 5$. TRUE

Contrapositive: If $6x \neq 30$, then $x \neq 5$. TRUE

Sometimes, as in this example, all four statements can be logically equivalent; however, the only statement that will always be logically equivalent to the original conditional is the contrapositive.

Sample Test Questions and Rationale

Rigorous

1. If $4x - (3 - x) = 7(x - 3) + 10$, then:

    A. $x = 8$

    B. $x = -8$

    C. $x = 4$

    D. $x = -4$

Answer: $x = 4$

Rationale: Solve for x.

$$4x - (3 - x) = 7(x - 3) + 10$$

$$4x - 3 + x = 7x - 21 + 10$$

$$5x = 7x - 11 + 3$$

$$5x - 7x = -8$$

$$-2x = -8$$

$$x = 4$$

SKILL 9.2 Judging the validity or logic of mathematical arguments

A valid argument is a statement made about a pattern or relationship between elements thought to be true, which is subsequently justified through repeated examples and logical reasoning. Another term for a valid argument is a *proof*.

For example, the statement that the sum of two odd numbers is always even could be tested through actual examples.

Two Odd Numbers	Sum	Validity of Statement
1+1	2 (even)	Valid
1+3	4 (even)	Valid
61+29	90 (even)	Valid
135+47	182 (even)	Valid
253+17	270 (even)	Valid
1,945+2,007	3,952 (even)	Valid
6,321+7,851	14,172 (even)	Valid

Adding two odd numbers always results in a sum that is even. It is a valid argument based on the justifications in the table above.

Here is another example: The statement that a fraction of a fraction can be determined by multiplying the numerator by the numerator and the denominator by the denominator can be proven through logical reasoning. For example, one-half of one-quarter of a candy bar can be found by multiplying $\frac{1}{2} \times \frac{1}{4}$. The answer would be one-eighth. The validity of this argument can be demonstrated as valid with a model.

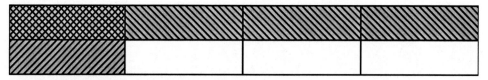

This entire rectangle represents one whole candy bar. The top half (four sections) of the model is shaded in one direction to demonstrate how much of the candy bar remains from the whole candy bar. The left quarter, shaded in a different direction, demonstrates that one-quarter of the candy bar has been given to a friend. Since the whole candy bar is not available to give out, the area that is double-shaded is the fractional part of the half candy bar that has been actually given away. That fractional part is one-eighth of the whole candy bar as shown in both the sketch and the algorithm.

SKILL 9.3 Drawing a valid conclusion based on stated conditions and evaluating conclusions involving simple and compound sentences

As stated in Skill 9.1, conditional statements can be diagrammed using a Venn diagram. A diagram can be drawn with one figure inside another figure. The inner figure represents the hypothesis. The outer figure represents the conclusion. If the hypothesis is taken to be true, then you are located inside the inner figure. If you are located in the inner figure then you are also inside the outer figure, so that proves the conclusion is true. Sometimes that conclusion can then be used as the hypothesis for another conditional, which can result in a second conclusion.

Suppose that these statements were given to you, and you are asked to try to reach a conclusion. The statements are:

All swimmers are athletes.
All athletes are scholars.

In "if-then" form, these would be:
If you are a swimmer, then you are an athlete.
If you are an athlete, then you are a scholar.

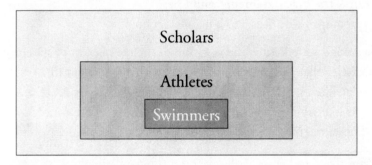

Clearly, if you are a swimmer, then you are also an athlete. This includes you in the group of scholars.

Suppose that these statements were given to you, and you are asked to try to reach a conclusion. The statements are:

All swimmers are athletes.
All wrestlers are athletes.

In "if-then" form, these would be:
If you are a swimmer, then you are an athlete.
If you are a wrestler, then you are an athlete.

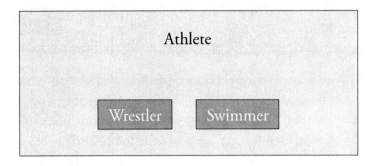

Clearly, if you are a swimmer or a wrestler, then you are also an athlete. This does NOT allow you to come to any other conclusions.

A swimmer may or may NOT also be a wrestler. Therefore, NO CONCLUSION IS POSSIBLE.

Suppose that these statements were given to you, and you are asked to try to reach a conclusion. The statements are:
All rectangles are parallelograms.
Quadrilateral ABCD is not a parallelogram.

In "if-then" form, the first statement would be:
If a figure is a rectangle, then it is also a parallelogram.

Note that the second statement is the negation of the conclusion of statement one. Remember also that the contrapositive is logically equivalent to a given conditional. That is, "**If ~ q, then ~ p.**" Since "ABCD is NOT a parallelogram" is like saying "**If ~ q,**" then you can come to the conclusion "**then ~ p.**" Therefore, the conclusion is ABCD is not a rectangle.

Looking at the Venn diagram below, if all rectangles are parallelograms, then rectangles are included as part of the parallelograms. Since quadrilateral ABCD is not a parallelogram, that it is excluded from anywhere inside the parallelogram box. This allows you to conclude that ABCD can not be a rectangle either.

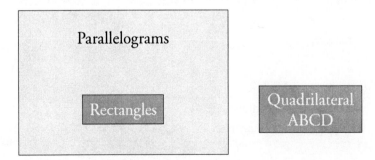

SKILL 9.4 Applying inductive reasoning to make mathematical conjectures

Inductive thinking is the process of finding a pattern from a group of examples. That pattern is the conclusion that this set of examples seemed to indicate. It may be a correct conclusion or it may be an incorrect conclusion because other examples may not follow the predicted pattern.

Deductive thinking is the process of arriving at a conclusion based on other statements that are all known to be true, such as theorems, axioms, or postulates. Conclusions found by deductive thinking based on true statements will always be true.

Example:
Suppose:

On Monday, Mr. Peterson eats breakfast at McDonald's.
On Tuesday, Mr. Peterson eats breakfast at McDonald's.
On Wednesday, Mr. Peterson eats breakfast at McDonald's.
On Thursday, Mr. Peterson eats breakfast at McDonald's again.
Conclusion: On Friday, Mr. Peterson will eat breakfast at McDonald's again.

This is a conclusion based on inductive reasoning. Based on several days of observations, you conclude that Mr. Peterson will eat at McDonald's. This may or may not be true, but it is a conclusion arrived at by inductive thinking.

SKILL 9.5 Using a variety of problem-solving strategies to model and solve problems, and evaluating the appropriateness of a problem-solving strategy (e.g., estimation, mental math, working backward, pattern recognition) in a given situation

Estimation and approximation may be used to check the reasonableness of answers.

Example: Estimate the answer.

$$\frac{58 \times 810}{1989}$$

58 becomes 60, 810 becomes 800, and 1,989 becomes 2,000.

$$\frac{60 \times 800}{2000} = 24$$

Word Problems

An estimate may sometimes be all that is needed to solve a problem.

Example: Janet goes into a store to purchase a CD on sale for $13.95. While shopping, she sees two pairs of shoes, priced $19.95 and $14.50. She only has $50. Can she purchase everything?

Solve by rounding:

$$\$19.95 \rightarrow \$20.00$$
$$\$14.50 \rightarrow \$15.00$$
$$\underline{\$13.95 \rightarrow \$14.00}$$
$$\$49.00$$

Yes, she can purchase the CD and the shoes.

SKILL 9.6 **Analyzing the usefulness of a specific model or mental math procedure for exploring a given mathematical, scientific, or technological idea or problem**

Examining the change in area or volume of a given figure requires first to find the existing area given the original dimensions and then finding the new area given the increased dimensions.

Sample problem: Given the rectangle below determine the change in area if the length is increased by 5 and the width is increased by 7.

7

4

Draw and label a sketch of the new rectangle.

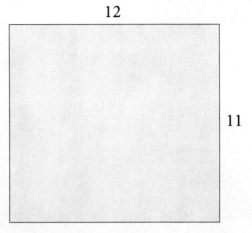

12

11

Find the areas.

Area of original = LW   Area of enlarged shape = LW
                 = (7)(4)   = (12)(11)
                 = 28 units^2 = 132 units^2

The change in area is $132 - 28 = 104$ units^2.

COMPETENCY 10

USE MATHEMATICAL TERMINOLOGY AND SYMBOLS TO INTERPRET, REPRESENT, AND COMMUNICATE MATHEMATICAL IDEAS AND INFORMATION

SKILL 10.1 Using mathematical notation to represent a given relationship

Mathematical operations include addition, subtraction, multiplication, and division.

- Addition can be indicated by the expressions: sum, greater than, and, more than, increased by, added to.

- Subtraction can be expressed by: difference, fewer than, minus, less than, decreased by.

- Multiplication can be expressed by: product, times, multiplied by, twice.

- Division can be expressed by: quotient, divided by, ratio.

Examples:

7 added to a number: n + 7

a number decreased by 8: n − 8

12 times a number divided by 7: 12n ÷ 7

28 less than a number: n − 28

the ratio of a number to 55: $\frac{n}{55}$

4 times the sum of a number and 21: 4(n + 21)

Sample Test Questions and Rationale

Average Rigor

1. **Which words in a test problem would indicate that an addition operation is needed?**

   A. each

   B. decreased by

   C. in each group

   D. increased by

Answer: D – increased by

Rationale: Addition can be indicated by the expressions: sum, greater than, and, more than, increased by, added to. Subtraction can be expressed by: difference, fewer than, minus, less than, decreased by. Multiplication is shown by: product, times, multiplied by, twice. Division is used for: quotient, divided by, ratio.

SKILL 10.2 Using appropriate models, diagrams, and symbols to represent mathematical concepts

Mathematical operations can be shown using manipulatives or drawings.

Multiplication can be shown using arrays.

   3 × 4

Addition and subtractions can be demonstrated with symbols.

   ψψψζζ

   3 + 4 = 7

   7 − 3 = 4

Fractions can be clarified using pattern blocks, fraction bars, or paper folding.

SKILL 10.3 Using appropriate vocabulary to express given mathematical ideas and relationships

To read a bar graph or a pictograph, read the explanation of the scale that was used in the legend. Compare the length of each bar with the dimensions on the axes and calculate the value each bar represents. On a pictograph count the number of pictures used in the chart and calculate the value of all the pictures.

To read a circle graph, find the total of the amounts represented on the entire circle graph. To determine the actual amount that each sector of the graph represents, multiply the percent in a sector times the total amount number.

To read a chart, read the row and column headings on the table. Use this information to evaluate the given information in the chart.

Mathematical vocabulary includes models to facilitate mathematical thinking and equations and expressions to define mathematical relationships. Models can include such things as charts to represent algebraic functions, graphs to show relationships between quantities, as well as objects to represent quantities.

Mathematical vocabulary also helps students in logical thinking processes. Being able to describe processes using this vocabulary helps students understand exactly what they are doing in the process. Writing about mathematical processes using this vocabulary also helps clarify processes for students.

Mathematic vocabulary is grade-specific. Lower grades have less mathematical terms to explain operations and relationships than do higher grades. Higher grades also have more exposure to operations and relationships that require specific vocabulary terms.

SKILL 10.4 Relating the language of ordinary experiences to mathematical language and symbols

A popular theory of math learning is *constructivism*. Constructivism argues that prior knowledge greatly influences the learning of math and learning is cumulative and vertically structured. Thus, it is important for teachers to recognize the knowledge and ideas about a subject that students already possess. Instruction must build on the innate knowledge of students and address any common misconceptions. Teachers can gain insight into the prior knowledge of students by beginning each lesson with open questions that allow students to share their thoughts and ideas on the subject or topic.

There are levels of experience with language and concepts. Math learning progresses in a spiral nature, with early learning experiences being merely an introduction and later learning experiences building on earlier ones. As the individual progresses through the spiral, later experiences become more and more abstract and difficult. Exposing the student from an early age to math language in everyday experiences helps them develop expertise in later math concepts.

Math is the language of symbols. Math helps us describe both similarities and differences and also helps us think and solve practical problems. The language of math helps us understand the relationship and patterns of numbers and the way they change. Through math language the individual makes sense out of numbers, measurement, and geometrical experiences in the environment.

Mathematical language skills include the abilities to read with comprehension, to express mathematical thoughts clearly, to reason logically, and to recognize and employ common patterns of mathematical thought. Mathematical results are expressed in a foreign language—a language that, like other languages, has its own grammar, syntax, vocabulary, word order, synonyms, negations, conventions, abbreviations, sentence structure, and paragraph structure. Just as one must be proficient in language to understand what is read, so must one be proficient in mathematical language to understand math concepts.

SKILL 10.5 Translating among graphic, numeric, symbolic, and verbal representations of mathematical relationships and concepts

Recognition and understanding of the relationships between concepts and topics is of great value in mathematical problem solving and the explanation of more complex processes.

For instance, multiplication is simply repeated addition. This relationship explains the concept of variable addition. We can show that the expression $4x + 3x = 7x$ is true by rewriting 4 times x and 3 times x as repeated addition, yielding the expression $(x + x + x + x) + (x + x + x)$. Thus, because of the relationship between multiplication and addition, variable addition is accomplished by coefficient addition.

Mathematical problem solving can be approached by using graphic representation, numeric solutions, symbols, and verbal explanations. Each of these methods is important in helping the student understand math concepts.

In solving a problem using a new concept, the student may be led to draw pictures representing the problem situation. This will assist the student in visualizing the problem solving process.

Once the concept is grasped the student should be encouraged to move to numeric representation of the concept. At this stage, there is still dependence on graphic representation combined with numeric representation. There should be a gradual move toward using only numbers to describe and solve the problem.

The next step is to represent mathematical concepts using numbers and symbols. The graphic part of the representation should at this time be dropped from the solution process. The concept should become so ingrained that the student will understand symbolic representation.

The highest level of mathematical language is verbal representation. Once the concept is thoroughly internalized, the student should be able to explain the concept and solution verbally. This can be done orally or in written form. Once the student can accurately write the solution, he or she has fully internalized the concept.

SKILL 10.6 **Using mathematical representations to model and interpret physical, social, and mathematical phenomena**

Manipulatives

Example: Using tiles to demonstrate both geometric ideas and number theory.

Give each group of students 12 tiles and instruct them to build rectangles. Students draw their rectangles on paper.

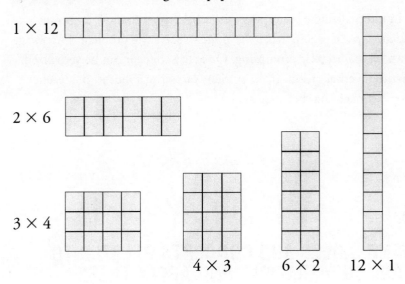

1 × 12

2 × 6

3 × 4

4 × 3   6 × 2   12 × 1

Encourage students to describe their reactions. Extend to 16 tiles. Ask students to form additional problems.

Using Mathematical Representations

Addition, subtraction, multiplication, and division can be represented using counters. Before performing paper and pencil solutions, the student should be exposed to manipulative representations. Let the student have plenty of time to explore the concept of each operation, i.e., combining sets of manipulatives for addition, taking some away for subtraction, forming equal groups for multiplication, and separating a total into groups of equal size for division. Even the concept of remainders in division can be represented with a left over number when groups are formed.

Base ten, or place value, blocks can be used to teach renaming concepts and place value. Using mats marked with hundreds, tens, and ones, later adding thousands and ten thousands, can help the student visualize what the larger numbers mean.

Once the concept has been introduced thoroughly the student should be moved to using graphic representations, or drawings. This can be done using drawings of sets for operations, and drawings of base ten blocks for place value and renaming. This is a step toward numeric representation.

Once the student is competent solving problems using graphic representations, it is time to move toward complete numeric representation. This is best done by using a combination of graphic and numeric representation, slowly moving toward complete numeric representation.

The final step in internalizing a concept is the verbal representation. Begin by having the student explain exactly what was done to solve the problem. Encourage them through the verbal step by prompting. Once the concept can be verbalized, move toward written verbalization. If the student can write about it, the teacher can be assured the concept has been grasped.

COMPETENCY 11

UNDERSTAND SKILLS AND CONCEPTS RELATED TO NUMBER AND NUMERATION, AND APPLY THESE CONCEPTS TO REAL-WORLD SITUATIONS

SKILL 11.1 Selecting the appropriate computational and operational method to solve given mathematical problems

The use of supplementary materials in the classroom can greatly enhance the learning experience by stimulating student interest and satisfying different learning styles. Manipulatives, models, and technology are examples of tools available to teachers.

MANIPULATIVES are materials that students can physically handle and move. Manipulatives allow students to understand mathematic concepts by allowing them to see concrete examples of abstract processes. Manipulatives are attractive to students because they appeal to the students' visual and tactile senses. Available for all levels of math, manipulatives are useful tools for reinforcing operations and concepts. They are not, however, a substitute for the development of sound computational skills.

MANIPULATIVES: materials that students can physically handle and move

MODELS are other means of representing mathematical concepts by relating the concepts to real-world situations. Teachers must choose wisely when devising and selecting models because, to be effective, models must be applied properly. For example, a building with floors above and below ground is a good model for introducing the concept of negative numbers. It would be difficult, however, to use the building model in teaching subtraction of negative numbers.

Finally, there are many forms of technology available to math teachers. For example, students can test their understanding of math concepts by working on skill-specific computer programs and Web sites. Graphing calculators can help students visualize the graphs of functions. Teachers can also enhance their lectures and classroom presentations by creating multimedia presentations.

> **MODELS:** other means of representing mathematical concepts by relating the concepts to real-world situations

---

SKILL 11.2 **Demonstrating an understanding of the commutative, distributive, and associative properties**

Field Properties

Real numbers exhibit the following addition and multiplication properties, where a, b, and c are real numbers.

Note: Multiplication is implied when there is no symbol between two variables. Thus,

$a \times b$ can be written ab.

Multiplication can also be indicated by a raised dot $\cdot$ (a $\cdot$ b).

Closure

$a + b$ is a real number

Example: Since 2 and 5 are both real numbers, 7 is also a real number.

ab is a real number

Example: Since 3 and 4 are both real numbers, 12 is also a real number. The sum or product of two real numbers is a real number.

Commutative

$a + b = b + a$

Example: $5 + (-8) = -8 + 5 = -3$

$ab = ba$

Example: $-2 \times 6 = 6 \times -2 = -12$

The order of the addends or factors does not affect the sum or product.

Associative

$(a + b) + c = a + (b + c)$

Example: $(-2 + 7) + 5 = -2 + (7 + 5)$
$5 + 5 = -2 + 12 = 10$

$(ab)c = a(bc)$

Example: $(3 \times -7) \times 5 = 3 \times (-7 \times 5)$
$-21 \times 5 = 3 \times -35 = -105$

The grouping of the addends or factors does not affect the sum or product.

Distributive

$a(b + c) = ab + ac$

Example: $6 \times (-4 + 9) = (6 \times -4) + (6 \times 9)$
$6 \times 5 = -24 + 54 = 30$

To multiply a sum by a number, multiply each addend by the number, then add the products.

Additive Identity (Property of Zero)

$a + 0 = a$

Example: $17 + 0 = 17$

The sum of any number and zero is that number.

Multiplicative Identity (Property of One)

$a \cdot 1 = a$

Example: $-34 \times 1 = -34$

The product of any number and one is that number.

Additive Inverse (Property of Opposites)

$a + -a = 0$

Example: $25 + -25 = 0$

The sum of any number and its opposite is zero.

Multiplicative Inverse (Property of Reciprocals)

$a \times \frac{1}{a} = 1$

Example: $5 \times \frac{1}{5} = 1$

The product of any number and its reciprocal is one.

Property of Denseness

Between any pair of rational numbers, there is at least one rational number. The set of natural numbers is *not* dense because between two consecutive natural numbers there may not exist another natural number.

Example: Between 7.6 and 7.7, there is the rational number 7.65 in the set of real numbers.

Between 3 and 4 there exists no other natural number.

SKILL 11.3 **Using ratios, proportions, and percents to model and solve problems**

PROPORTIONS can be used to solve word problems whenever relationships are compared.

Some situations include scale drawings and maps, similar polygons, speed, time and distance, cost, and comparison shopping.

> **PROPORTIONS:**
> can be used to solve word problems whenever relationships are compared

Example: Which is the better buy, 6 items for $1.29 or 8 items for $1.69?

Find the unit price.

$$\frac{6}{1.29} = \frac{1}{x}$$
$$6x = 1.29$$
$$x = 0.21\dot{5}$$

$$\frac{8}{1.69} = \frac{1}{x}$$
$$8x = 1.69$$
$$x = 0.21125$$

Thus, 6 items for $1.29 is the better buy.

Example: A car travels 125 miles in 2.5 hours. How far will it go in 6 hours?

Write a proportion comparing the distance and time. $\frac{miles}{hours}$

$$\frac{125}{2.5} = \frac{x}{6}$$
$$2.5x = 750$$
$$x = 300$$

Thus, the car can travel 300 miles in 6 hours.

Example: The scale on a map is ¾ inch = 6 miles. What is the actual distance between two cities if they are 1½ inch apart on the map?

Write a proportion comparing the scale to the actual distance.

$$\overset{scale}{} \quad \overset{actual}{}$$
$$\frac{\frac{3}{4}}{1\frac{1}{2}} = \frac{6}{x}$$

$$\frac{3}{4}x = 1\frac{1}{2} \times 6$$

$$\frac{3}{4}x = 9$$

$$x = 12$$

Thus, the actual distance between the cities is 12 miles.

SKILL 11.4 Comparing and ordering fractions, decimals, and percents

To convert a fraction to a decimal, simply divide the numerator (top) by the denominator (bottom). Use long division if necessary.

If a decimal has a fixed number of digits, the decimal is said to be terminating. To write such a decimal as a fraction, first determine what place value the farthest right digit is in, for example: tenths, hundredths, thousandths, ten thousandths, hundred thousands, etc. Then drop the decimal and place the string of digits over the number given by the place value.

If a decimal continues forever by repeating a string of digits, the decimal is said to be repeating. To write a repeating decimal as a fraction, follow these steps.

1. Let x = the repeating decimal
   ($x = 0.716716716\ldots$)

2. Multiply x by the multiple of ten that will move the decimal just to the right of the repeating block of digits.
   ($1000x = 716.716716\ldots$)

3. Subtract the first equation from the second.
   ($1000x - x = 716.716716\ldots - 0.716716\ldots$)

4. Simplify and solve this equation. The repeating block of digits will subtract out.
   ($999x = 716$ so $x = \frac{716}{999}$)

5. The solution will be the fraction for the repeating decimal.

In ordering and comparing fractions, the student needs to be introduced to the concept that the larger the denominator, the smaller the fraction. This is best done using manipulative and graphic representation. Cutting an actual object, or a card stock or paper representation, into more and more equal pieces shows the student that the larger the number of pieces, the smaller each piece will be. This is a hard

UNDERSTAND SKILLS AND CONCEPTS RELATED TO NUMBER AND NUMERATION,
AND APPLY THESE CONCEPTS TO REAL-WORLD SITUATIONS

concept for the student just beginning work with fractions, because normally the larger number is the largest.

An important concept for teaching comparing and ordering decimals is the concept of the zero placed at the end of a number following the decimal. Such a zero doesn't change the value. However, a zero added before the decimal does change the number. Resorting to using base ten blocks to teach decimal concepts will help the student visualize the concept.

> ### SKILL Solving problems using equivalent forms of numbers (e.g., integer, 11.5 fraction, decimal, percent, exponential and scientific notation), and problems involving number theory (e.g., primes, factors, multiples)

Word problems involving percents can be solved by writing the problem as an equation, then solving the equation. Keep in mind that "**of**" means "*multiplication*" and "**is**" means "*equals*."

Example: The Ski Club has 85 members. 80% of the members are able to attend the meeting. How many members attend the meeting?

Restate the problem.

What is 80% of 85?

Write an equation.

$n = 0.8 \times 85$

Solve.

$n = 68$

Sixty-eight members attend the meeting.

Example: There are 64 dogs in the kennel. 48 are collies. What percent are collies?

Restate the problem.

48 is what percent of 64?

Write an equation.

$48 = n \times 64$

Solve.

$$\frac{48}{64} = n$$
$$n = \frac{3}{4} = 75\%$$

75% of the dogs are collies.

EACHER CERTIFICATION STUDY GUIDE   123

Example: The auditorium was filled to 90% capacity. There were 558 seats occupied. What is the capacity of the auditorium?

Restate the problem.

90% of what number is 558?

Write an equation.

0.9n = 558

Solve.

$$n = \frac{588}{0.9}$$
$$n = 620$$

The capacity of the auditorium is 620 people.

Example: Shoes cost $42.00. Sales tax is 6%. What is the total cost of the shoes?

Restate the problem.

What is 6% of 42?

Write an equation.

n = 0.06 × 42

Solve.

n = 2.52

Add the sales tax to the cost. $42.00 + $2.52 = $44.52

The total cost of the shoes, including sales tax, is $44.52.

COMMON EQUIVALENTS				
$\frac{1}{2}$	=	0.5	=	50%
$\frac{1}{3}$	=	$0.33\frac{1}{3}$	=	$33\frac{1}{3}\%$
$\frac{1}{4}$	=	0.25	=	25%
$\frac{1}{5}$	=	0.2	=	20%
$\frac{1}{6}$	=	$0.16\frac{2}{3}$	=	$16\frac{2}{3}\%$
$\frac{1}{8}$	=	$0.12\frac{1}{2}$	=	$12\frac{1}{2}\%$

Table continued on next page

$\frac{1}{10}$	=	0.1	=	10%
$\frac{2}{3}$	=	$0.66\frac{2}{3}$	=	$66\frac{2}{3}$%
$\frac{5}{6}$	=	$0.83\frac{1}{3}$	=	$83\frac{1}{3}$%
$\frac{3}{8}$	=	$0.37\frac{1}{2}$	=	$37\frac{1}{2}$%
$\frac{5}{8}$	=	$0.62\frac{1}{2}$	=	$62\frac{1}{2}$%
$\frac{7}{8}$	=	$0.87\frac{1}{2}$	=	$87\frac{1}{2}$%
1	=	1.0	=	100%

PRIME NUMBERS are numbers that can only be factored into 1 and the number itself. When factoring into prime factors, all the factors must be numbers that cannot be factored again (without using 1). Initially numbers can be factored into any 2 factors. Check each resulting factor to see if it can be factored again. Continue factoring until all remaining factors are prime. This is the list of prime factors. Regardless of what way the original number was factored, the final list of prime factors will always be the same.

> **PRIME NUMBERS:** numbers that can only be factored into 1 and the number itself

Example: Factor 30 into prime factors.
Factor 30 into any 2 factors.

$5 \cdot 6$

Now factor the 6.

$5 \cdot 2 \cdot 3$

These are all prime factors.

Factor 30 into any 2 factors.

$3 \cdot 10$

Now factor the 10.

$3 \cdot 2 \cdot 5$

These are the same prime factors even though the original factors were different.

Example: Factor 240 into prime factors.
Factor 240 into any 2 factors.

$24 \cdot 10$

Now factor both 24 and 10.

$4 \cdot 6 \cdot 2 \cdot 5$

Now factor both 4 and 6.

$2 \cdot 2 \cdot 2 \cdot 3 \cdot 2 \cdot 5$

These are prime factors.

This can also be written as $2^4 \cdot 3 \cdot 5$.

Sample Test Questions and Rationale

Average Rigor

1. A sofa sells for $520. If the retailer makes a 30% profit, what was the wholesale price?

   A. $400

   B. $676

   C. $490

   D. $364

   Answer: A – $400

   Rationale: Let x be the wholesale price, then $x + .30x = 520$, $1.30x = 520$. Divide both sides by 1.30.

Rigorous

2. An item that sells for $375 is put on sale at $120. What is the percent of decrease?

   A. 25%

   B. 28%

   C. 68%

   D. 34%

   Answer: C – 68%

   Rationale: Use $(1 - x)$ as the discount. $375x = 120$.
   $375 (1 - x) = 120 \rightarrow$
   $375 - 375x = 120 \rightarrow$
   $375x = 255 \rightarrow$
   $x = 0.68 = 68\%$

SKILL 11.6 Analyzing the number properties used in operational algorithms *(e.g., multiplication, long division)*

The **Order of Operations** is to be followed when evaluating algebraic expressions. Follow these steps in order:

1. Simplify inside grouping characters such as parentheses, brackets, square roots, fraction bars, etc.

2. Multiply out expressions with exponents

3. Do multiplication or division, from left to right

4. Do addition or subtraction, from left to right

Samples of simplifying expressions with exponents:

$(-2)^3 = -8$ $-2^3 = -8$

$(-2)^4 = 16$ $-2^4 = 16$ Note change of sign.

$(\frac{2}{3})^3 = \frac{8}{27}$

$5^0 = 1$

$4^{-1} = \frac{1}{4}$

SKILL 11.7   Applying number properties to manipulate and simplify algebraic expressions

The EXPONENT FORM is a shortcut method to write repeated multiplication. The BASE is the factor. The EXPONENT tells how many times that number is multiplied by itself.

> **EXPONENT FORM:** a shortcut method to write repeated multiplication

Example: 3^4 is $3 \times 3 \times 3 \times 3 = 81$ where 3 is the base and 4 is the exponent.

x^2 is read "x squared"

y^3 is read "y cubed"

$a^1 = a$ for all values of a; thus $17^1 = 17$

$b^0 = 1$ for all values of b; thus $24^0 = 1$

> **BASE:** the factor

> **EXPONENT:** tells how many times that number is multiplied by itself

When 10 is raised to any power, the exponent tells the numbers of zeroes in the product.

Example: $10^7 = 10,000,000$

To simplify a radical, follow these steps:

1. Factor the number or coefficient completely.

2. For square roots, group like factors in pairs. For cube roots, arrange like factors in groups of three. For n^{th} roots, group like factors in groups of n.

3. For each of these groups, put one of that number outside the radical. Any factors that cannot be combined in groups should be multiplied together and left inside the radical.

4. The index number of a radical is the little number on the front of the radical. For a cube root, the index is 3. If no index appears, then the index is 2 for square roots.

5. For variables inside the radical, divide the index number of the radical into each exponent. The quotient (the answer to the division) is the new exponent

Remember that the square root of a negative number can be designated by replacing the negative sign inside that square root with an "i" in front of the radical (to signify an imaginary number). Then simplify the remaining positive radical by the normal method. Include the i outside the radical as part of the answer.

to be written on the variable outside the radical. The remainder from the division is the new exponent on the variable remaining inside the radical sign. If the remainder is zero, then the variable no longer appears in the radical sign.

If the index number is an odd number, you can still simplify the radical to get a negative solution.

Example:
$$\sqrt{50a^4b^7} = \sqrt{5 \cdot 5 \cdot 2 \cdot a^4b^7} = 5a^2b^3\sqrt{2b}$$

Example:
$$7x\sqrt[3]{16x^5} = 7x\sqrt[3]{2 \cdot 2 \cdot 2 \cdot 2 \cdot x^5} = 7x \cdot 2x\sqrt[3]{2x^2} = 14x^2\sqrt[3]{2x^2}$$

A mnemonic devise to help the student keep the order of operations straight is the saying, "**P**lease **E**xcuse **M**y **D**ear **A**unt **S**ally." Another is to teach the acronym PEMDAS, or parenthesis, exponents, multiplication/division, and addition/subtraction. Explain that multiplication/division and addition/subtraction are done left to right, without reference to which comes first in the acronym.

COMPETENCY 12
UNDERSTAND PATTERNS AND APPLY THE PRINCIPLES AND PROPERTIES OF LINEAR ALGEBRAIC RELATIONS AND FUNCTIONS

SKILL 12.1 Recognizing and describing mathematical relationships

The function or relationship between two quantities may be analyzed to determine how one quantity depends on the other. For example, the function below shows a relationship between y and x:

$$y = 2x + 1$$

The relationship between two or more variables can be analyzed using a table, graph, written description, or symbolic rule. The function, $y = 2x + 1$, is written as a symbolic rule. The same relationship is also shown in this table:

x	0	2	3	6	9
y	1	5	7	13	19

A relationship could be written in words by saying the value of y is equal to two times the value of x, plus one. This relationship could be shown on a graph by plotting given points such as the ones shown in the table above.

Another way to describe a function is as a process in which one or more numbers are input into an imaginary machine that produces another number as the output. If 5 is input, (x), into a machine with a process of $x + 1$, the output, (y), will equal 6.

In real situations, relationships can be described mathematically. The function, $y = x + 1$, can be used to describe the idea that people age one year on their birthday. To describe the relationship in which a person's monthly medical costs are 6 times a person's age, we could write $y = 6x$. The monthly cost of medical care could be predicted using this function. A 20-year-old person would spend $120 per month ($120 = 20 \times 6$). An 80-year-old person would spend $480 per month ($480 = 80 \times 6$). Therefore, one could analyze the relationship to say: as you get older, medical costs increase $6.00 each year.

SKILL **Using a variety of representations** *(e.g., manipulatives, figures, numbers,*
12.2 *calculators)* **to recognize and extend patterns**

Arithmetic Sequences

When given a set of numbers where the common difference between the terms is constant, use the following formula:

$$a_n = a_1 + (n - 1)d$$

where a_1 = the first term
n = the nth term (general term)
d = the common difference

Example: Find the 8th term of the arithmetic sequence 5, 8, 11, 14, ...

$a_n = a_1 + (n - 1)d$
$a_1 = 5$ Identify the 1st term.
$d = 8 - 5 = 3$ Find d.
$a_n = 5 + (8 - 1)3$ Substitute.
$a_n = 26$

Example: Given two terms of an arithmetic sequence, find a_1 and d.

$a_n = a_1 + (n - 1)d$ $a_4 = 21$

$21 = a_1 + (4 - 1)d$ $a_6 = 32$

$32 = a_1 + (6 - 1)d$ $a_4 = 21, n = 4$

                           $a_6 = 32, n = 6$

$21 = a_1 + 3d$ Solve the system of equations.

$32 = a_1 + 5d$

$21 = a_1 + 3d$

$\underline{^-32 = ^-a_1 - 5d}$ Multiply by ⁻1.

$^-11 = ^-2d$ Add the equations.

$5.5 = d$

$21 = a_1 + 3(5.5)$ Substitute d = 5.5, into one of the equations.

$21 = a_1 + 16.5$

$a_1 = 4.5$

The sequence begins with 4.5 and has a common difference of 5.5 between numbers.

Geometric Sequences

When using geometric sequences, consecutive numbers are compared to find the common ratio.

$$r = \frac{a_{n+1}}{a}$$

where r = common ratio

a = the nth term

The ratio is then used in the geometric sequence formula:

$a_n = a_1 r^{n-1}$

Example: Find the 8th term of the geometric sequence 2, 8, 32, 128 ...

$$r = \frac{a_{n+1}}{a_n}$$

                             Use common ratio formula to find ratio.

$r = \frac{8}{2}$ Substitute $a_n = 2$ $a_{n+1} = 8$.

$r = 4$

$a_n = a_1 \cdot r^{n-1}$ Use r = 4 to solve for the 8th term.

$a_n = 2 \cdot 4^{8-1}$

$a_n = 32{,}768$

SKILL Analyzing mathematical relationships and patterns using tables, 12.3 verbal rules, equations, and graphs

A relationship between two quantities can be shown using a table, graph or rule. In this example, the rule $y = 9x$ describes the relationship between the total amount earned, y, and the total amount of $9 sunglasses sold, x.

A table using this data would appear as:

number of sunglasses sold	1	5	10	15
total dollars earned	9	45	90	135

Each (x,y) relationship between a pair of values is called the coordinate pair and can be plotted on a graph. The coordinate pairs (1,9), (5,45), (10,90), and (15,135), are plotted on the graph below.

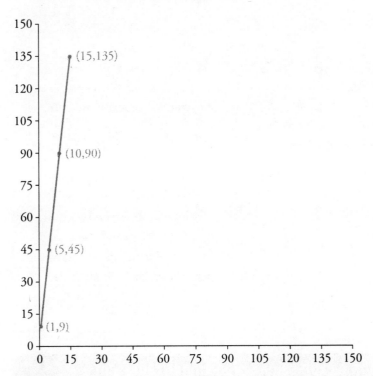

This graph shows a linear relationship. A linear relationship is one in which two quantities are proportional to each other. Doubling x also doubles y. On a graph, a straight line depicts a linear relationship.

Another type of relationship is a nonlinear relationship. This is one in which a change in one quantity does not affect the other quantity to the same extent. Nonlinear graphs have a curved line such as the following graph below.

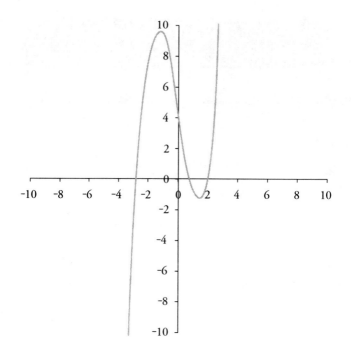

Sample Test Questions and Rationale

Easy

1. Each (*x,y*) relationship between a pair of values is called the _____ and can be plotted on a graph.

   A. coordinate pair

   B. parallel value

   C. symbolic rule

   D. proportional function

Answer: A – coordinate pair

Rationale: Each (*x,y*) relationship between a pair of values is called the coordinate pair and can be plotted on a graph. The relationship between two or more variables can be analyzed using a table, graph, written description or symbolic rule.

SKILL 12.4 Deriving an algebraic expression or function to represent a relationship or pattern from the physical or social world

Exercise: Interpreting Slope as a Rate of Change

Connection: Social Sciences/Geography

Real-life Application: Slope is often used to describe a constant or average rate of change. These problems usually involve units of measure such as miles per hour or dollars per year.

Problem: The town of Verdant Slopes has been experiencing a boom in population growth. By the year 2000, the population had grown to 45,000, and by 2005, the population had reached 60,000.

Communicating about Algebra:

a. Using the formula for slope as a model, find the average rate of change in population growth, expressing your answer in people per year.

Extension:

b. Using the average rate of change determined in a., predict the population of Verdant Slopes in the year 2010.

Solution:

a. Let t represent the time and p represent population growth. The two observances are represented by (t_1, p_1) and (t_2, p_2).

   1st observance = (t_1, p_1) = (2000, 45,000)
   2nd observance = (t_2, p_2) = (2005, 60,000)

Use the formula for slope to find the average rate of change.

   Rate of change $= \dfrac{p_2 - p_1}{t_2 - t_1}$

Substitute values.
   $$\dfrac{60000 - 45000}{2005 - 2000}$$

Simplify.
   $\dfrac{15000}{5} = 3{,}000$ people/year

The average rate of change in population growth for Verdant Slopes between the years 2000 and 2005 was 3,000 people/year.

   3,000 people/year $\times$ 5 years = 15,000 people
   60,000 people/year + 1,500 people = 75,000 people

At a continuing average rate of growth of 3,000 people/year, the population of Verdant Slopes could be expected to reach 75,000 by the year 2010.

SKILL Using algebraic functions to describe given graphs, to plot points,
12.5 and to determine slopes

To find the y-intercept, substitute 0 for y and solve for x. This is the x-intercept.
   Find the slope and intercepts of $3x + 2y = 14$.
   $3x + 2y = 14$
   $2y = -3x + 14$
   $y = -3/2x + 7$

The slope of the line is -3/2 , the value of m.
The *y*-intercept of the line is 7.

The intercepts can also be found by substituting 0 in place of the other variable in the equation.

To find the *y*-intercept:
let $x = 0$; $3(0) + 2y = 14$
$0 + 2y = 14$
$2y = 14$
$y = 7$
$(0,7)$ is the *y*-intercept.

To find the *x*-intercept:
let $y = 0$; $3x + 2(0) = 14$
$3x + 0 = 14$
$3x = 14$
$x = 14/3$
$(14/3,0)$ is the *x*-intercept.

Find the slope and the intercepts (if they exist) for these equations:
$5x + 7y = -70$
$x - 2y = 14$
$5x + 3y = 3(5 + y)$
$2x + 5y = 15$

Example: Sketch the graph of the line represented by 2x + 3y = 6.
Let $x = 0$; $2(0) + 3y = 6$
    $3y = 6$
    $y = 2$
    $(0,2)$ is the *y*-intercept

Let $y = 0$; $2x + 3(0) = 6$
    $2x = 6$
    $x = 3$
    $(3,0)$ is the *x*-intercept

Let $x = 1$; $2(1) + 3y = 6$
    $2 + 3y = 6$
    $3y = 4$
    $y = 4/3$
    $(1,4/3)$ is the third point.

Plotting the three points on the coordinate system, we get the following:

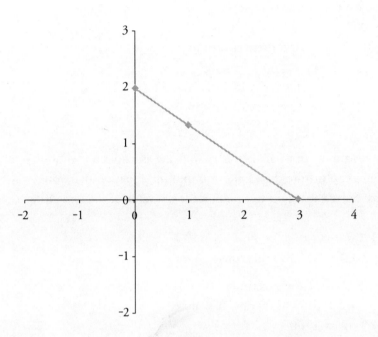

SKILL 12.6 Performing algebraic operations to solve equations and inequalities

Word problems can sometimes be solved by using a system of two equations in 2 unknowns. This system can then be solved using **substitution**, or the **addition-subtraction method**.

Example: Farmer Greenjeans bought 4 cows and 6 sheep for $1,700. Mr. Ziffel bought 3 cows and 12 sheep for $2,400. If all the cows were the same price and all the sheep were another price, find the price charged for a cow or for a sheep.

Let x = price of a cow; let y = price of a sheep

Then Farmer Greenjeans' equation would be: $4x + 6y = 1700$

Mr. Ziffel's equation would be: $3x + 12y = 2400$

To solve by **addition-subtraction**:

Multiply the first equation by -2: $-2(4x + 6y = 1700)$

Keep the other equation the same: $3x + 12y = 2400$

By doing this, the equations can be added to each other to eliminate one variable and solve for the other variable.

$-8x - 12y = -3400$

$\underline{3x + 12y = 2400}$ Add these equations.

$-5x = -1000$

$x = 200$ The price of a cow was $200.

Solving for y, $y = 150$ The price of a sheep, $150.

To solve by **substitution**:

Solve one of the equations for a variable. (Try to make an equation without fractions if possible.) Substitute this expression into the equation that you have not yet used. Solve the resulting equation for the value of the remaining variable.

$4x + 6y = 1700$

$3x + 12y = 2400$ Solve this equation for x.

It becomes $x = 800 - 4y$. Now substitute $800 - 4y$ in place of x in the OTHER equation. $4x + 6y = 1700$ now becomes:

$4(800 - 4y) + 6y = 1700$

$3200 - 16y + 6y = 1700$

$3200 - 10y = 1700$

$-10y = -1500$

$y = 150$, or $150 for a sheep.

Substituting 150 back into an equation for y, find x.

$4x + 6(150) = 1700$

$4x + 900 = 1700$

$4x = 800$ so $x = 200$ for a cow.

Word problems can sometimes be solved by using a system of three equations in 3 unknowns. This system can then be solved using substitution or the addition-subtraction method.

Example: Mrs. Allison bought 1 pound of potato chips, a 2 pound beef roast, and 3 pounds of apples for a total of $8.19. Mr. Bromberg bought a 3 pound beef roast and 2 pounds of apples for $9.05. Kathleen Kaufman bought 2 pounds of potato chips, a 3 pound beef roast, and 5 pounds of apples for $13.25. Find the per pound price of each item.

Let x = price of a pound of potato chips

Let y = price of a pound of roast beef

Let z = price of a pound of apples

Mrs. Allison's equation would be: $1x + 2y + 3z = 8.19$

Mr. Bromberg's equation would be: $3y + 2z = 9.05$

K. Kaufman's equation would be: $2x + 3y + 5z = 13.25$

To solve by **substitution**:

Take the first equation and solve it for x. (This was chosen because x is the easiest variable to get alone in this set of equations.) This equation would become:

$x = 8.19 - 2y - 3z$

Substitute this expression into the other equations in place of the letter x:

$3y + 2z = 9.05$ Equation 2

$2(8.19 - 2y - 3z) + 3y + 5z = 13.25$ Equation 3

Simplify the equation by combining like terms:

$3y + 2z = 9.05$ Equation 2

$\times -1y - 1z = -3.13$ Equation 3

Solve equation 3 for either y or z:

$y = 3.13 - z$

Substitute this into equation 2 for y:

$3(3.13 - z) + 2z = 9.05$ Equation 2

$-1y - 1z = -3.13$ Equation 3

Combine like terms in equation 2:

$9.39 - 3z + 2z = 9.05$

$z = .34$ per pound price of apples

Substitute .34 for z in the starred equation above to solve for y:

$y = 3.13 - z$ becomes $y = 3.13 - .34$, so

$y = 2.79$ per pound price of roast beef

Substituting .34 for z and 2.79 for y in one of the original equations, solve for x:

$1x + 2y + 3z = 8.19$

$1x + 2(2.79) + 3(.34) = 8.19$

$x + 5.58 + 1.02 = 8.19$

$x + 6.60 = 8.19$

$x = 1.59$ per pound of potato chips

$(x, y, z) = (1.59, 2.79, .34)$

To solve by **addition-subtraction**:

Choose a letter to eliminate. Since the second equation is already missing an x, let's eliminate x from equations 1 and 3.

1) $1x + 2y + 3x = 8.19$ Multiply by -2 below.

2) $3y + 2z = 9.05$

3) $2x + 3y + 5z = 13.25$

$-2(1x + 2y + 3z = 8.19) = -2x - 4y - 6z = -16.38$

Keep equation 3 the same: $\underline{2x + 3y + 5z = 13.25}$

By doing this, the equations $-y - z = -3.13$ Equation 4 can be added to each other to eliminate one variable.

The equations left to solve are equations 2 and 4:

$-y - z = -3.13$ Equation 4

$3y + 2z = 9.05$ Equation 2

Multiply equation 4 by 3: $3(y - z = -3.13)$

Keep equation 2 the same: $3y + 2z = 9.05$

$3y - 3z = -9.39$

$\underline{3y + 2z = 9.05}$ Add these equations.

$-1z = -.34$

$z = .34$ per pound price of apples

solving for y, $y = 2.79$ per pound roast beef price

solving for x, $x = 1.59$ potato chips, per pound price

To solve by **substitution**:

Solve one of the 3 equations for a variable. (Try to make an equation without fractions if possible.) Substitute this expression into the other 2 equations that you have not yet used.

1) $1x + 2y + 3x = 8.19$ Solve for x.

2) $3y + 2z = 9.05$

3) $2x + 3y + 5z = 13.25$

Equation 1 becomes $x = 8.19 - 2y - 3z$.

Substituting this into equations 2 and 3, they become:

2) $3y + 2z = 9.05$

3) $2(8.19 - 2y - 3z) + 3y + 5z = 13.25$

      $16.38 - 4y - 6z + 3y + 5z = 13.25$

        $-y - z = -3.13$

The equations left to solve are:

$3y + 2z = 9.05$

$-y - z = -3.13$ Solve for either y or z.

It becomes $y = 3.13 - z$. Now substitute $3.13 - z$ in place of y in the OTHER equation. $3y + 2z = 9.05$ now becomes:

$3(3.13 - z) + 2z = 9.05$

$9.39 - 3z + 2z = 9.05$

$9.39 - z \; 9.05$

$-z = -.34$

$z = .34$, or $.34$/lb of apples

Substituting .34 back into an equation for z, find y.

$3y + 2z = 9.05$

$3y + 2(.34) = 9.05$

$3y + .68 = 9.05$, so $y = 2.79$ /lb of roast beef

Substituting .34 for z and 2.79 for y into one of the original equations, it becomes:

$2x + 3y + 5z = 13.25$

$2x + 3(2.79) + 5(.34) = 13.25$

$2x + 8.37 + 1.70 = 13.25$

$2x + 10.07 = 13.25$, so $x = 1.59$/lb of potato chips

To graph an inequality, solve the inequality for y. This gets the inequality in **slope intercept form**, (for example: $y < mx + b$). The point (0,b) is the y-intercept and m is the line's slope.

If the inequality solves to $x \geq$ any number, then the graph includes a **vertical line**.

If the inequality solves to $y \leq$ any number, then the graph includes a **horizontal line**.

When graphing a linear inequality, the line will be dotted if the inequality sign is $<$ or $>$. If the inequality signs are either $\geq$ or $\leq$, the line on the graph will be a solid line. Shade above the line when the inequality sign is $\geq$ or $>$. Shade below the line when the inequality sign is $\leq$ or $<$. For inequalities of the forms $x > $ number, $x \leq$ number, $x <$ number, or $x \geq$ number, draw a vertical line (solid or dotted). Shade to the right for $>$ or $\geq$. Shade to the left for $<$ or $\leq$.

Use these rules to graph and shade each inequality. The solution to a system of linear inequalities consists of the part of the graph that is shaded for each inequality. For instance, if the graph of one inequality was shaded with red, and the graph of another inequality was shaded with blue, then the overlapping area would be shaded purple. The purple area would be the points in the solution set of this system.

Example: Solve by graphing:

$x + y \leq 6$

$x - 2y \leq 6$

Solving the inequalities for y, they become:

$y \leq -x + 6$ (y-intercept of 6 and slope = -1)

$y \geq 1.2x - 3$ (y-intercept of -3 and slope = 1/2)

A graph with shading is shown below:

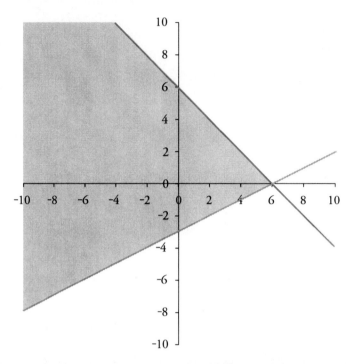

SKILL 12.7 Analyzing how changing one variable changes the other variable for linear and nonlinear functions

Word problems can sometimes be solved by using a system of two equations in 2 unknowns. This system can then be solved using substitution, the addition-subtraction method, or graphing.

Example: Mrs. Winters bought 4 dresses and 6 pairs of shoes for $340. Mrs. Summers went to the same store and bought 3 dresses and 8 pairs of shoes for $360. If all the dresses were the same price and all the shoes were the same price, find the price charged for a dress and for a pair of shoes.

Let x = price of a dress

Let y = price of a pair of shoes

    Then Mrs. Winters' equation would be: $4x + 6y = 340$

    Mrs. Summers' equation would be: $3x + 8y = 360$

To solve by **addition-subtraction**:

    Multiply the first equation by 4:

        $4(4x + 6y = 340)$

Multiply the other equation by -3:

$-3(3x + 8y = 360)$

By doing this, the equations can be added to each other to eliminate one variable and solve for the other variable.

$16x + 24y = 1360$

$-9x - 24y = -1080$

$7x = 280$

$x = 40$, the price of a dress was $40

solving for y, $y = 30$, the price of a pair of shoes, $30

Example: Aardvark Taxi charges $4 initially plus $1 for every mile traveled. Baboon Taxi charges $6 initially plus $.75 for every mile traveled. Determine when it is cheaper to ride with Aardvark Taxi or to ride with Baboon Taxi.

Aardvark Taxi's equation: $y = 1x + 4$

Baboon Taxi's equation: $y = .75x + 6$

Using **substitution**: $.75x + 6 = x + 4$

Multiplying by 4:

$3x + 24 = 4x + 16$

Solving for x:

$8 = x$

This tells you that at 8 miles the total charge for the 2 companies is the same. If you compare the charge for 1 mile, Aardvark charges $5 and Baboon charges $6.75. Clearly Aardvark is cheaper for distances up to 8 miles, but Baboon Taxi is cheaper for distances greater than 8 miles.

This problem can also be solved by graphing the 2 equations.

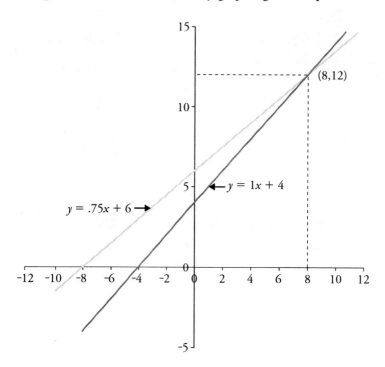

The lines intersect at (8,12), therefore at 8 miles both companies charge $12. At values less than 8 miles, Aardvark Taxi charges less (the graph is below Baboon). Greater than 8 miles, Aardvark charges more (the graph is above Baboon).

Equations and inequalities can be used to solve various types of word problems. Examples follow.

Example: The YMCA wants to sell raffle tickets to raise at least $32,000. If they must pay $7,250 in expenses and prizes out of the money collected from the tickets, how many tickets worth $25 each must they sell?
Solution: Since they want to raise **at least $32,000**, that means they would be happy to get 32,000 **or more**. This requires an inequality.

Let x = number of tickets sold
    Then $25x$ = total money collected for x tickets
    Total money minus expenses is greater than $32,000.
        $25x - 7250 \geq 32000$
        $25x \geq 39250$
        $x \geq 1570$

If they sell **1,570 tickets or more**, they will raise AT LEAST $32,000.

Example: The Simpsons went out for dinner. All 4 of them ordered the aardvark steak dinner. Bert paid for the 4 meals and included a tip of $12 for a total of $84.60. How much was an aardvark steak dinner?

Let x = the price of one aardvark dinner.

So $4x$ = the price of 4 aardvark dinners.

$4x + 12 = 84.60$

$x = \$18.15$ for each dinner

Here is another example. Some word problems can be solved using a **system of equations** or **inequalities**. Watch for words like *greater than*, *less than*, *at least*, or no more than which indicate the need for inequalities.

Graph these 2 inequalities:

$y \leq 8 - 1/2x$

$y \geq 4 - 4/5x$

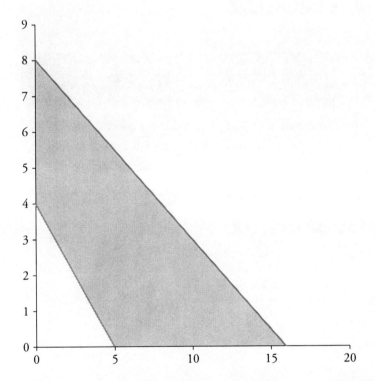

Realize that $x \geq 0$ and $y \geq 0$, since the number of bikes assembled can not be a negative number. Graph these as additional constraints on the problem. The number of bikes assembled must always be an integer value, so points within the shaded area of the graph must have integer values. The maximum profit will occur at or near a corner of the shaded portion of this graph. Those points occur at (0,4), (0,8), (16,0), or (5,0).

Since profits are \$60/3-speed or \$75/10-speed, the profit would be:

(0,4) $60(0) + 75(4) = 300$
(0,8) $60(0) + 75(8) = 600$
(16,0) $60(16) + 75(0) = 960$ maximum profit
(5,0) $60(5) + 75(0) = 300$

The maximum profit would occur if 16 3-speed bikes are made daily.

COMPETENCY 13

UNDERSTAND THE PRINCIPLES AND PROPERTIES OF GEOMETRY AND TRIGONOMETRY, AND APPLY THEM TO MODEL AND SOLVE PROBLEMS

SKILL 13.1 Identifying relationships among two- and three-dimensional geometric shapes

In order to represent three-dimensional figures, we need three coordinate axes (X, Y, and Z) which are all mutually perpendicular to each other. Since we cannot draw three mutually perpendicular axes on a two-dimensional surface, we use oblique representations.

Example: Represent a cube with sides of 2.
We draw three sides along the three axes to make things easier.

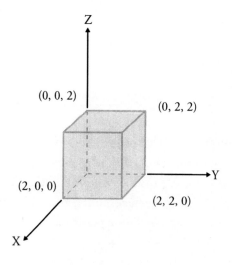

Each point has three coordinates (X, Y, Z).

SKILL **Applying knowledge of basic geometric figures to solve real-world**
13.2 **problems involving more complex patterns** *(e.g., area and perimeter of composite figures)*

The lateral area is the area of the faces excluding the bases.

The surface area is the total area of all the faces, including the bases.

The volume is the number of cubic units in a solid. This is the amount of space a figure holds.

Right prism

$V = Bh$ (where B = area of the base of the prism and h = the height of the prism)

Rectangular right prism

$S = 2(lw + hw + lh)$ (where l = length, w = width, and h = height)
$V = lwh$

Example: Find the height of a box whose volume is 120 cubic meters and the area of the base is 30 square meters.

$V = Bh$
$120 = 30h$
$h = 4$ meters

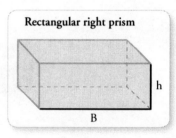

Rectangular right prism

Regular pyramid

$V = \frac{1}{3} Bh$

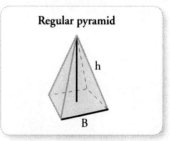

Regular pyramid

Right circular cylinder

$S = 2\pi r(r + h)$ (where r is the radius of the base)
$V = \pi r^2 h$

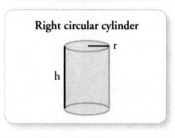

Right circular cylinder

Right circular cone

$V = \frac{1}{3} Bh$

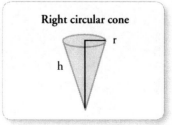

Right circular cone

Sample Test Questions and Rationale

Rigorous

1. **If the radius of a right circular cylinder is doubled, how does its volume change?**

    A. no change

    B. also is doubled

    C. four times the original

    D. pi times the original

Answer: C – four times the original

Rationale: If the radius of a right circular cylinder is doubled, the volume is multiplied by four because in the formula, the radius is squared; therefore the new volume is 2×2 or four times the original.

SKILL Applying the concepts of similarity and congruence to model and
13.3 solve problems

Example:

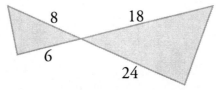

The two triangles are similar since the sides are proportional and vertical angles are congruent.

Example: Given two similar quadrilaterals, find the lengths of sides x, y, and z.

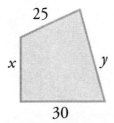

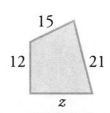

Since corresponding sides are proportional:

$\frac{15}{25} = \frac{3}{5}$ so the scale is $\frac{3}{5}$

$\frac{12}{x} = \frac{3}{5}$ $\frac{21}{y} = \frac{3}{5}$ $\frac{z}{30} = \frac{3}{5}$

$3x = 60$ $3y = 105$ $5z = 90$

$x = 20$ $y = 35$ $z = 18$

Polygons are similar if and only if there is a one-to-one correspondence between their vertices such that the corresponding angles are congruent and the lengths of corresponding sides are proportional.

Given the rectangles below, compare the area and perimeter.

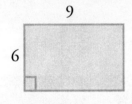
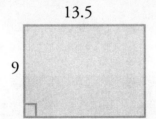

$A = LW$	$A = LW$	1. Write formula.
$A = (6)(9)$	$A (9)(13.5)$	2. Substitute known values.
$A = 54$ sq. units	$A = 121.5$ sq. units	3. Compute.
$P = 2(L + W)$	$P = 2(L + W)$	1. Write formula.
$P = 2(6 + 9)$	$P = 2(9 + 13.5)$	2. Substitute known values.
$P = 30$ units	$P = 45$ units	3. Compute.

Notice that the areas relate to each other in the following manner:

Ratio of sides $9/13.5 = 2/3$

Multiply the first area by the square of the reciprocal $(2/3)^2$ to get the second area.

$54 \times (2/3)^2 = 121.5$

The perimeters relate to each other in the following manner:

Ratio of sides $9/13.5 = 2/3$

Multiply the perimeter of the first by the reciprocal of the ratio to get the perimeter of the second

$30 \times 3/2 = 45$

Sample Test Questions and Rationale

Average Rigor

1. **In similar polygons, if the perimeters are in a ratio of x:y, the sides are in a ratio of:**

   A. x: y

   B. x^2: y^2

   C. 2x: y

   D. 1/2 x: y

Answer: A – x: y

Rationale: The sides are in the same ratio.

SKILL 13.4 Applying inductive and deductive reasoning to solve problems in geometry

See Skills 9.1 and 9.4

Try These:

What conclusion, if any, can be reached? Assume each statement is true, regardless of any personal beliefs.

1. If the Red Sox win the World Series, I will die.
   I died.

2. If an angle's measure is between 0° and 90°, then the angle is acute.
   Angle B is not acute.

3. Students who do well in geometry will succeed in college.
   Annie is doing extremely well in geometry.

4. Left-handed people are witty and charming.
   You are left-handed.

A counterexample is an exception to a proposed rule or conjecture that disproves the conjecture. For example, the existence of a single nonbrown dog disproves the conjecture "all dogs are brown." Thus, any nonbrown dog is a counterexample.

In searching for mathematic counterexamples, one should consider extreme cases near the ends of the domain of an experiment and special cases where an additional property is introduced. Examples of extreme cases are numbers near zero and obtuse triangles that are nearly flat. An example of a special case for a problem involving rectangles is a square because a square is a rectangle with the additional property of symmetry.

Example: Identify a counterexample for the following conjectures.

1. If n is an even number, then n + 1 is divisible by 3.

   n = 4

   n + 1 = 4 + 1 = 5

   5 is not divisible by 3.

2. If n is divisible by 3, then $n^2 - 1$ is divisible by 4.

   n = 6

   $n^2 - 1 = 6^2 - 1 = 35$

   35 is not divisible by 4.

DEFINITIONS are explanations of all mathematical terms except those that are undefined.

POSTULATES are mathematical statements that are accepted as true statements without providing a proof.

THEOREMS are mathematical statements that can be proven to be true based on postulates, definitions, algebraic properties, given information, and previously proved theorems.

The following algebraic postulates are frequently used as reasons for statements in two-column geometric properties:

Addition Property: If a = b and c = d, then a + c = b + d.
Subtraction Property: If a = b and c = d, then a − c = b − d.
Multiplication Property: If a = b and c ≠ 0, then ac = bc.
Division Property: If a = b and c ≠ 0, then a/b = b/c.
Reflexive Property: a = a
Symmetric Property: If a = b, then b = a.
Transitive Property: If a = b and b = c, then a = c.
Distributive Property: a(b + c) = ab + ac
Substitution Property: If a = b, then b may be substituted for a in any other expression (a may also be substituted for b).

In a two-column proof, the left side of the proof should be the given information, or statements that could be proved by deductive reasoning. The right column of the proof consists of the reasons used to determine that each statement to the left was verifiably true. The right side can identify given information, or

DEFINITIONS:
explanations of all mathematical terms except those that are undefined

POSTULATES:
mathematical statements that are accepted as true statements without providing a proof

THEOREMS:
mathematical statements that can be proven to be true based on postulates, definitions, algebraic properties, given information, and previously proved theorems

state theorems, postulates, definitions, or algebraic properties used to prove that particular line of the proof is true.

To write indirect proofs, assume the opposite of the conclusion. Keep your hypothesis and given information the same. Proceed to develop the steps of the proof, looking for a statement that contradicts your original assumption or some other known fact. This contradiction indicates that the assumption you made at the beginning of the proof was incorrect; therefore, the original conclusion has to be true.

SKILL 13.5 Using coordinate geometry to represent and analyze properties of geometric figures

We can represent any two-dimensional geometric figure in the Cartesian or rectangular coordinate system. The Cartesian or rectangular coordinate system is formed by two perpendicular axes (coordinate axes): the x-axis and the y-axis. If we know the dimensions of a two-dimensional, or planar, figure, we can use this coordinate system to visualize the shape of the figure.

Example: Represent an isosceles triangle with two sides of length 4.
Draw the two sides along the x- and y-axes and connect the points (vertices).

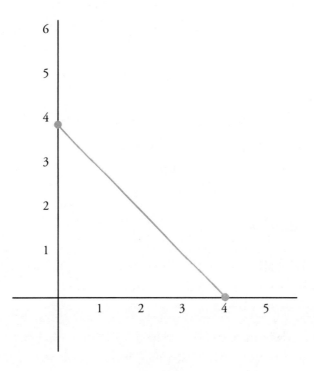

SKILL **Applying transformations** *(e.g., reflections, rotations, dilations)* **and**
13.6 **symmetry to analyze properties of geometric figures**

A transformation is a change in the position, shape, or size of a geometric figure. Transformational geometry is the study of manipulating objects by flipping, twisting, turning and scaling. Symmetry is exact similarity between two parts or halves, as if one were a mirror image of the other.

A translation is a transformation that "slides" an object a fixed distance in a given direction. The original object and its translation have the same shape and size, and they face in the same direction.

> An example of a translation in architecture would be stadium seating. The seats are the same size and the same shape and face in the same direction.

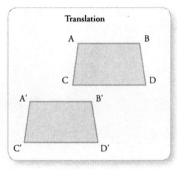

A rotation is a transformation that turns a figure about a fixed point called the center of rotation. An object and its rotation are the same shape and size, but the figures may be turned in different directions. Rotations can occur in either a clockwise or a counterclockwise direction.

> Rotations can be seen in wallpaper and art; a Ferris wheel is an example of rotation.

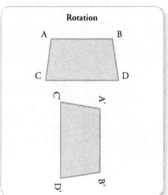

An object and its reflection have the same shape and size, but the figures face in opposite directions.

> The line (where a mirror may be placed) is called the line of reflection. The distance from a point to the line of reflection is the same as the distance from the point's image to the line of reflection.

A glide reflection is a combination of a reflection and a translation.

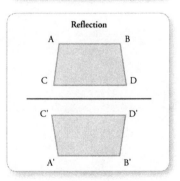

Another type of transformation is dilation. Dilation is a transformation that "shrinks" or "makes it bigger."

Example: Using dilation to transform a diagram.
Starting with a triangle whose center of dilation is point P,

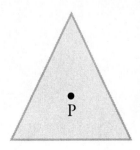

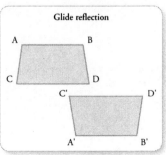

we dilate the lengths of the sides by the same factor to create a new triangle.

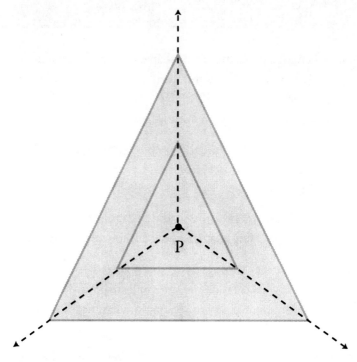

Sample Test Questions and Rationale

Average Rigor

1. Kindergarten students are doing a butterfly art project. They fold paper in half. On one half, they paint a design. Then they fold the paper closed and reopen. The resulting picture is a butterfly with matching sides. What math principle does this demonstrate?

   A. slide

   B. rotate

   C. symmetry

   D. transformation

Answer: C – symmetry

Rationale: By folding the painted paper in half, the design is mirrored on the other side, creating symmetry and reflection. The butterfly design is symmetrical about the center.

COMPETENCY 14

UNDERSTAND CONCEPTS, PRINCIPLES, SKILLS, AND PROCEDURES RELATED TO THE CUSTOMARY AND METRIC SYSTEMS OF MEASUREMENT

SKILL 14.1 Demonstrating knowledge of fundamental units of customary and metric measurement

Nonstandard units are sometimes used when standard instruments might not be available. For example, students might measure the length of a room by their arm-spans. An inch originated as the length of three barley grains placed end to end. Seeds or stones might be used for measuring weight. In fact, our current "carat," used for measuring precious gems, was derived from carob seeds. In ancient times, baskets, jars, and bowls were used to measure capacity.

To estimate measurement of familiar objects, it is first necessary to determine the units to be used.

When you can measure what you are speaking about and express it in numbers, you know something about it; but when you cannot measure it, when you cannot express it in numbers, your knowledge is of a meager and unsatisfactory kind.
—Lord Kelvin

Examples:

LENGTH	
The coastline of Florida	miles or kilometers
The width of a ribbon	inches or millimeters
The thickness of a book	inches or centimeters
The length of a football field	yards or meters
The depth of water in a pool	feet or meters

WEIGHT OR MASS	
A bag of sugar	pounds or grams
A school bus	tons or kilograms
A dime	ounces or grams

CAPACITY	
Paint to paint a bedroom	gallons or liters
Glass of milk	cups or liters
Bottle of soda	quarts or liters
Medicine for child	ounces or milliliters

Sample Test Questions and Rationale

Easy

1. **What measure could be used to report the distance traveled in walking around a track?**

   A. degrees

   B. square meters

   C. kilometers

   D. cubic feet

   Answer: C – kilometers

   Rationale: Degrees measures angles, square meters measure area, cubic feet measure volume, and kilometers measures length. Kilometers is the only reasonable answer.

Average Rigor

2. **The mass of a cookie is closest to:**

   A. 0.5 kg

   B. 0.5 grams

   C. 15 grams

   D. 1.5 grams

   Answer: C – 15 grams

   Rationale: A cookie is measured in grams.

SKILL 14.2 **Selecting an appropriate unit to express measures of length, area, capacity, weight, volume, time, temperature, and angle**

See Skill 14.1

**SKILL Estimating and converting measurements using standard and
14.3 nonstandard measurement units within customary and metric
systems**

The units of length in the customary system are inches, feet, yards, and miles.

12 inches (in.)	=	1 foot (ft.)
36 in.	=	1 yard (yd.)
3 ft.	=	1 yd.
5280 ft.	=	1 mile (mi.)
1760 yd.	=	1 mi.

To change from a **larger unit to a smaller unit, multiply**.

To change from a **smaller unit to a larger unit, divide**.

Example:
4 mi. = _____ yd.
Since 1760 yd. = 1 mile, multiply 4 × 1760 = 7040 yd.

Example:
21 in. = _____ ft.
21 ÷ 12 = 1 ft.

The units of weight are ounces, pounds, and tons.

16 ounces (oz.)	=	1 pound (lb.)
2,000 lb.	=	1 ton (T.)

Example:
$2\frac{2}{3}$ T. = _____ lb.
$2\frac{2}{3}$ × 2,000 = 5,500 lb.

The units of capacity are fluid ounces, cups, pints, quarts, and gallons.

8 fluid ounces (fl. oz.)	=	1 cup (c.)
2 c.	=	1 pint (pt.)
4 c.	=	1 quart (qt.)
2 pt.	=	1 qt.
4 qt.	=	1 gallon (gal.)

Example:

3 gal. = _____ qt.

$3 \times 4 = 12$ qt.

Example:

$1\frac{1}{4}$ cups = _____ oz.

$1\frac{1}{4} \times 8 = 10$ oz.

Example:

7 c. = _____ pt.

$7 \div 2 = 3\frac{1}{2}$ pt.

Square units

Square units can be derived with knowledge of basic units of length by squaring the equivalent measurements.

1 square foot (sq. ft.)	=	144 sq. in.
1 sq. yd.	=	9 sq. ft.
1 sq. yd.	=	1296 sq. in.

Example:

14 sq. yd. = _____ sq. ft.

$14 \times 9 = 126$ sq. ft.

Metric units

The metric system is based on multiples of **ten**. Conversions are made by simply moving the decimal point to the left or right.

kilo-	1000	thousands
hecto-	100	hundreds
deca-	10	tens
deci-	.1	tenths
centi-	.01	hundredths
milli-	.001	thousandths

The basic unit for **length** is the meter. One meter is approximately one yard.

The basic unit for **weight** or mass is the gram. A paper clip weighs about one gram.

The basic unit for **volume** is the liter. One liter is approximately a quart.

These are the most commonly used units.

1 m = 100 cm	1000 mL = 1 L
1 m = 1000 mm	1 kL = 1000 L
1 cm = 10 mm	1000 mg = 1 g
1000 m = 1 km	1 kg = 1000 g

The prefixes are commonly listed from left to right for ease in conversion.
K H D U D C M

Example:
63 km = _____ m
Since there are 3 steps from **Kilo** to **Unit**, move the decimal point 3 places to the right.
63 km = 63,000 m

Example:

14 mL = _____ L

Since there are 3 steps from **Milli** to **Unit**, move the decimal point 3 places to the left.

14 mL = 0.014 L

Example:

56.4 cm = _____ mm

56.4 cm = 564 mm

Example:

9.1 m = _____ km

9.1 m = 0.0091 km

Example:

75 kg = _____ m

75 kg = 75,000,000 m

Sample Test Questions and Rationale

Rigorous

1. **3 km is equivalent to:**

    A. 300 cm

    B. 300 m

    C. 3000 cm

    D. 3000 m

Answer: D – 3000 m

Rationale: To change kilometers to meters, move the decimal 3 places to the right.

SKILL 14.4 Developing and using formulas to determine the perimeter and area of two-dimensional shapes and the surface area and volume of three-dimensional shapes

The perimeter of any polygon is the sum of the lengths of the sides.

P = sum of sides

Since the opposite sides of a rectangle are congruent, the perimeter of a rectangle equals twice the sum of the length and width or

$P_{rect} = 2l + 2w$ or $2(l + w)$

Similarly, since all the sides of a square have the same measure, the perimeter of a square equals four times the length of one side or

$P_{square} = 4s$

The area of a polygon is the number of square units covered by the figure.

$A_{rect} = l \times w$
$A_{square} = s^2$

Example: Find the perimeter and the area of this rectangle.

16 cm

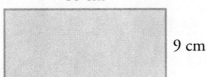

9 cm

$\begin{aligned} P_{rect} &= 2l + 2w \\ &= 2(16) + 2(9) \\ &= 32 + 18 = 50 \text{ cm} \end{aligned}$ $\qquad$ $\begin{aligned} A_{rect} &= l \times w \\ &= 16(9) \\ &= 144 \text{ cm}^2 \end{aligned}$

Example: Find the perimeter and area of this square.

3.6 in.

$\begin{aligned} P_{square} &= 4s \\ &= 4(3.6) \\ &= 14.4 \text{ in.} \end{aligned}$ $\qquad$ $\begin{aligned} A_{square} &= s^2 \\ &= (3.6)(3.6) \\ &= 12.96 \text{ in}^2 \end{aligned}$

In the following formulas, b = the base and h = the height of an altitude drawn to the base.

$A_{parallelogram} = bh$ $\qquad$ $A_{triangle} = \frac{1}{2}bh$ $\qquad$ $A_{trapezoid} = \frac{1}{2}h(b_1 + b_2)$

Example: Find the area of a parallelogram whose base is 6.5 cm and the height of the altitude to that base is 3.7 cm.

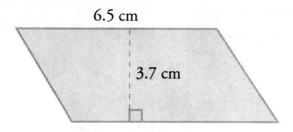

6.5 cm

3.7 cm

$A_{parallelogram} = bh$
$A_{parallelogram} = (3.7)(6.5)$
$A_{parallelogram} = 24.05 \text{ cm}^2$

Example: Find the area of this triangle.

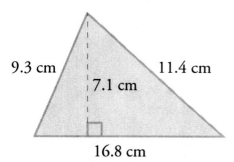

9.3 cm 11.4 cm

7.1 cm

16.8 cm

$A_{triangle} = \frac{1}{2}bh$
$= 0.5\,(16.8)\,(7.1)$
$= 59.64 \text{ cm}^2$

Note that the altitude is drawn to the base measuring 16.8 cm. The lengths of the other two sides are unnecessary information.

Example: Find the area of a right triangle whose sides measure 10 inches, 24 inches and 26 inches.

Since the hypotenuse of a right triangle must be the longest side, then the two perpendicular sides must measure 10 and 24 inches.

$A_{triangle} = \frac{1}{2}bh$

$= \frac{1}{2}(10)\,(24)$
$= 120 \text{ sq. in.}$

Example: Find the area of this trapezoid.

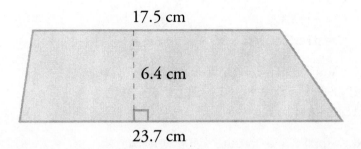

The area of a trapezoid equals one-half the sum of the bases times the altitude.

$$A_{trapezoid} = \frac{1}{2}h(b_1 + b_2)$$
$$= 0.5\ (6.4)\ (17.5 + 23.7)$$
$$= 131.84\ cm^2$$

Compute the area remaining when sections are cut out of a given figure composed of triangles, squares, rectangles, parallelograms, trapezoids, or circles.

Example: You have decided to fertilize your lawn. The shapes and dimensions of your lot, house, pool, and garden are given in the diagram below. The shaded area will not be fertilized. If each bag of fertilizer costs $7.95 and covers 4,500 square feet, find the total number of bags needed and the total cost of the fertilizer.

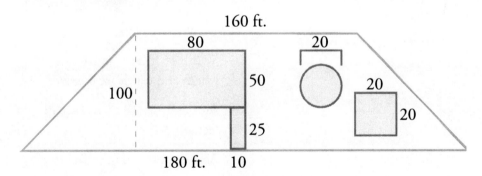

Area of Lot

$$A = \frac{1}{2}h(b_1 + b_2)$$

$$= \frac{1}{2}(100)(180 + 160)$$
$$= 17,000\ sq\ ft$$

Area of House

$$A = L$$

$$= (80)(50)$$
$$= 4,000\ sq\ ft$$

Area of Driveway	Area of Pool	Area of Garden
$A = LW$	$A = \pi r^2$	$A = s^2$
$= (10)(25)$	$= \pi(10)^2$	$= (20)^2$
$= 250$ sq ft	$= 314.159$ sq ft	$= 400$ sq ft

Total area to fertilize = Lot area − (House + Driveway + Pool + Garden)

$\qquad = 17,000 - (4,000 + 250 + 314.159 + 400)$

$\qquad = 12,035.841$ sq ft

Number of bags needed = Total area to fertilize/4,500 sq ft. bag

$\qquad = 12,035.841/4,500$

$\qquad = 2.67$ bags

Since we cannot purchase 2.67 bags we must purchase 3 full bags.

Total cost = Number of bags × \$7.95

$\qquad = 3 \times \$7.95$

$\qquad = \$23.85$

Sample Test Questions and Rationale

Rigorous

1. **What is the area of a square whose side is 13 feet?**

   A. 169 feet

   B. 169 square feet

   C. 52 feet

   D. 52 square feet

Answer: B − 169 square feet

Rationale: Area = length times width (*lw*).

Length = 13 feet

Width = 13 feet (square, so length and width are the same).

Area = 13 × 13 = 169 square feet.

Area is measured in square feet.

SKILL 14.5 Solving measurement problems involving derived measurements *(e.g., velocity, density)*

Some problems can be solved using equations with rational expressions. First write the equation. To solve it, multiply each term by the least common denominator (LCD) of all fractions. This will cancel out all of the denominators and give an equivalent algebraic equation that can be solved.

Example: The denominator of a fraction is two less than three times the numerator. If 3 is added to both the numerator and denominator, the new fraction equals 1/2.

original fraction: $\dfrac{x}{3x-2}$

revised fraction: $\dfrac{x+3}{3x+1}$ $\dfrac{x+3}{3x+1} = \dfrac{1}{2}$

$2x + 6 = 3x + 1$ $x = 5$

original fraction: $\dfrac{5}{13}$

Elly Mae can feed the animals in 15 minutes. Jethro can feed them in 10 minutes. How long will it take them if they work together.

Solution: If Elly Mae can feed the animals in 15 minutes, then she could feed 1/15 of them in 1 minute, 2/15 of them in 2 minutes, x/15 of them in x minutes. In the same fashion Jethro could feed x/10 of them in x minutes. Together they complete 1 job. The equation is:

$$\dfrac{x}{15} + \dfrac{x}{10} = 1$$

Multiply each term by the LCD of 30:

$2x + 3x = 30$ $x = 6$ minutes

Example: A salesman drove 480 miles from Pittsburgh to Hartford. The next day he returned the same distance to Pittsburgh in half an hour less time than his original trip took, because he increased his average speed by 4 mph. Find his original speed.

Since distance = rate $\times$ time, then time $= \dfrac{\text{distance}}{\text{rate}}$

original time $-$ 1/2 hour = shorter return time

$$\dfrac{480}{x} - \dfrac{1}{2} = \dfrac{480}{x+4}$$

Multiplying by the LCD of $2x(x + 4)$, the equation becomes:

$480[2(x + 4)] - 1[x(x + 4)] = 480 (2x)$

$960x + 3840 - x^2 - 4x = 960x$

$x^2 + 4x - 3840 = 0$

$(x + 64)(x - 60) = 0$

$x = 60$

60 mph is the original speed, 64 mph is the faster return speed.

Try these:

1. Working together, Larry, Moe, and Curly can paint an elephant in 3 minutes. Working alone, it would take Larry 10 minutes or Moe 6 minutes to paint the elephant. How long would it take Curly to paint the elephant if he worked alone?

2. The denominator of a fraction is 5 more than twice the numerator. If the numerator is doubled, and the denominator is increased by 5, the new fraction is equal to 1/2. Find the original number.

3. A trip from Augusta, Maine, to Galveston, Texas, is 2,108 miles. If one car drove 6 mph faster than a truck and got to Galveston 3 hours before the truck, find the speeds of the car and truck.

Sample Test Questions and Rationale

Rigorous

1. Given the formula d = *rt*, (where d = distance, r = rate, and t = time), calculate the time required for a vehicle to travel 585 miles at a rate of 65 miles per hour.

   A. 8.5 hours

   B. 6.5 hours

   C. 9.5 hours

   D. 9 hours

   Answer: D – 9 hours

   Rationale: We are given d = 585 miles and r = 65 miles per hour and d = rt. Solve for t. $585 = 65t \rightarrow$ = 9 hours.

Average Rigor

2. $(\frac{-4}{9}) + (\frac{-7}{10}) =$

   A. $\frac{23}{90}$

   B. $\frac{-23}{90}$

   C. $\frac{103}{90}$

   D. $\frac{-103}{90}$

   Answer: D – $\frac{-103}{90}$

   Rationale: Find the LCD of $\frac{-4}{9}$ and $\frac{-7}{10}$. The LCD is 90, so you get $\frac{-40}{90} + \frac{-63}{90} = \frac{-103}{90}$

SKILL 14.6 Applying the Pythagorean theorem and right triangle trigonometry to solve measurement problems

Pythagorean theorem states that the square of the length of the hypotenuse is equal to the sum of the squares of the lengths of the legs. Symbolically, this is stated as:

$$c^2 = a^2 + b^2$$

Example: Given the right triangle below, find the missing side.

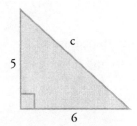

$c^2 = a^2 + b^2$	1. Write formula.
$c^2 = 5^2 + 6^2$	2. Substitute known values.
$c^2 = 61$	3. Take square root.
$c = \sqrt{61}$ or 7.81	4. Solve.

The converse of the Pythagorean Theorem states that if the square of one side of a triangle is equal to the sum of the squares of the other two sides, then the triangle is a right triangle.

Example: Given △XYZ, with sides measuring 12, 16, and 20 cm. Is this a right triangle?

$c^2 = a^2 + b^2$

$20^2 \underline{\ ?\ } 12^2 + 16^2$

$400 \underline{\ ?\ } 144 + 256$

$400 = 400$

Yes, the triangle is a right triangle.

This theorem can be expanded to determine if triangles are obtuse or acute.

If the square of the longest side of a triangle is greater than the sum of the squares of the other two sides, then the triangle is an obtuse triangle.

and

If the square of the longest side of a triangle is less than the sum of the squares of the other two sides, then the triangle is an acute triangle.

Example: Given △LMN with sides measuring 7, 12, and 14 inches. Is the triangle right, acute, or obtuse?

$14^2 \underline{\ ?\ } 7^2 + 12^2$

$196 \underline{\ ?\ } 49 + 144$

$196 > 193$

Therefore, the triangle is obtuse.

Real-World Example: Find the area and perimeter of a rectangle if its length is 12 inches and its diagonal is 15 inches.

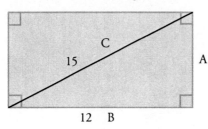

1. Draw and label sketch.
2. Since the height is still needed use Pythagorean formula to find missing leg of the triangle.

$$A^2 + B^2 = C^2$$
$$A^2 + 12^2 = 15^2$$
$$A^2 = 15^2 - 12^2$$
$$A^2 = 81$$
$$A = 9$$

Now use this information to find the area and perimeter.

A = LW	P = 2(L + W)	1. Write formula.
A = (12)(9)	P = 2(12 + 9)	2. Substitute.
A = 108 in²	P = 42 inches	3. Solve.

Real-World Example: Given the figure below, find the area by dividing the polygon into smaller shapes.

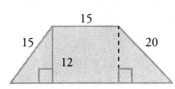

1. Divide the figure into two triangles and a rectangle.
2. Find the missing lengths.
3. Find the area of each part.
4. Find the sum of all areas.

Find base of both right triangles using Pythagorean Formula:

$a^2 + b^2 = c^2$	$a^2 + b^2 = c^2$
$a^2 + 12^2 = 15^2$	$a^2 + 12^2 = 20^2$
$a^2 = 225 - 144$	$a^2 = 400 - 144$
$a^2 = 81$	$a^2 = 256$
$a = 9$	$a = 16$

Area of triangle 1	Area of triangle 2	Area of rectangle
$A = \frac{1}{2}bh$	$A = \frac{1}{2}bh$	A = LW
$A = \frac{1}{2}(9)(12)$	$A = \frac{1}{2}(16)(12)$	A = (15)(12)
A = 54 sq. units	A = 96 sq. units	A = 180 sq. units

Find the sum of all three figures.
54 + 96 + 180 = 330 sq. units

Given triangle right ABC, the adjacent side and opposite side can be identified for each angle A and B.

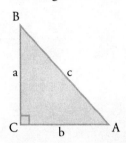

Looking at angle A, it can be determined that side b is adjacent to angle A and side a is opposite angle A.

If we now look at angle B, we see that side a is adjacent to angle B and side b is opposite angle B.
The longest side (opposite the 90° angle) is always called the hypotenuse.

The basic trigonometric ratios are listed below:

$$\text{Sine} = \frac{\text{opposite}}{\text{hypotenuse}} \quad \text{Cosine} = \frac{\text{adjacent}}{\text{hypotenuse}} \quad \text{Tangent} = \frac{\text{opposite}}{\text{adjacent}}$$

Sample problem: Use triangle ABC to find the sin, cos, and tan for angle A.

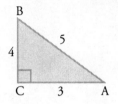

sin = 4/5
cos = 3/5
tan = 4/3

Use the **basic trigonometric ratios** of sine, cosine, and tangent to solve for the missing sides of right triangles when given at least one of the acute angles.

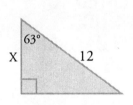

In the triangle ABC, an acute angle of 63° and the length of the hypotenuse (12). The missing side is the one adjacent to the given angle.

The appropriate trigonometric ratio to use would be cosine since we are looking for the adjacent side and we have the length of the hypotenuse.

$\cos x = \frac{\text{adjacent}}{\text{hypotenuse}}$ 1. Write formula.

$\cos 63 = \frac{x}{12}$ 2. Substitute known values.

$0.454 = \frac{x}{12}$
$x = 5.448$ 3. Solve.

Example: Find the missing side or angle.

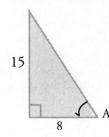

$\tan A = \frac{\text{opposite}}{\text{adjacent}}$

$\tan A = \frac{15}{8} = 1.875$

Looking on the trigonometric chart, the angle whose tangent is closest to 1.875 is 62°.

Thus $\angle A \approx 62°$.

Example:

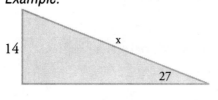

$$\sin A = \frac{\text{opposite}}{\text{hypotenuse}}$$

$$\sin 27° = \frac{14}{x}$$

$$0.4540 \approx \frac{14}{x}$$

$$x \approx \frac{14}{.454}$$

$$x \approx 30.8$$

Example:

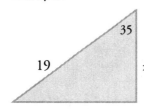

$$\cos A = \frac{\text{adjacent}}{\text{hypotenuse}}$$

$$\cos 35° = \frac{x}{19}$$

$$x \approx 19 \times .5636$$

$$x \approx 10.9$$

COMPETENCY 15

UNDERSTAND CONCEPTS AND SKILLS RELATED TO DATA ANALYSIS, PROBABILITY, AND STATISTICS, AND APPLY THIS UNDERSTANDING TO EVALUATE AND INTERPRET DATA AND TO SOLVE PROBLEMS

SKILL 15.1 Demonstrating the ability to collect, organize, and analyze data using appropriate graphic and nongraphic representations

MEAN: the average of the data items

MEDIAN: the item in the middle (or the average of the two items in the middle)

MODE: the most frequently occurring item

Mean, median and mode are three measures of central tendency. The MEAN is the average of the data items. The MEDIAN is found by putting the data items in order from smallest to largest and selecting the item in the middle (or the average of the two items in the middle). The MODE is the most frequently occurring item.

RANGE is a measure of variability. It is found by subtracting the smallest value from the largest value.

Sample problem: Find the mean, median, mode, and range of the test score listed below:

85	77	65	75	80	69
92	90	54	85	88	60
88	85	70	72	74	95

> **RANGE:** a measure of variability found by subtracting the smallest value from the largest value

Mean (X) = sum of all scores ÷ number of scores
  = 78

Median = put numbers in order from smallest to largest. Pick middle number.

54 60 65 69 70 72 74 75 $\boxed{77\ 80}$ 85 85 85 88 88 90 92 95

both in middle

Therefore, median is average of two numbers in the middle or 78.5.

Mode = most frequent number
  = 85

Range = largest number minus the smallest number
  = 95 − 54
  = 41

Sample Test Questions and Rationale

Average Rigor

1. **Corporate salaries are listed for several employees. Which would be the best measure of central tendency?**

$24,000	$24,000
$26,000	$28,000
$30,000	$120,000

   A. mean

   B. median

   C. mode

   D. no difference

Answer: B – median

Rationale: The median provides the best measure of central tendency in this case where the mode is the lowest number and the mean would be disproportionately skewed by the outlier $120,000.

> **CORRELATION:** a measure of association between two variables

CORRELATION is a measure of association between two variables. It varies from -1 to 1, with 0 being a random relationship, 1 being a perfect positive linear relationship, and -1 being a perfect negative linear relationship.

The correlation coefficient (r) is used to describe the strength of the association between the variables and the direction of the association.

Example:

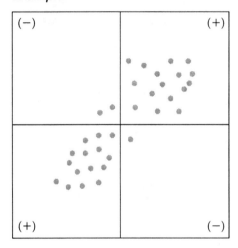

Horizontal and vertical lines are drawn through the point of averages which is the point on the averages of the x and y values. This divides the scatter plot into four quadrants. If a point is in the lower left quadrant, the product of two negatives is positive; in the upper right, the product of two positives is positive. The positive quadrants are depicted with the positive sign (+). In the two remaining quadrants (upper left and lower right), the product of a negative and a positive is negative. The negative quadrants are depicted with the negative sign (−). If r is positive, then there are more points in the positive quadrants and if r is negative, then there are more points in the two negative quadrants.

> **REGRESSION:** a form of statistical analysis used to predict a dependent variable (y) from values of an independent variable (z)

REGRESSION is a form of statistical analysis used to predict a dependent variable (y) from values of an independent variable (z). A regression equation is derived from a known set of data.

The simplest regression analysis models the relationship between two variables using the following equation: $y = a + bx$, where y is the dependent variable and x is the independent variable. This simple equation denotes a linear relationship between x and y. This form would be appropriate if, when you plotted a graph of x and y, you tended to see the points roughly form along a straight line.

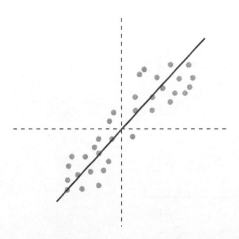

The line can then be used to make predictions.

If all of the data points fell on the line, there would be a perfect correlation ($r = 1$) between the x and y data points. These cases represent the best scenarios for prediction. A positive or negative r value represents how y varies with x. When r is positive, y increases as x increases. When r is negative y decreases as x increases.

SKILL 15.3 **Computing probabilities using a variety of methods** *(e.g., ratio and proportion, tree diagrams, tables of data, area models)*

Bar, Line, Picto, and Circle graphs

	Test 1	Test 2	Test 3	Test 4	Test 5
Evans, Tim	75	66	80	85	97
Miller, Julie	94	93	88	97	98
Thomas, Randy	81	86	88	87	90

Bar graphs are used to compare various quantities.

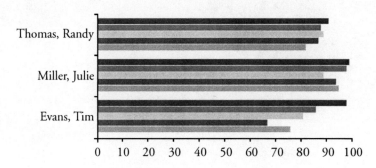

Line graphs are used to show trends, often over a period of time.

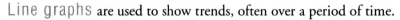

A **pictograph** shows comparison of quantities using symbols. Each symbol represents a number of items.

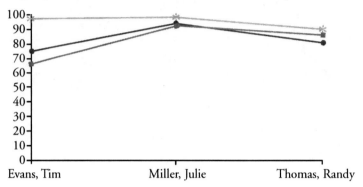

Circle graphs show the relationship of various parts to each other and the whole. Percents are used to create circle graphs.

Julie spends 8 hours each day in school, 2 hours doing homework, 1 hour eating dinner, 2 hours watching television, 10 hours sleeping, and the rest of the time doing other things.

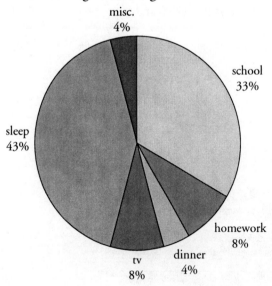

Sample Test Questions and Rationale

Easy

1. The following chart shows the yearly average number of international tourists visiting Palm Beach for 1990–1994. How many more international tourists visited Palm Beach in 1994 than in 1991?

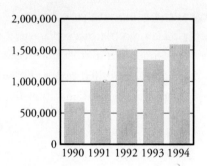

A. 100,000

B. 600,000

C. 1,600,000

D. 8,000,000

Answer: B – 600,000

Rationale: The number of tourists in 1991 was 1,000,000 and the number in 1994 was 1,600,000. Subtract to get a difference of 600,000.

Average rigor

2. Which type of graph uses symbols to represent quantities?

A. bar graph

B. line graph

C. pictograph

D. circle graph

Answer: C – pictograph

Rationale: A pictograph shows comparison of quantities using symbols. Each symbol represents a number of items.

SKILL Using simulations *(e.g., spinners, multisided die, random number generators)*
15.4 to estimate probabilities

Dependent events occur when the probability of the second event depends on the outcome of the first event. For example, consider the two events: (A) it is sunny on Saturday and (B) you go to the beach. If you intend to go to the beach on Saturday, rain or shine, then A and B may be independent. If, however, you plan to go to the beach only if it is sunny, then A and B may be dependent. In this situation, the probability of event B will change depending on the outcome of event A.

Suppose you have a pair of dice, one red and one green. If you roll a three on the red die and then roll a four on the green die, we can see that these events do not depend on the other. The total probability of the two independent events can be found by multiplying the separate probabilities.

$$P(A \text{ and } B) = P(A) \times P(B)$$
$$= 1/6 \times 1/6$$
$$= 1/36$$

Many times, however, events are not independent. Suppose a jar contains 12 red marbles and 8 blue marbles. If you randomly pick a red marble, replace it, and then randomly pick again, the probability of picking a red marble the second time remains the same. However, if you pick a red marble, and then pick again without replacing the first red marble, the second pick becomes dependent upon the first pick.

$$P(\text{Red and Red}) \text{ with replacement} = P(\text{Red}) \times P(\text{Red})$$
$$= 12/20 \times 12/20$$
$$= 9/25$$

$$P(\text{Red and Red}) \text{ without replacement} = P(\text{Red}) \times P(\text{Red})$$
$$= 12/20 \times 11/19$$
$$= 33/95$$

Sample Test Questions and Rationale

Rigorous

1. **Given a drawer with 5 black socks, 3 blue socks, and 2 red socks, what is the probability that you will draw two black socks in two draws in a dark room?**

   A. 2/9

   B. 1/4

   C. 17/18

   D. 1/18

Answer: A – 2/9

Rationale: In this example of conditional probability, the probability of drawing a black sock on the first draw is 5/10. It is implied in the problem that there is no replacement, therefore the probability of obtaining a black sock in the second draw is 4/9. Multiply the two probabilities and reduce to lowest terms.

SKILL 15.5 Applying measures of central tendency *(mean, median, mode)* and spread *(e.g., range, percentiles, variance)* to analyze data in graphic or nongraphic form

Different situations require different information. If we examine the circumstances under which an ice cream store owner may use statistics collected in the store, we find different uses for different information.

Over a seven-day period, the store owner collected data on the ice cream flavors sold. He found the mean number of scoops sold was 174 per day. The most frequently sold flavor was vanilla. This information was useful in determining how much ice cream to order in all and in what amounts for each flavor.

In the case of the ice cream store, the median and range had little business value for the owner.

Consider the set of test scores from a math class: 0, 16, 19, 65, 65, 65, 68, 69, 70, 72, 73, 73, 75, 78, 80, 85, 88, and 92. The mean is 64.06 and the median is 71. Since there are only three scores less than the mean out of the eighteen score, the median (71) would be a more descriptive score.

SKILL 15.6 Formulating and designing statistical experiments to collect, analyze, and interpret data

The **Addition Principle of Counting** states:

If A and B are events, $n(A or B) = n(A) + n(B) - n(A \cap B)$.

Example: In how many ways can you select a black card or a Jack from an ordinary deck of playing cards?

Let B denote the set of black cards and let J denote the set of Jacks.

Then, $n(B) = 26$, $n(J) = 4$, $n(B \cap J) = 2$ and

$$n(B or J) = n(B) + n(J) - n(B \cap J)$$
$$= 26 + 4 - 2$$
$$= 28$$

The **Addition Principle of Counting for Mutually Exclusive Events** states:

If A and B are mutually exclusive events, $n(A or B) = n(A) + n(B) - n(A \cap B)$.

Example: A travel agency offers 40 possible trips: 14 to Asia, 16 to Europe and 10 to South America. In how many ways can you select a trip to Asia or Europe through this agency?

Let A denote trips to Asia and let E denote trips to Europe. Then, $A \cap E = \varnothing$ and

$$n(AorE) = 26 + 4 - 2$$
$$= 28$$

Therefore, the number of ways you can select a trip to Asia or Europe is 30.

The **Multiplication Principle of Counting for Dependent Events** states:
Let A be a set of outcomes of Stage 1 and B a set of outcomes of Stage 2. Then the number of ways $n(AandB)$, that A and B can occur in a two-stage experiment is given by:

$$n(AandB) = n(A)n(B|A),$$

where $n(B|A)$ denotes the number of ways can occur given that has already occurred.

Example: How many ways from an ordinary deck of 52 cards can two Jacks be drawn in succession if the first card is drawn but not replaced in the deck and then the second card is drawn?

This is a two-stage experiment for which we wish to compute $n(AandB)$, where A is the set of outcomes for which a Jack is obtained on the first draw and B is the set of outcomes for which a Jack is obtained on the second draw.

If the first card drawn is a Jack, then there are only three remaining Jacks left to choose from on the second draw. Thus, drawing two cards without replacement means the events A and B are dependent.

$$n(AandB) = n(A)n(B|A) = 4 \cdot 3 = 12$$

The **Multiplication Principle of Counting for Independent Events** states:
Let A be a set of outcomes of Stage 1 and B a set of outcomes of Stage 2. If A and B are independent events then the number of ways $n(AandB)$, that A and B can occur in a two-stage experiment is given by: $n(AandB) = n(A)n(B)$

Example: How many six-letter code "words" can be formed if repetition of letters is not allowed?

Since these are code words, a word does not have to look like a word; for example, abcdef could be a code word. Since we must choose a first letter and a second letter and a third letter and a fourth letter and a fifth letter and a sixth letter, this experiment has six stages.

Since repetition is not allowed there are 26 choices for the first letter; 25 for the second; 24 for the third; 23 for the fourth; 22 for the fifth; and 21 for the sixth. Therefore, we have:

n(six-letter code words without repetition of letters)

$= 26 \cdot 25 \cdot 24 \cdot 23 \cdot 22 \cdot 21$

$= 165,765,600$

SKILL 15.7 Identifying patterns and trends in data and making predictions based on those trends

The absolute probability of some events cannot be determined. For instance, one cannot assume that the probability of winning a tennis match is ½ because, in general, winning and losing are not equally likely. In such cases, past results of similar events can be used to help predict future outcomes. The relative frequency of an event is the number of times an event has occurred divided by the number of attempts.

$$\text{Relative frequency} = \frac{\text{number of successful trials}}{\text{total number of trials}}$$

For example, if a weighted coin flipped 50 times lands on heads 40 times and tails 10 times, the relative frequency of heads is 40/50 = 4/5. Thus, one can predict that if the coin is flipped 100 times, it will land on heads 80 times.

Example: Two tennis players, John and David, have played each other 20 times. John has won 15 of the previous matches and David has won 5.
(1) Estimate the probability that David will win the next match.
(2) Estimate the probability that John will win the next 3 matches.

Solution:
(1) David has won 5 out of 20 matches. Thus, the relative frequency of David winning is 5/20 or ¼. We can estimate that the probability of David winning the next match is ¼.

(2) John has won 15 out of 20 matches. The relative frequency of John winning is 15/20 or ¾. We can estimate that the probability of John winning a future match is ¾. Thus, the probability that John will win the next three matches is ¾ $\times$ ¾ $\times$ ¾ = 27/64.

Sample Test Questions and Rationale

Rigorous

1. What is the probability of drawing 2 consecutive aces from a standard deck of cards?

   A. $\frac{3}{51}$

   B. $\frac{1}{221}$

   C. $\frac{2}{104}$

   D. $\frac{2}{52}$

Answer: B – $\frac{1}{221}$

Rationale: There are 4 aces in the 52 card deck.

P(first ace) = $\frac{4}{52}$.

P(second ace) = $\frac{3}{51}$.

P(first ace and second ace) = P(one ace)xP(second ace|first ace) = $\frac{4}{52} \times \frac{3}{51} = \frac{1}{221}$.

DOMAIN III
SCIENCE AND TECHNOLOGY

Enhanced features only available in our ebook edition:

 eStickynotes: allows you take digital notes anywhere in the ebook edition. It further allows you to aggregate and print all enotes for easy studying.

 eFlashcards: a digital representation of a card represented with words, numbers or symbols or any combination of each and briefly displayed as part of a learning drill. eFlashcards takes away the burden of carrying around traditional cards that could easily be disarranged, dropped, or soiled.

 More Sample Tests: more ways to assess how much you know and how much further you need to study. Ultimately, makes you more prepared and attain mastery in the skills and techniques of passing the test the FIRST TIME!

Visit www.XAMonline.com
and click on ebook.

PERSONALIZED STUDY PLAN

PAGE	COMPETENCY AND SKILL	KNOWN MATERIAL/ SKIP IT	BRIEFLY REVIEW eSTICKYNOTES	MAKE eFLASHCARDS	TAKE ADDITIONAL SAMPLE TESTS
181	**16: Scientific Inquiry and Investigation**	☐	☐	☐	☐
	16.1: Forming hypotheses	☐	☐	☐	☐
	16.2: Evaluating a proposed scientific investigation	☐	☐	☐	☐
	16.3: Mathematical rules for analyzing data	☐	☐	☐	☐
	16.4: Basic data interpretation	☐	☐	☐	☐
	16.5: Valid scientific conclusions	☐	☐	☐	☐
193	**17: Physical Science**	☐	☐	☐	☐
	17.1: Celestial interactions	☐	☐	☐	☐
	17.2: Interactions among air, water, and land	☐	☐	☐	☐
	17.3: Physical and chemical properties of matter	☐	☐	☐	☐
	17.4: Forms of energy	☐	☐	☐	☐
	17.5: Effects of forces on objects	☐	☐	☐	☐
	17.6: Inferring physical science principles	☐	☐	☐	☐
205	**18: The Living Environment**	☐	☐	☐	☐
	18.1: Characteristics of living things	☐	☐	☐	☐
	18.2: Processes that contribute to life	☐	☐	☐	☐
	18.3: Changes in organisms and species over time	☐	☐	☐	☐
	18.4: Basic life functions	☐	☐	☐	☐
	18.5: Effect of the environment on living organisms	☐	☐	☐	☐
	18.6: Life science principle	☐	☐	☐	☐
211	**19: Technology and Engineering**	☐	☐	☐	☐
	19.1: Technological systems	☐	☐	☐	☐
	19.2: Engineering design and optimization	☐	☐	☐	☐
	19.3: Technological solutions	☐	☐	☐	☐
	19.4: Designing and constructing a technological product	☐	☐	☐	☐
	19.5: Appropriate technological tests	☐	☐	☐	☐
	19.6: Effects of technology on society	☐	☐	☐	☐
220	**20: Common Mathematics, Science, and Technology Applications**	☐	☐	☐	☐
	20.1: Making connections	☐	☐	☐	☐
	20.2: Modeling	☐	☐	☐	☐
	20.3: Exploring phenomenon from other disciplines	☐	☐	☐	☐
	20.4: Designing solutions to problems	☐	☐	☐	☐
	20.5: Effect of human activities on the environment	☐	☐	☐	☐

COMPETENCY 16

UNDERSTAND AND APPLY THE PRINCIPLES AND PROCESSES OF SCIENTIFIC INQUIRY AND INVESTIGATION

> **SKILL** Formulate hypotheses based on reasoning and preliminary results
> **16.1** or information

SCIENCE may be defined as a body of knowledge that is systematically derived from study, observations, and experimentation. Its goal is to identify and establish principles and theories that may be applied to solve problems. Pseudoscience, on the other hand, is a belief that is not warranted. There is no scientific methodology or application. Some of the more classic examples of pseudoscience include witchcraft, alien encounters, or any topics that are explained by hearsay.

Scientific inquiry starts with observation. Observation is a very important skill by itself, since it leads to experimentation and finally communicating the experimental findings to the society/public. After observing, a question is formed, which starts with "why" or "how." To answer these questions, experimentation is necessary. Between observation and experimentation, there are three more important steps. These are: gathering information (or researching about the problem), hypothesis, and designing the experiment.

Designing an experiment is very important since it involves identifying control, constants, independent variables, and dependent variables. A control/standard is something we compare our results with at the end of the experiment. It is like a reference. Constants are the factors we have to keep constant in an experiment to get reliable results. Independent variables are factors we change in an experiment. It is very important to bear in mind that there should be more constants than variables to obtain reproducible results in an experiment.

Classifying is grouping items according to their similarities. It is important for students to realize relationships and similarity as well as differences to reach a reasonable conclusion in a lab experience.

After the experiment is done, it is repeated and results are graphically presented. The results are then analyzed and conclusions drawn.

It is the responsibility of the scientists to share the knowledge they obtain through their research.

> **SCIENCE:** a body of knowledge that is systematically derived from study, observations, and experimentation

After the conclusion is drawn, the final step is communication. In this age, lot of emphasis is put on the way and the method of communication. The conclusions must be communicated by clearly describing the information using accurate data, visual presentation like graphs (bar/line/pie), tables/charts, diagrams, artwork, and other appropriate media like PowerPoint presentations. Modern technology must be used whenever it is necessary. The method of communication must be suitable to the audience.

Written communication is as important as oral communication. This is essential for submitting research papers to scientific journals, newspapers, other magazines, etc.

Sample Test Questions and Rationale

Rigorous

1. **In an experiment measuring the growth of bacteria at different temperatures, what is the independent variable?**

   A. Number of bacteria.

   B. Growth rate of bacteria.

   C. Temperature.

   D. Size of bacteria.

   Answer: C – Temperature

   Rationale: To answer this question, recall that the independent variable in an experiment is the entity that is changed by the scientist, in order to observe the effects (the dependent variable(s)). In this experiment, temperature is changed in order to measure growth of bacteria, so (C) is the answer. Note that answer (A) is the dependent variable, and neither (B) nor (D) is directly relevant to the question.

Average rigor

2. **Which is the correct order of methodology?**
   1. **collecting data**
   2. **planning a controlled experiment**
   3. **drawing a conclusion**
   4. **hypothesizing a result**
   5. **revisiting a hypothesis to answer a question**

   A. 1,2,3,4,5

   B. 4,2,1,3,5

   C. 4,5,1,3,2

   D. 1,3,4,5,2

   Answer: B – 4,2,1,3,5

   Rationale: The correct methodology for the scientific method is first to make a meaningful hypothesis (educated guess), then plan and execute a controlled experiment to test that hypothesis. Using the data collected in that experiment, the scientist then draws conclusions and attempts to answer the original question related to the hypothesis. This is consistent only with answer (B).

SKILL 16.2 Evaluate the soundness and feasibility of a proposed scientific investigation

The scientific method is the basic process behind science. It involves several steps beginning with hypothesis formulation and working through to the conclusion.

The scientific method is the basic process behind science

Posing a Question	Although many discoveries happen by chance, the standard thought process of a scientist begins with forming a question to research. The more limited the question, the easier it is to set up an experiment to answer it.
Form a Hypothesis	Once the question is formulated, take an educated guess about the answer to the problem or question. This "best guess" is your hypothesis.
Doing the Test	To make a test fair, data from an experiment must have a VARIABLE such as temperature or mass. A good test will try to manipulate as few variables as possible so as to see which variable is responsible for the result. This requires a second example of a CONTROL.
Observe and Record the Data	Reporting of the data should state specifics of how the measurements were calculated. A graduated cylinder needs to be read with proper procedures. As beginning students, technique must be part of the instructional process so as to give validity to the data.
Drawing a Conclusion	After recording data, you compare your data with that of other groups. A conclusion is the judgment derived from the data results.
Graphing Data	Graphing utilizes numbers to demonstrate patterns. The patterns offer a visual representation, making it easier to draw conclusions.

VARIABLE: any condition that can be changed

CONTROL: an extra setup in which all the conditions are the same except for the variable being tested

Apply Knowledge of Designing and Performing Investigations

Normally, knowledge is integrated in the form of a lab report. A report has many sections. It should include a specific title and tell exactly what is being studied. The ABSTRACT is a summary of the report written at the beginning of the paper. The PURPOSE should always be defined and will state the problem. The purpose should include the HYPOTHESIS (educated guess) of what is expected from the outcome of the experiment. The entire experiment should relate to this problem.

It is important to describe exactly what was done to prove or disprove a hypothesis. A control is necessary to prove that the results occurred from the changed conditions and would not have happened normally. Only one variable should be

ABSTRACT: a summary of the report written at the beginning of the paper

PURPOSE: defines and states the problem

HYPOTHESIS: an educated guess of what is the expected outcome

OBSERVATIONS AND RESULTS: the recorded outcomes of the experiment

manipulated at a time. OBSERVATIONS and RESULTS of the experiment should be recorded including all results from data. Drawings, graphs, and illustrations should be included to support information. Observations are objective, whereas analysis and interpretation is subjective. A CONCLUSION should explain why the results of the experiment either proved or disproved the hypothesis.

CONCLUSION: explains why the results proved or disproved the hypothesis

A scientific theory is an explanation of a set of related observations based on a proven hypothesis. A scientific law usually lasts longer than a scientific theory and has more experimental data to support it.

SKILL Apply mathematical rules or formulas (including basic statistics) 16.3 to analyze given experimental or observational data

See Domain II

SKILL Interpret data presented in one or more graphs, charts, or tables to 16.4 determine patterns or relationships

Science uses the metric system, as it is accepted worldwide and allows easier comparison among experiments done by scientists around the world. Learn the following basic units and prefixes:

UNIT	meter	liter	gram
MEASURE OF	length	volume	mass

UNIT	THE BASE UNIT
deca-(meter, liter, gram)	10X
deci-(meter, liter, gram)	1/10
hecto-(meter, liter, gram)	100X
centi-(meter, liter, gram)	1/100
kilo-(meter, liter, gram)	1000X
milli-(meter, liter, gram)	1/1000

GRAPHING is an important skill to visually display collected data for analysis. The two types of graphs most commonly used are the line graph and the bar graph (histogram).

Line graphs are set up to show two variables represented by one point on the graph. The X axis is the horizontal axis and represents the dependent variable. Dependent variables are those that would be present independent of the experiment. A common example of a dependent variable is time. Time proceeds regardless of anything else occurring. The Y axis is the vertical axis and represents the independent variable. Independent variables are manipulated by the experiment, such as the amount of light, or the height of a plant. Graphs should be calibrated at equal intervals. If one space represents one day, the next space may not represent ten days. A "best fit" line is drawn to join the points and may not include all the points in the data. Axes must always be labeled, for the graph to be meaningful. A good title will describe both the dependent and the independent variable. Bar graphs are set up similarly in regards to axes, but points are not plotted. Instead, the dependent variable is set up as a bar where the X axis intersects with the Y axis. Each bar is a separate item of data and is not joined by a continuous line.

Indirect Evidence and Models

Some things happen at too fast or too slow a rate or are too small or too large for use to see. In these cases, we have to rely on indirect evidence to develop models of what is intangible. Once data have been collected and analyzed, it is useful to generalize the information by creating a model. A model is a conceptual representation of a phenomenon. Models are useful in that they clarify relationships, helping us to understand the phenomenon and make predictions about future outcomes. The natural sciences and social sciences employ modeling for this purpose.

Many scientific models are mathematical in nature and contain a set of variables linked by logical and quantitative relationships. These mathematical models may include functions, tables, formulas, and graphs. Typically, such mathematical models include assumptions that restrict them to very specific situations. Often this means they can only provide an approximate description of what occurs in the natural world. These assumptions, however, prevent the model from become overly complicated. For a mathematical model to fully explain a natural or social phenomenon, it would have to contain many variables and could become too cumbersome to use. Accordingly, it is critical that assumptions be carefully chosen and thoroughly defined.

Certain models are abstract and simply contain sets of logical principles rather than relying on mathematics. These types of models are generally more vague and

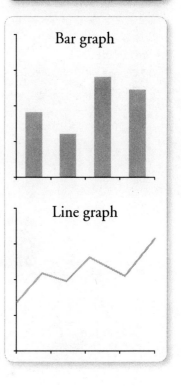

GRAPHING: visually displays collected data for analysis

Bar graph

Line graph

are more useful for discovering and understanding new ideas. Abstract models can also include actual physical models built to make concepts more tangible. Abstract models, to an even greater extent than mathematical models, make assumptions and simplify actual phenomena.

Proper scientific models must be able to be tested and verified using experimental data.

Proper scientific models must be able to be tested and verified using experimental data. Often these experimental results are necessary to demonstrate the superiority of a model when two or more conflicting models seek to explain the same phenomenon. Computer simulations are increasingly used in both testing and developing mathematical and even abstract models. These types of simulations are especially useful in situations, such as ecology or manufacturing, where experiments are not feasible or variables are not fully under control.

SKILL 16.5 Evaluating the validity of a scientific conclusion in a given situation

In scientific experimental investigations, conclusions are very important. These are the very significant because they highlight the interpretation of results. Conclusions are the inferences of the experimental results. They are important because those are the ideas people look at. The general public is not really interested in the variables, constants, methodology, or any other thing about the experiment, since it is not aware of it. What all the public is interested in, is the end product, the conclusions and their practical use to society. Society needs to be benefited by any type of research.

With this background information, we will examine the validity of conclusions.

Validity of conclusions is the most important aspect in any research.

Conclusion validity is the degree to which conclusions we reach about our data are reasonable. Conclusion validity is the least considered and the most misunderstood. It was originally labeled as statistical conclusion validity and the mere mention of the word statistics scared people because of the numbers involved in that.

In fact, conclusion validity is the most important of the validity types. It is relevant whenever we are trying to identify patterns and relationships in our data obtained from the scientific investigations. It is important both in qualitative and quantitative research and, hence, has lot of practical uses and potential.

In order to understand validity of conclusions, we need to bear in mind that there is always a relationship between variables and the dependent variable, the factor that is measured in an experiment. There are two more terms connected with validity of conclusions. One is "reliability" and the other is "reproducibility." Both are interdependent because without reproducibility there is no reliability and vice versa. For conclusions to be valid, the results we have on hand must be reproducible and only then we will be able to say with confidence that our results are reliable.

Reproducibility and reliability are the two keys giving our conclusions validity.

Hence, we can safely say that when we identify patterns, trends, and relationships in our experiments, the conclusions we draw are very valid and that's what makes any experiment outstanding and scientifically sound.

Such valid conclusions have the potential to become theories. Though theories are open to criticism and the threat of being rejected, they are still based on valid conclusions.

To summarize, validity of conclusions is dependent on reproducible results and reliable data.

SKILL 16.6 **Apply procedures for the safe and appropriate use of equipment and the care and humane treatment of animals in the laboratory**

Appropriate Care and Treatment of Laboratory Animals

Dissections

Animals that are not obtained from recognized sources should not be used. Decaying animals or those of unknown origin may harbor pathogens and/or parasites. Specimens should be rinsed before handling. Latex gloves are desirable. If gloves are not available, students with sores or scratches should be excused from the activity. Formaldehyde is a carcinogen and should be avoided or disposed of according to district regulations. Students objecting to dissections for moral reasons should be given an alternative assignment.

Live Specimens

No dissections may be performed on living mammalian vertebrates or birds. Lower order life and invertebrates may be used.

Biological experiments may be done with all animals except mammalian vertebrates or birds. No physiological harm may result to the animal. All animals housed and cared for in the school must be handled in a safe and humane manner. Animals are not to remain on school premises during extended vacations unless adequate care is provided. Many state laws stipulate that any instructor who intentionally refuses to comply with the laws may be suspended or dismissed.

Microbiology

Pathogenic organisms must never be used for experimentation. Students should adhere to the following rules at all times when working with microorganisms to avoid accidental contamination:

- Treat all microorganisms as if they were pathogenic

- Maintain sterile conditions at all times

If you are taking a national level exam you should check the Department of Education for your state for safety procedures. You will want to know what your state expects of you not only for the test but also for performance in the classroom and for the welfare of your students.

Appropriate Use and Management of Laboratory Equipment

Bunsen Burners

Hot plates should be used whenever possible to avoid the risk of burns or fire. If Bunsen burners are used, the following precautions should be followed:

- Know the location of fire extinguishers and safety blankets and train students in their use. Long hair and long sleeves should be secured and out of the way.

- Turn the gas all the way on and make a spark with the striker. The preferred method to light burners is to use strikers rather than matches.

- Adjust the air valve at the bottom of the Bunsen burner until the flame shows an inner cone.

- Adjust the flow of gas to the desired flame height by using the adjustment valve.

- Do not touch the barrel of the burner (it is hot).

Graduated Cylinder

These are used for precise measurements. They should always be placed on a flat surface. The surface of the liquid will form a meniscus (lens-shaped curve). The measurement is read at the *bottom* of this curve.

Balance

Electronic balances are easier to use, but more expensive. An electronic balance should always be tarred (returned to zero) before measuring and used on a flat

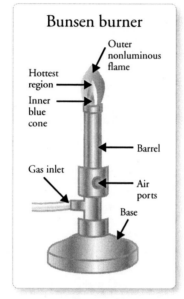

Bunsen burner

Outer nonluminous flame
Hottest region
Inner blue cone
Barrel
Gas inlet
Air ports
Base

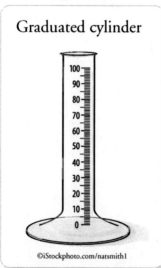

Graduated cylinder

©iStockphoto.com/natsmith1

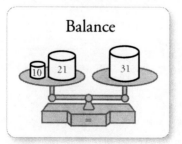

Balance

surface. Substances should always be placed on a piece of paper to avoid spills and/or damage to the instrument. Triple beam balances must be used on a level surface. There are screws located at the bottom of the balance to make any adjustments. Start with the largest counterweight first and proceed toward the last notch that does not tip the balance. Do the same with the next largest, and so on, until the pointer remains at zero. The total mass is the total of all the readings on the beams. Again, use paper under the substance to protect the equipment.

Buret

A buret is used to dispense precisely measured volumes of liquid. A stopcock is used to control the volume of liquid being dispensed at a time.

Light Microscopes

These are commonly used in laboratory experiments. Several procedures should be followed to properly care for this equipment:

- Clean all lenses with lens paper only

- Carry microscopes with two hands; one on the arm and one on the base

- Always begin focusing on low power, then switch to high power

- Store microscopes with the low power objective down

- Always use a coverslip when viewing wet mount slides

- Bring the objective down to its lowest position then focus by moving up to avoid breaking the slide or scratching the lens

Wet mount slides should be made by placing a drop of water on the specimen and then putting a glass coverslip on top of the drop of water. Dropping the coverslip at a forty-five degree angle will help avoid air bubbles. Total magnification is determined by multiplying the ocular (usually 10X) and the objective (usually 10X on low, 40X on high).

Appropriate Alternative Sources of and Substitutions for Laboratory Materials

Lab materials are readily available from the many school suppliers that routinely send their catalogues to schools. Often, common materials are available at the local grocery store. The use of locally available flora and fauna both reduces the cost and familiarizes students with the organisms where they live. Innovation and networking with other science teachers will assist in keeping costs of lab materials to a minimum.

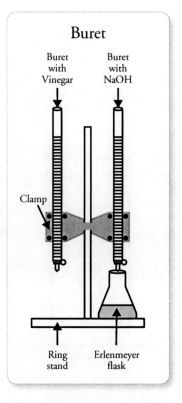

Buret

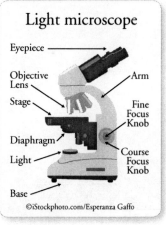

Light microscope

©iStockphoto.com/Esperanza Gaffo

Procedures for Safe Preparation, Use, Storage, and Disposal of Chemicals and Other Materials

All science labs should contain safety equipment. The following items are requirements by law.

- Fire blanket which is visible and accessible.

- Ground Fault Circuit Interrupters (GFCI) within two feet of water supplies.

- Emergency shower capable of providing a continuous flow of water.

- Signs designating room exits.

- Emergency eye wash station, which can be activated by the foot or forearm.

- Eye protection for every student and a means of sanitizing equipment.

- Emergency exhaust fans providing ventilation to the outside of the building.

- Master cut-off switches for gas, electric, and compressed air. Switches must have permanently attached handles. Cut-off switches must be clearly labeled.

- An ABC fire extinguisher.

- Storage cabinets for flammable materials.

Also recommended, but not required by law:

- Chemical spill control kit.

- Fume hood with a motor which is spark proof.

- Protective laboratory aprons made of flame retardant material.

- Signs that will alert people to potential hazardous conditions.

- Containers for broken glassware, flammables, corrosives, and waste.

- Labels on all containers.

It is the responsibility of teachers to provide a safe environment for their students. Proper supervision greatly reduces the risk of injury and a teacher should never leave a class for any reason without providing alternate supervision. After an accident, two factors are considered: foreseeability and negligence.

FORESEEABILITY is the anticipation that an event may occur under certain circumstances. NEGLIGENCE is the failure to exercise ordinary or reasonable care. Safety procedures should be a part of the science curriculum and a well managed classroom is important to avoid potential lawsuits.

The RIGHT TO KNOW LAW statutes cover science teachers who work with potentially hazardous chemicals. Briefly, the law states that employees must be informed of potentially toxic chemicals. An inventory must be made available if requested.

Ground Fault
Circuit Interrupter

FORESEEABILITY: the anticipation that an event may occur under certain circumstances

NEGLIGENCE: the failure to exercise ordinary or reasonable care

RIGHT TO KNOW LAW: employees must be informed of potentially toxic chemicals

The inventory must contain information about the hazards and properties of the chemicals. Training must be provided in the safe handling and interpretation of the Material Safety Data Sheet.

These chemicals are potential carcinogens and are not allowed in school facilities:

- Acrylonitriel
- Arsenic compounds
- Asbestos
- Bensidine
- Benzene
- Cadmium compounds
- Chloroform
- Chromium compounds
- Ethylene oxide
- Ortho-toluidine
- Nickel powder
- Mercury

All laboratory solutions should be prepared as directed in the lab manual. Care should be taken to avoid contamination. All glassware should be rinsed thoroughly with distilled water before using and cleaned well after use. Safety goggles should be worn while working with glassware in case of an accident. All solutions should be made with distilled water as tap water contains dissolved particles that may affect the results of an experiment. Chemical storage should be located in a secured, dry area. Chemicals should be stored in accordance with reactability. Acids are to be locked in a separate area. Used solutions should be disposed of according to local disposal procedures. Any questions regarding safe disposal or chemical safety may be directed to the local fire department.

Sample Test Questions and Rationale

Average rigor

1. **Accepted procedures for preparing solutions should be made with _____ .**

   A. alcohol

   B. hydrochloric acid

   C. distilled water

   D. tap water

   Answer: C – distilled water

   Rationale: The correct answer is distilled water. Alcohol and hydrochloric acid should never be used to make solutions unless instructed to do so. All solutions should be made with distilled water as tap water contains dissolved particles which may affect the results of an experiment

Easy

2. **Chemicals should be stored:**

   A. in the principal's office

   B. in a dark room

   C. according to their reactivity with other substances

   D. in a double locked room

   Answer: C – according to their reactivity with other substances

   Rationale: Chemicals should be stored with other chemicals of similar properties (e.g. acids with other acids), to reduce the potential for either hazardous reactions in the storeroom, or mistakes in reagent use. Certainly, chemicals should not be stored in anyone's office, and the light intensity of the room is not very important because light-sensitive chemicals are usually stored in dark containers. In fact, good lighting is desirable in a storeroom, so that labels can be read easily. Chemicals may be stored off-site, but that makes their use inconvenient.

COMPETENCY 17

UNDERSTAND AND APPLY CONCEPTS, PRINCIPLES, AND THEORIES PERTAINING TO THE PHYSICAL SETTING (INCLUDING EARTH SCIENCE, CHEMISTRY, AND PHYSICS)

SKILL Analyze interactions among the earth, the moon, and the sun
17.1 *(e.g., seasonal changes, the phases of the moon)*

Earth is the third planet away from the Sun in our solar system. Earth's numerous types of motion and states of orientation greatly affect global conditions, such as seasons, tides, and lunar phases. The Earth orbits the Sun with a period of 365 days. During this orbit, the average distance between the Earth and Sun is 93 million miles. The shape of the Earth's orbit around the Sun deviates from the shape of a circle only slightly. This deviation, known as the Earth's eccentricity, has a very small affect on the Earth's climate. The Earth is closest to the Sun at perihelion, occurring around January 2 of each year, and is farthest from the Sun at aphelion, occurring around July 2. Because the Earth is closest to the sun in January, the northern winter is slightly warmer than the southern winter.

Seasons

The rotation axis of the Earth is not perpendicular to the orbital (ecliptic) plane. The axis of the Earth is tilted 23.45° from the perpendicular. The tilt of the Earth's axis is known as the obliquity of the ecliptic and is mainly responsible for the four seasons of the year by influencing the intensity of solar rays received by the Northern and Southern Hemispheres.

The four seasons—spring, summer, fall, and winter—are extended periods of characteristic average temperature, rainfall, storm frequency, and vegetation growth or dormancy. The effect of the Earth's tilt on climate is best demonstrated at the solstices, the two days of the year when the Sun is farthest from the Earth's equatorial plane. At the Summer Solstice (June Solstice), the Earth's tilt on its axis causes the Northern Hemisphere to the lean toward the Sun, while the Southern Hemisphere leans away. Consequently, the Northern Hemisphere receives more intense rays from the Sun and experiences summer during this time, while the Southern Hemisphere experiences winter. At the Winter Solstice (December Solstice), it is the Southern Hemisphere that leans toward the Sun and thus experiences summer. Spring and fall are produced by varying degrees of the same leaning toward or away from the Sun.

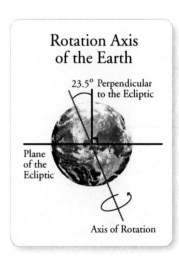

Rotation Axis of the Earth

23.5° Perpendicular to the Ecliptic

Plane of the Ecliptic

Axis of Rotation

Tides

The orientation of and gravitational interaction between the Earth and the Moon are responsible for the ocean tides that occur on Earth. The term TIDE refers to the cyclic rise and fall of large bodies of water. Gravitational attraction is defined as the force of attraction between all bodies in the universe. At the location on Earth closest to the Moon, the gravitational attraction of the Moon draws seawater toward the Moon in the form of a tidal bulge. On the opposite side of the Earth, another tidal bulge forms in the direction away from the Moon because at this point, the Moon's gravitational pull is the weakest. "Spring tides" are especially strong tides that occur when the Earth, Sun, and Moon are in line, allowing both the Sun and the Moon to exert gravitational force on the Earth and increase tidal bulge height. These tides occur during the full moon and the new moon. "Neap tides" are especially weak tides occurring when the gravitational forces of the Moon and the Sun are perpendicular to one another. These tides occur during quarter moons.

Lunar Phases

Teaching lunar phases:

http://www. moonconnection.com/ moon_phases.phtml

The Earth's orientation in respect to the solar system is also responsible for our perception of the phases of the Moon. As the Earth orbits the Sun with a period of 365 days, the Moon orbits the Earth every 27 days. As the Moon circles the Earth, its shape in the night sky appears to change. The changes in the appearance of the Moon from Earth are known as "lunar phases." These phases vary cyclically according to the relative positions of the Moon, the Earth, and the Sun. At all times, half of the Moon is facing the Sun and is thus illuminated by reflecting the Sun's light. As the Moon orbits the Earth and the Earth orbits the Sun, the half of the Moon that faces the Sun changes. However, the Moon is in synchronous rotation around the Earth, meaning that nearly the same side of the Moon faces the Earth at all times. This side is referred to as the near side of the Moon. Lunar phases occur as the Earth and Moon orbit the Sun and the fractional illumination of the Moon's near side changes.

When the Sun and Moon are on opposite sides of the Earth, observers on Earth perceive a full Moon, meaning the Moon appears circular because the entire illuminated half of the Moon is visible. As the Moon orbits the Earth, the Moon "wanes" as the amount of the illuminated half of the Moon that is visible from Earth decreases. A gibbous Moon is between a full Moon and a half Moon, or between a half Moon and a full Moon. When the Sun and the Moon are on the same side of Earth, the illuminated half of the Moon is facing away from Earth, and the Moon appears invisible. This lunar phase is known as the new Moon. The time between each full Moon is approximately 29.53 days.

LUNAR PHASES		
New Moon		The moon is invisible or the first signs of a crescent appear
Waxing Crescent		The right crescent of the moon is visible
First Quarter		The right quarter of the moon is visible
Waxing Gibbous		Only the left crescent is not illuminated
Full Moon		The entire illuminated half of the moon is visible
Waning Gibbous		Only the right crescent of the moon is not illuminated
Last Quarter		The left quarter of the moon is illuminated
Waning Crescent		Only the left crescent of the moon is illuminated

Viewing the moon from the Southern Hemisphere would cause these phases to occur in the opposite order.

SKILL 17.2 Analyze the effects of interactions among components of air, water, and land *(e.g., weather, volcanism, erosion)*

EROSION is the inclusion and transportation of surface materials by another moveable material, usually water, wind, or ice. The most important cause of erosion is running water. Streams, rivers, and tides are constantly at work removing weathered fragments of bedrock and carrying them away from their original location.

EROSION: the inclusion and transportation of surface materials by another moveable material, usually water, wind, or ice

A stream erodes bedrock by the grinding action of the sand, pebbles, and other rock fragments. This grinding against each other is called abrasion. Streams also erode rocks by dissolving or absorbing their minerals. Limestone and marble are readily dissolved by streams.

WEATHERING is the breaking down of rocks at or near to the earth's surface. Weathering breaks down these rocks into smaller and smaller pieces. There are two types of weathering: physical weathering and chemical weathering.

WEATHERING: the breaking down of rocks at or near to the earth's surface

Physical weathering is the process by which rocks are broken down into smaller fragments without undergoing any change in chemical composition. Physical weathering is mainly caused by the freezing of water, the expansion of rock, and the activities of plants and animals.

Frost wedging is the cycle of daytime thawing and refreezing at night. This cycle causes large rock masses, especially the rocks exposed on mountain tops, to be broken into smaller pieces.

The peeling away of the outer layers from a rock is called exfoliation. Rounded mountain tops are called exfoliation domes and have been formed in this way.

Chemical weathering is the breaking down of rocks through changes in their chemical composition. An example would be the change of feldspar in granite to clay. Water, oxygen, and carbon dioxide are the main agents of chemical weathering. When water and carbon dioxide combine chemically, they produce a weak acid that breaks down rocks.

Deposition, also known as sedimentation, is the term for the process by which material from one area is slowly deposited into another area. This is usually due to the movement of wind, water, or ice containing particles of matter. When the rate of movement slows down, particles filter out and remain behind, causing a build up of matter. Note that this is a result of matter being eroded and removed from another site.

Features, Functions, and Characteristics of the Atmospheric Layers

Dry air is composed of three basic components; dry gas, water vapor, and solid particles (dust from soil, etc.).

MOST ABUNDANT DRY GASES IN THE ATMOSPHERE		
Chemical Symbol	Gas	% in atmosphere
N_2	Nitrogen	78.09
O_2	Oxygen	20.95
AR	Argon	0.93
CO_2	Carbon Dioxide	0.03

FOUR MAIN LAYERS OF ATMOSPHERE (BASED ON TEMPERATURE)	
Troposphere	Closest to the Earth's surface, all weather phenomena occur here as it is the layer with the most water vapor and dust. Air temperature decreases with increasing altitude. The average thickness of the troposphere is 7 miles (11 km).
Stratosphere	Containing very little water, clouds within this layer are extremely rare. The ozone layer is located in the upper portions of the stratosphere. Air temperature is fairly constant but does increase somewhat with height due to the absorption of solar energy and ultraviolet rays from the ozone layer.
Mesosphere	Air temperature again decreases with height in this layer. It is the coldest layer with temperatures in the range of -1000° C at the top.
Thermosphere	Extends upward into space. Oxygen molecules in this layer absorb energy from the Sun, causing temperatures to increase with height. The lower part of the thermosphere is called the ionosphere. Here charged particles or ions and free electrons can be found. When gases in the ionosphere are excited by solar radiation, the gases give off light and glow in the sky. These glowing lights are called the Aurora Borealis in the Northern Hemisphere and Aurora Australis in Southern Hemisphere. The upper portion of the thermosphere is called the exosphere. Gas molecules are very far apart in this layer. Layers of exosphere are also known as the Van Allen Belts and are held together by Earth's magnetic field.

CLOUD TYPES	
Cirrus	White and feathery; high in the sky
Cumulus	Thick, white, fluffy
Stratus	Layers of clouds cover most of the sky
Nimbus	Heavy, dark clouds that represent thunderstorm clouds

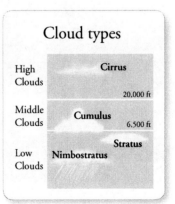

Cloud types

High Clouds — Cirrus — 20,000 ft
Middle Clouds — Cumulus — 6,500 ft
Low Clouds — Stratus / Nimbostratus

Teaching cloud formations:

http://www.summitpost. org/article/171461/cloud-formations.html

Variations on the clouds mentioned above include Cumulo-nimbus and Strato-nimbus.

Atmospheric Conditions and Weather

El Niño refers to a sequence of changes in the ocean and atmospheric circulation across the Pacific Ocean. The water around the equator is unusually hot every two to seven years. Trade winds normally blow east to west across the equatorial latitudes, piling warm water into the western Pacific. A huge mass of heavy thunderstorms usually forms in the area and produces vast currents of rising air that displace heat poleward. This helps create the strong midlatitude jet streams. The world's climate patterns are disrupted by this change in location of thunderstorm activity.

Air masses moving toward or away from the Earth's surface are called air currents. Air moving parallel to Earth's surface is called wind. Weather conditions are generated by winds and air currents carrying large amounts of heat and moisture from one part of the atmosphere to another. Wind speeds are measured by instruments called anemometers.

The wind belts in each hemisphere consist of convection cells that encircle Earth like belts. There are three major wind belts on Earth:

1. Trade winds

2. Prevailing westerlies

3. Polar easterlies

Wind belt formation depends on the differences in air pressures that develop in the doldrums, the horse latitudes, and the polar regions. The doldrums surround the equator. Within this belt, heated air usually rises straight up into Earth's atmosphere. The horse latitudes are regions of high barometric pressure with calm and light winds, and the Polar regions contain cold dense air that sinks to the Earth's surface.

Winds caused by local temperature changes include sea breezes and land breezes.

SEA BREEZES are caused by the unequal heating of the land and an adjacent, large body of water. Land heats up faster than water. The movement of cool ocean air toward the land is called a sea breeze. Sea breezes usually begin blowing about midmorning; ending about sunset.

A breeze that blows from the land to the ocean or a large lake is called a **LAND BREEZE**.

SEA BREEZE: caused by the unequal heating of the land and an adjacent, large body of water

LAND BREEZE: a breeze that blows from the land to the ocean or a large lake

MONSOONS are huge wind systems that cover large geographic areas and that reverse direction seasonally. The monsoons of India and Asia are examples of these seasonal winds. They alternate wet and dry seasons. As denser cooler air over the ocean moves inland, a steady seasonal wind called a summer or wet monsoon is produced.

The air temperature at which water vapor begins to condense is called the DEW POINT.

RELATIVE HUMIDITY is the actual amount of water vapor in a certain volume of air compared to the maximum amount of water vapor this air could hold at a given temperature.

Knowledge of Types of Storms

A THUNDERSTORM is a brief, local storm produced by the rapid upward movement of warm, moist air within a cumulo-nimbus cloud. Thunderstorms always produce lightning and thunder and are accompanied by strong wind gusts and heavy rain or hail.

A severe storm with swirling winds that may reach speeds of hundreds of km per hour is called a TORNADO. Such a storm is also referred to as a "twister." The sky is covered by large cumulo-nimbus clouds and violent thunderstorms; a funnel-shaped swirling cloud may extend downward from a cumulo-nimbus cloud and reach the ground. Tornadoes are storms that leave a narrow path of destruction on the ground.

A swirling, funnel-shaped cloud that extends downward and touches a body of water is called a WATERSPOUT.

HURRICANES are storms that develop when warm, moist air carried by trade winds rotate around a low-pressure "eye." A large, rotating, low-pressure system accompanied by heavy precipitation and strong winds is called a tropical cyclone (better known as a hurricane). In the Pacific region, a hurricane is called a typhoon.

Storms that occur only in the winter are known as blizzards or ice storms. A blizzard is a storm with strong winds, blowing snow, and frigid temperatures. An ice storm consists of falling rain that freezes when it strikes the ground, covering everything with a layer of ice.

MONSOONS: huge wind systems that cover large geographic areas and that reverse direction seasonally

DEW POINT: the air temperature at which water vapor begins to condense

RELATIVE HUMIDITY: the actual amount of water vapor in a certain volume of air compared to the maximum amount of water vapor this air could hold at a given temperature

THUNDERSTORM: a brief, local storm produced by the rapid upward movement of warm, moist air within a cumulo-nimbus cloud

TORNADO: a severe storm with swirling winds that may reach speeds of hundreds of km per hour

WATERSPOUT: a swirling, funnel-shaped cloud that extends downward and touches a body of water

HURRICANES: storms that develop when warm, moist air carried by trade winds rotate around a low-pressure "eye"

SKILL 17.3 Distinguishing between physical and chemical properties of matter and between physical and chemical changes in matter

The kinetic theory states that matter consists of molecules, possessing kinetic energies, in continual random motion.

The kinetic theory states that matter consists of molecules, possessing kinetic energies, in continual random motion. The state of matter (solid, liquid, or gas) depends on the speed of the molecules and the amount of kinetic energy the molecules possess. The molecules of solid matter merely vibrate allowing strong intermolecular forces to hold the molecules in place. The molecules of liquid matter move freely and quickly throughout the body and the molecules of gaseous matter move randomly and at high speeds.

Matter changes state when energy is added or taken away. The addition of energy, usually in the form of heat, increases the speed and kinetic energy of the component molecules. Faster moving molecules more readily overcome the intermolecular attractions that maintain the form of solids and liquids. In conclusion, as the speed of molecules increases, matter changes state from solid to liquid to gas (melting and evaporation).

As matter loses heat energy to the environment, the speed of the component molecules decreases. Intermolecular forces have greater impact on slower moving molecules. Thus, as the speed of molecules decrease, matter changes from gas to liquid to solid (condensation and freezing).

Kinetic motion

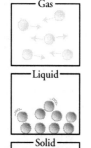

Gas

Liquid

Solid

SKILL 17.4 Distinguishing among forms of energy and identifying the transformations of energy observed in everyday life

HEAT: a measure of energy

TEMPERATURE: the measure of how hot (or cold) a body is with respect to a standard object

THERMAL EQUILIBRIUM: when two objects are in thermal contact, eventually they will have the same temperature.

THERMOMETER: used to measure temperature

Heat and temperature are different physical quantities. HEAT is a measure of energy. TEMPERATURE is the measure of how hot (or cold) a body is with respect to a standard object.

Two concepts are important in the discussion of temperature changes. Objects are in thermal contact if they can affect each other's temperatures. Set a hot cup of coffee on a desk top. The two objects are in thermal contact with each other and will begin affecting each other's temperatures. The coffee will become cooler and the desktop warmer. Eventually, they will have the same temperature. When this happens, they are in THERMAL EQUILIBRIUM.

We can not rely on our sense of touch to determine temperature because the heat from a hand may be conducted more efficiently by certain objects, making them feel colder. THERMOMETERS are used to measure temperature. A small amount of mercury in a capillary tube will expand when heated. The thermometer and the object whose temperature it is measuring are put in contact long enough for them to reach thermal equilibrium. Then the temperature can be read from the thermometer scale.

Three temperature scales are used:

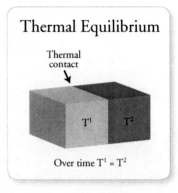

Thermal Equilibrium

Thermal contact

Over time T¹ = T²

Celcius	Freezing point of water: 0; Steam (boiling) point: 100. The interval between the two is divided into 100 equal parts called degrees Celsius. Celsius to Fahrenheit: F = (9/5) C + 32; Celsius to Kelvin: K = C + 273.15
Fahrenheit	Freezing point of water: 32; Boiling point: 212. The interval between is divided into 180 equal parts called degrees Fahrenheit. Fahrenheit to Celsius: C = 5/9 (F − 32)
Kelvin	Kelvin Scale has degrees the same size as the Celsius scale, but the zero point is moved to the triple point of water. Water inside a closed vessel is in thermal equilibrium in all three states (ice, water, and vapor) at 273.15 degrees Kelvin. This temperature is equivalent to .01 degrees Celsius. Because the degrees are the same in the two scales, temperature changes are the same in Celsius and Kelvin. Kelvin to Celsius: C = K − 273.15

Heat is a measure of energy. If two objects that have different temperatures come into contact with each other, heat flows from the hotter object to the cooler.

There are a number of ways that heat is measured. In each case, the measurement is dependent upon raising the temperature of a specific amount of water by a specific amount. These conversions of heat energy and work are called the MECHANICAL EQUIVALENT OF HEAT.

MECHANICAL EQUIVALENT OF HEAT: the conversion of heat energy and work

The CALORIE is the amount of energy that it takes to raise one gram of water one degree Celsius.

The kilocalorie is the amount of energy that it takes to raise one kilogram of water by one degree Celsius. Food calories are kilocalories.

In the International System of Units (SI), the calorie is equal to 4.184 joules.

CALORIE: the amount of energy that it takes to raise one gram of water one degree Celsius

A British thermal unit (BTU) = 252 calories = 1.054 kJ

**SKILL Analyze the effects of forces on objects in given situations
17.5**

There are generally four types of forces that may act on an object:

- Air resistance (drag) occurs when an object moves through the air. The force of air resistance acts in the opposite direction to the motion. Air resistance depends on the shape of the object and its speed.

- Contact force happens when two objects are pushed together. They exert equal and opposite forces on each other. The contact force from the ground pushes up on your feet as you push down to walk forwards.

- Friction is the force that resists movement between two surfaces that are in contact.

- Gravity is the force that pulls objects towards the Earth. We call the pull of gravity on an object its weight. The Earth pulls with a force of about 9.8 newtons on every kilogram of mass.

Mass and weight are two different properties. An object's mass is constant and reflects the amount of matter in an object. In contrast, an object's weight can vary depending on the force of the gravitational field. In the International System of Units, mass is given as kilograms. Weight is calculated by multiplying an object's mass by the gravitational force, approximately 9.8 newtons. These two properties explain how a person of a constant mass can weigh 200 pounds on earth and be weightless in space where the gravitational force is zero.

There are usually several forces acting on an object an any given time. The forces might change the speed of a moving object, change the direction of a moving object or change the shape of an object. When you write with a pen you exert a force. When you peddle your bike, blow your nose, turn on a faucet, chew your gum, or swimming in a pool, you are exerting forces on other objects. We would never be able to move without exerting forces on things.

Consider a parachutist falling at 20 m/s.

While in free fall, the parachutist has the force of gravity pulling down toward the earth. Air resistance (drag) pushes on the canopy of the parachute.

Consider pushing down on a basketball on the floor.

There are three forces acting on the ball. The ball is being squashed by the hand pushing down and the contact force from the floor is pushing up on the ball. Gravity is pulling down on the ball.

Now consider a car moving at 2 m/s.

There are multiple forces acting on the car. Gravity is pulling down on the car. The contact force from the road pushes up on the wheels. The driving force from the engine is pushing the car along. There is friction between the road and the tires. There is also friction in the wheel bearings. Last, air resistance is acting on the front of the car.

Sample Test Questions and Rationale

Average rigor

1. The measure of the pull of the earth's gravity on an object is called _____

   A. mass number

   B. atomic number

   C. mass

   D. weight

Answer: D – weight

Rationale: Weight. To answer this question, recall that mass number is the total number of protons and neutrons in an atom, atomic number are the number of protons in an atom, and mass is the amount of matter in an object. The only remaining choice is (D), weight, which is correct because weight is the force of gravity on an object.

SKILL Inferring the physical science principle *(e.g., effects of common forces, 17.6 conservation of energy)* **illustrated in a given situation**

The law of conservation of energy states that energy is neither created nor destroyed. Thus, energy changes form when energy transactions occur in nature. Because the total energy in the universe is constant, energy continually transitions between forms. For example, an engine burns gasoline converting the chemical energy of the gasoline into mechanical energy, a plant converts radiant energy of the sun into chemical energy found in glucose, or a battery converts chemical energy into electrical energy.

CHEMICAL REACTIONS are the interactions of substances resulting in chemical change, and change in energy. Chemical reactions involve changes in electron motion and the breaking and forming of chemical bonds. Reactants are the

CHEMICAL REACTIONS: the interactions of substances resulting in chemical change and change in energy

NUCLEAR OR ATOMIC REACTIONS: reactions that change the composition, energy, or structure of atomic nuclei

FUSION: the joining of atomic nuclei, which results in the release of large amounts of energy

Nuclear Fusion

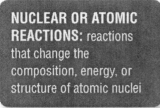

small nucleus   small nucleus

heat energy

○ neutron
● proton

1 Small like-charged nuclei fuse
2 Formation of a heavier nucleus
3 Formation of a nucleus with a different number of neutrons and protons
4 Energy is released

FISSION: the splitting of an atomic nucleus, which releases large amounts of enregy

Nuclear Fission

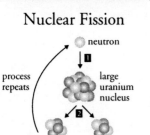

○ neutron

process repeats   large uranium nucleus

heat energy

○ neutron
● proton

1 Neutron collides with uranium nucleus
2 Uranium nucleus splits into smaller nuclei and neutrons
3 Neutrons collide with more uranium nuclei releasing energy

original substances that interact to form distinct products. Endothermic chemical reactions consume energy while exothermic chemical reactions release energy with product formation. Chemical reactions occur continually in nature and are also induced by man for many purposes.

NUCLEAR REACTIONS, or ATOMIC REACTIONS, are reactions that change the composition, energy, and/or structure of atomic nuclei. Nuclear reactions change the number of protons and neutrons in the nucleus. The two main types of nuclear reactions are: FUSION and FISSION. The fusion of small nuclei such as hydrogen releases more energy than is required to cause the nuclei to fuse and are therefore exothermic reactions. In contrast, the fusion of large nuclei requires more energy than is produced and are therefore endothermic reactions. The opposite is true for fission reactions. The fission of heavy atomic nuclei are exothermic reactions, while the fission of smaller nuclei are endothermic reactions. The fission of large nuclei such as uranium releases large amounts of energy because the products of fission undergo further nuclear reactions that are self-sustaining. Fission and fusion reactions can occur naturally, but are most recognized as man-made events. Particle acceleration and bombardment with neutrons are two methods of inducing nuclear reactions.

The law of conservation can also be applied to physical and biological processes. For example, when a rock is weathered, it does not just lose pieces, instead it is broken down into its composite minerals, many of which enter the soil. Biology takes advantage of decomposers to recycle decaying material. Since energy is neither created or destroyed, we know it must change form. An animal may die, but its body will be consumed by other animals or decay into the ecosystem. Either way, it enters another form and the matter still exists—it was not destroyed.

Sample Test Questions and Rationale

Rigorous

1. **Which parts of an atom are located inside the nucleus?**

   A. Electrons and neutrons

   B. Protons and neutrons

   C. Protons only

   D. Neutrons only

Answer: B – Protons and neutrons

Rationale: Protons and neutrons are located in the nucleus, while electrons move around outside the nucleus.

COMPETENCY 18

UNDERSTAND AND APPLY CONCEPTS, PRINCIPLES, AND THEORIES PERTAINING TO THE LIVING ENVIRONMENT

> **SKILL** Recognizing the characteristics of living things and common life
> **18.1** processes

Essential elements are recycled through an ecosystem. At times, the element needs to be "fixed" in a useable form. Cycles are dependent on plants, algae, and bacteria to fix nutrients for use by animals.

Water Cycle	Two percent of all the available water is fixed and held in ice or the bodies of organisms. Available water includes surface water (lakes, ocean, and rivers) and ground water (aquifers, wells). Ninety-six percent of all available water is from ground water. Water is recycled through the processes of evaporation and precipitation. The water present now is the water that has been here since our atmosphere formed.
Carbon Cycle	Ten percent of all available carbon in the air (from carbon dioxide gas) is fixed by photosynthesis. Plants fix carbon in the form of glucose, animals eat the plants and are able to obtain their source of carbon. When animals release carbon dioxide through respiration, the plants again have a source of carbon to fix.
Nitrogen Cycle	Eighty percent of the atmosphere is in the form of nitrogen gas. Nitrogen must be fixed and taken out of the gaseous form to be incorporated into an organism. Only a few genera of bacteria have the correct enzymes to break the triple bond between nitrogen atoms. These bacteria live within the roots of legumes (peas, beans, alfalfa) and add bacteria to the soil so it may be taken up by the plant. Nitrogen is necessary to make amino acids and the nitrogenous bases of DNA.
Phosphorus Cycle	Phosphorus exists as a mineral and is not found in the atmosphere. Fungi and plant roots have structures called mycorrhizae that are able to fix insoluble phosphates into useable phosphorus. Urine and decayed matter returns phosphorus to the earth where it can be fixed in the plant. Phosphorus is needed for the backbone of DNA and for the manufacture of ATP.

> **SKILL** Analyzing the processes that contribute to the continuity of life
> **18.2** (e.g., reproduction and development, inheritance of genetic information)

NATURAL SELECTION:
the process in nature in which only organisms best adapted to their environment evolve

Darwin defined the theory of NATURAL SELECTION in the mid-1800s. Through the study of finches on the Galapagos Islands, Darwin theorized that nature selects the traits that are advantageous to the organism. Those that do not possess the desirable trait die and do not pass on their genes. Those more fit to survive reproduce, thus increasing that gene in the population. Darwin listed four principles to define natural selection:

1. The individuals in a certain species vary from generation to generation.

2. Some of the variations are determined by the genetic makeup of the species.

3. More individuals are produced than will survive.

4. Some genes allow for better survival of an animal.

Causes of Evolution	Certain factors increase the chances of variability in a population, thus leading to evolution. Items that increase variability include mutations, sexual reproduction, immigration, and large population. Items that decrease variation would be natural selection, emigration, small population, and random mating.
Sexual Selection	Genes that happen to come together determine the makeup of the gene pool. Animals that use mating behaviors may be successful or unsuccessful. An animal that lacks attractive plumage or has a weak mating call will not attract the female, thereby eventually limiting that gene in the gene pool. Mechanical isolation, where sex organs do not fit the female, has an obvious disadvantage.

> SKILL Analyzing the factors that contribute to change in organisms and
> 18.3 species over time

See Skill 20.5

> SKILL Comparing the ways a variety of organisms carry out basic life
> 18.4 functions and maintain dynamic equilibrium *(e.g., obtaining nutrients, maintaining water balance)*

POPULATION: a group of the same species in a specific area

COMMUNITY: a group of populations residing in the same area

BIOMES: communities that are ecologically similar in regard to temperature, rainfall, and the species that live there

Ecology is the study of organisms, where they live and their interactions with the environment. A POPULATION is a group of the same species in a specific area. A COMMUNITY is a group of populations residing in the same area. Communities that are ecologically similar in regard to temperature, rainfall, and the species that live there are called BIOMES.

Specific biomes include:

Marine	Covers seventy-five of the earth. This biome is organized by the depth of the water. The intertidal zone is from the tide line to the edge of the water. The littoral zone is from the water's edge to the open sea. It includes coral reef habitats and is the most densely populated area of the marine biome. The open sea zone is divided into the epipelagic zone and the pelagic zone. The epipelagic zone receives more sunlight and has a larger number of species. The ocean floor is called the benthic zone and is populated with bottom feeders.
Tropical Rain Forest	Temperature is constant (25 degrees C), rainfall exceeds 200 cm per year. Located around the area of the equator, the rain forest has abundant, diverse species of plants and animals.
Savanna	Temperatures range from 0-25 degrees C depending on the location. Rainfall is from 90 to 150 cm per year. Plants include shrubs and grasses. The savanna is a transitional biome between the rain forest and the desert.
Desert	Temperatures range from 10 to 38 degrees C. Rainfall is under 25 cm per year. Plant species include xerophytes and succulents. Lizards, snakes, and small mammals are common animals.
Temperate Deciduous Forest	Temperature ranges from -24 to 38 degrees C. Rainfall is between 65 to 150 cm per year. Deciduous trees are common, as well as deer, bear, and squirrels.
Taiga	Temperatures range from -24 to 22 degrees C. Rainfall is between 35 to 40 cm per year. Taiga is located very north and very south of the equator, getting close to the poles. Plant life includes conifers and plants that can withstand harsh winters. Animals include weasels, mink, and moose.
Tundra	Temperatures range from -28 to 15 degrees C. Rainfall is limited, ranging from 10 to 15 cm per year. The tundra is located even further north and south than the taiga. Common plants include lichens and mosses. Animals include polar bears and musk ox.
Polar or Permafrost	Temperature ranges from -40 to 0 degrees C. It rarely gets above freezing. Rainfall is below 10 cm per year. Most water is bound up as ice. Life is limited.

Succession

SUCCESSION is an orderly process of replacing a community that has been damaged or beginning one where no life previously existed.

- Primary succession occurs after a community has been totally wiped out by a natural disaster or where life never existed before, as in a flooded area.

- Secondary succession takes place in communities that were once flourishing but were disturbed by some source, either man or nature, yet were not totally stripped.

SUCCESSION: an orderly process of replacing a community that has been damaged or beginning one where no life previously existed

A climax community is a community that is established and flourishing.

FEEDING RELATIONSHIPS	
Parasitism	Two species that occupy a similar place; the parasite benefits from the relationship, the host is harmed.
Commensalism	Two species that occupy a similar place; neither species is harmed or benefits from the relationship.
Mutualism (symbiosis)	Two species that occupy a similar place; both species benefit from the relationship.
Competition	Two species that occupy the same habitat or eat the same food are said to be in competition with each other.
Predation	Animals that eat other animals are called predators. The animals they feed on are called the prey. Population growth depends upon competition for food, water, shelter, and space. The amount of predators determines the amount of prey, which in turn affects the number of predators.
Carrying Capacity	This is the total amount of life a habitat can support. Once the habitat runs out of food, water, shelter, or space, the carrying capacity decreases, and then stabilizes.

ECOLOGICAL PROBLEMS CAUSED BY MAN	
Biological Magnification	Chemicals and pesticides accumulate along the food chain. Tertiary consumers have more accumulated toxins than animals at the bottom of the food chain.
Simplification of the Food Web	Three major crops feed the world (rice, corn, wheat). The planting of these foods wipe out habitats and push animals residing there into other habitats causing overpopulation or extinction.
Fuel Sources	Strip mining and the overuse of oil reserves have depleted these resources. At the current rate of consumption, conservation or alternate fuel sources will guarantee our future fuel sources.
Pollution	Although technology gives us many advances, pollution is a side effect of production. Waste disposal and the burning of fossil fuels have polluted our land, water and air. Global warming and acid rain are two results of the burning of hydrocarbons and sulfur.
Global Warming	Rainforest depletion and the use of fossil fuels and aerosols have caused an increase in carbon dioxide production. This leads to a decrease in the amount of oxygen which is directly proportional to the amount of ozone. As the ozone layer depletes, more heat enters our atmosphere and is trapped. This causes an overall warming effect which may eventually melt polar ice caps, causing a rise in water levels and changes in climate that will affect weather systems worldwide.

Table continued on next page

Endangered Species	Construction of homes to house people in our overpopulated world has caused the destruction of habitat for other animals leading to their extinction.
Overpopulation	The human race is still growing at an exponential rate. Carrying capacity has not been met due to our ability to use technology to produce more food and housing. Space and water cannot be manufactured and eventually our nonrenewable resources will reach a crisis state. Our overuse affects every living thing on this planet.

Sample Test Questions and Rationale

Rigorous

1. **A biome is which of the following:**

   A. set of surroundings within which members of a species normally live

   B. a large area of land with characteristic climate, soil, and mixture of plants and animals

   C. a community (of any size) consisting of a physical environment and the organisms that live within it.

   D. none of the above

   Answer: B – a large area of land with characteristic climate, soil, and mixture of plants and animals

   Rationale: A biome is a large area of land with characteristic climate, soil, and mixture of plants and animals. Biomes are made up of groups of ecosystems. Major biomes are: desert, chaparral, savanna, tropical rain forest, temperate grassland, temperate deciduous forest, taiga, and tundra.

Average Rigor

2. **A condition in which two organisms of different species are able to live in the same environment over an extended period of time without harming one another is called:**

   A. symbiosis

   B. biodiversity

   C. habitat

   D. ecosystem

   Answer: A – symbiosis

   Rationale: Symbiosis is a condition in which two organisms of different species are able to live in the same environment over an extended period of time without harming one another. In some cases one species may benefit without harming the other. In other cases both species benefit.

SKILL Analyzing the effects of environmental conditions *(e.g., temperature,* 18.5 *availability of water and sunlight)* on living organisms and the relationships between plants and animals within a community

Identify the biotic and abiotic factors that influence population density.

BIOTIC FACTORS: living things in an ecosystem: plants, animals, bacteria, fungi, etc.

- BIOTIC FACTORS are living things in an ecosystem; plants, animals, bacteria, fungi, etc. If one population in a community increases, it affects the ability of another population to succeed by limiting the available amount of food, water, shelter, and space.

ABIOTIC FACTORS: nonliving aspects of an ecosystem: soil quality, rainfall, and temperature

- ABIOTIC FACTORS are nonliving aspects of an ecosystem; soil quality, rainfall, and temperature. Changes in climate and soil can cause effects at the beginning of the food chain, thus limiting or accelerating the growth of populations.

Abiotic factors vary in the environment. It is also difficult to determine the types and numbers of organisms that exist in that environment. Factors that determine the types and numbers of organisms of a species in an ecosystem are called limiting factors. Many limiting factors restrict the growth of populations in nature.

The arrival of human species has greatly altered the biotic and abiotic factors for much of life on earth. An example of this would include how annual average temperature common to the Arctic restricts the growth of trees as the subsoil is permanently frozen. Another example is the effect that climate change has on migratory birds. The anticipated increase in cloudiness over the arctic could itself become a factor in ozone depletion. The clouds, formed from condensed nitric acid and water, tend to increase snowfall, which accelerates depletion of stratospheric nitrogen. There is a circular relationship between how biotic and abiotic factors influence environment conditions and then how environmental conditions in turn affect biotic and abiotic factors.

SKILL Inferring the life science principle *(e.g., adaptation, homeostasis)* 18.6 illustrated in a given situation

HOMEOSTASIS: the result of regulatory mechanisms that help maintain an organism's internal environment within tolerable limits

All living organisms respond and adapt to their environments. HOMEOSTASIS is the result of regulatory mechanisms that help maintain an organism's internal environment within tolerable limits.

The molecular composition of the immediate environment outside of the organism is not the same as it is inside and the temperature outside may not be optimal for metabolic activity within the organism. Homeostasis is the control of these differences between internal and external environments.

There are three homeostatic systems to regulate these differences.

1. Osmoregulation deals with maintenance of the appropriate level of water and salts in body fluids for optimum cellular functions.

2. Excretion is the elimination of metabolic waste products from the body including excess water.

3. Thermoregulation maintains the internal, or core, body temperature of the organism within a tolerable range for metabolic and cellular processes. For example, in humans and mammals, constriction and dilation of blood vessels near the skin help maintain body temperature.

COMPETENCY 19

APPLY KNOWLEDGE OF TECHNOLOGY AND THE PRINCIPLES OF ENGINEERING DESIGN

SKILL Demonstrating an understanding of technological systems (e.g.,
19.1 transportation system) and the principles on which technological systems are constructed (e.g., the use of component subsystems)

A TECHNOLOGICAL SYSTEM is a system that consists of different parts and uses scientific knowledge to solve problems. It means that a system designed to solve a problem or helping people. We often use the word system in many different ways—fuel system, digestive system, communication system, to name a few.

Systems are made up of subsystems or components. All systems have some basic parts that include:

- Inputs: the resources used by the system
- Processes: the actions taken to use the inputs
- Outputs: the result of the system
- Feedback: adjustments made to the processes to improve the outputs
- Goals: reason for the system

TECHNOLOGICAL SYSTEM: a system that consists of different parts and uses scientific knowledge to solve problems

All technological systems have these five parts.

> **CASE STUDY**
>
> As an example of a technological system, let's discuss transportation system: Transportation is the movement of people and goods from one place to another. Transportation technology is built around the vehicle. The vehicle in use must be designed to serve the purpose.
>
> Every vehicle must have:
>
> - A structure
> - A guidance system
> - A means of propulsion
> - Control systems
> - A means of transmission
> - Measurement devices

Most technological systems have two major goals:

1. The first goal is to meet human needs, such as moving people and goods used by people from place to place. In a city like New York City, the transport system is crucial for people because of the long distances they have to travel and the cost of driving a car and the time involved in reaching the destination.

2. The second goal is to profit. It is the reward earned by owners of the transportation system for taking financial risks. But, one thing is very important—the best technological system will be useless unless it helps people live better.

SUBCOMPONENTS OF THE TRANSPORTATION SYSTEM	
Modern Forms of Transport	These include road, rail, water, air, etc. These are very important because each has its own use to people using them. Each has its merits and demerits.
Intermodal Transport	Today, passengers move from one mode of transport (e.g., subway) to another (bus). There are facilities called intermodal facilities to help people and to make them comfortable during transit. An intermodal station may serve air, rail, and highway transportation.
Nodes and Stops	Stations are an important component of any public transportation system. Airport, heliport, airport terminal, bus stop, metro station, park and ride, ship terminal, ferry slip, pier or wharf are examples of Nodes and stops.
Ticket Systems	This is a very important component because it generates income. There are various types of tickets (passes, one-time tickets, multiuse tickets, discount cards, city cards, etc.). Depending on their use, passengers buy these cards or tickets.

When we analyze transportation systems, we become aware of various components and their uses. Ultimately, the single most important use of transportation systems is to move people and goods from one place to another and, while doing this, the owners make money.

SKILL 19.2 Analyzing the roles of modeling and optimization in the engineering design process

Albert Einstein, the famous physicist once said, "Scientists investigate that which already is; engineers create that which has never been."

ENGINEERING DESIGN PROCESS (EDP) is a process by which engineers design equipment or any piece of machinery to solve problems and to help people to have better quality of life. The range of these machines could be anything from a simple machine, such as a knife, to a very complicated one, such as a computer. The objective is to help people and enhance the quality of their lives. This could also be a motorized wheel chair for a person who is unable to walk or a dialysis machine for someone whose kidneys are not functioning properly.

> **ENGINEERING DESIGN PROCESS (EDP):** a series of steps that engineers use to guide them as they solve problems

Just like the scientists who use scientific method to explore and investigate, engineers use EDP to design a particular instrument, machine, etc. Just like the scientific process, the EDP also consists of a number of steps. However, it must be emphasized that EDP is not always a step-by-step process.

The five steps that constitute EDP are:

1. Define the problem (Engagement)

2. Research/investigate (Exploration)

3. Propose design ideas (Explanation)

4. Analysis (Application)

5. Choose final design (Evaluation and Communication)

Of particular interest here is the Engineering Design Process for Children.

The EDP is a series of steps that engineers use to guide them as they solve problems. Many variations of the basic model exist. Engineers do not follow these steps in a rigid manner and often do not perform all the steps. They may do a few steps and pass it on to the next team to complete. Because elementary children are younger, a much simpler version of EDP is formulated. Children can start this process at any point and carry on. It is flexible, positive, and yields good results.

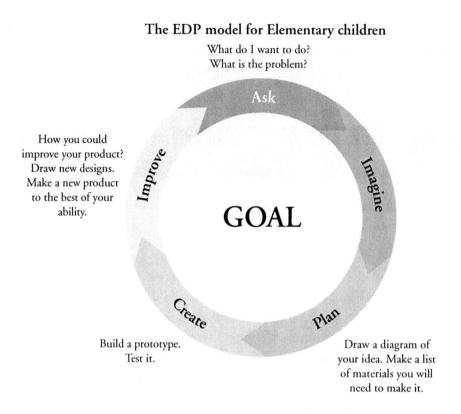

The EDP model for Elementary children

What do I want to do?
What is the problem?

Ask

How you could improve your product? Draw new designs. Make a new product to the best of your ability.

Improve

Imagine

GOAL

Create

Plan

Build a prototype.
Test it.

Draw a diagram of your idea. Make a list of materials you will need to make it.

Modeling is very useful for understanding the structure and functioning of any system, whether a human system, an animal/plant system, or even an engineering system. Models have revolutionized our understanding of science and technology. Models are also used extensively in other areas of learning. The models in science and technology are unique in that they can enlarge a structure or minimize it, if it is very big. The understanding we get when we look at the model of a gene is astounding. Modeling plays a very crucial role in constructing systems and understanding how they function. This helps the scientists/engineers to improve on the model and to come up with a better design that functions well. The ultimate goal of all this is to help the society.

SKILL 19.3 Evaluating a proposed technological solution to a given problem or need

See Skill 16.2

Science investigation is a very important part of science. Science investigation consists of a number of steps designed to solve a problem. This is important because it helps in solving scientific problems and to gather new information. Scientists start with a problem and solve it in an orderly fashion called the scientific method. This is made up of a series of steps, which, when applied properly, solve scientific problems. The key to the success of this method lies in minimizing human prejudice. As human beings, we tend to have bias. The steps of the scientific process consist of identifying the problem, gathering information, formulating a hypothesis, experimental design, interpreting data, and drawing conclusions.

If the hypothesis is tested and the results are repeated in further experimentation, a theory could be formulated. A theory is a hypothesis that is tested repeatedly by different scientists and has yielded the same results. A theory has more validity because it could be used to predict future events.

Scientific inquiries should end in formulating an explanation or model. Models should be physical, conceptual, and mathematical. While drawing conclusions, a lot of discussion and arguments are generated. There may be several possible explanations for any given sets of results: not all of them are reasonable. Carefully evaluating and analyzing the data creates a reasonable conclusion. The conclusion needs to be backed up by scientific criteria.

After the conclusion is drawn, the final step is communication. In this age, much emphasis is put on the method of communication. The conclusions must be communicated by clearly describing the information using accurate data, visual presentation like graphs (bar/line/pie), tables/charts, diagrams, artwork, and other appropriate media like PowerPoint presentations. Modern technology must be used whenever it is necessary. The method of communication must be suitable to the audience.

> *The steps of the scientific process consist of identifying the problem, gathering information, formulating a hypothesis, experimental design, interpreting data, and drawing conclusions.*

Sample Test Questions and Rationale

Rigorous

1. **In an experiment measuring the growth of bacteria at different temperatures, what is the independent variable?**

    A. Number of bacteria

    B. Growth rate of bacteria

    C. Temperature

    D. Size of bacteria

Answer: C – Temperature

Rationale: To answer this question, recall that the independent variable in an experiment is the entity that is changed by the scientist, in order to observe the effects (the dependent variable(s)). In this experiment, temperature is changed in order to measure growth of bacteria, so (C) is the answer. Note that answer (A) is the dependent variable, and neither (B) nor (D) is directly relevant to the question.

SKILL 19.4 Applying a criteria for selecting tools, materials, and other resources to design and construct a technological product or service

TECHNOLOGICAL SERVICE: a service that is provided to the society using the scientific knowledge

A TECHNOLOGICAL SERVICE can be defined as a service that is provided to the society using the scientific knowledge. Any service that is provided to the society is for the benefit of that society. Here we are going to discuss one of the most important services for the society—education. Education is absolutely important to any society because it breaks down the barriers that divide us on the basis of gender, race, socioeconomic status, etc. Education has the capacity to even out these differences to a significant level. It is not possible to have a society without any differences and tiers. If we had an ideal society, we would be bored to death, since there would be no controversy, competition, etc.

In a typical society, education is very valuable. It is the single most important thing that can bring changes in the clients who are pursuing it. Education is a very effective technological service.

But the technology used must also be human-centered, although the nonliving resources—the buildings, the transport system—are also important. Finances are crucial because this service is money hungry. Wise spending of money on this product will influence generations to come in a positive manner.

Sample Test Questions and Rationale

Easy

1. **An ecosystem is defined by its _____.**

   A. Climate

   B. indigenous plants/animals

   C. location to the equator

   D. Answers A and B

Answer: D – Answers A and B

Rationale: Answers A (climate) and B (indigenous plants/animals). The region of the Earth and its atmosphere in which living things are found is known as the biosphere. The biosphere is made up of distinct areas called ecosystems, each of which has its own characteristic climate, soils, and communities of plants and animals.

SKILL 19.5 Recognizing appropriate tests of a given technological solution

A TECHNOLOGICAL SOLUTION is a solution using the knowledge of science to solve a problem. This problem could be human-related or non-human-related.

> **TECHNOLOGICAL SOLUTION:** a solution using the knowledge of science to solve a problem

CASE STUDY

As an example, let us discuss the technological solution for patients whose kidneys are not functioning. A machine that is used for daily haemodialysis by individuals is called a Personal Haemodialysis System (PHD). Daily haemodialysis has been tried with excellent clinical results for more than three decades, but the attempts were short-lived for two reasons—lack of suitable equipment and adequate reimbursement.

The benefits of daily haemodialysis are:

- Improved blood pressure control
- Cardiac morphology and function
- Endocrine function
- Energy
- Physical activity
- Vitality
- Haematocrit
- Mental health
- Mineral metabolism
- Nutrition
- Social functioning
- Sexual function
- Patient survival
- Use of drugs, mortality, and hospitalization decreased.

Although haemodialysis technology has improved in recent decades; it was not specifically prepared for frequent home haemodialysis. With this background information on daily haemodialysis, we will discuss here the appropriate tests for this technological solution called PHD.

TESTS FOR PHD	
Simplicity of the Design	The design of the system must be relatively simple because all patients may not be well-acquainted or comfortable with the use of modern technology. It must be user-friendly.
Efficiency	As a machine, it has to perform with high efficiency rate and do all the functions for which it is made.
Cost Effective	This machine must be relatively cheap, making it affordable to majority of the patients who use it. Ideally, it should be affordable to all sections of the society. Realistically, some members of the society will definitely need federal/charitable organizations' support to buy it.
Time	The treatment time it takes must be reasonably short. Some people may not dialyze themselves properly and completely if it takes too long.

Table continued on next page

Size	The size of the machine is critical, because it may neet to be carried along by patients when they travel.
Power Supply/ Battery Operated	It is absolutely essential that this machine can be operated even when there is no power, for example, while in transit.

SKILL 19.6 Analyzing the positive and negative effects of technology on individuals, society, and the environment

Science and technology, while distinct concepts, are closely related. Science attempts to investigate and explain the natural world, while technology attempts to solve human adaptation problems. Technology often results from the application of scientific discoveries and advances in technology that can increase the impact of scientific discoveries. For example, Watson and Crick used science to discover the structure of DNA and their discovery led to many biotechnological advances in the manipulation of DNA. These technological advances greatly influenced the medical and pharmaceutical fields. The success of Watson and Crick's experiments, however, was dependent on the technology available. Without the necessary technology, the experiments would not have been possible.

The combination of biology and technology has improved the human standard of living in many ways. However, the negative impact of increasing human life expectancy and population on the environment is problematic. In addition, advances in biotechnology (e.g., genetic engineering, cloning) produce ethical dilemmas that society must consider. Scientists use a variety of tools and technologies to perform tests, collect and display data, and analyze relationships. Examples of commonly used tools include computer-linked probes, spreadsheets, and graphing calculators.

Scientists can also transfer data and displays to computers for further analysis. Finally, scientists connect computer-linked probes, used to collect data, to graphing calculators to ease the collection, transmission, and analysis of data.

Sample Test Questions and Rationale

Average Rigor

1. **An appropriate method for graphically representing data to the scientific community would be _____.**

   A. computer-linked probes

   B. graphing calculators

   C. both A and B

   D. neither A nor B

Answer: C – both A and B

Rationale: Scientific information and/or experimental results must be communicated by clearly describing the information using accurate data, visual presentations (including bar/line/pie graphs), tables/charts, diagrams, artwork, power point presentation, and other appropriate media. Modern technology must be used whenever it is necessary. The method of communication must be suitable to the audience. Written communication is as important as oral communication. This is essential for submitting research papers to scientific journals, newspapers, other magazines etc.

COMPETENCY 20

UNDERSTAND THE RELATIONSHIPS AMONG AND COMMON THEMES THAT CONNECT MATHEMATICS, SCIENCE, AND TECHNOLOGY, AND THE APPLICATION OF KNOWLEDGE AND SKILLS IN THESE DISCIPLINES TO OTHER AREAS OF LEARNING

> **SKILL 20.1** **Making connections among the common themes of mathematics, science, and technology** (e.g., systems, models, magnitude and scale, equilibrium and stability, patterns of change)

The combination of science, mathematics, and technology forms the scientific endeavor and makes science a success. It is impossible to study science on its own without the support of other disciplines like mathematics, technology, geology, and physics.

Science is tentative. By definition it is searching for information by making educated guesses. It must be replicable. Another scientist must be able to achieve the same results under the same conditions at a later time. The term EMPIRICAL means it must be assessed through tests and observations. Science changes over time. Science is limited by the available technology. An example of this would be the relationship of the discovery of the cell and the invention of the microscope. As our technology improves, more hypotheses will become theories and, possibly, laws. Science is also limited by the data that can be collected. Data may be interpreted differently on different occasions. Science limitations cause explanations to be changeable as new technologies emerge. New technologies gather previously unavailable data and enable us to build upon current theories with new information.

> **EMPIRICAL:** assessed through tests and observations

Ancient history followed the GEOCENTRIC THEORY, which was displaced by the HELIOCENTRIC THEORY developed by Copernicus, Ptolemy, and Kepler. Newton's laws of motion by Sir Isaac Newton were based on mass, force, and acceleration, and state that the force of gravity between any two objects in the universe depends upon their mass and distance. These laws are still widely used today. In the twentieth century, Albert Einstein was the most outstanding scientist for his work on relativity, which led to his theory that $E = mc^2$. Early in the twentieth century, Alfred Wegener proposed his theory of continental drift, stating that continents moved away from the supercontinent, Pangaea. This theory was accepted in 1960s when more evidence was collected to support his theory. John Dalton and Lavosier made significant contributions in the

> **GEOCENTRIC THEORY:** having the Earth as the center

fields of atoms and matter. The Curies and Ernest Rutherford contributed greatly to radioactivity and the splitting of atom, which have lot of practical applications. Charles Darwin proposed his theory of evolution and Gregor Mendel's experiments on peas helped us to understand heredity. The most significant improvement was the industrial revolution in Britain, in which science was applied practically to increase the productivity and also introduced a number of social problems like child labor.

The nature of science primarily consists of three important elements:

1. The scientific world view. This includes some very important issues— for instance, it is possible to understand this highly organized world and its complexities with the help of latest technology. Scientific ideas are subject to change. After repeated experiments, a theory is established, but this theory could be changed or supported in future. Only laws that occur naturally do not change. Scientific knowledge may not be discarded but is modified— Albert Einstein didn't discard the Newtonian principles but modified them in his theory of relativity. Also, science can't answer all of our questions. We can't find answers to questions related to our beliefs, moral values, and norms.

2. Scientific inquiry. Scientific inquiry starts with a simple question. This simple question leads to information gathering, an educated guess otherwise known as HYPOTHESIS. To prove the hypothesis, an experiment has to be conducted, which yields data and the conclusion. All experiments must be repeated at least twice to get reliable results. Thus scientific inquiry leads to new knowledge or verifying established theories. Science requires proof or evidence. Science is dependent on accuracy, not on bias or prejudice. In science, there is no place for preconceived ideas or premeditated results. By using their senses and modern technology, scientists will be able to get reliable information. Science is a combination of logic and imagination. A scientist needs to think, imagine, and be able to reason.

> **HYPOTHESIS:** an educated guess that leads to information gathering

Science explains, reasons, and predicts. These three are interwoven and inseparable. While reasoning is absolutely important for science, there should be no bias or prejudice. Science is not authoritarian because it has been shown that scientific authority can be wrong. No one can determine or make decisions for others on any issue.

3. Scientific enterprise. Science is a complex activity involving various people and places. A scientist may work alone or in a laboratory, classroom or for that matter, anywhere. Mostly, it is a group activity requiring the social skills of cooperation, communication of results or findings, consultations, discussions, etc. Science demands a high degree of communication to the governments, funding authorities, and the public.

> *Connecting science, math and technology in the classroom:*
>
> *http://archives.math.utk.edu/k12.html*
>
> *http://www.hbsponline.com/resources/planlaba.pdf*
>
> *http://www.challenger.org/teachers/lessons/index.cfm*
>
> *http://www.challenger.org/teachers/tools/multimedia.cfm*

SYSTEMS AND MODELS COMMON TO ALL SCIENTIFIC DISCIPLINES	
Systems, Order, and Organization	Because the natural world is so complex, the study of science involves the organization of items into smaller groups based on interaction or interdependence. These groups are called systems. Examples of organization are the periodic table of elements and the five-kingdom classification scheme for living organisms. Examples of systems are the solar system, cardiovascular system, Newton's laws of force and motion, and the laws of conservation. Order refers to the behavior and measurability of organisms and events in nature. The arrangement of planets in the solar system and the life cycle of bacterial cells are examples of order.
Evidence, Models, and Explanation	Scientists use evidence and models to form explanations of natural events. Models are miniaturized representations of a larger event or system. Evidence is anything that furnishes proof.
Constancy, Change, and Measurement	Constancy and change describe the observable properties of natural organisms and events. Scientists use different systems of measurement to observe change and constancy. For example, the freezing and melting points of given substances and the speed of sound are constant under constant conditions. Growth, decay, and erosion are all examples of natural change.
Evolution and Equilibrium	Evolution is the process of change over a long period of time. While biological evolution is the most common example, one can also classify technological advancement, changes in the universe, and changes in the environment as evolution. Equilibrium is the state of balance between opposing forces of change. Homeostasis and ecological balance are examples of equilibrium.
Form and Function	Form and function are properties of organisms and systems that are closely related. The function of an object usually dictates its form and the form of an object usually facilitates its function. For example, the form of the heart (e.g., muscle, valves) allows it to perform its function of circulating blood through the body.

Sample Test Questions and Rationale

Easy

1. Which of the following scientists proposed the relative theory of $E = mc^2$?

   A. Albert Einstein

   B. Sir Isaac Newton

   C. Thomas Edison

   D. Charles Darwin

Answer: A – Albert Einstein

Rationale: Albert Einstein was the most outstanding scientist for his work on relativity, which led to his theory that $E = mc^2$. Sir Isaac Newton's laws of motion were based on mass, force and acceleration, and state that the force of gravity between any two objects in the universe depends upon their mass and distance.

SKILL Applying principles of mathematics, science, and technology to 20.2 model a given situation *(e.g., the movement of energy and nutrients between a food chain and the physical environment)*

All living organisms respond and adapt to their environments. Homeostasis is the result of regulatory mechanisms that help maintain an organism's internal environment within tolerable limits.

The molecular composition of the immediate environment outside of the organism is not the same as it is inside and the temperature outside may not be optimal for metabolic activity within the organism. Homeostasis is the control of these differences between internal and external environments. There are three homeostatic systems to regulate these differences.

1. OSMOREGULATION deals with maintenance of the appropriate level of water and salts in body fluids for optimum cellular functions.

2. EXCRETION is the elimination of metabolic waste products, including excess water, from the body.

3. THERMOREGULATION maintains the internal, or core, body temperature of the organism within a tolerable range for metabolic and cellular processes. For example, in humans and mammals, constriction, and dilation of blood vessels near the skin help maintain body temperature.

OSMOREGULATION: deals with maintenance of the appropriate level of water and salts in body fluids for optimum cellular functions

THERMO REGULATION: maintains the internal, or core, body temperature of the organism within a tolerable range for metabolic and cellular processes

Interactions of biotic and abiotic factors within a system to the flow of matter and energy

Biogeochemical cycling is the movement of chemicals between the biotic (living) and abiotic (nonliving) parts of an ecosystem. Respiration and photosynthesis play an important role in the cycling of oxygen and carbon. RESPIRATION is the process by which an individual organism uses oxygen and releases carbon dioxide to the atmosphere during energy producing reactions. PHOTOSYNTHESIS, the reverse of respiration, is the process in which an individual plant or microorganism uses the carbon from carbon dioxide to produce carbohydrates with oxygen as a by-product.

Two major forms of carbon in the environment are carbon dioxide gas in the atmosphere and organic macromolecules in living things. Photosynthesis by plants and microorganisms converts carbon dioxide to carbohydrates, removing carbon from the atmosphere and storing it as biomass. Conversely, aerobic and anaerobic respiration by plants, animals, and microorganisms returns carbon to the environment in the form of carbon dioxide or methane gas, respectively.

The main driving force in the oxygen cycle is photosynthesis. Plants and microorganisms perform photosynthesis to produce glucose, releasing oxygen gas to the environment as a by-product. Animals, plants, and microorganisms remove oxygen from the environment, using it to break down glucose in an energy yielding reaction that produces carbon dioxide and water.

> **RESPIRATION:** the process in which an individual organism uses oxygen and releases carbon dioxide to the atmosphere during energy producing reactions

> **PHOTOSYNTHESIS:** the process in which an individual plant or microorganism uses the carbon from carbon dioxide to produce carbohydrates with oxygen as a by-product

> **SKILL Apply principles of mathematics, science, and technology to**
> **20.3 explore phenomena from other areas of learning** *(e.g., applying statistical methodologies to examine census data)*

The fields of mathematics, science, and technology are fully integrated and allow us to observe and analyze data from within and between these different fields. An example of one such analysis would be the use of statistical methodologies to examine census data. Data limitations are the greatest factor influencing the outcome of statistical analyses. The consistency and quality of the data pool will have a direct impact on the integrity of the statistical analysis.

When considering census data, there are three basic statistical methods appropriate for the analysis.

1. Tracking and trend analysis. Examining time trends in census data is helpful in identifying the growth for a specific area. The changes in population over a specific period of time allow city planners to make appropriate decisions regarding zoning, parks and recreation, and utilities.

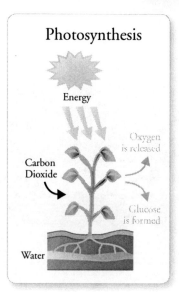

Photosynthesis

Energy

Oxygen is released

Carbon Dioxide

Glucose is formed

Water

2. Spatial analysis and geographic distribution. This analysis allows the researcher to find commonalities between population and other factors including health, wealth, education, etc. Such analysis allows for more in-depth understanding of the socio-economic indicators of a specific area.

3. Geographic correlation studies. These studies model the interrelationships of census data between population centers allowing us to compare and contrast different regions including rates of death and disease.

It is the mathematical field of statistics that allows us to examine scientific data and this is often done using computer technology. Computer programs continue to advance the level of analysis and comparison we may achieve with data such as census data. When used properly statistical analysis or any other research method allows us to link the fields of mathematics and science. Most research in the field of science is completed and analyzed using mathematic principals. They are more interdependent than not, and it is important to recognize the impact they have on one another. Other examples of this interconnectedness include the use of zero as a symbol in keeping track of time using calendars, binary numbers and computers, the mathematic of sound in creating Cochlear implants, and exponential growth when looking at the population and the environment.

SKILL 20.4 Design solutions to problems in the physical and social worlds using mathematical, scientific, and technological reasoning and procedures

Technological design is the identification of a problem and the application of scientific knowledge to solve the problem. The technological design process has five basic steps:

- Identify a problem

- Propose designs and choose between alternative solutions. Scientists often utilize simulations and models in evaluating possible solutions.

- Implement the proposed solution. Scientists use various tools depending on the problem, solution, and technology. They may use both physical tools and objects and computer software.

- Evaluate the solution and its consequences against predetermined criteria. Scientists must consider the negative consequences as well as the planned benefits.

- Report results. Scientists must communicate results in different ways — orally, written, models, diagrams, and demonstrations.

Current technology

Computer technology	Has greatly improved the collection and interpretation of scientific data. Molecular findings have been enhanced through the use of computer images. Technology has revolutionized access to data via the Internet and shared databases. The manipulation of data is enhanced by sophisticated software capabilities. Computer engineering advances have produced such products as MRIs and CT scans in medicine. Laser technology has numerous applications with refining precision.
Satellites	Have improved our ability to communicate and transmit radio and television signals. Navigational abilities have been greatly improved through the use of satellite signals. Sonar uses sound waves to locate objects and is especially useful underwater. The sound waves bounce off the object and are used to assist in location. Seismographs record vibrations in the earth and allow us to measure earthquake activity.

SKILL **Analyzing the effects of human activities** *(e.g., burning fossil fuels, clear-*
20.5 *cutting forests)* **on the environment and evaluating the use of science and technology in solving problems related to these effects**

RENEWABLE RESOURCE: one that is replaced naturally such as lumber

A RENEWABLE RESOURCE is one that is replaced naturally. Living renewable resources would be plants and animals. Plants are renewable because they grow and reproduce. Sometimes renewal of the resource doesn't keep up with the demand. Such is the case with trees. Since the housing industry uses lumber for frames and homebuilding, trees are often cut down faster than new ones can grow. Now there are specific tree farms. Special methods allow trees to grow faster.

A second renewable resource is animals. They renew by the process of reproduction. Some wild animals need protection on refuges. As the population of humans increases resources are used more quickly. Cattle are used for their hides and for food. Some animals like deer are killed for sport. Each state has an environmental protection agency with divisions of forest management and wildlife management.

Nonliving renewable resources would be water, air, and soil. Water is renewed in a natural cycle called the water cycle. Air is a mixture of gases. Oxygen is given off by plants and taken in by animals that in turn expel the carbon dioxide that the plants need. Soil is another renewable resource. Fertile soil is rich in minerals. When plants grow they remove the minerals and make the soil less fertile. Chemical treatments are one way or renewing the composition. It is also accomplished naturally when the plants decay back into the soil. The plant material is used to make compost to mix with the soil.

NONRENEWABLE RESOURCES are not easily replaced in a timely fashion. Minerals are nonrenewable resources. Quartz, mica, salt, and sulfur are some examples. Mining depletes these resources so society that may benefit. Glass is made from quartz, electronic equipment from mica, and salt has many uses. Sulfur is used in medicine, fertilizers, paper, and matches.

Metals are among the most widely used nonrenewable resource. Metals must be separated from the ore. Iron is our most important ore. Gold, silver, and copper are often found in a more pure form called native metals.

Identify causes and effects of pollutants

POLLUTANTS are impurities in air and water that may be harmful to life. Spills from barges carrying large quantities of oil pollute beaches and harm fish.

All acids contain hydrogen. Acidic substances from factories and car exhausts dissolve in rain water forming acid rain. ACID RAIN forms predominantly from pollutant oxides in the air (usually nitrogen-based NOx or sulfur-based SOx), which become hydrated into their acids (nitric or sulfuric acid). When the rain falls onto stone, the acids can react with metallic compounds and gradually wear the stone away.

RADIOACTIVITY is the breaking down of atomic nuclei by releasing particles or electromagnetic radiation. Radioactive nuclei give off radiation in the form of streams of particles or energy. Alpha particles are positively charged particles consisting of two protons and two neutrons. It is the slowest form of radiation. It can be stopped by paper! Beta particles are electrons. It is produced when a neutron in the nucleus breaks up into a proton and an electron. The proton remains inside the nucleus, increasing its atomic number by one, but the electron is given off. They can be stopped by aluminum.

Gamma rays are electromagnetic waves with extremely short wavelengths. They have no mass. They have no charge so they are not deflected by an electric field. Gamma rays travel at the speed of light. It takes a thick block of lead to stop them.

Uranium is the source of radiation and therefore is radioactive. Marie Curie discovered new elements called radium and polonium that actually give off more radiation than uranium.

NONRENEWABLE RESOURCE: not easily replaced in a timely fashion such as oil, iron, gold

POLLUTANTS: impurities in air and water that may be harmful to life

ACID RAIN: rains containing acids that form in the atmosphere when industrial gas emissions combine with water

RADIOACTIVITY: the breaking down of atomic nuclei by releasing particles or electromagnetic radiation

The major concern with radioactivity is in the case of a nuclear disaster. Medical misuse is also a threat. Radioactivity ionizes the air it travels through. It is strong enough to kill cancer cells or dangerous enough to cause illness or even death. Gamma rays can penetrate the body and damage cells. Protective clothing is needed when working with gamma rays. Electricity from nuclear energy uses uranium 235. The devastation of the Russian nuclear power plant disaster in Chernobyl caused entire regions to be evacuated as the damage to the land and food source will last for hundreds of years.

DOMAIN IV
SOCIAL STUDIES

Enhanced features only available in our ebook edition:

 eStickynotes: allows you take digital notes anywhere in the ebook edition. It further allows you to aggregate and print all enotes for easy studying.

 eFlashcards: a digital representation of a card represented with words, numbers or symbols or any combination of each and briefly displayed as part of a learning drill. eFlashcards takes away the burden of carrying around traditional cards that could easily be disarranged, dropped, or soiled.

 More Sample Tests: more ways to assess how much you know and how much further you need to study. Ultimately, makes you more prepared and attain mastery in the skills and techniques of passing the test the FIRST TIME!

Visit www.XAMonline.com
and click on ebook.

PERSONALIZED STUDY PLAN

PAGE	COMPETENCY AND SKILL	KNOWN MATERIAL/ SKIP IT	BRIEFLY REVIEW eSTICKYNOTES	MAKE eFLASHCARDS	TAKE ADDITIONAL SAMPLE TESTS
233	**21: Major Historical Themes in the United States and New York**	☐	☐	☐	☐
	21.1: Conceptual historical terminology	☐	☐	☐	☐
	21.2: Social effects of major historical developments	☐	☐	☐	☐
	21.3: Ancient civilizations	☐	☐	☐	☐
	21.4: Historical periodization	☐	☐	☐	☐
	21.5: European and indigenous cultures	☐	☐	☐	☐
	21.6: Individual and group contributions in history	☐	☐	☐	☐
265	**22: Geographic Concepts and Phenomenon**	☐	☐	☐	☐
	22.1: Important geographic terms and concepts	☐	☐	☐	☐
	22.2: Six essential elements of geography	☐	☐	☐	☐
	22.3: Physical characteristics of the Earth's surface	☐	☐	☐	☐
	22.4: Social, political, cultural, and religious systems	☐	☐	☐	☐
	22.5: Influence of demographic changes	☐	☐	☐	☐
	22.6: Impact of human activity on the environment	☐	☐	☐	☐
285	**23: Human Development and Interactions**	☐	☐	☐	☐
	23.1: Social phenomenon related to intercultural understanding	☐	☐	☐	☐
	23.2: Personal identity	☐	☐	☐	☐
	23.3: Development and transmission of culture	☐	☐	☐	☐
	23.4: Social groups and institutions	☐	☐	☐	☐
	23.5: Individual and group beliefs	☐	☐	☐	☐
	23.6: Social and cultural change	☐	☐	☐	☐
290	**24: Historical and Contemporary Developments**	☐	☐	☐	☐
	24.1: Important economic and political terms	☐	☐	☐	☐
	24.2: Basic structure and ideas of the U.S. economic system	☐	☐	☐	☐
	24.3: Major models of economic organization	☐	☐	☐	☐
	24.4: Key features of the American constitutional democracy	☐	☐	☐	☐
	24.5: Differing perspectives on economics and politics	☐	☐	☐	☐
	24.6: U.S. influence on other nations	☐	☐	☐	☐
300	**25: Citizenship**	☐	☐	☐	☐
	25.1: Personal and political rights	☐	☐	☐	☐
	25.2: Core values of the U.S. democratic system	☐	☐	☐	☐
	25.3: U.S. election process and parties	☐	☐	☐	☐
	25.4: Citizenship in a democratic society	☐	☐	☐	☐
	25.5: Rights and responsibilities of individuals	☐	☐	☐	☐
	25.6: Twentieth century U.S. political life	☐	☐	☐	☐

PERSONALIZED STUDY PLAN

PAGE	COMPETENCY AND SKILL	KNOWN MATERIAL/ SKIP IT	BRIEFLY REVIEW eSTICKYNOTES	MAKE eFLASHCARDS	TAKE ADDITIONAL SAMPLE TESTS
320	**26: Social Studies Skills**	☐	☐	☐	☐
	26.1: Evaluating historical data	☐	☐	☐	☐
	26.2: Mapping geographical information	☐	☐	☐	☐
	26.3: Information in social studies	☐	☐	☐	☐
	26.4: Interpreting graphic representations	☐	☐	☐	☐
	26.5: Historical narrative	☐	☐	☐	☐

COMPETENCY 21

UNDERSTAND MAJOR IDEAS, ERAS, THEMES, DEVELOPMENTS, AND TURNING POINTS IN THE HISTORY OF NEW YORK STATE, THE UNITED STATES, AND THE WORLD

SKILL 21.1 Defining important conceptual terms and using them to analyze general historical phenomena and specific historical events

History is the study of the past, especially the aspects of the human past, political and economic events as well as cultural and social conditions. Students study history through textbooks, research, field trips to museums and historical sights, and other methods. Most nations set the requirements in history to study the country's heritage, usually to develop an awareness and feeling of loyalty and patriotism. History is generally divided into the three main divisions: **time periods**, **nations**, and **specialized topics**. Study is accomplished through research, reading, and writing.

In Europe, the system of FEUDALISM was a system of loyalty and protection. The strong protected the weak that returned the service with farm labor, military service, and loyalty. Life was lived out on a vast estate, owned by a nobleman and his family, called a "manor." It was a complete village supporting a few hundred people, mostly peasants. Improved tools and farming methods made life more bearable although most never left the manor or traveled from their village during their lifetime.

> **FEUDALISM:** system of loyalty and protection whereby the strong protected the weak in return for labor and service

In feudal societies a very small number of people (or no one) owned land. Instead, they held it as a hereditary trust from some social or political superior in return for services. The superiors were a small percentage of the people, a fighting and ruling aristocracy. The vast majority of the people were simply workers. One of the largest landowners of the time was the Roman Catholic Church. It was estimated that during the twelfth and thirteenth centuries the Church controlled one third of the useable land in Western Europe.

Also coming into importance at this time was the era of knighthood and its code of chivalry as well as the tremendous influence of the Roman Catholic Church. Until the period of the Renaissance, the Church was the only place where people could be educated. The Bible and other books were hand-copied by monks in the monasteries. Cathedrals were built and were decorated with art depicting religious subjects.

> *Lesson plans and resources for teaching history:*
>
> http://www.csun.edu/~hcedu013/plans.html
>
> HTUhttp://www.emsc.nysed.gov/guides/social/
>
> http://www.historyteacher.net/

With the increase in trade and travel, cities sprang up and began to grow. Craft workers in the cities developed their skills to a high degree, eventually organizing guilds to protect the quality of the work and to regulate the buying and selling of their products. City government developed and flourished centered on strong town councils. Active in city government and the town councils were the wealthy businessmen who made up the rising middle class.

The end of the feudal manorial system was sealed by the outbreak and spread of the infamous Black Death, which killed over one-third of the total population of Europe. Those who survived and were skilled in any job or occupation were in demand and many serfs or peasants found freedom and, for that time, a decidedly improved standard of living. Strong nation-states became powerful and people developed a renewed interest in life and learning.

From its beginnings, Japan morphed into an imperial form of government, with the divine emperor being able to do no wrong and, therefore, serving for life. Kyoto, the capital, became one of the largest and most powerful cities in the world. Slowly, though, as in Europe, the rich and powerful landowners, the nobles, grew powerful. Eventually, the nobles had more power than the emperor which required an attitude change in the minds of the Japanese people.

The nobles were lords of great lands and were called Daimyos. They were of the highest social class and people of lower social classes worked for them, including the lowly peasants, who had few privileges other than being allowed to work for the great men that the Daimyos told everyone they were. The Daimyos had serving them warriors known as Shogun, who were answerable only to the Daimyo. The Shogun code of honor was an exemplification of the overall Japanese belief that every man was a soldier and a gentleman. The contradiction that the emerging social classes identified didn't seem to get noticed much, nor did the needs of women.

The main economic difference between imperial and feudal Japan was that the money that continued to flow into the country from trade with China, Korea, and other Asian countries and from good, old-fashioned plundering on the high seas, made its way into the pockets of the Daimyos rather than the emperor's coffers.

Feudalism developed in Japan later than it did in Europe and lasted longer as well. Japan dodged one huge historical bullet when a huge Mongol invasion was driven away by the famed kamikaze, or "divine wind," in the twelfth century. Japan was thus free to continue to develop itself as it saw fit and to refrain from interacting with the West, especially. This isolation lasted until the nineteenth century.

During the eighteenth and especially the nineteenth centuries, NATIONALISM emerged as a powerful force in Europe and elsewhere in the world. Strictly speaking, nationalism was a belief in one's own nation, or country, people. The people of the European nations began to think in terms of a nation of people who had similar beliefs, concerns, and needs. This was partly a reaction to a growing discontent with the autocratic governments of the day and also just a general realization that there was more to life than the individual. People could feel a part of something like their nation, making themselves more than just an insignificant soul struggling to survive.

> **NATIONALISM:** a belief in one's own nation, or country, people

Nationalism precipitated several changes in government, most notably in France; it also brought large groups of people together, as with the unifications of Germany and Italy. What it didn't do, however, is provide sufficient outlets for this sudden rise in national fervor. Especially in the 1700s and 1800s, European powers and people began looking to Africa and Asia in order to find colonies: rich sources of goods, trade, and cheap labor. Africa, especially, suffered at the hands of European imperialists, bent on expanding their reach outside the borders of Europe. Asia suffered colonial expansion, most notably in India and Southeast Asia.

This colonial expansion would come back to haunt the European imperialists in a very big way, as colonial skirmishes spilled over into alliance that dragged the European powers into World War I. Some of these colonial battles were still being fought as late as the start of World War II as well.

In 1957, the formation of the Southern Christian Leadership Conference by Martin Luther King, Jr., John Duffy, Rev. C. D. Steele, Rev. T. J. Jemison, Rev. Fred Shuttlesworth, Ella Baker, A. Philip Randolph, Bayard Rustin, and Stanley Levison provided training and assistance to local efforts to fight segregation. Nonviolence was its central doctrine and its major method of fighting segregation and racism, a belief or doctrine that biological differences determine success or cultural achievement and that one's own race is superior and has the right to rule over others.

Sample Test Questions and Rationale

Easy

1. **The end of the feudal manorial system was caused by:**

   A. the Civil War

   B. the Black Death

   C. the Christian riots

   D. westward expansion

   Answer: B – The Black Death

   Rationale: The end of the feudal manorial system was sealed by the outbreak and spread of the infamous Black Death, which killed over one-third of the total population of Europe.

2. **In 1957 the formation of the Southern Christian Leadership Conference was started by:**

   A. Martin Luther King, Jr

   B. Rev. T. J. Jemison

   C. Ella Baker

   D. All of the above

   Answer: D – All of the above

   Rationale: In 1957 the formation of the Southern Christian Leadership Conference by Martin Luther King, Jr., John Duffy, Rev. C. D. Steele, Rev. T. J. Jemison, Rev. Fred Shuttlesworth, Ella Baker, A. Philip Randolph, Bayard Rustin and Stanley Levison provided training and assistance to local efforts to fight segregation.

SKILL 21.2 Analyzing the social effects of major developments in human history

SCIENTIFIC REVOLUTION: characterized by a shift in scientific approach and ideas

The SCIENTIFIC REVOLUTION was characterized by a shift in scientific approach and ideas. Near the end of the sixteenth century, Galileo Galilei introduced a radical approach to the study of motion. He moved from attempts to explain why objects move the way they do and began to use experiments to describe precisely how they move. He also used experimentation to describe how forces affect nonmoving objects. Other scientists continued in the same approach. This was the period when experiments dominated scientific study. This method was particularly applied to the study of physics.

The AGRICULTURAL REVOLUTION occurred first in England. It was marked by experimentation that resulted in increased production of crops from the land and a new and more technical approach to the management of agriculture. The revolution in agricultural management and production was hugely enhanced by the industrial revolution and the invention of the steam engine. The introduction of steam-powered tractors greatly increased crop production and significantly decreased labor costs. Developments in agriculture were also enhanced by the scientific revolution and the learning from experimentation that led to philosophies of crop rotation and soil enrichment. Improved system of irrigation and harvesting also contributed to the growth of agricultural production.

The INDUSTRIAL REVOLUTION, which began in Great Britain and spread elsewhere, was the development of power-driven machinery (fueled by coal and steam) leading to the accelerated growth of industry with large factories replacing homes and small workshops as work centers. The lives of people changed drastically and a largely agricultural society changed to an industrial one. In Western Europe, the period of empire and colonialism began. The industrialized nations seized and claimed parts of Africa and Asia in an effort to control and provide the raw materials needed to feed the industries and machines in the "mother country." Later developments included power based on electricity and internal combustion, replacing coal and steam.

The INFORMATION REVOLUTION refers to the sweeping changes during the latter half of the twentieth century as a result of technological advances and a new respect for the knowledge or information provided by trained, skilled, and experienced professionals in a variety of fields. This approach to understanding a number of social and economic changes in global society arose from the ability to make computer technology both accessible and affordable. In particular, the development of the computer chip has led to such technological advances as the Internet, the cell phone, cybernetics, wireless communication, and the related ability to disseminate and access a massive amount of information quite readily.

In terms of economic theory and segmentation, it is now very much the norm to think of three basic economic sectors: agriculture and mining, manufacturing, and "services." Indeed, labor is now often divided between manual labor and informational labor. The fact that businesses are involved in the production and distribution, processing and transmission of information has, according to some, created a new business sector.

The Information Revolution has clearly changed modern life in many ways, such as the creation of devices and processes that actually control much of the world as it is experienced by the average person. It has most certainly revolutionized the entertainment industry, as well as influencing the way people spend their time. In education, new technology has made information on virtually any subject instantly accessible. It has also thoroughly altered the minute-to-minute knowledge people have of world events. Sixty years ago, news from the war front became available by radio for the first time. Visual images, however, were primarily

Outstanding scientists of the period included:

- Johannes Kepler
- Evangelista Torricelli
- Blaise Pascal
- Isaac Newton
- Gottfried Leibniz

AGRICULTURAL REVOLUTION: marked by experimentation that resulted in increased production of crops from the land and a new and more technical approach to the management of agriculture

INDUSTRIAL REVOLUTION: the development of power-driven machinery leading to the accelerated growth of industry with large factories replacing homes and small workshops as work centers

INFORMATION REVOLUTION: the sweeping changes during the latter half of the twentieth century as a result of technological advances and a new respect for the knowledge or information provided by trained, skilled and experienced professionals in a variety of fields

available through the weekly newsreels shown in motion picture theaters. Today, live pictures from the battlefield are instantly available to people, no matter where they are. This technology has also made it possible for "smart wars" to be fought, reducing the number of civilian casualties.

SKILL 21.3 Understanding major political, social, economic, and geographic characteristics of ancient civilizations and the connections and interactions among these civilizations

---

PREHISTORY: the period of man's achievements before the development of writing

PREHISTORY is defined as the period of man's achievements before the development of writing. In the Stone Age cultures, there were three different periods:

- Lower Paleolithic Period, with the use of crude tools.
- Upper Paleolithic Period, exhibiting a greater variety of better-made tools and implements, the wearing of clothing, highly organized group life, and skills in art.
- Neolithic Period, which showed domesticated animals, food production, the arts of knitting, spinning and weaving cloth, starting fires through friction, building houses rather than living in caves, the development of institutions including the family, religion, and a form of government or the origin of the state.

Ancient civilizations were those cultures which developed to a greater degree and were considered advanced. These included the following eleven with their major accomplishments.

Egypt

Egypt made numerous significant contributions including construction of the great pyramids; development of hieroglyphic writing; preservation of bodies after death; making paper from papyrus; contributing to developments in arithmetic and geometry; the invention of the method of counting in groups of 1–10 (the decimal system); completion of a solar calendar; and laying the foundation for science and astronomy.

CODE OF HAMMURABI: a Babylonian code of laws

The ancient civilization of the **Sumerians** invented the wheel; developed irrigation through use of canals, dikes, and devices for raising water; devised the system of cuneiform writing; learned to divide time; and built large boats for trade. The Babylonians devised the famous CODE OF HAMMURABI, a code of laws.

The ancient **Assyrians** were warlike and aggressive due to a highly organized military and used horse drawn chariots.

The **Hebrews**, also known as the ancient Israelites, instituted MONOTHEISM, which is the worship of one God, Yahweh, and combined the sixty-six books of the Hebrew and Christian Greek scriptures into the Bible we have today.

> **MONOTHEISM:** the worship of one God

The **Minoans** had a system of writing using symbols to represent syllables in words. They built palaces with multiple levels containing many rooms, water, and sewage systems with flush toilets, bathtubs, hot and cold running water, and bright paintings on the walls.

The **Mycenaeans** changed the Minoan writing system to aid their own language and used symbols to represent syllables.

The **Phoenicians** were sea traders well known for their manufacturing skills in glass and metals and the development of their famous purple dye. They became so very proficient in the skill of navigation that they were able to sail by the stars at night. Further, they devised an alphabet using symbols to represent single sounds, which was an improved extension of the Egyptian writing system.

India

In India, the caste system was developed, the principle of zero in mathematics was discovered, and the major religion of Hinduism was begun. In India, Hinduism was a continuing influence along with the rise of Buddhism. Industry and commerce developed along with extensive trading with the Near East. Outstanding advances in the fields of science and medicine were made along with being one of the first to be active in navigation and maritime enterprises during this time.

China

China began building the Great Wall, practiced crop rotation and terrace farming, increased the importance of the silk industry, and developed caravan routes across Central Asia for extensive trade. Also, the Chinese increased proficiency in rice cultivation and developed a written language based on drawings or pictographs (no alphabet symbolizing sounds as each word or character had a form different from all others). China is considered by some historians to be the oldest uninterrupted civilization in the world and was in existence around the same time as the ancient civilizations founded in **Egypt**, **Mesopotamia**, and the **Indus Valley**. The Chinese studied nature and weather; stressed the importance of education, family, and a strong central government; followed the religions of Buddhism, Confucianism, and Taoism; and invented such things as gunpowder, paper, printing, and the magnetic compass.

The **Tang Dynasty** extended from 618 to 907. Its capital was the most heavily populated of any city in the world at the time. Buddhism was adopted by the imperial family (Li) and became an integral part of Chinese culture. The emperor, however, feared the monasteries and began to take action against them in the tenth century. Confucianism experienced a rebirth during the time of this dynasty as an instrument of state administration.

Following a civil war, the central government lost control of local areas. Warlords arose in 907, and China was divided into north and south. These areas came to be ruled by short-lived minor dynasties. A major political accomplishment of this period was the creation of a class of career government officials, who functioned between the populace and the government. This class of "SCHOLAR-OFFICIALS" continued to fulfill this function in government and society until 1911.

The period of the Tang Dynasty is generally considered a pinnacle of Chinese civilization. Through contact with the Middle East and India, the period of the Tang Dynasty was marked by great creativity in many areas. Block printing was invented, and made much information and literature available to wide audiences.

In science, astronomers calculated the paths of the sun and the moon and the movements of the constellations. This facilitated the development of the calendar. In agriculture, such technologies as cultivating the land by setting it on fire, the curved-shaft plow, separate cultivation of seedlings, and sophisticated irrigation system increased productivity. Hybrid breeds of horses and mules were created to strengthen the labor supply. In medicine, there were achievements like the understanding of the circulatory system and the digestive system and great advances in pharmacology. Ceramics was another area in which great advances were made. A new type of glazing was invented that gave Tang Dynasty porcelain and earthenware its unique appearance through three-colored glazing.

In literature, the poetry of the period is generally considered the best in the entire history of Chinese literature. The rebirth of Confucianism led to the publication of many commentaries on the classical writings. Encyclopedias on several subjects were produced, as well as histories and philosophical works.

> **SCHOLAR-OFFICIALS:** a class of career government officials, who functioned between the populace and the government

Persia

The ancient Persians developed an alphabet; contributed the religions/philosophies of **Zoroastrianism**, **Mithraism**, and **Gnosticism**; and allowed conquered peoples to retain their own customs, laws, and religions.

Greece

The classical civilization of Greece reached the highest levels in man's achievements based on the foundations already laid by such ancient groups as the Egyptians, Phoenicians, Minoans, and Mycenaeans.

Among the more important contributions of Greece were the Greek alphabet derived from the Phoenician letters that formed the basis for the Roman alphabet and our present-day alphabet. Extensive trading and colonization resulted in the spread of the Greek civilization. The love of sports, with emphasis on a sound body, led to the tradition of the Olympic Games. Greece was responsible for the rise of independent, strong city-states. Note the complete contrast between independent, freedom-loving Athens with its practice of pure democracy (i.e., direct, personal, active participation in government by qualified citizens) and the rigid, totalitarian, militaristic Sparta. Other important areas that the Greeks are credited with influencing include drama, epic and lyric poetry, fables, myths centered on the many gods and goddesses, science, astronomy, medicine, mathematics, philosophy, art, architecture, and recording historical events. The conquests of Alexander the Great spread Greek ideas to the areas he conquered and brought to the Greek world many ideas from Asia including the value of ideas, wisdom, curiosity, and the desire to learn as much about the world as possible.

A most interesting and significant characteristic of the Greek, Hellenic, and Roman civilizations was SECULARISM where emphasis shifted away from religion to the state. Men were not absorbed in or dominated by religion as had been the case in Egypt and the nations located in Mesopotamia. Religion and its leaders did not dominate the state and its authority was greatly diminished.

> **SECULARISM:** when emphasis shifts away from religion to the state

Japan

Civilization in Japan appeared during this time, having borrowed much of their culture from China. It was the last of these classical civilizations to develop. Although they used, accepted, and copied Chinese art, law, architecture, dress, and writing, the Japanese refined these into their own unique way of life, including incorporating the religion of Buddhism into their culture.

Africa

The civilizations in Africa south of the Sahara were developing the refining and use of iron, especially for farm implements and later for weapons. Trading was overland using camels and at important seaports. The Arab influence was extremely important, as was their later contact with Indians, Christian Nubians, and Persians. In fact, their trading activities were probably the most important factor in the spread of and assimilation of different ideas and stimulation of cultural growth.

Vikings

The Vikings had a lot of influence at this time, spreading their ideas and knowledge of trade routes and sailing, accomplished first through their conquests and later through trade.

Byzantium and the Saracens

In other parts of the world were the Byzantine and Saracenic (or Islamic) civilizations, both dominated by religion. The major contributions of the Saracens were in the areas of science and philosophy. Included were accomplishments in astronomy, mathematics, physics, chemistry, medicine, literature, art, trade, manufacturing, agriculture, and a marked influence on the Renaissance period of history. The Byzantines (Christians) made important contributions in art and the preservation of Greek and Roman achievements including architecture (especially in Eastern Europe and Russia), the Code of Justinian and Roman law.

Ghana

The ancient empire of Ghana occupied an area that is now known as Northern Senegal and Southern Mauritania. There is no absolute certainty regarding the origin of this empire. Oral history dates the rise of the empire to the seventh century BCE. Most believe, however, that the date should be placed much later. Many believe the nomads who were herding animals on the fringes of the desert posed a threat to the early Soninke people, who were an agricultural community. In times of drought, it is believed the nomads raided the agricultural villages for water and places to pasture their herds. To protect themselves, it is believed that these farming communities formed a loose confederation that eventually became the empire of ancient Ghana.

The empire's economic vitality was determined by geographical location. It was situated midway between the desert, which was the major source of salt, and the gold fields. This location along the trade routes of the camel caravans provided exceptional opportunity for economic development. The caravans brought copper, salt, dried fruit, clothing, manufactured goods, etc. For these goods, the people of Ghana traded kola nuts, leather goods, gold, hides, ivory, and slaves. In addition, the empire collected taxes on every trade item that entered the boundaries of the empire. With the revenue from the trade goods tax, the empire supported a government, an army that protected the trade routes and the borders, the maintenance of the capital, and primary market centers. But it was control of the gold fields that gave the empire political power and economic prosperity. The location of the gold fields was a carefully guarded secret. By the tenth century, Ghana was very rich and controlled an area about the size of the state of Texas. Demand for this gold sharply increased in the ninth and tenth centuries as the Islamic states of Northern Africa began to mint coins. As the gold trade expanded, so did the empire. The availability of local iron ore enabled the early people of the Ghana kingdom to make more efficient farm implements and effective weapons.

Sample Test Questions and Rationale

Average Rigor

1. **This country is considered by some historians to be the oldest uninterrupted civilization in the world.**

    A. Japan

    B. China

    C. Canada

    D. Mexico

Answer: B – China

Rationale: China is considered by some historians to be the oldest uninterrupted civilization in the world and was in existence around the same time as the ancient civilizations founded in Egypt, Mesopotamia, and the Indus Valley.

SKILL 21.4 **Examining reasons for organizing periods of history in different ways and comparing alternative interpretations of key events and issues in New York State, U.S., and world history**

The practice of dividing time into a number of discrete periods or blocks of time is called PERIODIZATION. Because history is continuous, all systems of periodization are arbitrary to a greater or lesser extent. However, dividing time into segments facilitates understanding of changes that occur over time and identifying similarities of events, knowledge, and experience within the defined period. Further, some divisions of time into these periods apply only under specific circumstances.

PERIODIZATION: the practice of dividing time into a number of discrete periods or blocks of time

Divisions of time may be determined by date, by cultural advances or changes, by historical events, by the influence of particular individuals or groups, or by geography. The "World War II" era defines a particular period of time in which key historical, political, social, and economic events occurred. The "Jacksonian Era," however, has meaning only in terms of American history. Defining the "Romantic period" makes sense only in England, Europe, and countries under their direct influence.

Many of the divisions of time that are commonly used are open to some controversy and discussion. The use of BC and AD dating, for example, has clear reference only in societies that account time according to the Christian calendar. Similarly, "the year of the pig" has greatest meaning in China.

An example of the kind of questions that can be raised about designations of time periods can be seen in the use of "Victorian." Is it possible to speak of a Victorian era beyond England? Is literature that is written in the style of the English poets and writers "Victorian" if it is written beyond the borders of England? Some designations also carry both positive and negative connotations. "Victorian" is an example of potential negative connotations, as well. The term is often used to refer to class conflict, sexual repression, and heavy industry. These might be negative connotations. The term "Renaissance" is generally read with positive connotations.

Sometimes several designations can be applied to the same period. The period known as the "Elizabethan Period" in English history is also called the "English Renaissance." In some cases the differences in designation refer primarily to the specific aspect of history that is being considered. For example, one designation may be applied to a specific period of time when one is analyzing cultural history, while a different designation is applied to the same period of time when considering military history.

Civil War

In 1833, Congress lowered tariffs, this time at a level acceptable to South Carolina. Although President Jackson believed in states' rights, he also firmly believed in and determined to keep the preservation of the Union. A constitutional crisis had been averted but sectional divisions were getting deeper and more pronounced. The abolition movement was growing rapidly, becoming an important issue in the North. The slavery issue was at the root of every problem, crisis, event, decision, and struggle from then on. The next crisis involved the issue concerning Texas. By 1836, Texas was an independent republic with its own constitution. During its fight for independence, Americans were sympathetic to and supportive of the Texans and some recruited volunteers who crossed into Texas to help the struggle. Problems arose when the state petitioned Congress for statehood. Texas wanted to allow slavery but Northerners in Congress opposed admission to the Union because it would disrupt the balance between free and slave states and give Southerners in Congress increased influence.

A few years later, Congress took up consideration of new territories between Missouri and present-day Idaho. Again, heated debate over permitting slavery in these areas flared up. Those opposed to slavery used the MISSOURI COMPROMISE to prove their point showing that the land being considered for territories was part of the area the Compromise had been designated as banned to slavery. On May 25, 1854, Congress passed the infamous KANSAS-NEBRASKA ACT which nullified the provision creating the territories of Kansas and Nebraska. This provided for the people of these two territories to decide for themselves whether or not to permit slavery to exist there. Feelings were so deep and divided that any further attempts to compromise would meet with little, if any, success. Political and social turmoil swirled everywhere. Kansas was called "Bleeding Kansas" because of the extreme violence and bloodshed throughout the territory because two governments existed there, one pro-slavery and the other anti-slavery.

The Supreme Court, in 1857, handed down a decision guaranteed to cause explosions throughout the country. Dred Scott was a slave whose owner had taken him from slave state Missouri, then to free state Illinois, into Minnesota Territory, free under the provisions of the Missouri Compromise, then finally back to slave state Missouri. Abolitionists pursued the dilemma by presenting a court case, stating that since Scott had lived in a free state and free territory, he was in actuality a free man. Two lower courts had ruled before the Supreme Court became involved, one ruling in favor and one against. The Supreme Court decided that residing in a free state and free territory did not make Scott a free man because Scott (and all other slaves) was not a U.S. citizen or a state citizen of Missouri. Therefore, he did not have the right to sue in state or federal courts.

The Court went a step further and ruled that the old Missouri Compromise was now unconstitutional because Congress did not have the power to prohibit slavery in the Territories.

In 1858, Abraham Lincoln and Stephen A. Douglas were running for the office of U.S. Senator from Illinois and participated in a series of debates, which directly affected the outcome of the 1860 Presidential election. Douglas, a Democrat, was up for reelection and knew that if he won this race, he had a good chance of becoming President in 1860. Lincoln, a Republican, was not an abolitionist but he believed that slavery was morally wrong and he supported the Republican Party principle that slavery must not be allowed to extend any further.

The final straw came with the election of Lincoln to the presidency the next year. Due to a split in the Democratic Party, there were four candidates from four political parties. With Lincoln receiving a minority of the popular vote and a majority of electoral votes, the Southern states, one by one, voted to secede from the Union, as they had promised they would do if Lincoln and the Republicans were victorious. The die was cast.

MISSOURI COMPROMISE: Congressional solution to the addition of slave states to the union; it forbade slavery to areas north of latitude 36° 30'N

KANSAS-NEBRASKA ACT: Congressional act that allowed the territories of Kansas and Nebraska to decide for themselves whether to allow slavery; it repealed the Missouri Compromise

It is ironic that South Carolina was the first state to secede from the Union and the first shots of the war were fired on Fort Sumter in Charleston Harbor. Both sides quickly prepared for war. The North had more in its favor: a larger population; superiority in finances and transportation facilities; manufacturing, agricultural, and natural resources. The North possessed most of the nation's gold, had about ninety-two percent of all industries, and almost all known supplies of copper, coal, iron, and various other minerals. Most of the nation's railroads were in the North and Midwest, men and supplies could be moved wherever needed; food could be transported from the farms of the Midwest to workers in the East and to soldiers on the battlefields. Trade with nations overseas could go on as usual due to control of the navy and the merchant fleet. The Northern states numbered twenty-four and included western states (California and Oregon) and border states (Maryland, Delaware, Kentucky, Missouri, and West Virginia).

The eleven states of the Southern Confederacy were:

- South Carolina
- Mississippi
- North Carolina
- Georgia
- Louisiana
- Tennessee
- Florida
- Texas
- Arkansas
- Alabama
- Virginia

Although outnumbered in population, the South was completely confident of victory. They knew that all they had to do was fight a defensive war and protect their own territory.

The North had to invade and defeat an area almost the size of Western Europe. Another advantage of the South was that a number of its best officers had graduated from the U.S. Military Academy at West Point and had had long years of army experience. Many had exercised varying degrees of command in the Indian Wars and the war with Mexico. Men from the South were conditioned to living outdoors and were more familiar with horses and firearms than men from northeastern cities. Since cotton was such an important crop, Southerners felt that British and French textile mills were so dependent on raw cotton that they would be forced to help the Confederacy in the war.

The South won decisively until the Battle of Gettysburg, July 1 through 3, 1863. Until Gettysburg, Lincoln's commanders, McDowell and McClellan, were less than desirable, Burnside and Hooker, not what was needed. Lee, on the other hand, had many able officers: Jackson and Stuart were depended on heavily by him. Jackson died at Chancellorsville and was replaced by Longstreet. Lee decided to invade the North and depended on J.E.B. Stuart and his cavalry to keep him informed of the location of Union troops and their strengths.

The day after Gettysburg, on July 4, Vicksburg, Mississippi, surrendered to Union General Ulysses Grant, thus severing the western Confederacy from the eastern part. In September 1863, the Confederacy won its last important victory at Chickamauga. In November, the Union victory at Chattanooga made it possible for Union troops to go into Alabama and Georgia, splitting the eastern Confederacy in two. Lincoln gave Grant command of all Northern armies in March of 1864. Grant led his armies into battles in Virginia while Phil Sheridan and his cavalry did as much damage as possible. In a skirmish at a place called Yellow Tavern, Virginia, Sheridan's and Stuart's forces met. Stuart was fatally wounded.

The Civil War took more American lives than any other war in history, the South losing one-third of its soldiers in battle compared to about one-sixth for the North. More than half of the total deaths were caused by disease and the horrendous conditions of field hospitals. Both sides paid a tremendous economic price but the South suffered more severely from direct damages. Destruction was pervasive with towns, farms, trade, industry, lives, and homes of men, women, children all destroyed and an entire Southern way of life was lost. The South had no voice in the political, social, and cultural affairs of the nation, lessening to a great degree the influence of the more traditional Southern ideals. The Northern Yankee Protestant ideals of hard work, education, and economic freedom became the standard of the United States and helped influence the development of the nation into a modem, industrial power.

The effects of the Civil War were tremendous. It changed the methods of waging war and has been called the first modern war. It introduced weapons and tactics that, when improved later, were used extensively in wars of the late 1800s and 1900s.

- Civil War soldiers were the first to fight in trenches, first to fight under a unified command, and first to wage a defense called "major cordon defense," a strategy of advance on all fronts

- They were also the first to use repeating and breech loading weapons

- Observation balloons were first used during the war along with submarines, ironclad ships, and mines

- Telegraphy and railroads were put to use first in the Civil War

It was considered a modern war because of the vast destruction and was "total war," involving the use of all resources of the opposing sides. There was no way it could have ended other than total defeat and unconditional surrender of one side or the other.

By executive proclamation and constitutional amendment, slavery was officially ended, although there remained deep prejudice and racism, still raising its ugly head today. Also, the Union was preserved and the states were finally truly united. Sectionalism, especially in the area of politics, remained strong for another hundred years but not to the degree and with the violence as existed before 1861. It has been noted that the Civil War may have been American democracy's greatest failure because from 1861 to 1865, calm reason—basic to democracy—fell to human passion. Yet, democracy did survive.

The victory of the North established that no state has the right to end or leave the Union. Because of unity, the United States became a major global power. Lincoln never proposed to punish the South. He was most concerned with restoring the South to the Union in a program that was flexible and practical rather than rigid and unbending. In fact he never really felt that the states had succeeded in leaving the Union but that they had left the "family circle" for a short time.

World Wars

The American isolationist mood was given a shocking and lasting blow in 1941 with the Japanese attack on Pearl Harbor. The nation arose and forcefully entered the international arena as never before. Declaring itself "the arsenal of democracy," it entered the Second World War and emerged not only victorious, but also as the strongest power on the Earth. It would now, like it or not, have a permanent and leading place in world affairs.

In the aftermath of the Second World War, with the Soviet Union emerging as the second strongest power on Earth, the United States embarked on a policy known as "containment" of the Communist menace. This involved what came to be known as the Marshall Plan and the Truman Doctrine. The MARSHALL PLAN involved the economic aid that was sent to Europe in the aftermath of the Second World War aimed at preventing the spread of communism. To that end, the United States has devoted a larger and larger share of its foreign policy, diplomacy, and both economic and military might to combating it.

The TRUMAN DOCTRINE offered military aid to those countries that were in danger of communist upheaval. This led to the era known as the COLD WAR in which the United States took the lead along with the Western European nations against the Soviet Union and the Eastern Bloc countries. It was also at this time that the United States finally gave up on George Washington's advice against "European entanglements" and joined the North Atlantic Treaty Organization (NATO). This was formed in 1949 and was composed of the United States and several Western European nations for the purposes of opposing communist aggression.

MARSHALL PLAN: U.S. program for rebuilding the economic foundation of Western Europe following WWII

TRUMAN DOCTRINE: President Harry S. Truman's foreign policy declaring the United States "leader of the free world"

COLD WAR: the state of political tension and military rivalry between the Soviet Union and the West from the end of WWII to the 1980s

The UNITED NATIONS was formed in 1945 to replace the defunct League of Nations for the purposes of ensuring world peace. Even with American involvement, it would prove largely ineffective in its goals. In the 1950s, the United States embarked on what was called the "Eisenhower Doctrine," after the then-President Eisenhower. This aimed at trying to maintain peace in a troubled area of the world, the Middle East. However, unlike the Truman Doctrine in Europe, it would have little success.

The United States also became involved in a number of world conflicts in the ensuing years. Each had at the core the struggle against communist expansion. Among these were the **Korean War** (1950–1953), the **Vietnam War** (1965–1975), and various continuing entanglements in Central and South America and the Middle East. By the early 1970s under the leadership of then-Secretary of State Henry Kissinger, the United States and its allies embarked on the policy that came to be known as DÉTENTE. This was aimed at the easing of tensions between the United States and its allies and the Soviet Union and its allies.

By the 1980s, the United States embarked on what some saw as a renewal of the Cold War. This owed to the fact that the United States was becoming more involved in trying to prevent communist insurgency in Central America. A massive expansion of its armed forces and the development of space-based weapons systems were undertaken at this time. As this occurred, the Soviet Union, with a failing economic system and a foolhardy adventure in Afghanistan, found itself unable to compete. By 1989, events had come to a head. This ended with the breakdown of the Communist Bloc, the virtual end of the monolithic Soviet Union, and the collapse of the communist system by the early 1990s.

Now the United States remains active in world affairs in trying to promote peace and reconciliation, with a new specter rising to challenge it and the world—the specter of nationalism.

UNITED NATIONS: an international organization composed of most countries of the world and dedicated to promoting peace, security, and economic development

DÉTENTE: the easing of tensions or strained relations between rivals

Sample Test Questions and Rationale

Rigorous

1. The practice of dividing time into a number of discrete periods or blocks of time is called:

   A. eras

   B. chronological time

   C. periodization

   D. years

Answer: C – periodization

Rationale: The practice of dividing time into a number of discrete periods or blocks of time is called **periodization**. Dividing time into segments facilitates understanding of changes that occur over time and identifying similarities of events, knowledge, and experience within the defined period.

SKILL 21.5 Analyzing the effects of European contact with indigenous cultures and the effects of European settlement on New York State and the Northeast

The area now known as the State of New York was initially inhabited by several tribes that were part of one of two major Native American Nations. These were the Iroquois Nation and Algonquian Nation.

IROQUOIS: the confederacy of Haudenosaunee tribes, the League of Peace and Power

The confederacy of IROQUOIS tribes was known as the Haudenosaunee, the League of Peace and Power. They are often called the People of the Longhouse. Their original homeland was in upstate New York between the Adirondack Mountains and Niagara Falls. As a result of migration and conquest, they controlled most of the northeastern United States and Eastern Canada by the time of the first European contact. The confederacy had a constitution prior to the arrival of Europeans. It was known as the Gayanashagowa (Great Law of Peace). This was recorded in memory using a device in the form of special beads called wampum. There is no consensus among historians about the date of the origin of this constitution. Dating has ranged from 1142 to the early 1600s. The confederacy consisted of five nations, later six.

The name People of the Longhouse was derived from the traditional dwelling, the longhouse. Each longhouse was occupied by a matron, her daughters, and their husbands and children. The matrons controlled the clans, and the children belonged to their mother's clan.

THE ORIGINAL FIVE TRIBES OR NATIONS	
The Mohawk	Keepers of the Eastern Door of the symbolic longhouse (also known as the People of Flint)
The Oneida	The People of Stone
The Onondaga	The People on the Hill
The Cayuga	The People at the Mucky Land
The Seneca	The Great Hill People and the Keepers of the Western Door

After 1722, the Tuscarora were added to the confederation as a sixth, nonvoting member. The confederation was ruled by a council of fifty chiefs. Each nation was assigned a set number of chiefships. The men were elected by the clan matrons.

At the time of initial European contact, the Iroquois practiced hunting and gathering, which supplemented the basis of their economy, which was agriculture. It was primarily the women who practiced agriculture while the men functioned as hunters and warriors. This agricultural basis of the economy encouraged permanent settlements into villages. These villages moved only after depleting the soil (about every twenty years) through continuous harvesting of maize, beans, and squash. The Iroquois had a reputation as fierce warriors.

During the century prior to the AMERICAN REVOLUTION there were numerous wars with the Algonquin and other tribes of the Algonquian Nation. Their decision to oppose the colonists and support the British during the Revolutionary War was extremely unfortunate. As the American incursion into their territory gained pace after the Revolution, many of the Iroquois were driven into southern Ontario.

Much of the homeland of the Iroquois was ceded to New York land speculators through various treaties after the Revolutionary War. During the war, the confederation had been split in allegiance between support for the Americans and support for the British. In 1779, the alliance with Great Britain was defeated. In 1794, the Confederacy signed the Treaty of Canandaigua.

In many ways the Iroquois were not significantly different from neighboring tribes. But what made them unique was a sophisticated political system, with a system of checks, balances, and supreme law. The central authority of the league was very limited. This left each tribe the autonomy to pursue its own interests. They were also quite skilled in diplomacy. There is great discussion about the influence the Iroquois government exerted upon the Framers of the Articles of Confederation and the U.S. Constitution.

AMERICAN REVOLUTION: The war between the American colonies and Great Britain (1775–1783), which lead to the formation of the independent United States

The Dutch were the primary trading partners of the Iroquois people. They traded beaver and other furs for various European goods. The Algonquian people were a group of tribes that were united to greater or lesser degrees by a shared language family. The Long Island Algonquians are generally Mohegan Indians; the New York Algonquians are generally Mahicans and Munsee Delawares. The Algonquian tribe called themselves Anishinabe.

Algonquian territories and the Ottawa River were critical locations in trade routes. This facilitated cultural exchange, as well as commerce. They allied themselves with the French under Champlain in 1603. In 1632, after Sir David Kirke's occupation of New France, the French began to trade muskets with the Algonquians and other native people. As French settlements grew, French Jesuits began to convert the native people to Roman Catholicism. They were the traditional enemies of the Iroquois, a factor that encouraged the Iroquois to side with the British.

The first Europeans to arrive in New York were the Dutch led by Henry Hudson in 1609. Searching for a shortcut to India, and not finding one, they sailed on very quickly. Long Island was explored in 1614 by Adriaen Block, a Dutchman, who first mapped the island and gave it its name. The first settlements in New York were established in 1624 when the Dutch West India Company sent out a contingent of colonists. Most of these people settled in the northern Hudson Valley near what is now Albany. The next group of settlers arrived the next year and settled on the lower tip of Manhattan. This settlement came to be known as New Amsterdam. But in 1635, Charles I of England gave all of Long Island to the Earl of Sterling.

Peter Minuit, one of the early Dutch settlers and the first governor of New Amsterdam purchased Manhattan Island from the local people for trinkets valued at about $24. The colony was then named New Netherland. It grew slowly because the Dutch West India Company was more interested in the West Indies than in the Northern territories. They traded with the native peoples, primarily for furs. In 1629, the company offered its members large estates, which were called patroonships, if they would send new settlers to the region. There was little interest. In 1637, the company appointed Willem Kieft Director-General of the colony. His efforts to rule as a dictator sparked a series of disputes and wars with the local Algonquian tribes. He was replaced in 1647 by Peter Stuyvesant, who also tried to rule as a dictator. His imposition of high taxes on imports was unpopular. In 1650, Stuyvesant was forced to cede all of Long Island east of Oyster Bay to Connecticut, which was a British colony.

In 1664, King Charles II decided to claim the entire New York region on the basis of explorations made for England by John Cabot in 1497 and 1498. Charles granted his brother James, Duke of York and Albany, all the land between the

Connecticut and Delaware rivers. Within a matter of months, the English forced the Dutch to give up claims to New Amsterdam, which then became known as New York. The Dutch settlement near Fort Orange was renamed Albany.

In 1665, the first governor of the colony, refusing to create an assembly to govern the colony, drafted the Duke's Laws. This permitted the people to elect their own town boards and constables. It also guaranteed freedom of religion. These rights were extended to the rest of the colony later.

In 1682, Thomas Dongan became governor. He created a representative assembly of settlers, which adopted the Charter of Liberties and Privileges the next year. This charter provided for an elected legislature which was empowered to levy taxes and make laws. It guaranteed trial by jury and religious freedom.

New York and Albany were granted charters and allowed limited home rule and trading rights. He also created goodwill with the Iroquois. The next year, the Duke of York and Albany became king as James II. He incorporated New York within the New England colony, placing it within strict control of a royal governor. This new governor ruled from Boston, which enraged the colonists. The English governors gave huge land grants to their friends. The result was that most of the land was controlled by a very small number of landowners. Most were more interested in speculation than settlement. Particularly important was the establishment of the manors. This, in turn, placed the control of colonial affairs in the hands of the small number of landowners and the wealthy merchants of New York City.

When news reached the colony that James II had been overthrown in the Glorious Revolution and the colonial governor had been captured by rebels in Boston, an uprising persuaded Jacob Leisler to take command of the colony. He was able to establish control of the entire colony and establish an assembly before a new British representative of the new King William III arrived. Leisler was immediately tried, convicted of treason, and executed.

The population was composed of farmers and others who held jobs associated with agriculture. The growth of crafts and trades was determined by the needs of the community. These farmers grew crops and husbanded livestock. The economy was based on the barter system. The coastal areas developed a large fishing industry. Whaling was also a major part of the economy. The export of whale oil began in the seventeenth century, but did not become truly profitable until the nineteenth century.

Intellectually, two primary movements, the SCIENTIFIC REVOLUTION and the ENLIGHTENMENT, promoted scientific knowledge, a skepticism toward beliefs that could not be verified by science or logic, and scientific explanation of many things

SCIENTIFIC REVOLUTION: a period in the seventeenth century when great scientific advancements were made

ENLIGHTENMENT: a philosophical movement in the eighteenth century that held that reason could be used to scrutinize previously accepted doctrines and traditions about the natural world that were previously unexplained. Enlightenment thinking fostered several attacks on traditional religious beliefs. Partially in response to these attacks, the American colonies experienced a rebirth of religious fervor known as The First Great Awakening. Revival ministers during the 1730s and 1740s preached against the emptiness of materialism, talked about the corruption of human nature, and called for immediate repentance and a renewal of inner religious consciousness. Two of the leading revivalists were George Whitfield and Jonathan Edwards. This resulted in a polarization of Christians along the lines of "enthusiasm" and created a number of new churches, denominations, and sects, as well as schools and universities that would teach according to their principles.

Colonial economy developed around the European policy of mercantilism. This theory is based upon the idea that a nation must export more than it imports in order to build a strong and stable economy. As a result, Great Britain implemented a number of measures aimed at achieving this favorable trade balance, particularly the four NAVIGATION ACTS.

NAVIGATION ACTS: a series of British laws that restricted use of foreign shipping for trade between England and its colonies

During colonial times, **Middle** or **Middle Atlantic colonies** included New York, New Jersey, Pennsylvania, Delaware, and Maryland. New York and New Jersey were at one time the Dutch colony of New Netherlands and Delaware at one time was New Sweden. These five colonies, from their beginnings were considered "melting pots," with settlers from many different nations and backgrounds. The main economic activity was farming and settlers scattered over the countryside cultivating rather large farms. The Indians were not as much of a threat as in New England so colonists did not have to settle in small farming villages. The soil was very fertile, the land was gently rolling, and a milder climate provided a longer growing season.

These farms produced a large surplus of food, not only for the colonists themselves but also for sale. This colonial region became known as the "breadbasket" of the New World and the New York and Philadelphia seaports were constantly filled with ships being loaded with meat, flour, and other foodstuffs for the West Indies and England. There were other economic activities such as shipbuilding, iron mines, and factories producing paper, glass, and textiles.

STAMP ACT: the first direct tax on the American colonies, which imposed a tax on the transfer of certain documents

The earliest signs of the American Revolution became evident over the issue of trade and taxation. In 1765, the British Parliament passed the STAMP ACT, which directly taxed trade in the American colonies. As primary colonial harbors, New York City and Boston would have felt the sting from this tax most severely. In 1765, New York was the site of the Stamp Act Congress, a collection of representatives from the colonies which united in opposition to the Stamp Act, claiming that only colonial governments had the right to pass taxes on the colonial trade. New York merchants led a boycott on British goods in protest, and were later joined by Boston merchants. In 1765, when the Stamp Act was to have gone into effect, violence erupted in New York City and an effigy of the colonial governor was burned. The New York assembly also refused a direct request from the British military to enforce the Quartering Act, which required colonists to house and feed British troops. Fearing revolution, King George III repealed the Stamp Act in 1766. At the same time, however, Parliament passed a series of acts designed to give Britain even more power over colonial affairs. New York continued to refuse to enforce the Quartering Act as tensions grew and revolution sparked.

New York was a principal battleground of the Revolutionary War, with nearly one third of the battles of the war fought within its boundaries. The British recognized its importance as both a major harbor and its strategic location between New England and the rest of the colonies. The Battle of Long Island in 1776 resulted in Washington's defeat by Howe, and established a British foothold that would endure throughout the Revolution. George Washington retreated to Brooklyn Heights, then to Manhattan. Earlier in the hostilities, Ethan Allen had led a successful attack on Fort Ticonderoga on Lake Champlain, securing much needed military supplies, including cannons, which were removed to Boston. Now the British retook the fort and marched toward Albany to drive a wedge through the center of the colonies. Having been driven across the Delaware River to Pennsylvania, Washington and the main army began to move back north, winning key victories in New Jersey. The Battle of Saratoga, New York between the British under General Burgoyne and American troops led by Benedict Arnold was a critical turning point in the War. In two battles, the American forces weakened the British troops to the point of surrender, thereby foiling the British strategy to use New York as a dividing wedge. The decisive victory at Saratoga convinced France to enter the fray on the side of the American colonies. This alliance with France was crucial in the eventual American victory.

Sample Test Questions and Rationale

Average Rigor

1. **New York was initially inhabited by what two native peoples?**

    A. Sioux and Pawnee

    B. Micmac and Wampanoag

    C. Iroquois and Algonquin

    D. Nez Perce and Cherokee

    Answer: C – Iroquois and Algonquin

    Rationale: The area now known as the State of New York was initially inhabited by several tribes that were part of one of two major Native American Nations. These were the Iroquois Nation and the Algonquian Nation. (A) Sioux and Pawnee tribal lands were found primarily in Minnesota and Nebraska respectively. (B) Micmac and Wampanoag are tribes primarily found in New England and Canada. (D) Nez Perce and Cherokee were found in the Pacific Northwest and the Eastern parts of the United States respectively.

SKILL 21.6 **Analyze how the roles and contributions of individuals and groups helped shape U.S. social, political, economic, cultural, and religious life**

During the colonial period, political parties, as the term is now understood, did not exist. The issues, which divided the people, were centered on the relations of the colonies to the mother country. There was initially little difference of opinion on these issues. About the middle of the eighteenth century, after England began to develop a harsher colonial policy, two factions arose in America. One favored the attitude of home government and the other declined to obey and demanded a constantly increasing level of self-government. The former came to be known as TORIES, the latter as WHIGS. During the course of the American Revolution a large number of Tories left the country either to return to England or move to Canada.

From the beginning of the Confederation, there were differences of opinion about the new government. One faction favored a loose confederacy in which the individual state would retain all powers of sovereignty except the absolute minimum required for the limited cooperation of all the states. The other faction, which steadily gained influence, demanded that the central government be granted all

TORIES: favored the attitude of home government

WHIGS: declined to obey and demanded a constantly increasing level of self-government

the essential powers of sovereignty and the what should be left to the states was only the powers of local self-government. The inadequacy of the Confederation demonstrated that the latter were promoting a more effective point of view.

The first real party organization developed soon after the inauguration of George Washington as president. His cabinet included people of both factions. Hamilton was the leader of the Nationalists—the Federalist Party—and Jefferson was the spokesman for the Anti-Federalists, later known as Republicans, Democratic-Republicans, and finally Democrats. Several other parties formed over the years including the Anti-Masonic Party and the Free Soil Party, which existed for the 1848 and 1852 elections only. They opposed slavery in the lands acquired from Mexico. The Liberty Party of this period was abolitionist.

The American Party was called the "Know Nothings." They lasted from 1854 to 1858 and were opposed to Irish-Catholic immigration. The Constitution Union Party was formed in 1860. It was made up of entities from other extinguished political powers. They claim to support the Constitution above all and thought this would do away with the slavery issue. The National Union Party of 1864 was formed only for the purpose of the Lincoln election. That was the only reason for its existence. There were many more to follow.

> **Coming up:**
> • Westward Expansion
> • Social Reform Movement
> • Religious Revival
> • Cultural Growth

Westward Expansion

The Industrial Revolution had spread from Great Britain to the United States. Before 1800, most manufacturing activities were done in small shops or in homes. However, starting in the early 1800s, factories with modern machines were built making it easier to produce goods faster. The eastern part of the country became a major industrial area although some developed in the West. At about the same time, improvements began to be made in building roads, railroads, canals, and steamboats. The increased ease of travel facilitated the westward movement and boosted the economy with faster and cheaper shipment of goods and products, covering larger areas. Some of the innovations include the Erie Canal connecting the interior and Great Lakes with the Hudson River and the coastal port of New York.

Westward expansion occurred for a number of reasons, most important being economic. Cotton had become most important to most of the people who lived in the southern states. The effects of the Industrial Revolution, which began in England, were now being felt in the United States. With the invention of power-driven machines, the demand for cotton fiber greatly increased for the yarn needed in spinning and weaving. Eli Whitney's cotton gin made the separation of the seeds from the cotton much more efficient and faster. This, in turn, increased the demand and more and more farmers became involved in the raising and selling of cotton.

The innovations and developments of better methods of long-distance transportation moved the cotton in greater quantities to textile mills in England as well as the areas of New England and Middle Atlantic states in the United States. As prices increased along with increased demand, southern farmers began expanding by clearing increasingly more land to grow more cotton. Movement, settlement, and farming headed west to utilize the fertile soils. This, in turn, demanded increased need for a large supply of cheap labor. The system of slavery expanded, both in numbers and in the movement to lands "west" of the South.

Cotton farmers and slave owners were not the only ones heading west. Many, in other fields of economic endeavor, began the migration: trappers, miners, merchants, ranchers, and others were all seeking their fortunes. The Lewis and Clark expedition stimulated the westward push. Fur companies hired men, known as Mountain Men, to go westward, searching for the animal pelts to supply the market and meet the demands of the East and Europe. These men in their own way explored and discovered the many passes and trails that would eventually be used by settlers in their trek to the west. The California gold rush also had a very large influence on the movement west.

In the American Southwest, the results were exactly the opposite. Spain had claimed this area since the 1540s, had spread northward from Mexico City and, in the 1700s, had established missions, forts, villages, towns, and very large ranches. After the purchase of the Louisiana Territory in 1803, Americans began moving into Spanish territory. A few hundred American families in what is now Texas were allowed to live there but had to agree to become loyal subjects to Spain. In 1821, Mexico successfully revolted against Spanish rule, won independence, and chose to be more tolerant toward the American settlers and traders. The Mexican government encouraged and allowed extensive trade and settlement, especially in Texas. Many of the new settlers were Southerners and brought with them their slaves. Slavery was outlawed in Mexico and technically illegal in Texas, although the Mexican government looked the other way.

The Red River Cession was the next acquisition of land and came about as part of a treaty with Great Britain in 1818:

- It included parts of **North** and **South Dakota** and **Minnesota**.

- In 1819, **Florida**, both east and west, was ceded to the United States by Spain along with parts of **Alabama**, **Mississippi**, and **Louisiana**.

- **Texas** was annexed in 1845.

- After the war with Mexico in 1848 the government paid $15 million for what would become the states of **California**, **Utah**, **Nevada**, and parts of four other states.

- In 1846, the **Oregon Country** was ceded to the United States, which extended the western border to the Pacific Ocean. The northern U.S. boundary was established at the 49th parallel. The states of **Idaho**, **Oregon**, and **Washington** were formed from this territory.

- In 1853, the **Gadsden Purchase** rounded out the present boundary of the 48 conterminous states with payment to Mexico of $10 million for land that makes up the present states of New **Mexico** and **Arizona**.

The election of Andrew Jackson as president signaled a swing of the political pendulum from government influence of the wealthy, aristocratic Easterners to the interests of the Western farmers and pioneers and the era of the "common man." Jacksonian democracy was a policy of equal political power for all. After the War of 1812, Henry Clay and supporters favored economic measures that came to be known as the American System. This involved tariffs protecting American farmers and manufacturers from having to compete with foreign products, stimulating industrial growth and employment. With more people working, more farm products would be consumed, prosperous farmers would be able to buy more manufactured goods, and the additional monies from tariffs would make it possible for the government to make needed internal improvements. To get this going, in 1816, Congress not only passed a high tariff, but also chartered a second Bank of the United States. Upon becoming President, Jackson fought to get rid of the bank.

Many social reform movements began during this period, including:

- education
- women's rights
- labor and working conditions
- temperance
- prisons and insane asylums

But the most intense and controversial was the abolitionists' efforts to end slavery, an effort alienating and splitting the country, hardening Southern defense of slavery, and leading to four years of bloody war. The abolitionist movement had political fallout, affecting admittance of states into the Union and the government's continued efforts to keep a balance between total numbers of free and slave states. Congressional legislation after 1820 reflected this.

Robert Fulton's *Clermont*, the first commercially successful steamboat, led the way in the fastest way to ship goods, making it the most important way to do so. Later, steam-powered railroads soon became the biggest rival of the steamboat as a means of shipping, eventually being the most important transportation method opening the West. With expansion into the interior of the country, the United States became the leading agricultural nation in the world. The hardy pioneer farmers produced a vast surplus and emphasis went to producing products with a high-sale value. These implements, such as the cotton gin and reaper, improved production. Travel and shipping were greatly assisted in areas not yet touched by railroad or, by improved or new roads, such as the National Road in the East and in the West the Oregon and Santa Fe Trails.

People were exposed to works of literature, art, newspapers, drama, live entertainment, and political rallies. With better communication and travel, more information was desired about previously unknown areas of the country, especially the West. The discovery of gold and other mineral wealth resulted in a literal surge of settlers and even more interest.

Public schools were established in many of the states with more and more children being educated. With more literacy and more participation in literature and the arts, the young nation was developing its own unique culture becoming less and less influenced by and dependent on that of Europe.

More industries and factories required more and more labor. Women, children, and, at times, entire families worked the long hours and days, until the 1830s. By that time, the factories were getting even larger and employers began hiring immigrants who were coming to America in huge numbers. Before then, efforts were made to organize a labor movement to improve working conditions and increase wages. It never really caught on until after the Civil War, but the seed had been sown.

In between the growing economy, expansion westward of the population, and improvements in travel and mass communication, the federal government did face periodic financial depressions. Contributing to these downward spirals were land speculations, availability and soundness of money and currency, failed banks, failing businesses, and unemployment. Sometimes conditions outside the nation would help trigger it; at other times, domestic politics and presidential elections affected it. The growing strength and influence of two major political parties with opposing philosophies and methods of conducting government did not ease matters at times.

As 1860 began, the nation had extended its borders north, south, and west. Industry and agriculture were flourishing. Although the United States did not involve itself actively in European affairs, the relationship with Great Britain was much improved and it and other nations that dealt with the young nation accorded it more respect and admiration. Nevertheless, war was on the horizon. The country was deeply divided along political lines concerning slavery and the election of Abraham Lincoln.

Religion has always been a factor in American life. Many early settlers came to America in search of religious freedom. Religion, particularly Christianity, was an essential element of the value and belief structure shared by the Founding Fathers. Yet the Constitution prescribes a separation of Church and State.

- The First Great Awakening was a religious movement within American Protestantism in the 1730s and 1740s. This was primarily a movement among Puritans seeking a return to strict interpretation of morality and values as well as emphasizing the importance and power of personal religious or spiritual experience. Many historians believe the First Great Awakening unified the people of the original colonies and supported the independence of the colonists.

- The Second Great Awakening (the Great Revival) was a broad movement within American Protestantism that led to several kinds of activities that were distinguished by region and denominational tradition. In general terms, the Second Great Awakening, which began in the 1820s, was a time of recognition that "awakened religion" must weed out sin on both a personal and a social level. It inspired a wave of social activism. In New England, the Congregationalists established missionary societies to evangelize the West. Publication and education societies arose, most notably the American Bible Society. This social activism gave rise to the temperance movement, prison reform efforts, and help for the handicapped and mentally ill. This period was particularly notable for the abolition movement. In the Appalachian region, the camp meeting was used to revive religion. The camp meeting became a primary method of evangelizing new territory.

- The Third Great Awakening (the Missionary Awakening) gave rise to the Social Gospel Movement. This period (1858 to 1908) resulted in a massive growth in membership of all major Protestant denominations through their missionary activities. This movement was partly a response to claims that the Bible was fallible. Many churches attempted to reconcile or change biblical teaching to fit scientific theories and discoveries. Colleges associated with Protestant churches began to appear rapidly throughout the nation. In terms of social and political movements, the Third Great Awakening was the most expansive and profound. Coinciding with many changes in production and labor, it won battles against child labor and stopped the exploitation of women in factories. Compulsory elementary education for children came from this movement, as did the establishment of a set work day. Much was also done to protect and rescue children from abandonment and abuse, to improve the care of the sick, to prohibit the use of alcohol and tobacco, as well as numerous other "social ills."

Numerous conflicts, often called the Indian Wars, broke out between the U.S. army and many different native tribes. Many treaties were signed with the various

Major writers and works of the Harlem Renaissance:

- *Langston Hughes (The Weary Blues)*
- *Nella Larsen (Passing)*
- *Zora Neale Hurston (Their Eyes Were Watching God)*
- *Claude McKay*
- *Countee Cullen*
- *Jean Toomer*

The leading jazz musicians of the time included:

- *Buddy Bolden,*
- *Joseph "King" Oliver*
- *Duke Ellington*
- *Louis Armstrong*
- *Jelly Roll Morton.*

Notable musicians of the Big Band era:

- *Bing Crosby*
- *Frank Sinatra*
- *Don Redman*
- *Fletcher Henderson*
- *Count Basie*
- *Benny Goodman*
- *Billie Holiday*
- *Ella Fitzgerald*
- *The Dorsey Brothers*

tribes, but most were broken by the government for a variety of reasons. Two of the most notable battles were the Battle of Little Bighorn in 1876, in which native people defeated General Custer and his forces, and the massacre of Native Americans in 1890 at Wounded Knee. In 1876, the U.S. government ordered all surviving Native Americans to move to reservations.

As African Americans left the rural South and migrated to the North in search of opportunity, many settled in Harlem in New York City. By the 1920s Harlem had become a center of life and activity for people of color. The music, art, and literature of this community gave birth to a cultural movement known as the Harlem Renaissance. The artistic expressions that emerged from this community in the 1920s and 1930s celebrated the black experience, black traditions, and the voices of black America.

Many refer to the decade of the 1920s as The Jazz Age. The decade was a time of optimism and exploration of new boundaries. It was a clear movement in many ways away from conventionalism. Jazz music, uniquely American, was the country's popular music at the time. The jazz musical style perfectly typified the mood of society. Jazz is essentially free-flowing improvisation on a simple theme with a four-beat rhythm. Jazz originated in the poor districts of New Orleans as an outgrowth of the Blues.

As jazz grew in popularity and in the intricacy of the music, it gave birth to Swing and the era of Big Band Jazz by the mid 1920s.

NINETEENTH CENTURY CULTURAL CONTRIBUTORS	
AMERICAN	**CONTRIBUTION**
Lucretia Mott and Elizabeth Cady Stanton	women's rights
Emma Hart Willard, Catharine Esther Beecher, and Mary Lyon	education for women
Dr. Elizabeth Blackwell	the first woman doctor
Antoinette Louisa Blackwell	the first female minister
Dorothea Lynde Dix	reforms in prisons and insane asylums
Elihu Burritt and William Ladd	peace movements

Table continued on next page

Robert Owen	a Utopian society
Horace Mann, Henry Barmard, Calvin E. Stowe, Caleb Mills, and John Swett	public education
Benjamin Lundy, David Walker, William Lloyd Garrison, Isaac Hooper, Arthur and Lewis Tappan, Theodore Weld, Frederick Douglass, Harriet Tubman, James G. Birney, Henry Highland Garnet, James Forten, Robert Purvis, Harriet Beecher Stowe, Wendell Phillips, and John Brown	abolition of slavery and the Underground Railroad
Louisa Mae Alcott, James Fenimore Cooper, Washington Irving, Walt Whitman, Henry David Thoreau, Ralph Waldo Emerson, Herman Melville, Richard Henry Dana, Nathaniel Hawthorne, Henry Wadsworth Longfellow, John Greenleaf Whittier, Edgar Allan Poe, Oliver Wendell Holmes	famous writers
John C. Fremont, Zebulon Pike, Kit Carson	explorers
Henry Clay, Daniel Webster, Stephen Douglas, John C. Calhoun	statesmen
Robert Fulton, Cyrus McCormick, Eli Whitney	inventors
Noah Webster	American dictionary and spellers

Hispanic Americans have contributed to American life and culture since before the Civil War. Hispanics have distinguished themselves in every area of society and culture. Mexicans taught Californians to pan for gold and introduced the technique of using mercury to separate silver from worthless ores. Six state names are of Hispanic origin.

Native Americans have made major contributions to the development of the nation and have been contributors, either directly or indirectly in every area of political and cultural life. In the early years of European settlement, Native Americans were both teachers and neighbors. Even during periods of extermination and relocation, their influence was profound.

Asian Americans, particularly in the West and in large cities, have made significant contributions despite immigration bans, mistreatment, and confinement. Asians were particularly important in the construction of the transcontinental railroad, mining metals, and providing other kinds of labor and service.

Sample Test Questions and Rationale

Easy

1. **What was the name of the cultural revival after the Civil War that took place in New York?**

    A. the Revolutionary War

    B. the Second Great Awakening

    C. the Harlem Renaissance

    D. the Gilded Age

Answer: C – The Harlem Renaissance

Rationale: As African Americans left the rural South and migrated to the North in search of opportunity, many settled in Harlem in New York City. By the 1920s Harlem had become a center of life and activity for persons of color. The music, art, and literature of this community gave birth to a cultural movement known as the Harlem Renaissance. (A) The Revolution War (1776) occurred prior to the Civil War. (B) The Second Great Awakening occurred in the 1920s but like the (D) Gilded Age (1878–1889) affected the entire United States.

COMPETENCY 22

UNDERSTAND GEOGRAPHIC CONCEPTS AND PHENOMENA AND ANALYZE THE INTERRELATIONSHIPS OF GEOGRAPHY, SOCIETY, AND CULTURE IN THE DEVELOPMENT OF NEW YORK STATE, THE UNITED STATES, AND THE WORLD.

SKILL 22.1 Defining important geographic terms and concepts and using them to analyze various geographic issues, problems, and phenomena

GEOGRAPHY involves studying location and how living things and Earth's features are distributed throughout the Earth. It includes where animals, people, and plants live and the effects of their relationship with Earth's physical features. Geographers also explore the locations of Earth's features, how they got there, and why it is so important.

GEOGRAPHY: the study of location and how living things and Earth's features are distributed throughout the Earth

AREAS OF GEOGRAPHICAL STUDY	
Regional	Elements and characteristics of a place or region.
Topical	One Earth feature or one human activity occurring throughout the entire world.
Physical	Earth's physical features, what creates and changes them, their relationships to each other, as well as human activities.
Human	Human activity patterns and how they relate to the environment including political, cultural, historical, urban, and social geographical fields of study.

Two of the most important terms in the study of geography are absolute and relative location. First, what is **location**? We want to know this in order to determine where something is and where we can find it. We want to point to a spot on a map and say, "That is where we are" or "That is where we want to be." In another way, we want to know where something is as compared to other things. It is very difficult for many people to describe something without referring to something else. Associative reasoning is a powerful way to think.

- Absolute location is the exact whereabouts of a person, place, or thing, according to any kind of geographical indicators you want to name. You could be talking about latitude and longitude or GPS or any kind of indicators at all. For example, Paris is at 48 degrees north longitude and 2 degrees east latitude. You can't get much more exact than that. If you had a map that showed every degree of latitude and longitude, you could pinpoint exactly where Paris was and have absolutely no doubt that your geographical depiction was accurate.

- **Relative location**, on the other hand, is always a description that involves more than one thing. When you describe a relative location, you tell where something is by describing what is around it. The same description of where the nearest post office is in terms of absolute location might be this: "It's down the street from the supermarket, on the right side of the street, next to the dentist's office."

ECOLOGY is the study of how living organisms interact with the physical aspects of their surroundings (their environment), including soil, water, air, and other living things. BIOGEOGRAPHY is the study of how the surface features of the Earth—form, movement, and climate—affect living things.

ECOLOGY: the study of how living organisms interact with the physical aspects of their surroundings (their environment), including soil, water, air, and other living things

BIOGEOGRAPHY: the study of how the surface features of the Earth—form, movement, and climate—affect living things

THREE LEVELS OF ENVIRONMENTAL UNDERSTANDING	
Ecosystem	A community (of any size) consisting of a physical environment and the organisms that live within it.
Biome	A large area of land with characteristic climate, soil, and mixture of plants and animals. Biomes are made up of groups of ecosystems. Major biomes are: desert, chaparral, savanna, tropical rain forest, temperate grassland, temperate deciduous forest, taiga, and tundra.
Habitat	The set of surroundings within which members of a species normally live. Elements of the habitat include soil, water, predators, and competitors.

Within habitats interactions between members of the species occur. These interactions occur among members of the same species and among members of different species. Interaction tends to be of three types:

1. **Competition.** Competition occurs between members of the same species or between members of different species for resources required to continue life, to grow, or to reproduce. For example, competition for acorns can occur between squirrels or it can occur between squirrels and woodpeckers. One species can either push out or cause the demise of another species if it is better adapted to obtain the resource. When a new species is introduced into a habitat, the result can be a loss of the native species and/or significant change to the habitat. For example, the introduction of the Asian plant Kudzu into

the American South has resulted in the destruction of several species because Kudzu grows and spreads very quickly and smothers everything in its path.

2. Predation. Predators are organisms that live by hunting and eating other organisms. The species best suited for hunting other species in the habitat will be the species that survives. Larger species that have better hunting skills reduce the amount of prey available for smaller and/or weaker species. This affects both the amount of available prey and the diversity of species that are able to survive in the habitat.

3. Symbiosis is a condition in which two organisms of different species are able to live in the same environment over an extended period of time without harming one another. In some cases one species may benefit without harming the other. In other cases both species benefit.

BIODIVERSITY refers to the variety of species and organisms, as well as the variety of habitats available on the Earth. Biodiversity provides the life-support system for the various habitats and species. The greater the degree of biodiversity, the more species and habitats will continue to survive.

> **BIODIVERSITY:** the variety of species and organisms, as well as the variety of habitats available on the Earth

When human and other population and migration changes, climate changes, or natural disasters disrupt the delicate balance of a habitat or an ecosystem, species either adapt or become extinct.

Natural changes can occur that alter habitats—floods, volcanoes, storms, earthquakes. These changes can affect the species that exist within the habitat, either by causing extinction or by changing the environment in a way that will no longer support the life systems. Climate changes can have similar effects. Inhabiting species, however, can also alter habitats, particularly through migration. Human civilization, population growth, and efforts to control the environment can have many negative effects on various habitats. Humans change their environments to suit their particular needs and interests. This can result in changes that result in the extinction of species or changes to the habitat itself. For example, deforestation damages the stability of mountain surfaces. One particularly devastating example is in the removal of the grasses of the Great Plains for agriculture. Tilling the ground and planting crops left the soil unprotected. Sustained drought dried out the soil into dust. When windstorms occurred, the topsoil was stripped away and blown all the way to the Atlantic Ocean.

SKILL
22.2
Demonstrating an understanding of the six essential elements of geography: the world in spatial terms, places and regions, physical settings, human systems, environment and society and the use of geography

SIX THEMES OF GEOGRAPHY	
Location	Including relative and absolute location. A relative location refers to the surrounding geography, e.g., "on the banks of the Mississippi River." Absolute location refers to a specific point, such as 41 degrees North latitude, 90 degrees West longitude, or 123 Main Street.
Spatial Organization	A description of how things are grouped in a given space. In geographical terms, this can describe people, places, and environments anywhere and everywhere on Earth. The most basic form of spatial organization for people is where they live. The vast majority of people live near other people, in villages and towns and cities and settlements. These people live near others in order to take advantage of the goods and services that naturally arise from cooperation. These villages and towns and cities and settlements are, to varying degrees, near bodies of water. Water is a staple of survival for every person on the planet and is also a good source of energy for factories and other industries, as well as a form of transportation for people and goods. For example, in a city, where are the factories and heavy industry buildings? Are they near airports or train stations? Are they on the edge of town, near major roads? What about housing developments? Are they near these industries, or are they far away? Where are the other industry buildings? Where are the schools and hospitals and parks? What about the police and fire stations? How close are homes to each of these things? Towns and especially cities are routinely organized into neighborhoods, so that each house or home is near to most things that its residents might need on a regular basis. This means that large cities have multiple schools, hospitals, grocery stores, fire stations, etc.
Place	A place has both human and physical characteristics. Physical characteristics include features such as mountains, rivers, and deserts. Human characteristics are the features created by human interaction with their environment such as canals and roads.
Human-Environmental Interaction	The theme of human-environmental interaction has three main concepts: humans adapt to the environment (wearing warm clothing in a cold climate); humans modify the environment (planting trees to block a prevailing wind); and humans depend on the environment (for food, water, and raw materials).
Movement	The theme of movement covers how humans interact with one another through trade, communications, immigration, and other forms of interaction.
Regions	A region is an area that has some kind of unifying characteristic, such as a common language or a common government. There are three main types of regions. Formal regions are areas defined by actual political boundaries, such as a city, county, or state. Functional regions are defined by a common function, such as the area covered by a telephone service. Vernacular regions are less formally defined areas that are formed by people's perception, e.g., the Middle East, and the South.

Geography involves studying location and how living things and Earth's features are distributed throughout the Earth. It includes where animals, people, and plants live and the effects of their relationship with Earth's physical features.

Geographers also explore the locations of Earth's features, how they got there, and why it is so important. Another way to describe where people live is by the geography and topography around them. The vast majority of people on the planet live in areas that are very hospitable. Yes, people live in the Himalayas and in the Sahara, but the populations in those areas are small indeed when compared to the plains of China, India, Europe, and the United States. People naturally want to live where they won't have to work really hard just to survive, and world population patterns reflect this.

Human communities subsisted initially as gatherers—gathering berries, leaves, etc. With the invention of tools it became possible to dig for roots, hunt small animals, and catch fish from rivers and oceans. Humans observed their environments and soon learned to plant seeds and harvest crops. As people migrated to areas in which game and fertile soil were abundant, communities began to develop. When people had the knowledge to grow crops and the skills to hunt game, they began to understand division of labor. Some of the people in the community tended to agricultural needs while others hunted game.

As habitats attracted larger numbers of people, environments became crowded and there was competition. The concept of division of labor and sharing of food soon followed. Groups of people focused on growing crops while others concentrated on hunting. Experience led to the development of skills and of knowledge that make the work easier. Farmers began to develop new plant species and hunters began to protect animal species from other predators for their own use. This ability to manage the environment led people to settle down, to guard their resources, and to manage them.

Camps soon became villages. Villages became year-round settlements. Animals were domesticated and gathered into herds that met the needs of the village. With the settled life it was no longer necessary to "travel light." Pottery was developed for storing and cooking food.

By 8000 BCE, culture was beginning to evolve in these villages. Agriculture was developed for the production of grain crops, which led to a decreased reliance on wild plants. Domesticating animals for various purposes decreased the need to hunt wild game. Life became more settled. It was then possible to turn attention to such matters as managing water supplies, producing tools, and making cloth. There was both the social interaction and the opportunity to reflect upon existence. Mythologies arose and various kinds of belief systems. Rituals arose that reenacted the mythologies that gave meaning to life.

As farming and animal husbandry skills increased, the dependence upon wild game and food gathering declined. With this change came the realization that a larger number of people could be supported on the produce of farming and animal husbandry.

Two things seem to have come together to produce CULTURES and CIVILIZATIONS: a society and culture based on agriculture and the development of centers of the community with literate social and religious structures.

The members of these hierarchies then managed water supplies and irrigation and ritual and religious life and exerted their own right to use a portion of the goods produced by the community for their own subsistence in return for their management.

Sharpened skills, development of more sophisticated tools, commerce with other communities, and increasing knowledge of their environment, the resources available to them, and responses to the needs to share good, order community life, and protect their possessions from outsiders led to further division of labor and community development.

As trade routes developed and travel between cities became easier, trade led to specialization. Trade enables a people to obtain the goods they desire in exchange for the goods they are able to produce. This, in turn, leads to increased attention to refinements of technique and the sharing of ideas. The knowledge of a new discovery or invention provides knowledge and technology that increases the ability to produce goods for trade. As each community learns the value of the goods it produces and improves its ability to produce the goods in greater quantity, industry is born.

> **CULTURE:** the set of values, conventions, or social practices associated with a particular group

> **CIVILIZATION:** a high level of cultural and technological development

Sample Test Questions and Rationale

Average Rigor

1. **The term spatial organization refers to:**

   A. latitude and longitude lines

   B. the alignment of the stars

   C. how things are grouped in a given space

   D. the space between point A and point B

Answer: C – how things are grouped in a given space

Rationale: Spatial organization is a description of how things are grouped in a given space. In geographical terms, this can describe people, places, and environments anywhere and everywhere on Earth. The most basic form of spatial organization for people is where they live.

The Earth's physical environment is divided into three major parts:

1. Atmosphere: the layer of air that surrounds the Earth

2. Hydrosphere: the water portion of the planet (seventy percent of the Earth is covered by water)

3. Lithosphere: the solid portion of the Earth

PHYSICAL CHARACTERISTICS OF THE EARTH	
Mountains	Mountains are landforms with rather steep slopes at least 2,000 feet or more above sea level. Mountains are found in groups called mountain chains or mountain ranges. At least one range can be found on six of the Earth's seven continents. North America has the Appalachian and Rocky Mountains; South America the Andes; Asia the Himalayas; Australia the Great Dividing Range; Europe the Alps; and Africa the Atlas, Ahaggar, and Drakensburg Mountains. Mountains are commonly formed by volcanic activity, when land is thrust upward where two tectonic plates collide.
Hills	Hills are elevated landforms rising to an elevation of about 500 to 2,000 feet. They are found everywhere on Earth including Antarctica, where they are covered by ice.
Plateaus	Plateaus are elevated landforms usually level on top. Depending on location, they range from being an area that is very cold to one that is cool and healthful. Some plateaus are dry because they are surrounded by mountains that keep out any moisture. Some examples include the Kenya Plateau in East Africa, which is very cool. The plateau extending north from the Himalayas is extremely dry while those in Antarctica and Greenland are covered with ice and snow. Plateaus can be formed by underground volcanic activity, erosion, or colliding tectonic plates.
Plains	Plains are described as areas of flat or slightly rolling land, usually lower than the landforms next to them. Sometimes called lowlands (and sometimes located along **seacoasts**) they support the majority of the world's people. Some are found inland and many have been formed by large rivers. This resulted in extremely fertile soil for successful cultivation of crops and numerous large settlements of people. In North America, the vast plains areas extend from the Gulf of Mexico north to the Arctic Ocean and between the Appalachian and Rocky Mountains. In Europe, rich plains extend east from Great Britain into central Europe on into the Siberian region of Russia. Plains in river valleys are found in China (the Yangtze River valley), India (the Ganges River valley), and Southeast Asia (the Mekong River valley).
Valleys	Valleys are land areas that are found between hills and mountains. Some have gentle slopes containing trees and plants; others have very steep walls and are referred to as canyons. One famous example is Arizona's Grand Canyon of the Colorado River, which was formed by erosion.

Table continued on next page

Deserts	Deserts are large dry areas of land receiving ten inches or less of rainfall each year. Among the better known deserts are Africa's large Sahara Desert, the Arabian Desert on the Arabian Peninsula, and the desert Outback covering roughly one third of Australia. Deserts are found mainly in the tropical latitudes and are formed when surrounding features such as mountain ranges extract most of the moisture from the prevailing winds.
Deltas	Deltas are areas of lowlands formed by soil and sediment deposited at the mouths of rivers. The soil is generally very fertile and most fertile river deltas are important crop-growing areas. One well-known example is the delta of Egypt's Nile River, known for its production of cotton.
Mesas	Mesas are the flat tops of hills or mountains usually with steep sides. Mesas are similar to plateaus, but smaller.
Basins	Basins are considered to be low areas drained by rivers or low spots in mountains.
Foothills	Foothills are generally considered a low series of hills found between a plain and a mountain range.
Marshes and Swamps	Marshes and swamps are wet lowlands providing growth of such plants as rushes and reeds.
Oceans	Oceans are the largest bodies of water on the planet. The four oceans of the Earth are the **Atlantic Ocean**, one-half the size of the Pacific and separating North and South America from Africa and Europe; the **Pacific Ocean**, covering almost one-third of the entire surface of the Earth and separating North and South America from Asia and Australia; the **Indian Ocean**, touching Africa, Asia, and Australia; and the ice-filled **Arctic Ocean**, extending from North America and Europe to the North Pole. The waters of the Atlantic, Pacific, and Indian Oceans also touch the shores of Antarctica.
Seas	Seas are smaller than oceans and are surrounded by land. Some examples include the Mediterranean Sea found between Europe, Asia, and Africa; and the Caribbean Sea, touching the West Indies, South and Central America.
Lakes	A lake is a body of water surrounded by land. The Great Lakes in North America are a good example.
Rivers	Rivers, considered a nation's lifeblood, usually begin as very small streams, formed by melting snow and rainfall, flowing from higher to lower land, emptying into a larger body of water, usually a sea or an ocean. Examples of important rivers for the people and countries affected by and/or dependent on them include the Nile, Niger, and Zaire Rivers of Africa; the Rhine, Danube, and Thames Rivers of Europe; the Yangtze, Ganges, Mekong, Hwang He, and Irrawaddy Rivers of Asia; the Murray-Darling in Australia; and the Orinoco in South America. River systems are made up of large rivers and numerous smaller rivers or tributaries flowing into them. Examples include the vast Amazon Rivers system in South America and the Mississippi River system in the United States.
Canals	Canals are manmade water passages constructed to connect two larger bodies of water. Famous examples include the **Panama Canal** across Panama's isthmus connecting the Atlantic and Pacific Oceans and the **Suez Canal** in the Middle East between Africa and the Arabian peninsulas connecting the Red and Mediterranean Seas.

World weather patterns are greatly influenced by ocean surface currents in the upper layer of the ocean. These current continuously move along the ocean surface in specific directions. Ocean currents that flow deep below the surface are called subsurface currents. These currents are influenced by such factors as the location of landmasses in the current's path and the Earth's rotation.

Surface currents are caused by winds and classified by temperature. Cold currents originate in the Polar regions and flow through surrounding water that is measurably warmer. Those currents with a higher temperature than the surrounding water are called warm currents and can be found near the equator. These currents follow swirling routes around the ocean basins and the equator.

The GULF STREAM and the CALIFORNIA CURRENT are the two main surface currents that flow along the coastlines of the United States. The Gulf Stream is a warm current in the Atlantic Ocean that carries warm water from the equator to the northern parts of the Atlantic Ocean. Benjamin Franklin studied and named the Gulf Stream. The California Current is a cold current that originates in the Artic regions and flows southward along the West Coast of the United States.

CLIMATE is average weather or daily weather conditions for a specific region or location over a long or extended period of time. Studying the climate of an area includes information gathered on the area's monthly and yearly temperatures and its monthly and yearly amounts of precipitation. In addition, a characteristic of an area's climate is the length of its growing season.

Natural changes can occur that alter habitats—floods, volcanoes, storms, earthquakes. These changes can affect the species that exist within the habitat, either by causing extinction or by changing the environment in a way that will no longer support the life systems. Climate changes can have similar effects. Inhabiting species can also alter habitats, particularly through migration.

PLATE TECTONICS, is a geological theory that explains continental drift, which is the large movements of the solid portions of the Earth's crust floating on the molten mantle. There are ten major tectonic plates, with several smaller plates. The surface of the Earth can be drastically affected at the boundaries of these plates. There are three types of plate boundaries:

1. Convergent boundaries occur where plates are moving toward one another. When this happens, the two plates collide and fold up against one another, called continental collision, or one plate slides under the other, called subduction. Continental collision can create high mountain ranges, such as the Andes and Himalayas. Subduction often results in volcanic activity along the boundary, as in the "Ring of Fire" along the northern coasts of the Pacific Ocean.

GULF STREAM: a warm current in the Atlantic Ocean that carries warm water from the equator to the North Atlantic

CALIFORNIA CURRENT: a cold current that originates in the Arctic and flows southward along the West Coast of the United States

CLIMATE: average weather or daily weather conditions for a region over a long period

PLATE TECTONICS: a geological theory that explains continental drift, which is the large movements of the solid portions of the Earth's crust floating on the molten mantle

2. **Divergent boundaries** occur where plates are moving away from one another, creating **rifts** in the surface. The Mid-Atlantic Ridge on the floor of the Atlantic Ocean, and the Great Rift Valley in east Africa are examples of rifts at divergent plate boundaries.

3. **Transform boundaries** are where plates are moving in opposite directions along their boundary, grinding against one another. The tremendous pressures that build along these types of boundaries often lead to earthquake activity when this pressure is released. The San Andreas Fault along the West Coast of North America is an example of a transform boundary.

FOUR PHYSICAL PROCESSES THAT RESHAPE THE EARTH	
Erosion	Erosion is the displacement of solid Earth surfaces such as rock and soil. Erosion is often a result of wind, water, or ice acting on surfaces with loose particles, such as sand, loose soils, or decomposing rock. Gravity can also cause erosion on loose surfaces. Factors such as slope, soil, and rock composition, plant cover, and human activity all affect erosion.
Weathering	Weathering is the natural decomposition of the Earth's surface from contact with the atmosphere. It is not the same as erosion, but can be a factor in erosion. Heat, water, ice and pressure are all factors that can lead to weathering. Chemicals in the atmosphere can also contribute to weathering.
Transportation	Transportation is the movement of eroded material from one place to another by wind, water or ice. Examples of transportation include pebbles rolling down a streambed and boulders being carried by moving glaciers.
Deposition	Deposition is the result of transportation, and occurs when the material being carried settles on the surface and is deposited. Sand dunes and moraines are formed by transportation and deposition of glacial material.

SKILL 22.4 Analyzing the development and interaction of social, political, cultural, and religious systems in different regions of New York State, the United States, and the world

CULTURAL IDENTITY: are influenced by their belonging to a particular group or culture

CULTURAL IDENTITY is the identification of individuals or groups as they are influenced by their belonging to a particular group or culture. This refers to the sense of who one is, what values are important, and what racial or ethnic characteristics are important in one's self-understanding and manner of interacting with the world and with others. In a nation with a well-deserved reputation as a "melting pot" the attachment to cultural identities can become a divisive factor in communities and societies. Cosmopolitanism, its alternative, tends to blur those cultural differences in the creation of a shared new culture.

Cross-cultural exchanges, however, can enrich every involved group of people with the discovery of shared values and needs, as well as an appreciation for unique cultural characteristics of each. For the most part, the history of the nation has been the story of successful enculturation and cultural enrichment. The notable failures, often resulting from one sort of prejudice and intolerance or another, are well known. For example, cultural biases have led to the oppression of the Irish or the Chinese immigrants in various parts of the country. Racial biases have led to various kinds of disenfranchisement and oppression of other groups of immigrants. Perhaps most notably, the bias of the European settlers against the civilization and culture of the Native peoples of North America has caused mass extermination, relocation, and isolation.

American popular music, for example, evolved from folk music. This was the music of the first half of the century, characterized by a consistent structure of two verses, a chorus, and a repetition of the chorus. The songs were written to be sung by average persons, and the tunes were usually harmonized. Much of this music originated in New York's Tin Pan Alley. Particularly notable during this period were Irving Berlin, George and Ira Gershwin, and a host of others. After WWII, teen music began to dominate. New forms emerged from various ethnic and regional groups including Blues, Rhythm and Blues and Rap from the African American community; Country music from the south and the southwest, folk music, jazz, rock and roll, and rock.

In art, the primary expression of the first half of the twentieth century was MODERNISM. The avant-garde perspective encouraged all types of innovation and experimentation. Key elements of this movement have been abstraction, cubism, surrealism, realism, and abstract expressionism. Notable among the artists of this period for the birth or perfection of particular styles are Henri Matisse, Pablo Picasso, George Rouault, Gustav Klimt, George Braque, Salvador Dali, Hans Arp, Rene Magrite, and Marcel Duchamp. In the United States realism tended to find regional expressions including the Ashcan School and Robert Henri, Midwestern Regionalism, and Grant Wood. Other particularly notable painters are Edward Hopper and Georgia O'Keeffe. The New York School came to be known for a style known as Abstract Expressionism and included such artists as Jackson Pollock, Willem de Kooning, and Larry Rivers. Other painters of the period were Mark Rothko, Clement Greenberg, Ellsworth Kelly, and the Op Art Movement.

MODERNISM: a genre of art that makes a self-conscious break with previous traditional genres

In painting and sculpture, the new direction of the decade was REALISM. In the early years of the 20th century, American artists had developed several realist styles, some of which were influenced by modernism, others that reacted against it. Several groups of artists of this period are particularly notable.

REALISM: the representation of objects as they actually are without idealizing them

- The Eight or The Ash Can School in New York developed around the work and style of Robert Henri. Their subjects were everyday urban life that was presented without adornment or glamour.

- The American Scene Painters produced a tight, detailed style of painting that focused on images of American life that were understandable to all. In the Midwest, a school within this group was called regionalism. One of the leading artists of regionalism was Grant Wood, best known for American Gothic.

- Other important realists of the day were Edward Hopper and Georgia O'Keeffe.

Statue of Liberty

©iStockphoto.com/Sami Suni

As one of the first colonized areas in the nation, New York was a major point of entry for immigrants. The melding of the Dutch, French, and British settlers into a unified colony was the first step along the way to becoming the melting pot that New York has been to this day. New York's large harbor and growing reputation of the state for business, industry, and commerce, made it a place of special opportunity for immigrants who were seeking freedom and opportunity.

The development of Ellis Island as an immigrant processing center made it the point of entry for millions who came to America in search of political or religious freedom, safe haven from political oppression, and the quest for the American dream. The gift of the Statue of Liberty and its placement in New York harbor, made New York the symbol of American opportunity and freedom. Throughout the history of America, New York has welcomed people from all parts of the world and created within the state a truly international and unique cultural Mecca.

SKILL 22.5 Examining ways in which economic, environmental, and cultural factors influence demographic change, and interpreting geographic relationships, such as population density and spatial distribution patterns

POPULATION: a group of people living within a certain geographic area

A POPULATION is a group of people living within a certain geographic area. Populations are usually measured on a regular basis by census, which also measures age, economic, ethnic and other data. Populations change over time due to many factors, and these changes can have significant impact on cultures.

When a population grows in size, it becomes necessary for it to either expand its geographic boundaries to make room for new people or to increase its density. Population density is simply the number of people in a population divided by the geographic area in which they live. Cultures with a high population density are likely to have different ways of interacting with one another than those with low density, as people live in closer to proximity to one another.

As a population grows, its economic needs change. More basic needs are required and more workers are needed to produce them. If a population's production or purchasing power does not keep pace with its growth, its economy can be adversely affected. The age distribution of a population can affect the economy as well, if the number of young and old people who are not working is disproportionate to those who are.

Growth in some areas may spur migration to other parts of a population's geographic region that are less densely populated. This redistribution of population also places demands on the economy, as infrastructure is needed to connect these new areas to older population centers, and land is put to new use.

Populations can grow naturally, when the rate of birth is higher than the rate of death, or by adding new people from other populations through IMMIGRATION.

Immigration is often a source of societal change as people from other cultures bring their institutions and language to a new area. Immigration also affects a population's educational and economic institutions as immigrants enter the workforce and place their children in schools.

Populations can also decline in number, when the death rate exceeds the birth rate or when people migrate to another area. War, famine, disease and natural disasters can also dramatically reduce a population. The economic problems from population decline can be similar to those from over population because economic demands may be higher than can be met. In extreme cases, a population may decline to the point where it can no longer perpetuate itself and its members and their culture either disappear or are absorbed into another population.

DEMOGRAPHY is the branch of science of statistics most concerned with the social well-being of people. Demographic tables may include:

- Analysis of the population on the basis of age, parentage, physical condition, race, occupation and civil position, giving the actual size and the density of each separate area

- Changes in the population as a result of birth, marriage, and death

- Statistics on population movements and their effects and their relations to given economic, social and political conditions

- Statistics of crime, illegitimacy, and suicide

- Levels of education and economic and social statistics

> **IMMIGRATION:** to enter and settle in a country or region to which one is not native

> **DEMOGRAPHY:** the branch of science of statistics most concerned with the social well being of people

Such information is also similar to that area of science known as vital statistics and as such is indispensable in studying social trends and making important legislative, economic, and social decisions. Such demographic information is gathered from census, and registrar reports and the like, and by state laws such information, especially the vital kind, is kept by physicians, attorneys, funeral directors, members of the clergy, and similar professional people. In the United States such demographic information is compiled, kept and published by the Public Health Service of the United States Department of Health, Education, and Welfare.

The most important element of this information is the so-called rate, which customarily represents the average of births and deaths for a unit of 1000 population over a given calendar year. These general rates are called crude rates, which are then subdivided into sex, color, age, occupation, locality, etc. They are then known as refined rates.

STATISTICS: the mathematical science that deals with the collection, organization, presentation, and analysis of various forms of numerical data

In examining STATISTICS and the sources of statistical data one must also be aware of the methods of statistical information gathering. For instance, there are many good sources of raw statistical data. Books such as *The Statistical Abstract of the United States*, published by the United States Chamber of Commerce; *The World Fact Book*, published by the Central Intelligence Agency; or *The Monthly Labor Review*, published by the United States Department of Labor are excellent examples that contain much raw data.

Simply put, statistics is the mathematical science that deals with the collection, organization, presentation, and analysis of various forms of numerical data and with the problems such as interpreting and understanding such data. The raw materials of statistics are sets of numbers obtained from enumerations or measurements collected by various methods of extrapolation, such as census taking, interviews, and observations.

CORROBORATED: the data presented is more consistent with this theory than with any other theory

CORRELATION: the joint movement of various data points

One important idea to understand is that statistics usually deal with a specific model, hypothesis, or theory that is being attempted to be proven. One should be aware, however, that a theory could never actually be proved correct; it can only be CORROBORATED. One should also be aware that what is known as CORRELATION does not infer CAUSATION. It is important that one take these aspects into account so that one can be in a better position to appreciate what the collected data is really saying.

CAUSATION: the change in one of those data points caused the other data points to change

Tests of reliability are used, bearing in mind the manner in which the data has been collected and the inherent biases of any artificially created model to be used to explain real world events. Indeed the methods used and the inherent biases and reasons actually for doing the study by the individual(s) involved must never be discounted.

Geography of New York State

The northern and eastern sections of New York are mountainous, while the remainder of the state is a region of low plateaus and rolling plains. Excluding Long Island, the surface of which is low and level, New York can be divided into several well-marked physical regions.

PHYSICAL REGIONS OF NEW YORK	
Eastern Mountain Belt	This is a region of rugged hills and low mountains, the continuation of the Green Mountains and of the Berkshire Hills of New England. It occupies the entire portion east of the Hudson River ("River of Steep Hills.").
The Plateau Region and the Catskill Mountains	West of the Hudson River is the plateau region, which extends through Southern and Central New York almost to Lake Erie. This region is the northern extension of the Allegheny plateau, which skirts the western base of the Appalachian Mountains. The eastern limit of this plateau is formed by the Catskill Mountains. The Catskills cover an area of about 500 square miles and are in the form of a group rather than a range. Many of their slopes are wooded, and the intervening valleys are fertile. The highest peak, Slide Mountain, has an altitude of 4,205 feet, and there are several peaks between 3,000 and 4,000 feet high. This entire extensive plateau region is divided by many deep and wide valleys, which have a general direction from north to south.
Adirondacks	The most notable feature of New York's surface is the roughly circular mountain region believed to have been the first mountains of the western world to emerge from the ocean and known as the Adirondacks. This region has an area of over 5,000 square miles and covers the northeastern portion of the state, extending south to the Mohawk Valley. The region is noted for its rugged peaks, primeval forests, and its hundreds of lakes and mountain streams. It contains many peaks between 3,000 and 4,000 feet high. Mount Marcy, at 5,344 feed, is the highest point of the state. To the west of the Adirondacks and north of the plateau region extends the lake-shore plain, which has a slightly undulating surface, sloping gently toward Lake Erie and Lake Ontario. The soil of this plain is very fertile, and the region is particularly suited to fruit-raising.
Mohawk Valley	This area, which extends from the Hudson River near Albany and west to Utica, is the low, narrow valley of the Mohawk River, dividing the Adirondacks from the Catskills. The Hudson-Mohawk Valley forms the only great break in the Appalachian system and the best access to the interior of the continent. It provided the only natural trade route between the Atlantic and the Great Lakes prior to the construction of the Erie Canal; the Hudson-Lake Champlain route was very important in the early years of the colonies.

Rivers

All parts of the state are well supplied with rivers, which find their way into the Atlantic Ocean by five different drainage basins. These navigable waters and the open valleys which lead out in all directions have been among the main factors which have contributed to give New York its leading commercial position. Foremost among them are the Hudson and the Mohawk. The rivers in the northern part of the state flow into Lakes Erie and Ontario and are drained through the Saint Lawrence River into the Atlantic Ocean. Among these rivers are the Genesee, which completely traverses the state from south to north, and the Oswego and its tributary the Seneca, which gather the waters of the Finger Lakes. The southern part of the state is drained by the Delaware, the Susquehanna, and the Allegheny.

Waterfalls

Many of these rivers flow through wide and fertile valleys during the greater part of their course, but at some points pass through deep gorges and form notable waterfalls. These falls are sources of water power, a fact that has caused the establishment of large industrial plants in their neighborhood.

Lakes

New York contains a large number of lakes, either wholly or partly within its boundaries. Most notable are Lake George and Lake Champlain. In the plateau region directly south of Lake Ontario there is a group of long, narrow, navigable lakes, nearly parallel to each other, with their greatest length extending from north to south. These are known as the Finger Lakes. Northeast of these is Lake Oneida. In the extreme southwestern part of the state is Lake Chautauqua.

During the glacial epoch, ice sheets covered most of the northern part of the continent, extending about as far south as New York Bay and the Ohio, Missouri, and Columbia Rivers. There was also extensive glaciation in the Rocky Mountains and in the Sierra Nevadas. The ice accumulated around several centers of dispersion. As it reached a significant thickness, it moved outward from the center in all directions, but primarily southward. At their greatest extent they covered hundreds of thousands of square miles and were several thousand feet thick, so that mountains such as the Adirondacks were completely buried in ice. As the ice advanced, it removed the soil and loose material down to the bedrock, into which it gouged deeply in places. Hilltops were ground down and valleys were deepened, and a large amount of rock material was removed and transported by the ice, sometimes for hundreds of miles.

In time, the ice sheets spread so far that their advance was stopped and the southern margins could not extend beyond where the ice melted as fast as it advanced. The transported material was deposited at the margin of the ice in an irregular, hummocky ridge called the terminal moraine, or was borne away by water flowing from the melting ice. When the advance of the glaciers had stopped, they began to melt away from the area they had occupied, leaving behind them great drift sheets formed of the transported material. In areas of little relief, such as the prairies of

Adirondacks

©iStockphoto.com/Lauri Wiberg

the North Central states, the thick blanket of drift obliterated the former topography and gave a new surface to the region.

On this surface was developed a new system of drainage, which in many regions is characterized by the abundance of lakes and swamps. During the disappearance of the ice, many temporary lakes formed in low places along the ice margin. When these lakes were drained, through the opening of lower outlets by the further melting of the ice, the silt deposited on their former beds became the fertile soil.

Sample Test Questions and Rationale

Rigorous

1. **Vital statistics, social trends, and crude rates are all apart of a branch of science of statistics which is concerned with the social well being of people. What is the name of this branch?**

   A. cartography

   B. sociology

   C. demography

   D. psychology

Answer: C – Demography

Rationale: Demography is the branch of science of statistics most concerned with the social well being of people. Demographic tables may include: analysis of the population on the basis of age, parentage, physical condition, race, occupation and civil position.

SKILL 22.6 Analyzing the impact of human activity on the physical environment

Environmental and geographic factors have affected the pattern of urban development in New York and the rest of the United States. In turn, urban infrastructure and development patterns are interrelated factors, which affect one another.

The growth of urban areas is often linked to the advantages provided by its geographic location. Before the advent of efficient overland routes of commerce such as railroads and highways, water provided the primary means of transportation of commercial goods. Most large American cities are situated along bodies of water. New York's major cities include Buffalo, on Lake Erie, Albany, on the Hudson River, and of course New York City, situated on a large harbor where two major rivers meet the Atlantic Ocean. Where water traffic was not provided for naturally, New Yorkers built a series of canals, including the Erie Canal, which sparked the growth of inland cities.

As transportation technology advanced, the supporting infrastructure was built to connect cities with one another and to connect remote areas to larger communities. The railroad, for example, allowed for the quick transport of agricultural products from rural areas to urban centers. This newfound efficiency not only further fueled the growth of urban centers it changed the economy of rural America. Where once farmers had practiced only subsistence farming—growing enough to support one's own family—the new infrastructure meant that one could convert agricultural products into cash by selling them at market.

For urban dwellers, improvements in building technology and advances in transportation allowed for larger cities. Growth brought with it a new set of problems unique to each location. The bodies of water that had made the development of cities possible in their early days also formed natural barriers to growth. Further infrastructure in the form of bridges, tunnels and ferry routes were needed to connect central urban areas with outlying communities.

As cities grew in population, living conditions became more crowded. As roads and bridges became better, and transportation technology improved, many people began to look outside the city for living space. Along with the development of these new suburbs came the infrastructure to connect them to the city in the form of commuter railroads and highways. In the case of New York City, which is situated mainly on islands, a mass transit system became crucial early on to bring essential workers from outlying areas into the commercial centers.

The growth of suburbs had the effect in many cities of creating a type of economic segregation. Working class people who could not afford new suburban homes and perhaps an automobile to carry them to and from work were relegated to closer, more densely populated areas. Frequently, these areas had to be passed through by those on their way to the suburbs, and rail lines and freeways sometimes bisected these urban communities. Acres of farmland and forest were cleared to make way for growing suburban areas.

In the modern age, advancements in telecommunications infrastructure may have an impact on urban growth patterns as information can pass instantly and freely between almost any two points on the globe, allowing access to some aspects of urban life to those in remote areas.

By nature, people are essentially social creatures. They generally live in communities or settlements of some kind and of some size. Settlements are the cradles of culture, political structure, education, and the management of resources.

The relative placement of these settlements or communities are shaped by the proximity to natural resources, the movement of raw materials, the production of finished products, the availability of a work force, and the delivery of finished products. Shared values, language, culture, religion, and subsistence will at least to some extent, determine the composition of communities.

Cities are the major hubs of human settlement. Almost half of the population of the world now lives in cities. These percentages are much higher in developed regions. Established cities continue to grow. The fastest growth, however, is occurring in developing areas. In some regions there are "metropolitan areas" made up of urban and suburban areas. In some places cities and urban areas have become interconnected into *megalopoli* (e.g., Tokyo-Kawasaki-Yokohama).

The concentrations of populations and the divisions of these areas among various groups that constitute the cities can differ significantly. North American cities are different from European cities in terms of shape, size, population density, and modes of transportation. While in North America, the wealthiest economic groups tend to live outside the cities, the opposite is true in Latin American cities.

There are significant differences among the cities of the world in terms of connectedness to other cities. While European and North American cities tend to be well linked both by transportation and communication connections, there are other places in the world in which communication between the cities of the country may be inferior to communication with the rest of the world.

NATURAL RESOURCES are naturally occurring substances that are considered valuable in their natural form. A commodity is generally considered a natural resource when the primary activities associated with it are extraction and purification, as opposed to creation. Thus, mining, petroleum extraction, fishing, and forestry are generally considered natural resource industries, while agriculture is not.

Natural resources are often classified into RENEWABLE and NONRENEWABLE resources. Renewable resources are generally living resources (fish, coffee, and forests, for example), which can restock (renew) themselves if they are not overharvested. Renewable resources can restock themselves and be used indefinitely if they are sustained. Once renewable resources are consumed at a rate that exceeds their natural rate of replacement, the standing stock will diminish and eventually run out. The rate of sustainable use of a renewable resource is determined by the replacement rate and amount of standing stock of that particular resource.

Nonliving renewable natural resources include soil, as well as water, wind, and solar radiation. Natural resources include soil, timber, oil, minerals, and other goods taken more or less as they are from the Earth.

NATURAL RESOURCES: naturally occurring substances that are considered valuable in their natural form such as fish and forests

RENEWABLE RESOURCES: generally living resources, which can restock themselves if not overharvested

NONRENEWABLE RESOURCES: resources that exceed their natural rate of replacement and can run out

In recent years, the depletion of natural capital and attempts to move to sustainable development has been a major focus of development agencies. This is of particular concern in rainforest regions, which hold most of the Earth's natural biodiversity—irreplaceable genetic natural capital. Conservation of natural resources is the major focus of Natural Capitalism, environmentalism, the ecology movement, and Green Parties. Some view this depletion as a major source of social unrest and conflicts in developing nations.

ENVIRONMENTAL POLICY is concerned with the sustainability of the Earth, the region under the administration of the governing group or individual or a local habitat. The concern of environmental policy is the preservation of the region, habitat or ecosystem.

Because humans, both individually and in community, rely upon the environment to sustain human life, social and environmental policy must be mutually supportable. Because humans, both individually and in community, live upon the Earth, draw upon the natural resources of the Earth, and affect the environment in many ways, environmental and social policy must be mutually supportive.

In an age of GLOBAL WARMING, unprecedented demand upon natural resources, and a shrinking planet, social and environmental policies must become increasingly interdependent if the planet is to continue to support life and human civilization.

For example, between 1870 and 1916, more than 25 million immigrants came into the United States adding to the phenomenal population growth taking place. This tremendous growth aided business and industry in two ways:

- The number of consumers increased creating a greater demand for products thus enlarging the markets for the products

- With increased production and expanding business, more workers were available for newly created jobs

The completion of the nation's transcontinental railroad in 1869 contributed greatly to the nation's economic and industrial growth. Many wealthy industrialists and railroad owners saw tremendous profits steadily increasing due to this improved method of transportation. Yet, natural resources were required to support the growing population and its needs.

ENVIRONMENTAL POLICY: concerned with the sustainability of the Earth, the region under the administration of the governing group or individual or a local habitat

GLOBAL WARMING: an increase in the average temperature of the Earth's atmosphere

Lesson plans and resources for teaching geography:

http://www.learner.org/resources/series161.html

http://geography.about.com/od/teachgeography/Teach_Geography.htm

http://www.educationworld.com/a_lesson/lesson/lesson071.shtml

http://www.sunysb.edu/libmap/nymaps.htm

http://www.geographyzone.com/new/index.php

COMPETENCY 23

UNDERSTAND CONCEPTS AND PHENOMENA RELATED TO HUMAN DEVELOPMENT AND INTERACTIONS

> **SKILL 23.1** Using concepts, theories, and modes of inquiry drawn from anthropology, psychology, and sociology to examine general social phenomena and issues related to intercultural understanding

The study of social phenomena can draw on the methods and theories of several disciplines.

- Anthropology is largely concerned with the institutions of a society and intercultural comparisons. Anthropologists observe people of a particular culture acting within their culture and interacting with people of other cultures, and interpret social phenomena. Anthropology relies on QUALITATIVE RESEARCH, such as researching the types of rituals a culture has, as well as QUANTITATIVE RESEARCH, such as measuring the relative sizes of ethnic groups.

- Psychology is mainly centered on the study of the individual and his behavior. As humans are social animals, the methods of psychology can be used to study society and culture by asking questions about how individuals behave within these groups, what motivates them, and the ways they find to express themselves.

- Sociology covers how humans act as a society and within a society, and examines the rules and mechanisms they follow as a society. Sociology also looks at groups within a society and how they interact. The field relies on research methods from several disciplines, including anthropology and psychology.

QUALITATIVE RESEARCH: such as researching the types of rituals a culture has

QUANTITATIVE RESEARCH: such as measuring the relative sizes of ethnic groups

THEORIES OF SOCIAL PHENOMENA	
Causality	The reason something happens, its cause, is a basic category of human thinking. We want to know the causes of some major event in our lives. Within the study of history, causality is the analysis of the reasons for change. The question we are asking is why and how a particular society or event developed in the particular way it did given the context in which it occurred.
Conflict	Conflict within history is opposition of ideas, principles, values or claims. Conflict may take the form of internal clashes of principles or ideas or claims within a society or group or it may take the form of opposition between groups or societies.

Table continued on next page

Bias	A prejudice or a predisposition either toward or against something. In the study of history, bias can refer to the persons or groups studied, in terms of a society's bias toward a particular political system, or it can refer to the historian's predisposition to evaluate events in a particular way.
Interdependence	A condition in which two things or groups rely upon one another, as opposed to independence, in which each thing or group relies only upon itself.
Identity	The state or perception of being a particular thing or person. Identity can also refer to the understanding or self-understanding of groups, nations, etc.
Nation–state	A particular type of political entity that provides a sovereign territory for a specific nation in which other factors also unites the citizens (e.g., language, race, ancestry, etc.).
Culture	The civilization, achievements, and customs of the people of a particular time and place.

SKILL 23.2 Evaluating factors that contribute to personal identity

Socialization is the process by which humans learn the expectations their society has for their behavior, in order that they might successfully function within that society.

Socialization takes place primarily in children as they learn and are taught the rules and norms of their culture. Children grow up eating the common foods of a culture and develop a "taste" for these foods, for example. By observing adults and older children, they learn about gender roles and appropriate ways to interact. The family is the primary influence in this kind of socialization and contributes directly to a person's sense of self-importance and personal identity.

Through socialization, a person gains a sense of belonging to a group of people with common ideals and behaviors. When a person encounters people affiliated with other groups, their own group affiliation can be reinforced in contrast, contributing to their own sense of personal identity.

SKILL 23.3 Recognizing how language, literature, the arts, media, architecture, traditions, beliefs, values, and behaviors influence and/or reflect the development and transmission of culture

The traditions and behaviors of a culture are based on the prevailing beliefs and values of that culture. Beliefs and values are similar and interrelated systems.

Beliefs are those things that are thought to be true. Beliefs are often associated with religion, but beliefs can also be based on political or ideological philosophies. "All men are created equal," is an example of an ideological belief.

Values are what a society thinks are right and wrong, and are often based on and shaped by beliefs. The value that every member of the society has a right to participate in his government might be considered to be based on the belief that "All men are created equal," for instance.

A culture's beliefs and values are reflected in the cultural products it produces, such as literature, the arts, media and architecture. These products become part of the culture and last from generation to generation, becoming one way that culture is transmitted through time. A common language among all members of a culture makes this transmission possible.

SKILL 23.4 Analyzing the roles and functions of social groups and institutions in the United States and their influence on individual and group interactions

Sociologists have identified five different types of institutions around which societies are structured: family, education, government, religion, and economy. These institutions provide a framework for members of a society to learn about and participate in a society, and allow for a society to perpetuate its beliefs and values to succeeding generations.

> *The five different types of institutions around which societies are structured: family, education, government, religion, and economy*

1. The family is the primary social unit in most societies. It is through the family that children learn the most essential skills for functioning in their society such as language and appropriate forms of interaction. The family is connected to ethnicity, which is partly defined by a person's heritage.

2. Education is an important institution in a society, as it allows for the formal passing on of a culture's collected knowledge. The institution of education is connected to the family, as that is where a child's earliest education

takes place. The United States has a public school system administered by the states that ensures a basic education and provides a common experience for most children.

3. A society's governmental institutions often embody its beliefs and values. Laws, for instance, reflect a society's values by enforcing its ideas of right and wrong. The structure of a society's government can reflect a society's ideals about the role of an individual in his society. The American form of democracy emphasizes the rights of the individual, but in return expects individuals to respect the rights of others, including those of ethnic or political minorities.

4. Religion is frequently the institution from which springs a society's primary beliefs and values and can be closely related to other social institutions. Many religions have definite teachings on the structure and importance of the family, for instance. The U.S. Constitution guarantees the free practice of religion, which has led to a large number of denominations practicing in the United States today.

5. A society's economic institutions define how an individual can contribute and receive economic reward from his society. The United States has a capitalist economy motivated by free enterprise. While this system allows for economic advancement for the individual, it can also produce areas of poverty and economic depression.

> ## SKILL 23.5 Analyzing why individuals and groups hold different or competing points of view on issues, events, or historical developments

Humans are social animals who naturally form groups based on familial, cultural, national, and other lines. Conflicts and differences of opinion are just as natural between these groups.

ETHNOCENTRISM:
the belief that one's own culture is the central and usually superior culture

One source of differing views among groups is ethnocentrism. ETHNOCENTRISM, as the word suggests, is the belief that one's own culture is the central and usually superior culture. An ethnocentric view usually considers different practices in other cultures as inferior or even "savage."

Psychologists have suggested that ethnocentrism is a naturally occurring attitude. For the large part, people are most comfortable among other people who share their same upbringing, language, and cultural background, and are likely to judge other cultural behaviors as alien or foreign.

Historical developments are likely to affect different groups in different ways, some positively and some negatively. These effects can strengthen the ties an individual feels to the group he or she belongs to and solidify differences between groups.

Sample Test Questions and Rationale

Average Rigor

1. _____ is the belief that one's own culture is the central and the superior culture.

   A. Ethnocentrism

   B. Egocentric

   C. Prejudice

   D. Superiority

Answer: A – Ethnocentrism

Rationale: Ethnocentrism, as the word suggests, is the belief that one's own culture is the central and usually superior culture. An ethnocentric view usually considers different practices in other cultures as inferior or even "savage."

SKILL 23.6 Understanding the processes of social and cultural change

- **Innovation** is the introduction of new ways of performing work or organizing societies, and can spur drastic changes in a culture. Prior to the innovation of agriculture, for instance, human cultures were largely nomadic and survived by hunting and gathering their food. Agriculture led directly to the development of permanent settlements and a radical change in social organization. Likewise, technological innovations in the Industrial Revolution of the nineteenth century changed the way work was performed and transformed the economic institutions of western cultures. Recent innovations in communications are changing the way cultures interact today.

- **Cultural diffusion** is the movement of cultural ideas or materials between populations independent of the movement of those populations. Cultural diffusion can take place when two populations are close to one another, through direct interaction, or across great distances, through mass media and via other routes. American movies are popular all over the world, for instance. Within the United States, hockey, traditionally a Canadian pastime, has become a popular sport. These are both examples of cultural diffusion.

- Adaptation is the process that individuals and societies go through in changing their behavior and organization to cope with social, economic and environmental pressures.

- Acculturation is an exchange or adoption of cultural features when two cultures come into regular direct contact. An example of acculturation is the adoption of Christianity and western dress by many Native Americans in the United States.

- Assimilation is the process of a minority ethnic group largely adopting the culture of the larger group it exists within. These groups are typically immigrants moving to a new country, as with the European immigrants who traveled to the United States at the beginning of the twentieth century who assimilated to American culture.

- Extinction is the complete disappearance of a culture. Extinction can occur suddenly, from disease, famine, or war when the people of a culture are completely destroyed, or slowly over time as a culture adapts, acculturates, or assimilates to the point where its original features are lost.

Teaching human development and interactions:

http://www.mrdonn.org/sociology.html

http://db.education-world.com/perl/browse?cat_id=2255

http://www.studysphere.com/Site/Sphere_6155.html

COMPETENCY 24

UNDERSTAND ECONOMIC AND POLITICAL PRINCIPLES, CONCEPTS, AND SYSTEMS, AND RELATE THIS KNOWLEDGE TO HISTORICAL AND CONTEMPORARY DEVELOPMENTS IN NEW YORK STATE, THE UNITED STATES, AND THE WORLD

SKILL 24.1 Defining important economic and political terms and use them to analyze general phenomena and specific issues

The fact that resources are scarce is the basis for the existence of economics. Economics is defined as a study of how scarce resources are allocated to satisfy unlimited wants. Resources refer to the four factors of production: labor, capital, land, and entrepreneurship. The individual has the right to supply whatever resources he wants to the market. The fact that the supply of these resources is finite means that society cannot have as much of everything that it wants. There is a constraint on production and consumption and on the kinds of goods and services that can be produced and consumed.

Scarcity means that choices have to be made. If society decides to produce more of one good, this means that there are fewer resources available for the production of other goods. Assume a society can produce two goods, good A and good B. The society uses resources in the production of each good. If producing one unit of good A results in an amount of resources used to produce three units of good B then producing one more unit of good A results in a decrease in 3 units of good B. In effect, one unit of good A "costs" three units of good B.

This cost is referred to as opportunity cost. OPPORTUNITY COST is the value of the sacrificed alternative, the value of what had to be given up in order to have the output of good A. Opportunity cost does not just refer to production. Your opportunity cost of studying with this guide is the value of what you are not doing because you are studying, whether it is watching TV, spending time with family, working, or whatever. Every choice has an opportunity cost.

The supply curve represents the selling and production decisions of the seller and is based on the costs of production. The costs of production of a product are based on the costs of the resources used in its production. The costs of resources are based on the scarcity of the resource. The scarcer a resource is, relatively speaking, the higher its price. A diamond costs more than paper because diamonds are scarcer than paper is. All of these concepts are embodied in the seller's supply curve. The same thing is true on the buying side of the market. The buyer's preferences, tastes, income, etc.—all of his or her buying decisions —are embodied in the demand curve.

Where the demand and supply curves intersect is where the buying decisions of buyers are equal to the selling decisions of sellers. The quantity that buyers want to buy at a particular price is equal to the quantity that sellers want to sell at that particular price. The market is in equilibrium.

Teaching economics:

http://fte.org/teachers/lessons/lessons.htm

http://www.teachingeconomics.org/

http://ecedweb.unomaha.edu/teachsug.htm

http://lessonplanz.com/Lesson_Plans/Social_Studies/__Grades_K-2/Economics/index.shtml

OPPORTUNITY COST: the value of the sacrificed alternative, the value of what had to be given up in order to have the output of good A

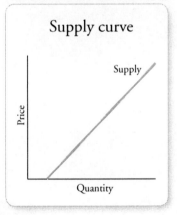
Supply curve

CASE STUDY

What happens when there is a change? Suppose a new big oil field is found. Also suppose there is a technology that allows its recovery and refining at a fraction of the present costs. The result is a big increase in the supply of oil at lower costs, as reflected by a rightward shifting oil supply curve. Oil is used as an input into almost all production. Firms now have lower costs. This means that the firm can produce the same amount of output at a lower cost or can produce a larger amount of output at the same cost. The result is a rightward shift of the firm's, and therefore, the industry supply curve. This means that sellers are willing and able to offer for sale larger quantities of output at each price. Assuming buyers' buying decisions stay the same, there is a new market equilibrium, or new point of intersection of the shifted supply curve with the buyers' demand curve. The result is a lower price with a larger quantity of output. The market has achieved a new equilibrium based on the increase in the quantity of a resource.

Firms in markets tend to grow over time. If there is a market for the firm's product, as it grows it experiences economies of scale, or lower per-unit costs. As firms grow they tend to become large relative to the market and the smaller more inefficient firms tend to go out of business. Larger firms have more market power and are able to influence their price and output. They can become monopolistic. Government counters this lessening of competition in a market by enacting antitrust legislation to protect the competitive nature of the market.

Sample Test Questions and Rationale

Rigorous

1. **Economics is defined as a study of:**

   A. how scarce resources are allocated to satisfy unlimited wants

   B. anything that is manufactured to be used in the production process

   C. anyone who sells his ability to produce goods and services

   D. decisions of buyers are equal to the selling decision of seller

Answer: A – how scarce resources are allocated to satisfy unlimited wants

Rationale: Economics is defined as a study of how scarce resources are allocated to satisfy unlimited wants. Capital is anything that is manufactured to be used in the production process. Market equilibrium occurs where the buying decisions of buyers are equal to the selling decision of seller.

SKILL 24.2 Analyzing the basic structure, fundamental ideas, accomplishments, and problems of the U.S. economic system

The U.S. economy consists of the **household** or **consumer sector**, the **business sector**, and the **government sector**. Households earn their incomes by selling their factors of production in the input market. Businesses hire their inputs in the factor market and use them to produce outputs. Households use their incomes earned in the factor market to purchase the output of businesses. Both households and businesses are active participants in both the input and output market. The function of organized labor was to help obtain a higher factor income for workers. They negotiate the work agreement, or contract, for their union members. This collective bargaining agreement states the terms and conditions of employment for the length of the contract, and is a contract between the worker and the employer. Households do not spend all of their income; they save some of it in banks. A well-organized smoothly functioning banking system is required for the operation of the economy.

MACROECONOMICS refers to the functioning of the economy on the national level and the functioning of the aggregate units that comprise the national economy. Macroeconomics is concerned with a study of the economy's overall economic performance, or what is called the GROSS DOMESTIC PRODUCT or GDP. The GDP is a measure of the economy's output during a specified time period. Tabulating the economy's output can be measured in two ways, both of which give the same result: the expenditures approach and the incomes approach. Basically, what is spent on the national output by each sectors of the economy is equal to what is earned producing the national output by each of the factors of production.

> **MACROECONOMICS:** study of the economy's overall economic performance, or what is called the Gross Domestic Product

> **GROSS DOMESTIC PRODUCT:** a measure of the economy's output during a specified time period

FOUR SECTORS OF A MACRO ECONOMY	
consumers	government
businesses	foreign interests

In the expenditures approach, GDP is determined by the amount of spending in each sector. GDP is equal to the consumption expenditures of consumers plus the investment expenditures of businesses plus spending of all three levels of government plus the net export spending in the foreign sector: GDP = C + I + G + (X−M).

When the economy is functioning smoothly, the amount of national output produced, or the aggregate supply, is just equal to the amount of national output purchased, or aggregate demand. Then we have an economy in a period of prosperity without economic instability. But market economies experience the fluctuations of the business cycle, the ups and downs in the level of economic activity.

FOUR PHASES OF ECONOMIC ACTIVITY	
boom	period of prosperity
recession	a period of declining GDP and rising unemployment
trough	the low point of the recession
recovery	a period of lessening unemployment and rising prices

There are no rules pertaining to the duration or severity of any of the phases. The phases result in periods of unemployment and periods of inflation.

Inflation results from too much spending in the economy. Buyers want to buy more than sellers can produce and bid up prices for the available output. Unemployment occurs when there is not enough spending in the economy. Sellers have produced more output than buyers are buying and the result is a surplus situation. Firms faced with surplus merchandise lower their production levels and layoff workers and there is unemployment. These are situations that require government policy actions.

The U.S. economy is based on the concepts of individual freedom of choice and competition. Economic agents are free to pursue their own interests. They can choose their occupation and undertake entrepreneurial ventures. If they are successful, they gain in the form of profits. The profit incentive is very important because people and businesses are willing to take risks for the possibility of gaining profit. The U.S. economy is one of the most successful economies in the world with the highest total GDP. Like any market economy, it is subject to the business cycle, the temporary bouts of inflation, and/or unemployment. When they occur, appropriate policies are implemented to counteract them.

SKILL 24.3 Recognizing and compare basic characteristics of major models of economic organization and various governmental systems

TRADITIONAL ECONOMY: an economy based on tradition and "old: ways of doing things

The TRADITIONAL ECONOMY is one based on custom. This usually describes the situation that exists in many less-developed countries. The people do things the way their ancestors did so they are not too technologically advanced. Since their whole mindset is directed toward tradition, they are not very interested in technology, equipment, and new ways of doing things. Technology and equipment are viewed as a threat to the old way of doing things and to their tradition. There is very little upward mobility for the same reason.

CAPITALISM: an economic system based on private ownership of capital

The model of CAPITALISM is based on private ownership of the means of production and operates on the basis of free markets, on both the input and output side. The free markets function to coordinate market activity and to achieve an efficient allocation of resources. Laissez-faire capitalism is based on the premise of no government intervention in the economy. The market will eliminate any unemployment or inflation that occurs. Government needs only to provide the framework for the functioning of the economy and to protect private property. The role of financial incentives is crucial for it results in risk-taking and research and development. Capitalist economies tend to have democratic forms of government because the system is based on competition and individual freedoms.

A COMMAND ECONOMY is almost the exact opposite of a market economy. A command economy is based on government ownership of the means of production and the use of planning to take the place of the market. Instead of the market determining the output mix and the allocation of resources, the bureaucracy fulfills this role by determining the output mix and establishing production target for the enterprises, which are publicly owned. The result is inefficiency. There is little interest in innovation and research because there is no financial reward for the innovator. A command economy tends to have an authoritarian form of government because a planning mechanism that replaces the market requires a planning authority to make decisions supplementing the freedom of choice of consumers and workers.

> **COMMAND ECONOMY:** an economy in which decisions about production and allocation are made by the governement

A MIXED ECONOMY uses a combination of markets and planning, with the degree of each varying according to country. The real world can be described as mixed economies, each with varying degrees of planning. The use of markets results in the greatest efficiency since markets direct resources in and out of industries according to changing profit conditions. However, government is needed to perform various functions. The degree of government involvement in the economy can vary in mixed economies. Government is needed to keep the economy stable during periods of inflation and unemployment.

> **MIXED ECONOMY:** an economy in which certain sectors are left to private ownership and the free market, while others are regulated by the government

All of the major economies of the world are mixed economies. They use markets but have different degrees of government involvement in the functioning of the markets and in the provision of public goods. For example, in some countries health care and education are provided by government and are not a part of the private sector. In the United States, most health care and higher education is private and at the expense of the consumer.

Sample Test Questions and Rationale

Rigorous

1. Laissez-faire capitalism is based on:

   A. government ownership of the means of production

   B. custom and usually exists in less developed countries

   C. the premise of no government intervention in the economy

   D. none of the above

Answer: C – the premise of no government intervention in the economy

Rationale: Laissez-faire capitalism is based on the premise of no government intervention in the economy. The market will eliminate any unemployment or inflation that occurs. Government needs only to provide the framework for the functioning of the economy and to protect private property.

SKILL 24.4 Analyzing values, principles, concepts, and key features of American constitutional democracy

The American nation was founded very much with the idea that the people would have a large degree of autonomy and liberty. The famous maxim no taxation without representation was a rallying cry for the Revolution, not only because the people didn't want to suffer the increasingly oppressive series of taxes imposed on them by the British Parliament, but also because the people could not in any way influence the lawmakers in Parliament in regard to those taxes. No American colonist had a seat in Parliament and no American colonist could vote for members of Parliament.

One of the most famous words in the Declaration of Independence is "liberty," the pursuit of which all people should be free to attempt. That idea, that a people should be free to pursue their own course, even to the extent of making their own mistakes, has dominated political thought in the 200-plus years of the American republic.

REPRESENTATION, the idea that a people can vote—or even replace—their lawmakers was not a new idea, except in America. Residents of other British colonies did not have these rights, of course, and America was only a colony, according to the conventional wisdom of the British government at the time. What the Sons of

REPRESENTATION: the idea that a people can vote

Liberty and other revolutionaries were asking for was to stand on an equal footing with the Mother Country. Along with the idea of representation comes the notion that key ideas and concepts can be deliberated and discussed, with theoretically everyone having a chance to voice their views. This applied to both lawmakers and the people who elected them. Lawmakers wouldn't just pass bills that became laws; rather, they would debate the particulars and go back and forth on the strengths and weaknesses of proposed laws before voting on them. Members of both houses of Congress had the opportunity to speak out on the issues, as did the people at large, who could contact their lawmakers and express their views. This idea ran very much counter to the experience that the Founding Fathers had before the Revolution—that of taxation without representation. The different branches of government were designed to serve as a mechanism of checks and balances on each other so that no one branch could become too powerful. They each have their own specific powers.

Another key concept in the American ideal is equality, the idea that every person has the same rights and responsibilities under the law. The Great Britain that the American colonists knew was one of a stratified society, with social classes firmly in place. Not everyone was equal under the law or in the coffers; and it was clear for all to see that the more money and power a person had, the easier it was for that person to avoid things like serving in the army and being charged with a crime. The goal of the Declaration of Independence and the Constitution was to provide equality for all who read those documents. The reality, though, was vastly different for large sectors of society, including women and nonwhite Americans.

Due process under law was also a big concern of the founders. Various amendments protect the rights of people. Amendments five through eight protect citizens who are accused of crimes and are brought to trial. Every citizen has the right to due process of law (due process as defined earlier being that the government must follow the same fair rules for everyone brought to trial). These rules include the right to a trial by an impartial jury, the right to be defended by a lawyer, and the right to a speedy trial. The last two amendments limit the powers of the federal government to those that are expressly granted in the Constitution; any rights not expressly mentioned in the Constitution, thus, belong to the states or to the people.

This feeds into the idea of basic opportunity. The "American Dream" is that every individual has an equal chance to make his or her fortune in a new land and that the United States welcomes and even encourages that initiative. The history of the country is filled with stories of people who ventured to America and made their fortunes in the Land of Opportunity. Unfortunately for anyone who wasn't a white male, that basic opportunity was sometimes a difficult thing to achieve.

SKILL 24.5 Comparing different perspectives regarding economic and political issues and policies in New York State and the United States

New York City has played a critical role in the development of the State of New York and the nation in many capacities. The huge harbor made the city an important port in colonial times. The construction of the wooden wall that was intended to keep out aggressors became both an actual and a symbolic center of economy and commerce. The tree at the end of the street where traders and dealers gathered informally later became the site of the New York Stock Exchange. This marked the beginning of New York's importance in the state's economy and the national economy. In time, it made the city a central point in international economy.

The construction of the Erie Canal, completed in 1825, further enhanced the importance of the port of New York. It was replaced in 1918 by the Barge Canal. This system of waterways was later expanded even more with the construction of the St. Lawrence Seaway. Transportation on land developed very quickly after the construction of a system of turnpikes, beginning in the 1880s. By 1853, railroads crossed the state and connected to those that crossed the nation.

New York City has one of the largest regional economies in the nation. It is a global center for business and commerce. With London, Hong Kong, Paris, and Tokyo, New York City is one of the main cities that controls world finance. Many consider it the financial capital of the world. In addition to finance and commerce, New York City is critical to the insurance and real estate industries. It is also the single most important center for publishing, mass media, and journalism in the country. In addition, it is critical in medical research, technology, fashion, and the arts. More Fortune 500 companies are based in New York City than any other city in the nation. Many international companies are also headquartered in the city.

New York City has historically been the point of entry into the United States for millions of immigrants. This made the city a major haven for oppressed people throughout the world and the point of entry that made the nation the "melting pot" that it is. The decision to locate the headquarters of the United Nations in New York has also made it a critical center of international politics and democracy.

FISCAL POLICY: changes in the levels of government spending and taxation

FISCAL POLICY refers to changes in the levels of government spending and taxation. All three levels of government engage in fiscal policy that has economic and social effects. At the state and local levels, the purpose of government spending and taxes is to run the state and local governments. When taxes are raised at the state or local level, the purpose is to provide revenues for the government to function, not to affect the level of aggregate spending in the economy. When New

York imposes taxes, the purpose is to pay for the programs and services that it provides to its population. These taxes have economic and social effects on the local population who have less money to spend. Local merchants may see a decrease in their revenues from less spending, in addition to having to pay taxes themselves. When state and local governments spend money through local programs, like repairing or building roads, the effect is to inject money into the local economy even though the purpose is to promote transportation. The purpose isn't to stimulate spending in the area.

Fiscal policy at the national level differs from that at the state and local levels because the purpose of the fiscal policy is to affect the level of aggregate spending in the economy. One of the functions of the federal government is to promote economic stabilization. This means to correct for inflation and unemployment. The way they do this is through changing the level of government spending and/ or the level of taxation. Inflation occurs when there is too high a level of aggregate spending. There is too much spending in the economy. Producers can't keep up with the demand and the result in rising prices. In this situation the government implements contractionary fiscal policy which consists of a decrease in government spending and/ or an increase in taxes. The purpose is to slow down an economy that is expanding too quickly by enacting policies that result in people having less money to spend. These policies, depending on how they are implemented, will affect the components of aggregate demand—consumption, investment, and government spending. Spending on imports will also decrease. The result of the contractionary fiscal policy will be, hopefully, to end the inflation.

Unemployment is another macroeconomic problem that requires expansionary fiscal policy. Unemployment occurs due to a lack of spending in the economy. There is not enough aggregate demand in the economy to fully employ the labor force. Here the role for government is to stimulate spending. If they can increase spending, producers will increase their output and hire more resources, including labor, thus eliminating the problem of unemployment.

Expansionary fiscal policy consists of increasing government spending and/ or lowering taxes. The increase in government spending injects money into the economy. Government programs to build roads mean more jobs. More jobs mean more spending and a higher level of aggregate demand. As producers see an increase in the demand for their product, they increase their output levels. As they expand, they require more resources, including labor. As more of the labor force works, the level of spending increases still further, and so on. Lowering taxes affects the consumption and possibly the investment components of aggregate demand leaving consumers and businesses with more money to spend, thus leading to a higher level of spending and eliminating unemployment.

SKILL 24.6 Analyzing ways in which the United States has influenced other nations and how other nations have influenced U.S. politics and culture

Because the United States is based on the principles of freedoms, it is active in trying to compel other nations to respect the rights of their own citizens. This concern for democratic principles and human rights has involved the United States in World War II and other skirmishes. Troops were sent to Serbia to halt the genocide that was taking place and to restore a democratic government to the area. The United States and other nations were instrumental in bringing Serbian leaders to trial for war crimes. The same is true of the situation in Iraq, where the U.S. invasion results in the overthrow of Saddam Hussein and the establishment of a democratic form of government. The same thing can be said of Vietnam and Korea and other places in the world where people have been oppressed.

Some of this is accomplished through the United Nations; some of this is accomplished outside of the United Nations

COMPETENCY 25

UNDERSTAND THE ROLES, RIGHTS, AND RESPONSIBILITIES OF CITIZENSHIP IN THE UNITED STATES AND THE SKILLS, KNOWLEDGE, AND ATTITUDES NECESSARY FOR SUCCESSFUL PARTICIPATION IN CIVIC LIFE

SKILL 25.1 Analyzing the personal and political rights guaranteed in the Declaration of Independence, the U.S. Constitution, the Constitution of the State of New York, and major civil rights legislation

The three most basic rights guaranteed by the Declaration of Independence are "life, liberty, and the pursuit of happiness."

1. Life. The first one is self-explanatory: Americans are guaranteed the right to live their lives in America.

2. **Liberty.** The second one is basic as well: Americans are guaranteed the right to live their lives free in America. (Although this principle has been violated for many people throughout our history; for example, Native Americans and slaves.)

3. **The Pursuit of Happiness.** The last basic right is more esoteric but no less important: Americans are guaranteed the right to pursue a happy life. First and foremost, they are allowed the ability to make a life for themselves in America, "the Land of Opportunity." That happiness also extends to the pursuit of life free from oppression or discrimination, two things that, again, some Americans have been deprived of throughout our history.

The DECLARATION OF INDEPENDENCE is an outgrowth of both ancient Greek ideas of democracy and individual rights and the ideas of the European Enlightenment and the Renaissance, especially the ideology of the political thinker John Locke. Thomas Jefferson (1743–1826) the principle author of the Declaration borrowed much from Locke's theories and writings. John Locke was one of the most influential political writers of the seventeenth century; he put great emphasis on human rights and put forth the belief that when governments violate those rights people should rebel. He wrote the book *Two Treatises of Government* in 1690, which had tremendous influence on political thought in the American colonies and helped to shape the U.S. Constitution and Declaration of Independence.

> **DECLARATION OF INDEPENDENCE:** founding document of the United States

The Declaration of Independence was the founding document of the United States of America. The ARTICLES OF CONFEDERATION were the first attempt of the newly independent states to reach a new understanding amongst their selves. The Declaration was intended to demonstrate the reasons that the colonies were seeking separation from Great Britain. Conceived by and written for the most part by Thomas Jefferson, it is not only important for what it says, but also for how it says it. The Declaration is in many respects a poetic document. Instead of a simple recitation of the colonists' grievances, it set out clearly the reasons why the colonists were seeking their freedom from Great Britain. They had tried all means to resolve the dispute peacefully.

> **ARTICLES OF CONFEDERATION:** the first constitution of the United States credited during the Revolutionary War

It was the right of a people, when all other methods of addressing their grievances have been tried and failed, to separate themselves from that power that was keeping them from fully expressing their rights to life, liberty, and the pursuit of happiness.

A convention met under the presidency of George Washington, with fifty-five of the sixty-five appointed members present. A constitution was written in four months. The CONSTITUTION OF THE UNITED STATES is the fundamental law of the republic. It is a precise, formal, written document of the extraordinary, or

> **CONSTITUTION OF THE UNITED STATES:** the fundamental law of the republic

supreme, type of constitution. The founders of the Union established it as the highest governmental authority. There is no national power superior to it. The foundations were so broadly laid as to provide for the expansion of national life and to make it an instrument which would last for all time. To maintain its stability, the framers created a difficult process for making any changes to it. No amendment can become valid until it is ratified by three fourths of all of the states. The British system of government was part of the basis of the final document. But significant changes were necessary to meet the needs of a partnership of states that were tied together as a single federation, yet sovereign in their own local affairs. This constitution established a system of government that was unique and advanced far beyond other systems of its day.

The constitution binds the states in a governmental unity in everything that affects the welfare of all. At the same time, it recognizes the right of the people of each state to independence of action in matters that relate only to them. Since the Federal Constitution is the law of the land, all other laws must conform to it.

The debates conducted during the Constitutional Congress represent the issues and the arguments that led to the compromises in the final document. The debates also reflect the concerns of the Founding Fathers that the rights of the people be protected from abrogation by the government itself and the determination that no branch of government should have enough power to continually dominate the others. There is, therefore, a SYSTEM OF CHECKS AND BALANCES.

SYSTEM OF CHECKS AND BALANCES: the determination that no branch of government should have enough power to continually dominate the others

The System of Checks and Balances

Executive (President)

Legislative (Congress)

Judicial (Courts)

©iStockphoto.com/Douglas Litchfield, Jeremy Edwards, Visual Field

The New York Constitution was adopted on April 20, 1777 and included New York's statement of independence from Britain. Drafted by John Jay, it was based on the colonial charter and created three sections of government, as the U.S. Constitution would later do. Powers were combined in the three branches in the New York constitution, however, with the legislature able to appoint executive positions and the courts having power to revise legislation. The governor had no direct veto power.

The New York constitution created the public university system and allowed for the assistance of the indigent. It remained in effect until it was superseded in 1821 by a new constitution. That constitution contained an enumerated bill of rights and has been extensively revised and amended. The powers and limitations of the three branches of government have been more clearly defined and brought closer in line with the federal system. Like most state constitutions, the New York Constitution has been extensively amended.

The New York Constitution is similar to the U.S. Constitution in many ways, providing for a division of labor of governmental powers between the three branches. The state Constitution is a bit older than the federal Constitution, having been passed back in 1777. One could make a strong case that many of the principles in New York's governmental blueprint found their way into that of the federal government, including the Bill of Rights.

Bill of Rights

The first ten amendments to the United States Constitution dealing with civil liberties and civil rights are collectively referred to as the Bill of Rights. James Madison was credited with writing most of them. They are in brief:

1. Freedom of religion

2. Right to bear arms

3. Security from the quartering of troops in homes

4. Right against unreasonable search and seizures

5. Right against self-incrimination

6. Right to trial by jury, right to legal council

7. Right to jury trial for civil actions

8. No cruel or unusual punishment allowed

9. These rights shall not deny other rights the people enjoy

10. Powers not mentioned in the Constitution shall be retained by the states or the people

Sample Test Questions and Rationale

Average Rigor

1. **The ability of the President to veto an act of Congress is an example of:**

   A. separation of powers

   B. checks and balances

   C. judicial review

   D. presidential prerogative

Answer: B – Checks and Balances

Rationale: The ability of the President too veto an act of Congress is an example of checks and balances. Judicial review is the checks and balances exerted by the Judicial on the Legislative Branch. The system of checks and balances prevents any one branch of the United States Government from becoming too powerful and corrupt.

SKILL 25.2 Recognizing the core values of the U.S. democratic system

Many of the core values in the U.S. democratic system can be found in the opening words of the Declaration of Independence, including the belief in equality and the rights of citizens to life, liberty and the pursuit of happiness.

The Declaration was a condemnation of the British king's tyrannical government, and these words emphasized the American colonists' belief that a government received its authority to rule from the people, and its function should not be to suppress the governed, but to protect the rights of the governed, including protection from the government itself. These two ideals, popular sovereignty and the rule of law are basic core values.

1. Popular sovereignty grants citizens the ability to directly participate in their own government by voting and running for public office. This ideal is based on a belief of equality that holds that all citizens have an equal right to engage in their own governance. The ideal of equality has changed over the years, as women and nonwhite citizens were not always allowed to vote or bring suit in court. Now all U.S citizens above the age of 18 are allowed to vote. This expansion of rights since the adoption of the Constitution demonstrates an American value of respect for minority rights.

The democratic system of election and representation is based on MAJORITY RULE. In the case of most public elections, the candidate receiving the most votes is awarded the office. Majority rule is also used to pass legislation in Congress. Majority rule is meant to ensure that authority cannot be concentrated in one small group of people.

2. The rule of law is the ideal that the law applies not only to the governed, but to the government as well. This core value gives authority to the justice system, which grants citizens protection from the government by requiring that any accusation of a crime be proved by the government before a person is punished. This is called DUE PROCESS and ensures that any accused person will have an opportunity to confront his accusers and provide a defense. Due process follows from the core value of a right to liberty. The government cannot take away a citizen's liberty without reason or without proof. The correlating ideal is also a core value—that someone who does harm to another or breaks a law will receive justice under the democratic system. The ideal of justice holds that a punishment will fit the crime and that any citizen can appeal to the judicial system if he or she feels he or she has been wronged.

Central to the ideal of justice is an expectation that citizens will act in a way that promotes the common good, that they will treat one another with honesty and respect and will exercise self-discipline in their interactions with others. These are among the basic responsibilities of a citizen of a democracy.

> **MAJORITY RULE:** the candidate receiving the most votes is awarded the office, meant to ensure that authority cannot be concentrated in one small group of people

> **DUE PROCESS:** grants citizens protection from the government by requiring that any accusation of a crime be proved by the government before a person is punished

---

SKILL 25.3 Understanding the U.S. election process and the roles of political parties, pressure groups, and special interests in the U.S. political system

The political party system in the United States has five main objects or lines of action:

1. To influence government policy

2. To form or shape public opinion

3. To win elections

4. To choose between candidates for office

5. To procure salaried posts for party leaders and workers

The U.S. electoral process has many and varied elements, from simple voting to complex campaigning for office. Everything in between is complex and detailed.

First, American citizens vote. They vote for laws and statues and referenda and elected officials. They have to register in order to vote, and at that time they can declare their intended membership in a political party. America has a large list of political parties, which have varying degrees of membership. The Democratic and Republican parties are the two with the most money and power, but other political parties abound. In some cases, people who are registered members of a political party are allowed to vote for only members of that political party. Elections are held at the local, state, and national level at designated times throughout the year.

Candidates affiliate themselves with political parties. Candidates then go about the business of campaigning, which includes getting the word on out on their candidacy, what they believe in, and what they will do if elected. All of this costs money, of course, unless a candidate relies entirely on word-of-mouth or some sort of e-mail campaign. Candidates sometimes get together for debates to showcase their views on important issues of the day and how those views differ from those of their opponents. Candidates give public speeches, attend public functions, and spout their views to reporters for coverage in newspapers and magazines and on radio and television. On election day candidates hope they've done enough. The results of elections are made known very quickly, sometimes instantly, thanks to computerized vote tallying. Once results are finalized, winning candidates give victory speeches and losing candidates give concession speeches.

Voters technically have the option to recall elected candidates; such a measure, however, is drastic and requires a large pile of signatures to get the motion on the ballot and then a large number of votes to have the measure approved. As such, recalls of elected candidates are relatively rare. One widely publicized recall in recent years was that of California Governor Gray Davis, who was replaced by movie star Arnold Schwarzenegger.

IMPEACHMENT: a formal process for charging a public official with misconduct in office

Another method of removing public officials from office is IMPEACHMENT. This is also rare but still a possibility. Both houses of the state or federal government get involved, and both houses have to approve the impeachment measures by a large margin. In the case of the federal government, the House of Representatives votes to impeach a federal official and the Senate votes to convict or acquit. Conviction means that the official must leave office immediately; acquittal results in no penalties or fines.

COLLEGE OF ELECTORS: the body of electors who formally elect the president of the United States

The COLLEGE OF ELECTORS—or the Electoral College, as it is more commonly known—has a long and distinguished history of mirroring the political will of the American voters. On some occasions, the results have not been entirely in sync with that political will.

Article II of the Constitution lists the specifics of the Electoral College. The Founding Fathers included the Electoral College as one of the famous "checks and balances" for two reasons:

1. To give states with small populations an equal weight in the presidential election

2. They didn't trust the common man (women couldn't vote then) to be able to make an informed decision on which candidate would make the best president

First of all, the same theory that created the U.S. Senate practice of giving two Senators to each state created the Electoral College. The large-population states had their populations reflected in the House of Representatives. New York and Pennsylvania, two of the states with the largest populations, had the highest number of members of the House of Representatives. But these two states still had only two senators, the exact same number that small-population states like Rhode Island and Delaware had. This was true as well in the Electoral College: Each state had just one vote, regardless of how many members of the House represented that state. So, the one vote that the state of New York cast would be decided by an initial vote of New York's Representatives. (If that initial vote was a tie, then that deadlock would have to be broken.)

Second, when the Constitution was being written, not many people knew a lot about government, politics, or presidential elections. The Founding Fathers thought that if "common people" could vote, they wouldn't necessarily make the best decision for the best president. So, the Electoral College was born.

Technically, the electors do not have to vote for anyone. The Constitution does not require them to do so. And throughout the history of presidential elections, some have indeed voted for someone else. But tradition holds that the electors vote for the candidate chosen by their state, and so the vast majority of electors do just that. The Electoral College meets a few weeks after the presidential election. Mostly, their meeting is a formality. When all the electoral votes are counted, the president with the most votes wins. In most cases, the candidate who wins the popular vote also wins in the Electoral College. However, this has not always been the case.

In 2000 in Florida, the election was decided by the Supreme Court. The Democratic Party's nominee was Vice President Al Gore. A presidential candidate himself back in 1988, Gore had served as vice president during both of President Bill Clinton's terms. As such, he was both a champion of Clinton's successes and a reflection of his failures. The Republican Party's nominee was George W. Bush, governor of Texas and son of former President George Bush. He campaigned on a platform of a strong national defense and an end to questionable ethics in the White House.

The election was hotly contested, and many states went down to the wire, being decided by only a handful of votes. The one state that seemed to be flip-flopping as Election Day turned into Election Night was Florida. In the end, Gore won the popular vote, by nearly 540,000 votes. But he didn't win the electoral vote. The vote was so close in Florida that a recount was necessary under federal law. Eventually, the Supreme Court weighed in and stopped all the recounts. The last count had Bush winning by less than a thousand votes. That gave him Florida and the White House.

LOBBYIST: someone who works for a political cause by attempting to influence lawmakers to vote a certain way on issues of the day

LOBBYISTS are a very visible and time-honored part of the political process. They wield power to varying degrees, depending on the issues involved and how much the parties they represent want to maintain the status quo or effect change.

A lobbyist is someone who works for a political cause by attempting to influence lawmakers to vote a certain way on issues of the day. For example, a lobbyist for an oil production company would urge lawmakers not to increase existing or create new taxes on oil. This urging can take many forms, among them direct communication, letter writing, or phone-in campaigns designed to stir up public sentiment for or against an issue or set of issues.

Lobbyists also serve to make lawmakers aware of information that they might not have, including how other lawmakers view the important issues of the day.

Lobbyists also attempt to influence one another. Some issues create strange bedfellows, and lobbyists who work for different employers might find themselves on the same side of an issue and end up working together for a larger cause to achieve a common goal.

Citizens wishing to engage in the political process to a greater degree have several paths open to them, such as participating in local government. Counties, states, and sometimes neighborhoods are governed by locally elected boards or councils that meet publicly. Citizens are usually able to address these boards, bringing their concerns and expressing their opinions on matters being considered. Citizens may even wish to stand for local election and join a governing board or seek support for higher office.

Supporting a political party is another means by which citizens can participate in the political process. Political parties endorse certain platforms that express general social and political goals and support member candidates in election campaigns. Political parties make use of much volunteer labor, with supporters making telephone calls, distributing printed material, and campaigning for the party's causes and candidates. Political parties solicit donations to support their efforts as well. Contributing money to a political party is another form of participation citizens can undertake.

First and foremost, money is needed to pay the people who will run a candidate's campaign. The faithful lieutenants of a campaign are paid performers. Money is also needed to buy or rent all of the tangible and intangible things that are needed to power a political campaign: office supplies, meeting places, transportation vehicles, and much more. Of course, the expense that gets the most exposure these days is media advertising, specifically television advertising. This is the most expensive kind of advertising but it also has the potential to reach the widest audience. TV ad prices can run into the hundreds of thousands of dollars, depending on when they run; but they have the potential to reach perhaps millions of viewers. Other forms of advertising include radio and Web ads, signs and billboards, and good old-fashioned flyers.

The sources of funds needed to run a successful political campaign are varied. A candidate might have a significant amount of money in his or her own personal coffers. In rare cases, the candidate finances the entire campaign. However, the most prevalent source of money is outside donations. A candidate's friends and family might donate funds to the campaign, as might the campaign workers themselves. State and federal governments will also contribute to most regional or national campaigns, provided that the candidate can prove that he or she can raise a certain amount of money first. The largest source of campaign finance money, however, comes from so-called special interests. A large company such as an oil company or a manufacturer of electronic goods will want to keep prices or tariffs down and so will want to make sure that laws lifting those prices or tariffs aren't passed.

To this end, the company will contribute money to the campaigns of candidates who are likely to vote to keep those prices or tariffs down. A candidate is not obligated to accept such a donation, of course, and further is not obligated to vote in favor of the interests of the special interest; however, doing the former might create a shortage of money and doing the latter might ensure that no further donations come from that or any other special interest. An oil company wants to protect its interests, and its leaders don't very much care which political candidate is doing that for them as long as it is being done.

Another powerful source of support for a political campaign is SPECIAL INTEREST GROUPS of a political nature. These are not necessarily economic powers but rather groups whose people want to effect political change or ensure that such change doesn't take place, depending on the status of the laws at the time.

A good example of a special interest group is a pro-life group or a pro-choice group. The abortion issue is still a divisive one in American politics, and many groups will want to protect or defend or ban—depending on which side they're on—certain rights and practices. This kind of social group usually has a large number of dedicated individuals who do much more than vote: They organize themselves into political action committees, attend meetings and rallies, and work to make sure that their message gets out to a wide audience. Methods of spreading

> **SPECIAL INTEREST GROUPS:** groups whose people want to effect political change or ensure that such change doesn't take place, depending on the status of the laws at the time

the word often include media advertising on behalf of their chosen candidates. This kind of expenditure is no doubt welcomed by the candidates, who will get the benefit of the exposure but won't have to spend that money because someone else is signing the checks.

> **SKILL 25.4** **Explaining what citizenship means in a democratic society and analyze the ways in which citizens participate in and influence the political process in the United States**

A person who lives in a democratic society theoretically has a list of rights guaranteed to him or her by the government. In the United States, this is the Constitution and its Amendments. Among these very important rights are:

- The right to speak out in public

- The right to pursue any religion

- The right for a group of people to gather in public for any reason that doesn't fall under a national security cloud

- The right not to have soldiers stationed in your home

- The right not to be forced to testify against yourself in a court of law

- The right to a speedy and public trial by a jury of your peers

- The right not to the victim of cruel and unusual punishment

- The right to avoid unreasonable search and seizure of your person, your house, and your vehicle

The average citizen of an authoritarian country has few if any of these rights and must watch his or her words, actions, and even magazine subscriptions and Internet visits in order to avoid the appearance of disobeying one of the many oppressive laws that help the government govern its people.

Both democratic-society and authoritarian-society citizens can serve in government. They can even run for election and can be voted in by their peers. One large difference exists, however: In an authoritarian society, the members of government will most likely be of the same political party. A country with this setup, like China, will have a government that includes representatives elected by the Chinese people, but all of those elected representatives will belong to the Communist Party, which runs the government and the country. When the voters cast their ballots, only Communist Party members are listed. In fact, in many cases, only one candidate is on the ballot for each office. China, in fact, chooses its head of government through a meeting of the Party leaders. In effect, the Party is higher in the governmental hierarchy than the leader of the country. Efforts to change this governmental structure and practice are discouraged.

On the other side of this spectrum is the citizen of the democratic society, who can vote for whomever he or she wants and can run for any office he or she wants. On those ballots will appear names and political parties that run the spectrum, including the Communist Party. Theoretically, any political party can get its candidates on ballots locally, statewide, or nationwide; varying degrees of effort have to be put in to do this, of course. Building on the First Amendment freedom to peacefully assembly, American citizens can have political party meetings, fundraisers, and even conventions without fearing reprisals from the government.

In a civil society, people are certainly free to pursue business interests both private and public. Private activities are less regulated than public ones, but public activities are not discouraged or dissuaded, as long as they don't violate laws or other people's rights.

In America and in other countries as well, a person has the right to pursue any kind of business strategy he or she wants. The age of Internet advertising and marketing has created opportunities abound for new and different businesses.

Rather than discourage people from starting businesses, the American government and its various associated entities actually encourage such endeavors. Prospective business owners can find whole libraries of information encouraging them and guiding them through the sometimes rigorous practice of starting a business. Entire organizations exist just to answer questions about this process.

America is a land full of groups—religious groups, political groups, social groups, and business and economic groups. All these groups meet in public and in private and the people who belong to these groups are free to associate with any groups that they choose, again as long as the practices of those groups are not illegal or harmful to other people.

Freedom to practice the faith of your choice finds extraordinary protection under U.S. law. The First Amendment guarantees every American the right to worship as he or she sees fit, without fear of reprisal by the government. Religious organizations, however, do not, for the most part, receive funding from governments to support their efforts. The First Amendment also denies the government the right to establish a religion, meaning that it can favor no one religion over others. Entities like parochial schools, which provide both education and religious training, routinely have to seek funding in places other than the federal or state governments.

Social groups are encouraged as well. The First Amendment gives the American people the right to peaceable assembly. Social organizations are made up of people with similar interests or experiences who come together on a regular basis to discuss those interests and experiences and to pursue a joint appreciation.

Public officials have an overwhelming need to communicate. They want other people to know what they're doing and why. They want to make sure that the voters who elected know what great jobs they're doing pursuing the agendas that are closest to their hearts. Ultimately, they want to do as much as they can to get themselves reelected or, if term limits won't allow such reelection, to leaving a memorable public legacy.

In the court of public opinion, the newspaper or radio offers politicians a fairly easy way to get noticed. Television began to change all that with its visual record of events. The proliferation of cable and satellite television channels has made it very difficult for a lawmaker not to get noticed if her or she does something remarkable these days. The Internet offers a vast, heterogeneous world of opportunities. Internet opportunities include not just news Web sites but personal Web sites and the eponymous blogs—public opinion pieces that may or may not be true.

The key thing to remember about information on Web pages: They might not have undergone the sort of scrutiny as comparable information released by major media outlets to newspapers, radio, and television. Those media processes have built-in safety measures called editors who will verify information before it is released to the world. In contrast, to blog all you need is access to a Web-enabled computer and time to write a column. Bloggers routinely do not use editors or run their copy by anyone else before publishing it; as such, they have lower standards of professionalism overall and need to be regarded as such.

PUBLIC RELATIONS: efforts intended to make the lawmakers look good in the eyes of their constituents

Public officials will hire one or more people or perhaps a whole department or an entire business to conduct PUBLIC RELATIONS, which are efforts intended to make the lawmakers look good in the eyes of their constituents. A public relations person or firm will have as its overreaching goal the happiness of the lawmaker who hired her or them and will gladly write press releases, arrange media events (like tours of schools or soup kitchens), and basically do everything else to keep their employer's name in the public eye in a good way. This includes making the lawmaker's position on important issues known to the public. Especially controversial issues will be embraced on the other side by lawmakers, and those lawmakers will want their constituents to know how they intend to vote those issues. It's also a good idea to find out what your constituents think about these issues of the day, since the fastest way to get yourself bad publicity or thrown out at reelection time is to ignore the weight of public opinion.

SKILL 25.5 Examining the rights, responsibilities, and privileges of individuals in relation to family, social group, career, community, and nation

The cause of human rights has been advanced significantly since the eighteenth century, both in theory and in fact. Several fundamental statements of human rights have extended and established human rights throughout the world.

The U.S. Declaration of Independence ratified in 1776 declared that certain truths are self-evident: all men are created equal, that they are inherently endowed with certain unalienable rights that no government should ever violate. These rights include the right to life, liberty, and the pursuit of happiness. When a government infringes upon those rights or fails to protect those rights, it is both the right and the duty of the people to overthrow that government and to establish in its place a new government that will protect those rights.

The Declaration of the Rights of Man and of the Citizen is a document created by the French National Assembly and issued in 1789. It sets forth the "natural, inalienable, and sacred rights of man." It proclaims the following rights:

- Men are born and remain free and equal in rights. Social distinctions may only be founded upon the general good.

- The aim of all political association is the preservation of the natural and imprescriptible rights of man: liberty, property, security, and resistance to oppression.

- All sovereignty resides essentially in the nation. No body or individual may exercise any authority which does not proceed directly from the nation.

- Liberty is the freedom to do everything which injures no one else; hence the exercise of these rights has no limits except those which assure to the other members of the society the enjoyment of the same rights. These limits can only be determined by law.

- Law can only prohibit such actions as are hurtful to society.

- Law is the expression of the general will. Every citizen has a right to participate in the formation of law. It must be the same for all. All citizens, being equal in the eyes of the law, are equally eligible to all dignities and to all public positions and occupations, according to their abilities.

- No person shall be accused, arrested, or imprisoned except in the cases and according to the forms prescribed by law.

- The law shall provide for such punishments only as are strictly and obviously necessary.

- All persons are held innocent until they have been declared guilty. If it is necessary to arrest a person, all harshness not essential to the securing of the prisoner's person shall be severely repressed by law.

- No one shall be disquieted on account of his opinions, including religious views, provided their manifestation does not disturb the peace.

- The free communication of ideas and opinions is one of the most precious of the rights of man.

- The security of the rights of man and of the citizen requires public military force. These forces are, therefore, established for the good of all and not for the personal advantage of those to whom they shall be entrusted.

- A common contribution is essential for the maintenance of the public forces and for the cost of administration. This should be equitably distributed among all the citizens in proportion to their means.

- All the citizens have a right to decide, either personally or by their representatives, as to the necessity of the public contribution.

- Society has the right to require of every public agent an account of his administration.

- A society in which the observance of the law is not assured, nor the separation of powers defined, has no constitution at all.

- Since property is an inviolable and sacred right, no one shall be deprived thereof except where public necessity, legally determined, shall clearly demand it, and then only on condition that the owner shall have been previously and equitably indemnified.

The United Nations Declaration of Universal Human Rights (1948) opens with these words: "Whereas recognition of the inherent dignity and of the equal and inalienable rights of all members of the human family is the foundation of freedom, justice, and peace in the world. Whereas disregard and contempt for human rights have resulted in barbarous acts which have outraged the conscience of mankind, and the advent of a world in which human beings shall enjoy freedom of speech and belief and freedom from fear and want has been proclaimed as the highest aspiration of the common people."

- All human beings are born free and equal in dignity and rights. They are endowed with reason and conscience and should act towards one another in a spirit of brotherhood.

- Everyone is entitled to all the rights and freedoms set forth in this Declaration, without distinction of any kind.

- Everyone has the right to life, liberty, and security of person.

- No one shall be held in slavery or servitude.

- No one shall be subjected to torture or to cruel, inhuman, or degrading treatment or punishment.

- Everyone has the right to recognition everywhere as a person before the law.

- All are equal before the law and are entitled without any discrimination to equal protection of the law.

- Everyone has the right to an effective remedy by the competent national tribunals for acts violating the fundamental rights granted him by the constitution of by law.

- No one shall be subjected to arbitrary arrest, detention, or exile.

- Everyone is entitled in full equality to a fair and public hearing by an independent and impartial tribunal, in the determination of his rights and obligations and of any criminal charge against him.

- Everyone charged with a penal offence has the right to be presumed innocent until proved guilty according to law in a public trial at which he has had all the guarantees necessary for his defence. No one shall be held guilty of any penal offence on account of any act or omission which did not constitute a penal offence, under national or international law, at the time when it was committed.

- No one shall be subjected to arbitrary interference with his privacy, family, home, or correspondence, nor to attacks upon his honour and reputation.

- Everyone has the right to freedom of movement and residence within the borders of each state. Everyone has the right to leave any country, including his own, and to return to his country.

- Everyone has the right to seek and to enjoy in other countries asylum from persecution. This right may not be invoked in the case of prosecutions genuinely arising from nonpolitical crimes or from acts contrary to the purposes and principles of the United Nations.

- Everyone has the right to a nationality. No one shall be arbitrarily deprived of his nationality nor denied the right to change his nationality.

- Men and women of full age have the right to marry and to found a family. They are entitled to equal rights as to marriage, during marriage, and at its dissolution. Marriage shall be entered into only with the free and full consent of the intending spouses. The family is the natural and fundamental group unit of society and is entitled to protection by society and the State.

- Everyone has the right to own property alone or in association with others. No one shall be arbitrarily deprived of his property.

- Everyone has the right to freedom of thought, conscience, and religion, including the right to change his religion or belief, and freedom to manifest his religion or belief in teaching, practice, worship, and observance.

- Everyone has the right to freedom of opinion and expression.

- Everyone has the right to freedom of peaceful assembly and association. No one may be compelled to belong to an association.

- Everyone has the right to take part in the government of his country, directly or through freely chosen representatives. Everyone has the right of equal access to public service in his country. The will of the people shall be the basis of the authority of government.

- Everyone has the right to social security and is entitled to realization of the economic, social, and cultural rights indispensable for his dignity and the free development of his personality.

- Everyone has the right to work. Everyone, without any discrimination, has the right to equal pay for equal work. Everyone who works has the right to just and favorable remuneration. Everyone has the right to form and to join trade unions for the protection of his interests.

- Everyone has the right to rest and leisure, including reasonable limitation of working hours and periodic holidays with pay.

- Everyone has the right to a standard of living adequate for the health and well-being of himself and his family, and the right to security in the event of unemployment, sickness, disability, widowhood, old age, or other lack of livelihood in circumstances beyond his control. Mothers and children are entitled to special care and assistance. All children shall enjoy the same social protection.

- Everyone has the right to education. Education shall be directed to the full development of the human personality and to the strengthening of respect for human rights and fundamental freedoms. Parents have a prior right to choose the kind of education that shall be given to their children.

- Everyone has the right freely to participate in the cultural life of the community. Everyone has the right to the protection of the moral and materials interests resulting from any scientific, literary, or artistic production of which he is the author.

- Everyone is entitled to a social and international order in which the rights and freedoms set forth in this Declaration can be fully realized.

The United Nations Convention on the Rights of the Child brings together the rights of children as they are enumerated in other international documents. In this document, those rights are clearly and completely stated, along with the explanation of the guiding principals that define the way society views children. The goal of the document is to clarify the environment that is necessary to enable every human being to develop to their full potential. The Convention calls for resources and contributions to be made to ensure the full development and survival of all children. The document also requires the establishment of appropriate means to protect children from neglect, exploitation and abuse. The document also recognizes that parents have the most important role in raising children.

SKILL 25.6 Analyzing factors that have expanded or limited the role of the individual in U.S. political life during the twentieth century

The WOMEN'S RIGHTS MOVEMENT is concerned with the freedoms of women as differentiated from broader ideas of human rights. These issues are generally different from those that affect men and boys because of biological conditions or social constructs. The rights the movement has sought to protect throughout history include:

WOMEN'S RIGHTS MOVEMENT: refers to the freedom and entitlements of women and girls

- The right to vote
- The right to work
- The right to fair wages
- The right to bodily integrity and autonomy
- The right to own property
- The right to an education
- The right to hold public office
- Marital rights
- Parental rights
- Religious rights
- The right to serve in the military
- The right to enter into legal contracts

The movement for women's rights has resulted in many social and political changes. Many of the ideas that seemed very radical merely 100 years ago are now normative. Some of the most famous leaders in the women's movement through-out American history are:

- Abigail Adams
- Susan B. Anthony
- Gloria E. Anzaldua
- Betty Friedan
- Olympe de Gouges
- Gloria Steinem
- Harriet Tubman
- Mary Wollstonecraft
- Virginia Woolf
- Germaine Greer

Many within the women's movement are primarily committed to justice and the natural rights of all people. This has led many members of the women's movement to be involved in the Black Civil Rights Movement, the gay rights movement, and the recent social movement to protect the rights of fathers.

After the Civil War, the rise of the Redeemer governments marked the beginning of the JIM CROW LAWS and official segregation. Blacks were still allowed to vote, but ways were found to make it difficult for them to do so, such as literacy tests and poll taxes. Reconstruction, which had set as its goal the reunification of the South with the North and the granting of civil rights to freed slaves was a limited success, at best, and in the eyes of blacks was considered a failure.

The National Association for the Advancement of Colored People (NAACP) was founded in 1909 to assist African Americans. In the early years, the work of the organization focused on working through the courts to overturn "Jim Crow" statutes that legalized racial discrimination. The group organized voters to oppose Woodrow Wilson's efforts to weave racial segregation into federal government policy. Between WWI and WWII, much energy was devoted to stopping the lynching of blacks throughout the country.

> **JIM CROW LAWS:** laws enacted in many southern States that promoted segregation between Blacks and Whites and restricted the rights of African Americans

CASE STUDY

Take for example the Birmingham Campaign of 1963-64. A campaign was planned to use sit-ins, kneel-ins in churches, and marches to the county building to launch a voter registration campaign. The City obtained an injunction forbidding all such protests. The protesters, including Martin Luther King, Jr., believed the injunction was unconstitutional and defied it. They were arrested. While in jail, King wrote his famous Letter from Birmingham Jail. When the campaign began to falter, the "Children's Crusade" called students to leave school and join the protests. The events became news when more than 600 students were jailed. The next day more students joined the protest. The media were present and broadcast to the nation vivid pictures of fire hoses being used to knock down children, and dogs attacking some of them. The resulting public outrage led the Kennedy administration to intervene. About a month later, a committee was formed to end hiring discrimination, arrange for the release of jailed protesters, and establish normative communication between blacks and whites. Four months later, the KKK bombed the Sixteenth Street Baptist Church, killing four girls.

Newspapers, then as now, influence the growth of political parties. Newspaper publishers and editors took sides on issues. Thus, from the very beginning, American newspapers and each new branch of the media have played an important role in helping to shape public opinion.

First and foremost, the media report on the actions taken and encouraged by leaders of the government. In many cases, these actions are common knowledge. Policy debates, discussions on controversial issues, struggles against foreign powers in economic and wartime endeavors—all are fodder for media reports. The First Amendment guarantees media in America the right to report on these things, and the media reporters take full advantage of that right and privilege in striving not only to inform the American public but also to keep the governmental leaders in check.

Sample Test Questions and Rationale

Average Rigor

1. **Jim Crow laws dealt with:**

   A. minority rights

   B. animal control

   C. segregation

   D. adoption

   Answer: C – segregation

   Rationale: The Jim Crow laws varied from state to state, but the most significant of them required separate school systems and libraries for blacks and whites and separate ticket windows, waiting rooms and seating areas on trains and, later, other public transportation. Restaurant owners were permitted or sometimes required to provide separate entrances and tables and counters for blacks and whites, so that the two races not see one another while dining. Public parks and playgrounds were constructed for each race. Landlords were not allowed to mix black and white tenants in apartment houses in some states.

COMPETENCY 26

UNDERSTAND AND APPLY SKILLS RELATED TO SOCIAL STUDIES, INCLUDING GATHERING, ORGANIZING, MAPPING, EVALUATING, INTERPRETING, AND DISPLAYING INFORMATION

> **SKILL 26.1** Evaluating the appropriateness of various resources and research methods for meeting specified information needs and apply procedures for retrieving information using traditional resources and current technologies

See Skill 22.5

LIBRARIES: offer resources such as survey information from various departments and bureaus of the federal and state government, magazines and periodicals in a wide range of topics, artifacts, encyclopedias and other reference materials, and usually access to the Internet

Historical data can come from a wide range of sources beginning with libraries, small local ones or very large university LIBRARIES. Records and guides are almost universally digitally organized and available for instant searching by era, topic, event, personality, or area. Libraries offer resources such as survey information from various departments and bureaus of the federal and state government, magazines and periodicals in a wide range of topics, artifacts, encyclopedias, and other reference materials, and usually access to the Internet.

The Internet offers unheard of possibilities for finding even the most obscure information. However, even with all these resources available, nothing is more valuable than a visit to the site being researched including a visit to historical societies, local libraries, sometimes even local schools.

The same things could be said about geographical data. It's possible to find a map of almost any area online; however, the best maps will be available locally as will knowledge and information about the development of the area.

SCIENTIFIC METHOD: the process by which researchers over time endeavor to construct an accurate representation of the world

The SCIENTIFIC METHOD is the process by which researchers over time endeavor to construct an accurate (that is, reliable, consistent, and nonarbitrary) representation of the world. Recognizing that personal and cultural beliefs influence both our perceptions and our interpretations of natural phenomena, standard procedures and criteria minimize those influences when developing a theory.

The scientific method has four steps:

1. Observation and description of a phenomenon or group of phenomena

2. Formulation of a hypothesis to explain the phenomena

3. Use of the hypothesis to predict the existence of other phenomena or to predict quantitatively the results of new observations

4. Performance of experimental tests of the predictions by several independent experimenters and properly performed experiments

While the researcher may bring certain biases to the study, it's important that bias not be permitted to enter into the interpretation. It's also important that data that don't fit the hypothesis not be ruled out. This is unlikely to happen if the researcher is open to the possibility that the hypothesis might turn out to be null. Another important caution is to be certain that the methods for analyzing and interpreting are flawless. Abiding by these mandates is important if the discovery is to make a contribution to human understanding.

The phenomena that interest social scientists are usually complex. Capturing that complexity more fully requires the assessment of simultaneous covariations along the following dimensions: the units of observation, their characteristics, and time. This is how behavior occurs. For example, to obtain a richer and more accurate picture of the progress of school children requires measuring changes in their attainment over time together with changes in the school over time. This acknowledges that changes in one arena of behavior are usually contingent on changes in other areas. Models used for research in the past were inadequate to handle the complexities suggested by multiple covariations. However, the evolution of computerized data processing has taken away that constraint.

While descriptions of the research project and presentation of outcomes along with analysis must be a part of every report, graphs, charts, and sometimes maps are necessary to make the results clearly understandable.

SKILL 26.2 Demonstrating an understanding of concepts, tools, and technologies for mapping information about the spatial distribution of people, places, and environments

Physical locations of the Earth's surface features include the four major hemispheres and the parts of the Earth's continents in them. Political locations are the political divisions, if any, within each continent. Both physical and political locations are precisely determined in two ways:

1. Surveying is done to determine boundary lines and distance from other features.

2. Exact locations are precisely determined by imaginary lines of latitude (parallels) and longitude (meridians). The intersection of these lines at

right angles forms a grid, making it impossible to pinpoint an exact location of any place using any two grip coordinates.

The process of putting the features of the Earth onto a flat surface is called projection. All maps are really map projections. There are many different types. Each one deals in a different way with the problem of distortion. Map projections are made in a number of ways. Some are done using complicated mathematics. However, the basic ideas behind map projections can be understood by looking at the three most common types:

Cylindrical Projections	These are done by taking a cylinder of paper and wrapping it around a globe. A light is used to project the globe's features onto the paper. Distortion is least where the paper touches the globe. For example, suppose that the paper was wrapped so that it touched the globe at the equator, the map from this projection would have just a little distortion near the equator.
	However, in moving north or south of the equator, the distortion would increase as you moved further away from the equator. The best known and most widely used cylindrical projection is the Mercator Projection. It was first developed in 1569 by Gerardus Mercator, a Flemish mapmaker.
Conical Projections	The name for these maps come from the fact that the projection is made onto a cone of paper. The cone is made so that it touches a globe at the base of the cone only. It can also be made so that it cuts through part of the globe in two different places. Again, there is the least distortion where the paper touches the globe. If the cone touches at two different points, there is some distortion at both of them. Conical projections are most often used to map areas in the middle latitudes. Maps of the United States are most often conical projections. This is because most of the country lies within these latitudes.
Flat-Plane Projections	These are made with a flat piece of paper. It touches the globe at one point only. Areas near this point show little distortion. Flat-plane projections are often used to show the areas of the north and south poles. One such flat projection is called a Gnomonic Projection. On this kind of map all meridians appear as straight lines, Gnomonic projections are useful because any straight line drawn between points on it forms a Great-Circle Route.

Great-Circle Routes can best be described by thinking of a globe and, when using the globe, the shortest route between two points on it can be found by simply stretching a string from one point to the other. However, if the string was extended in reality, so that it took into effect the globe's curvature, it would then make a great-circle. A great-circle is any circle that cuts a sphere, such as the globe, into two equal parts. Because of distortion, most maps do not show great-circle routes as straight lines. Gnomonic projections, however, do show the shortest distance between the two places as a straight line, because of this they are valuable for navigation. They are called Great-Circle Sailing Maps.

To properly analyze a given map one must be familiar with the various parts and symbols that most modern maps use. For the most part, this is standardized, with different maps using similar parts and symbols. These can include:

The Title	All maps should have a title, just like all books should. The title tells you what information is to be found on the map.
The Legend	Most maps have a legend. A legend tells the reader about the various symbols that are used on that particular map and what the symbols represent (also called a map key).
The Grid	A grid is a series of lines that are used to find exact places and locations on the map. There are several different kinds of grid systems in use however most maps do use the longitude and latitude system, known as the Geographic Grid System.
Directions	Most maps have some directional system to show which way the map is being presented. Often on a map, a small compass will be present, with arrows showing the four basic directions: north, south, east, and west.
The Scale	This is used to show the relationship between a unit of measurement on the map versus the real world measure on the Earth. Maps are drawn to many different scales. Some maps show a lot of detail for a small area. Others show a greater span of distance. Whichever is being used one should always be aware of just what scale is being used. For instance the scale might be something like 1 inch = 10 miles for a small area or for a map showing the whole world it might have a scale in which 1 inch = 1,000 miles. The point is that one must look at the map key in order to see what units of measurements the map is using.

Maps have four main properties. They are

1. The size of the areas shown on the map

2. The shapes of the areas

3. Consistent scales

4. Straight line directions

A map can be drawn so that it is correct in one or more of these properties. No map can be correct in all of them.

Equal Areas	One property that maps can have is that of equal areas. In an equal area map, the meridians and parallels are drawn so that the areas shown have the same proportions as they do on the Earth. For example, Greenland is about 118th the size of South America, thus it will be show as 118th the size on an equal area map. The Mercator projection is an example of a map that does not have equal areas. In it, Greenland appears to be about the same size of South America. This is because the distortion is very bad at the poles and Greenland lies near the North Pole.
Conformal Map	A second map property is conformal, or correct shapes. There are no maps that can show very large areas of the Earth in their exact shapes. Only globes can really do that, however Conformal Maps are as close as possible to true shapes. The United States is often shown by a Lambert Conformal Conic Projection Map.

Table continued on next page

Consistent Scales	Many maps attempt to use the same scale on all parts of the map. Generally, this is easier when maps show a relatively small part of the Earth's surface. For example, a map of Florida might be a Consistent Scale Map. Generally maps showing large areas are not consistent-scale maps. This is so because of distortion. Often such maps will have two scales noted in the key. One scale, for example, might be accurate to measure distances between points along the Equator. Another might be then used to measure distances between the North Pole and the South Pole. Maps showing physical features often try to show information about the elevation or **relief** of the land. **Elevation** is the distance above or below the sea level. The elevation is usually shown with colors, for instance, all areas on a map which are at a certain level will be shown in the same color.
Relief Maps	These show the shape of the land surface, flat, rugged, or steep. Relief maps usually give more detail than simply showing the overall elevation of the land's surface. Relief is also sometimes shown with colors, but another way to show relief is by using contour lines. These lines connect all points of a land surface that are the same height surrounding the particular area of land.
Thematic Maps	These are used to show more specific information, often on a single theme, or topic. Thematic maps show the distribution or amount of something over a certain given area—things such as population density, climate, economic information, cultural, political information, etc.

Sample Test Questions and Rationale

Rigorous

1. **The process of putting the features of the Earth onto a flat surface is called:**

   A. distortion

   B. projection

   C. cartography

   D. illustration

Answer: B – projection

Rationale: The process of putting the features of the Earth onto a flat surface is called projection. All maps are really map projections. It is impossible to reproduce exactly on a flat surface an object shaped like a sphere. In order to put the earth's features onto a map they must be stretched in some way. This stretching is called distortion. Cartographers are called mapmakers.

SKILL 26.3 Analyzing information in social studies

The struggle over what is to be the fair method to ensure equal political representation for all different groups in the United States continues to dominate the national debate. This has revolved around the problems of trying to ensure proper racial and minority representation. Various civil rights acts, notably the Voting Rights Act of 1965, sought to eliminate the remaining features of unequal suffrage in the United States.

Most recently, the question has revolved around the issue of what is called GERRYMANDERING, which involves the adjustment of various electoral districts in order to achieve a predetermined goal. Usually this is used in regard to the problem of minority political representation. The fact that gerrymandering sometimes creates odd and unusual looking districts (this is where the practice gets its name) and most often the sole basis of the adjustments is racial. This has led to the questioning of this practice being a fair, let alone a constitutional, way for society to achieve its desired goals. This promises to be the major issue in national electoral politics for some time to come. The debate has centered on those of the "left" (Liberals), who favor such methods, and the "right" (Conservatives), who oppose them. Overall, most Americans would consider themselves in the "middle" (Moderates).

> **GERRYMANDERING:**
> the adjustment of various electoral districts in order to achieve a predetermined goal

How best to move forward with ensuring civil liberties and civil rights for all continues to dominate the national debate. In recent times, issues seem to revolve not around individual rights, but what has been called "group rights" has been raised. At the forefront of the debate is whether some specific remedies like affirmative action, quotas, gerrymandering, and various other forms of preferential treatment are actually fair or just as bad as the ills they are supposed to cure. Currently, no easy answers seem to be forthcoming. It is a testament to the American system that it has shown itself able to enter into these debates, to find solutions, and then tended to come out stronger.

The sky is blue is a fact. The sky looks like rain is an opinion. This is because one is readily provable by objective empirical data, while the other is a subjective evaluation based upon personal bias. This means that facts are things that can be proved by the usual means of study and experimentation. We can look and see the color of the sky. Since the shade we are observing is expressed as the color blue and is an accepted norm, the observation that the sky is blue is therefore a fact. This brings us to our next idea: that it looks like rain. This is a subjective observation in that an individual's perception will differ from another. What looks like rain to one person will not necessarily look like that to another. This is an important concept to understand since much of what actually is studied in political science is, in reality, simply the opinions of various political theorists and philosophers. The truth of their individual philosophies is demonstrated by how well they work in the so-called real world.

The question thus remains as to how to differentiate fact from opinion. The best and only way is to ask oneself if what is being stated can be proved from other sources, by other methods, or by the simple process of reasoning.

Historians use primary sources from the actual time they are studying whenever possible. Ancient Greek records of interaction with Egypt, letters from an Egyptian ruler to regional governors, and inscriptions from the Fourteenth Egyptian Dynasty are all primary sources created at or near the actual time being studied. Letters from a nineteenth century Egyptologist would not be considered primary sources, as they were created thousands of years after the fact and may not actually be about the subject being studied. The resources used in the study of history can be divided into two major groups:[1]

- Primary sources: works, records, etc., that were created during the period being studied or immediately after it

- Secondary sources: works written significantly after the period being studied and based upon primary sources

> *Primary sources are works, records, etc., that were created during the period being studied or immediately after it. Secondary sources are works written significantly after the period being studied and based upon primary sources.*

SKILL 26.4 Interpreting information presented in one or more graphic representations and translate written or graphic information from one form to the other

Maps

Although maps have advantages over globes and photographs, they do have a major disadvantage. This problem must be considered as well. The major problem of all maps comes about because most maps are flat and the Earth is a sphere. It is impossible to reproduce exactly on a flat surface an object shaped like a sphere. In order to put the Earth's features onto a map they must be stretched in some way. This stretching is called distortion.

Distortion does not mean that maps are wrong; it simply means that they are not perfect representations of the Earth or its parts. Cartographers, or mapmakers, understand the problems of distortion. They try to design maps so that there is as little distortion as possible.

---

1   Norman F Cantor and Richard I. Schneider. How to Study History, Harlan Davidson, Inc., 1967, pp. 23-24.

Graphs

To apply information obtained from graphs one must understand the two major reasons why graphs are used:

1. To present a model or theory visually in order to show how two or more variables interrelate

2. To present real world data visually in order to show how two or more variables interrelate

The most-often used graphs are those known as bar graphs and line graphs. Graphs themselves are most useful when one wishes to demonstrate the sequential increase or decrease of a variable or to show specific correlations between two or more variables in a given circumstance.

Bar graphs are commonly used because they have a way of visually showing the difference in a given set of variables which is easy to see and understand. However, it is limited in that it can not really show the actual proportional increase, or decrease, of each given variable to each other. In order to show a decrease, a bar graph must show the "bar" under the starting line, thus removing the ability to really show how the various different variables would relate to each other.

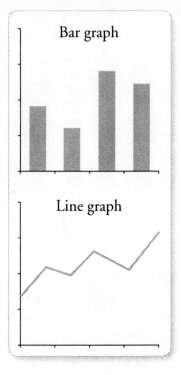

Thus, in order to accomplish this one must use a line graph. Line graphs can be of two types:

1. Linear graph: uses a series of straight lines

2. Nonlinear graph: uses a curved line

Though the lines can be either straight or curved, all of the lines are called curves.

A line graph uses a number line or axis. The numbers are generally placed in order, equal distances from one another, the number line is used to represent a number, degree, or some such other variable at an appropriate point on the line. Two lines are used, intersecting at a specific point. They are referred to as the X-axis and the Y-axis. The Y-axis is a vertical line the X-axis is a horizontal line. Together they form a coordinate system. The difference between a point on the line of the X-axis and the Y-axis is called the slope of the line, or the change in the value on the vertical axis divided by the change in the value on the horizontal axis. The Y-axis number is called the rise and the X-axis number is called the run, thus the equation for slope is:

$$\text{SLOPE} = \frac{\text{RISE (change in value on the vertical axis)}}{\text{RUN (change in value on the horizontal axis)}}$$

The slope tells the amount of increase or decrease of a given specific variable.

When using two or more variables one can plot the amount of difference between them in any given situation. This makes presenting information on a line graph more involved. It also makes it more informative and accurate than a simple bar graph. Knowledge of the term slope and what it is and how it is measured helps us to describe verbally the pictures we are seeing visually. For example, if a curve is said to have a slope of "zero," you should picture a flat line. If a curve has a slope of "1" you should picture a rising line that makes a 45-degree angle with the horizontal and vertical axis lines.

The preceding examples are of linear (straight line) curves. With nonlinear curves (the ones that really do curve) the slope of the curve is constantly changing so, as a result, we must then understand that the slope of the nonlinear curved line will be at a specific point. How is this done? The slope of a nonlinear curve is determined by the slope of a straight line that intersects the curve at that specific point. In all graphs, an upward sloping line represents a direct relationship between the two variables. A downward slope represents an inverse relationship between the two variables. In reading any graph, one must always be very careful to understand what is being measured, what can be deduced, and what cannot be deduced from the given graph.

Charts

To use charts correctly, one should remember the reasons one uses graphs. The general ideas are similar. It is usually a question as to which, a graph or chart, is more capable of adequately portraying the information one wants to illustrate. One can see the difference between them and realize that in many ways graphs and charts are interrelated. One of the most common types, because it is easiest to read and understand, even for the lay person, is the piechart.

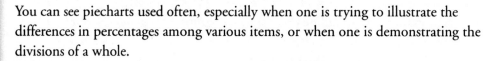

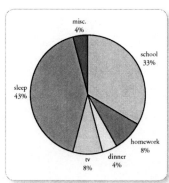

You can see piecharts used often, especially when one is trying to illustrate the differences in percentages among various items, or when one is demonstrating the divisions of a whole.

Sample Test Questions and Rationale

Easy

1. **The name for those who make maps is:**

   A. haberdasher

   B. geographer

   C. cartographer

   D. demographer

Answer: C – Cartographer

Rationale: (A) Haberdasher is a "British dealer in men's furnishings" according to the dictionary. (B) Geographers study mostly locations, conditions, and spatial relations. (C) Cartographers are people who make maps. (D) Demographers would be most concerned with the study of human populations.

SKILL 26.5 Summarizing the purpose or point of view of a historical narrative

A synthesis of information from multiple sources first requires an understanding of the content chosen for the synthesis. The writer of the synthesis will, no doubt, wish to incorporate his or her own ideas, particularly in any conclusions that are drawn, and show relationships to those of the chosen sources. That can only happen if the writer has a firm grip on what others have said or written. The focus is not so much on documentary methods but on techniques of critically examining and evaluating the ideas of others. Even so, careful documentation is extremely important in this type of presentation, particularly with regard to which particular edition is being read in the case of written sources; and date, location, etc., of online sources. The phrase "downloaded from such-and-such a Web site on such-and-such a date" is useful. If the conversation, interview, or speech is live, date, circumstances, and location must be indicated.

The purpose of a synthesis is to understand the works of others and to use that work in shaping a conclusion. The writer or speaker must clearly differentiate between the ideas that come from a source and his or her own.

Analyzing historical narratives involves using sources outside of a regular history textbook. Primary sources, such as letters, diaries, and printed resources must be considered when available. Even historical fiction can be a source of historical knowledge if written true to the era. It is up to the reader to determine the accuracy of historical information, based on a thorough analysis and comparison with known facts.

Analysis of historical narratives involves the ability to:

- Compare and contrast differing sets of ideas
- Consider multiple perspectives
- Analyze cause-and-effect relationships
- Draw comparisons across eras and regions in order to define enduring issues
- Distinguish between unsupported expressions of opinion and informed hypotheses grounded in historical evidence
- Compare competing historical narratives
- Challenge arguments of historical inevitability
- Hold interpretations of history as tentative
- Evaluate major debates among historians
- Hypothesize the influence of the past

DOMAIN V
THE FINE ARTS

Enhanced features only available in our ebook edition:

 eStickynotes: allows you take digital notes anywhere in the ebook edition. It further allows you to aggregate and print all enotes for easy studying.

 eFlashcards: a digital representation of a card represented with words, numbers or symbols or any combination of each and briefly displayed as part of a learning drill. eFlashcards takes away the burden of carrying around traditional cards that could easily be disarranged, dropped, or soiled.

 More Sample Tests: more ways to assess how much you know and how much further you need to study. Ultimately, makes you more prepared and attain mastery in the skills and techniques of passing the test the FIRST TIME!

Visit www.XAMonline.com
and click on ebook.

PERSONALIZED STUDY PLAN

PAGE	COMPETENCY AND SKILL	KNOWN MATERIAL/ SKIP IT	BRIEFLY REVIEW eSTICKYNOTES	MAKE eFLASHCARDS	TAKE ADDITIONAL SAMPLE TESTS
333	**27: Understanding the Visual Arts**	☐	☐	☐	☐
	27.1: Basic elements of art	☐	☐	☐	☐
	27.2: Two- and three-dimensional art	☐	☐	☐	☐
	27.3: Various art media	☐	☐	☐	☐
	27.4: Basic art tools and techniques	☐	☐	☐	☐
	27.5: How art reflects culture	☐	☐	☐	☐
	27.6: Comparing art of different cultures	☐	☐	☐	☐
346	**28: Understanding the Musical Arts**	☐	☐	☐	☐
	28.1: Comparing different instruments	☐	☐	☐	☐
	28.2: Common musical terms	☐	☐	☐	☐
	28.3: Science concepts to explain music-related terms	☐	☐	☐	☐
	28.4: Characteristics of music	☐	☐	☐	☐
	28.5: Basic musical techniques	☐	☐	☐	☐
	28.6: Cultural music	☐	☐	☐	☐
353	**29: Understanding Theater and Dance**	☐	☐	☐	☐
	29.1: Comparing dramatic and theatrical forms	☐	☐	☐	☐
	29.2: Dance characteristics	☐	☐	☐	☐
	29.3: Technical aspects of performance	☐	☐	☐	☐
	29.4: Methods of character development	☐	☐	☐	☐
	29.5: Cultural use of drama and dance	☐	☐	☐	☐

COMPETENCY 27

UNDERSTAND THE CONCEPTS, TECHNIQUES, AND MATERIALS OF THE VISUAL ARTS; ANALYZE WORKS OF VISUAL ART; AND UNDERSTAND THE CULTURAL DIMENSIONS AND CONTRIBUTIONS OF THE VISUAL ARTS

> **SKILL 27.1** **Identifying basic elements** *(e.g., line, color)* **and principles** *(e.g., unity, balance)* **of art, and recognizing how they are used to communicate meaning in works of art**

The components and strands of visual art encompass many areas. Students are expected to fine tune observation skills and be able to identify and recreate the experiences that teachers provide for them as learning tools. For example, students may walk as a group on a nature hike, taking in the surrounding elements, and then begin to discuss the repetition found in the leaves of trees, or the bricks of the sidewalk, or the size and shapes of the buildings and how they may relate. They may also use such an experience to describe lines, colors, shapes, forms, and textures. Beginning elements of perspective are noticed at an early age. The questions of why buildings look smaller when they are at a far distance and bigger when they are closer are sure to spark the imagination of early childhood students. Students can then take their inquiry to higher level of learning with some hands-on activities such as building three-dimensional buildings using paper and geometric shapes. Eventually students should acquire higher-level thinking skills such as analysis, in which they will begin to questions artists, art work, and many different aspects of visual art.

Students should have an early introduction to the principles of visual art and should become familiar with these terms:

Abstract	An image that reduces a subject to its essential visual elements, such as lines, shapes, and colors.
Background	Those portions or areas of composition that are behind the primary or dominant subject matter or design areas.

Table continued on next page

Balance	A principle of art and design concerned with the arrangement of one or more elements in a work of art so that they appear symmetrical or asymmetrical in design and proportion.
Contrast	A principle of art and design concerned with juxtaposing one or more elements in opposition, in order to show their differences.
Emphasis	A principle of art and design concerned with making one or more elements in a work of art stand out in such a way that they appear more important or significant.
Sketch	An image-development strategy; a preliminary drawing.
Texture	An element of art and design that pertains to the way something feels by representation of the tactile character of surfaces.
Unity	A principle of art and design concerned with the arrangement of one or more of the elements used to create a coherence of parts and a feeling of completeness or wholeness.

It is important that students learn the generic ideas for these terms and how they relate to the use of line, color, value, space, texture, and shape. An excellent opportunity is to create with the students an art sample book.

Such books could include a variety of sample materials that would help students make connections to such texture elements as sandpaper and cotton balls. Samples of square pieces of construction paper designed into various shapes could represent shape and string samples could represent the element of lines. The sampling of art should also focus clearly on colors. Color can be discussed in-depth when teaching about intensity or strength and value that relate to the lightness or darkness. Another valuable tool is the use of a color wheel, which allows students to experiment with the mixing of colors to create their own art experience.

The greatest works in art, literature, music, theater, and dance, all mirror universal themes. Universal themes are themes that reflect the human experience, regardless of time period, location, or socioeconomic standing. Universal themes tend to fall into broad categories, such as Man vs. Society, Man vs. Himself, Man vs. God, Man vs. Nature, and Good vs. Evil, to name the most obvious.

UNIVERSAL THEMES THROUGHOUT HISTORY	
Prehistoric Arts (circa 1,000,000–circa 8,000 BCE)	Major themes of this vast period appear to center around religious fertility rites and sympathetic magic, consisting of imagery of pregnant animals and faceless, pregnant women.
Mesopotamian Arts (circa 8,000–400 BCE)	The prayer statues and cult deities of the period point to the theme of polytheism in religious worship.
Egyptian Arts (circa 3,000–100 BCE)	The predominance of funerary art from ancient Egypt illustrates the theme of preparation for the afterlife and polytheistic worship. Another dominant theme, reflected by artistic convention, is the divinity of the pharaohs. In architecture, the themes were monumentality and adherence to ritual.
Greek Arts (800–100 BCE)	The sculpture of ancient Greece is replete with human figures, most nude and some draped. Most of these sculptures represent athletes and various gods and goddesses. The predominant theme is that of the ideal human, in both mind and body. In architecture, the theme was scale based on the ideal human proportions.
Roman Arts (circa 480 BCE–476 CE)	Judging from Roman arts, the predominant themes of the period deal with the realistic depiction of human beings and how they relate to Greek classical ideals. The emphasis is on practical realism. Another major theme is the glory in serving the Roman state. In architecture, the theme was rugged practicality mixed with Greek proportions and elements.
Middle Ages Arts (300–1400 CE)	Although the time span is expansive, the major themes remain relatively constant throughout. Since the Roman Catholic Church was the primary patron of the arts, most work was religious in nature. The purpose of much of the art was to educate. Specific themes varied from the illustration of Bible stories to interpretations of theological allegory, to lives of the saints, to consequences of good and evil. Depictions of the Holy Family were popular. Themes found in secular art and literature centered around chivalric love and warfare. In architecture, the theme was glorification of God and education of congregation to religious principles.

Table continued on next page

Renaissance Arts (circa 1400–1630 CE)	Renaissance themes include Christian religious depiction *(see also Middle Ages)*, but tend to reflect a renewed interest in all things classical. Specific themes include Greek and Roman mythological and philosophic figures, ancient battles, and legends. Dominant themes mirror the philosophic beliefs of Humanism, emphasizing individuality and human reason, such as those of the High Renaissance, which center around the psychological attributes of individuals. In architecture, the theme was scale based on human proportions.
Baroque Arts (1630–1700 CE)	The predominant themes found in the arts of the Baroque period include the dramatic climaxes of well-known stories, legends, and battles and the grand spectacle of mythology. Religious themes are found frequently, but it is drama and insight that are emphasized and not the medieval "salvation factor." Baroque artists and authors incorporated various types of characters into their works, careful to include minute details. Portraiture focused on the psychology of the sitters. In architecture, the theme was large scale grandeur and splendor.
Eighteenth Century Arts (1700–1800 CE)	Rococo themes of this century focused on religion, light mythology, portraiture of aristocrats, pleasure and escapism, and, occasionally, satire. In architecture, the theme was artifice and gaiety, combined with an organic quality of form. Neoclassic themes centered around examples of virtue and heroism, usually in classical settings, and historical stories. In architecture, classical simplicity and utility of design was regained.
Nineteenth Century Arts (1800–1900 CE)	Romantic themes include human freedom, equality, and civil rights, a love for nature, and a tendency toward the melancholic and mystic. The underlying theme is that the most important discoveries are made within the self, and not in the exterior world. In architecture, the theme was fantasy and whimsy, known as PICTURESQUE. Realistic themes included social awareness and a focus on society victimizing individuals. The themes behind Impressionism were the constant flux of the universe and the immediacy of the moment. In architecture, the themes were strength, simplicity, and upward thrust as skyscrapers entered the scene.

Table continued on next page

PICTURESQUE: the theme of fantasy and whimsy

Twentieth Century Arts (1900–2000 CE)	Diverse artistic themes of the century reflect a parting with traditional religious values and a painful awareness of man's inhumanity to man. Themes also illustrate a growing reliance on science, while simultaneously expressing disillusionment with man's failure to adequately control science. A constant theme is the quest for originality and self-expression, while seeking to express the universal in human experience. In architecture, "form follows function."

GENRES BY HISTORICAL PERIOD	
Ancient Greek Art (circa 800–323 BCE)	Dominant genres from this period were vase paintings—both black-figure and red-figure—and classical sculpture.
Roman Art (circa 480 BCE–476 CE)	Major genres from the Romans include FRESCOES (murals done in fresh plaster to affix the paint), classical sculpture, funerary art, state propaganda art, and relief work on cameos.
Middle Ages Art (circa 300–1400 CE)	Significant genres during the Middle Ages include Byzantine mosaics, illuminated manuscripts, ivory relief, altarpieces, cathedral sculpture, and fresco paintings in various styles.
Renaissance Art (1400–1630 CE)	Important genres from the Renaissance included Florentine fresco painting (mostly religious), High Renaissance painting and sculpture, Northern oil painting, Flemish miniature painting, and Northern printmaking.
Baroque Art (1630–1700 CE)	Pivotal genres during the Baroque era include Mannerism, Italian Baroque painting and sculpture, Spanish Baroque, Flemish Baroque, and Dutch portraiture. Genre paintings in still-life and landscape appear prominently in this period.
Eighteenth Century Art (1700–1800 CE)	Predominant genres of the century include Rococo painting, portraiture, social satire, Romantic painting, and Neoclassic painting and sculpture.

FRESCOES: murals done in fresh plaster to affix the paint

Table continued on next page

Nineteenth Century Art (1800–1900 CE)	Important genres include Romantic painting, academic painting and sculpture, landscape painting of many varieties, realistic painting of many varieties, Impressionism, and many varieties of post-Impressionism.
Twentieth Century Art (1900–2000 CE)	Major genres of the twentieth century include symbolism, art nouveau, fauvism, expressionism, cubism (both analytical and synthetic), futurism, non-objective art, abstract art, Surrealism, social realism, constructivism in sculpture, Pop and Op art, and conceptual art.

Sample Test Questions and Rationale

Average Rigor

1. Which of the following are universal themes in art, music, theater, and dance?

   A. Man vs. Society

   B. Man vs. Himself

   C. Good vs. Evil

   D. All of the above

   Answer: D – All of the above

   Rationale: The greatest works in art, literature, music, theater, and dance, all mirror universal themes. Universal themes are themes which reflect the human experience, regardless of time period, location, or socio-economic standing. Universal themes tend to fall into broad categories, such as Man vs. Society, Man vs. Himself, Man vs. God, Man vs. Nature, and Good vs. Evil, to name the most obvious.

Rigorous

2. Which time period of Arts does the themes of *"Roman mythology, Humanism, and Ancient legends"* reflect?

   A. Renaissance arts

   B. Baroque arts

   C. Mesopotamian arts

   D. Middle Ages arts

   Answer: A – Renaissance Arts

   Rationale: Renaissance themes include Christian religious depiction (see Middle Ages), but tend to reflect a renewed interest in all things classical. Specific themes include Greek and Roman mythological and philosophic figures, ancient battles, and legends. Dominant themes mirror the philosophic beliefs of Humanism, emphasizing individuality and human reason, such as those of the High Renaissance which center around the psychological attributes of individuals.

SKILL 27.2 Analyzing two-dimensional and three-dimensional works of art in terms of their visual and sensory characteristics

Teachers should be able to utilize and teach various techniques when analyzing works of art. Students will learn and then begin to apply what they have learned in the arts to all subjects across the curriculum. Using problem-solving techniques and creative skills, students will begin to master the techniques necessary to derive meaning from both the visual and sensory aspects of art. Students will be asked to review, respond, and analyze various types of art. Students should be critical and it is necessary that they relate to the human aspects of art. Students should be introduced to the wide range of opportunities to explore such art. Such opportunities may include exhibits, galleries, museums, libraries, and personal art collections.

Some opportunities for research include:

- Reproductions
- Art slides
- Films
- Print materials
- Electronic media

Once students are taught how to effectively research and use sources students should be expected to graduate to higher-level thinking skills. Students should begin to reflect on, interpret, evaluate, and explain how works of art and various styles of artwork explain social, psychological, cultural, and environmental aspects of life.

Several areas that must be mastered for students to explore and identify styles in the arts include:

- Understanding of various types of mediums, such as two-dimensional, three-dimensional, and electronic images
- Developing skills using electronic media to express visual ideas
- Awareness of cultural, environmental, and community opportunities that will provide options for exploring art images and consulting artists
- Awareness of potential careers in the field of arts
- Developing a variety of ways to use art materials/mediums

Some examples of mastery include:

- Drawing or painting using a computer graphics program
- Visiting a museum or art festival and writing a report telling about the experience
- Engaging in an interview or conversation with an artist regarding what he or she does and why they have chosen art as a profession
- Mixing and painting with a range of colors

SKILL 27.3 Applying knowledge of the characteristics of various art media (e.g., two-dimensional, three-dimensional, electronic) to select a medium appropriate for a given artistic purpose or intent

Students should create and experience works of art that will explore different types of subject matter, themes, and topics. Students need to understand the sensory elements and organizational principles of art and expression of images. Students should be able to select and use mediums and processes that actively communicate and express the intended meaning or their art works and exhibit competence in at least two mediums. For example, students should be able to select a process or medium for their intended work of art and describe their reasons for that selection. Students must also use the computer and electronic media to express their visual ideas and demonstrate a variety of different approaches to their selected medium. An excellent example would be for students to produce works using mixed media, such as a work of art that uses the computer, the camera, the copy machine, or other types of electronic equipment. At any age, students should be asked to compile their best works of art using different types of media. This is typically referred to as a portfolio. Early childhood students all the way through high school students benefit from the use of a portfolio.

The portfolio should begin with an early sample of the student's work, what is called a rough draft or a sketch. It can then be tracked to see the progress of the individual throughout the course of building the portfolio. By the end of the portfolio experience, the student's growth in use of medium and techniques should be clear. Progress can be tracked through the use of a rubric or by observation.

Some of the areas that students should master and that can be modeled by the teacher include:

- Experimentation through works of art using a variety of mediums, drawing, painting, sculpture, ceramics, printmaking, and video
- Producing a collection of art works (portfolio) and using a variety of mediums, topics, themes, and subject matters

- Conveying meaning through which art works were chosen

- Creating and evaluating different art works and which types of media chosen

- Reflecting on their work and others' works

Portfolios should include:

- Examples of mixing paint in ranges of shades and tints

- A sample of an idea for sculpting designed on the computer

- Works that display at least two mediums

- At least ten works of art in each portfolio

- Early sketches, including research and development of each project

- Research on a design, such as for a building or a landmark, and a completed design based on the research

- A painting made with tempera or watercolor, recalling a specific experience or memory

SKILL 27.4 Applying knowledge of basic tools and techniques for working with various materials (e.g., clay, textiles, wood)

It is vital that students learn to identify the materials, techniques, and processes employed in the visual arts and that are necessary to establish a connection between art and daily life. Younger children should begin to experience art in a variety of forms. It is important to reach many areas at an early age to establish a strong artistic foundation for young students. Students should be taught to recognize simple patterns found in the art environment. They should also be able to identify art materials such as clay, paint, and crayons. Each of these types of material should be used in daily lessons with young children.

Young students will need to be introduced to items that are developmentally appropriate for their age and for fine motor skills. Many pre-kindergarten and kindergarten students use oversized pencils and crayons for the first semester. Typically after this first semester enough development occurs to enable children to gradually begin using smaller sized materials. Students should begin to explore artistic expression at this age using colors and mixing.

It is vital for young children and students to learn the uses of primary colors and secondary colors using a color wheel. By the middle of the school year students should be able to explain this process. For example, a student needs orange paint but only has a few colors. Students should be able to determine that orange can be

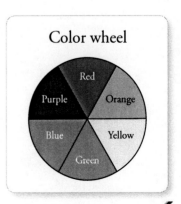
Color wheel

created by mixing red and yellow. Teachers should plan lessons using many different principles of design. By using common environmental figures such as people, animals, and buildings, teachers can base many art lessons on the characteristics of readily available examples.

Students should be introduced to as many techniques as possible to ensure that all strands of the visual arts and materials are experienced at a variety of levels. By using original works of arts, students should be able to identify visual and actual textures of art and based their judgments of objects found in everyday scenes. Good examples are landscapes, portraits, and still lifes. The major areas that young students should experience include:

- Painting: using tempera or watercolors

- Sculpture: typically using clay or Play-Doh

- Architecture: building or structuring design using 3D materials, such as cardboard and poster-board

- Ceramics: (another term for pottery) using a hollow clay sculpture and pots made from clay and fired in a kiln using high temperature to strengthen them

- Metalworking: (another term for engraving) cutting a design or letters into metal with a sharp tool

- Printmaking: lithography is an example of plan graphics, where a design is drawn on a surface and then the print is lifted from the surface

SKILL 27.5 **Analyzing how works of art reflect the cultures in which they were produced** (e.g., materials or techniques used, subject matter, style)

Although the elements of design have remained consistent throughout history, the emphasis on specific aesthetic principles has periodically shifted. Aesthetic standards or principles vary from time period to time period and from society to society.

An obvious difference in aesthetic principles occurs between works created by Eastern and Western cultures. Eastern works of art are more often based on spiritual considerations, while much Western art is secular in nature. In attempting to convey reality, Eastern artists generally prefer to use line, local color, and a simplistic view. Western artists tend toward a literal use of line, shape, color, and texture to convey a concise, detailed, complicated view. Eastern artists portray the human figure with symbolic meanings and little regard for muscle structure, resulting in a mystical view of the human experience. Western artists use the "principle of pondering," which requires the knowledge of both human anatomy and an expression of the human spirit.

In attempts to convey the illusion of depth or visual space in a work of art, Eastern and Western artists use different techniques. Eastern artists prefer a diagonal projection of eye movement into the picture plane, and often leave large areas of the surface untouched by detail. The result is the illusion of vast space, an infinite view that coincides with the spiritual philosophies of the Orient. Western artists rely on several techniques, such as overlapping planes, variation of object size, object position on the picture plane, linear and aerial perspective, color change, and various points of perspective to convey the illusion of depth. The result is space that is limited and closed.

In the application of color, Eastern artists use arbitrary choices of color. Western artists generally rely on literal color usage or emotional choices of color. The result is that Eastern art tends to be more universal in nature, while Western art is more individualized.

An interesting change in aesthetic principles occurred between the Renaissance and Baroque periods in Europe.

The Renaissance period was concerned with the rediscovery of the works of classical Greece and Rome. The art, literature, and architecture was inspired by classical orders, which tended to be formal, simple, and concerned with the ideal human proportions. This means that the painting, sculpture, and architecture was of a Teutonic, or closed nature, composed of forms that were restrained and compact. For example, consider the visual masterpieces of the period: Raphael's painting *The School of Athens*, with its precise use of space; Michelangelo's sculpture *David*, with its compact mass; and the facade of the Palazzo Strozzi, with its defined use of the rectangle, arches, and rustication of the masonry.

Compare the Renaissance characteristics to those of the Baroque period. The word *Baroque* means grotesque, which was the contemporary criticism of the new style. In comparison to the styles of the Renaissance, the Baroque was concerned with the imaginative flights of human fancy. The painting, sculpture, and architecture were of an a-Teutonic, or open, nature, composed of forms that were whimsical and free-flowing. Consider again the masterpieces of the period: Ruben's painting *The Elevation of the Cross*, with its turbulent forms of light and dark tumbling diagonally through space; Puget's sculpture *Milo of Crotona*, with its use of open space and twisted forms; and Borromini's *Chapel of St. Ivo*, with a facade that plays convex forms against concave ones.

Although artists throughout time have used the same elements of design to compose their various artistic works, the emphasis on specific aesthetic principles has periodically shifted. Aesthetic principles vary from time period to time period and from society to society.

In the 1920s and 1930s, the German art historian, Professor Wolfflin outlined these shifts in aesthetic principles in his influential book *Principles of Art History*. He arranged these changes into five categories of "visual analysis," sometimes referred to as the "categories of stylistic development." Wolfflin was careful to point out that no style is inherently superior to any other. They are simply indicators of the phase of development of that particular time or society. However, Wolfflin goes on to state, correctly or not, that once the evolution occurs, it is impossible to regress. These modes of perception apply to drawing, painting, sculpture, and architecture. They are:

WOLFFLIN'S CATEGORIES OF ANALYSIS	
From a Linear Mode to a Painterly Mode	This shift refers to stylistic changes that occur when perception or expression evolves from a linear form that is concerned with the contours and boundaries of objects, to perception or expression that stresses the masses and volumes of objects. From viewing objects in isolation, to seeing the relationships between objects are an important change in perception. Linear mode implies that objects are stationary and unchanging, while the painterly mode implies that objects and their relationships to other objects is always in a state of flux.
From Plane to Recession	This shift refers to perception or expression that evolves from a planar style, when the artist views movement in the work in an "up and down" and "side to side" manner, to a recessional style, when the artist views the balance of a work in an "in and out" manner. The illusion of depth may be achieved through either style, but only the recessional style uses an angular movement forward and backward through the visual plane.
From Closed to Open Form	This shift refers to perception or expression that evolves from a sense of enclosure, or limited space, in "closed form," to a sense of freedom in "open form." The concept is obvious in architecture, as in buildings that clearly differentiate between "outside" and "inside" space, and buildings that open up the space to allow the outside to interact with the inside.
From Multiplicity to Unity	This shift refers to an evolution from expressing unity through the use of balancing many individual parts, to expressing unity by subordinating some individual parts to others. Multiplicity stresses the balance between existing elements, whereas unity stresses emphasis, domination, and accent of some elements over other elements.
From Absolute to Relative Clarity	This shift refers to an evolution from works which clearly and thoroughly express everything there is to know about the object, to works that express only part of what there is to know, and leave the viewer to fill in the rest from his own experiences. Relative clarity, then, is a sophisticated mode, because it requires the viewer to actively participate in the "artistic dialogue." Each of the previous four categories is reflected in this, as linearity is considered to be concise while painting is more subject to interpretation. Planarity is more factual, while recessional movement is an illusion, and so on.

Sample Test Questions and Rationale

Average Rigor

1. **Aesthetic art principles vary from culture to culture. Which of the following is NOT an element of Eastern art?**

   A. more universal in nature

   B. portray the human figure with symbolic meanings

   C. convey a concise, detailed and complicated view

   D. use arbitrary choices of color

Answer: C – convey a concise, detailed and complicated view

Rationale: An obvious difference in aesthetic principles occurs between works created by Eastern and Western cultures. In attempting to convey reality, eastern artists generally prefer to use line, local color, and a simplistic view. Western artists tend toward a literal use of line, shape, color, and texture to **convey a concise, detailed, complicated view**. Eastern artists portray the human figure with symbolic meanings and little regard for muscle structure, resulting in a mystical view of the human experience. In the application of color, Eastern artists use arbitrary choices of color. Western artists generally rely on literal color usage or emotional choices of color. The end result is that eastern art tends to be more universal in nature, while Western art is more individualized.

**SKILL
27.6 Comparing works of art of different cultures, eras, and artists in terms of characteristics such as theme, imagery, and style**

See Skill 27.1

COMPETENCY 28

UNDERSTAND CONCEPTS, TECHNIQUES, AND MATERIALS FOR PRODUCING, LISTENING TO, AND RESPONDING TO MUSIC; ANALYZE WORKS OF MUSIC; AND UNDERSTAND THE CULTURAL DIMENSIONS AND CONTRIBUTIONS OF MUSIC

> **SKILL 28.1** **Comparing various types of instruments** *(e.g., strings, percussion, woodwind, brass, electronic)* **in terms of the sounds they produce**

Types of Musical Instruments

Instruments are categorized by the mechanism that creates its sound.

FOUR BASIC CATEGORIES OF MUSICAL INSTRUMENTS	
String Instruments	String instruments all make their sounds through strings. The sound of the instrument depends on the thickness and length of the strings. The slower a string vibrates, the lower the resulting pitch. Also, the way the strings are manipulated varies among string instruments. Some strings are plucked (e.g., guitar) while others use a bow to cause the strings to vibrate (e.g., violin). Some are even connected to keys (e.g., piano). Other common string instruments include the viola, double bass, cello, and piano.
Wind Instruments	The sound of wind instruments is caused by wind vibrating in a pipe or tube. Air blows into one end of the instrument and, in many wind instruments, air passes over a reed that causes the air to vibrate. The pitch depends on the air's frequency as it passes through the tube, and the frequency depends on the tube's length or size. Larger tubes create deeper sounds in a wind instrument. The pitch is also controlled by holes or values. As fingers cover the holes or press the valve, the pitch changes for the notes the musician intends. Common wind instruments include pipe organ, oboe, clarinet, and saxophone.
Brass Instruments	Brass instruments are similar to wind instruments because music from brass instruments also results from air passing through an air chamber. They are called brass instruments, however, because they are made from metal or brass. Pitch on a brass instrument is controlled by the size or length of the air chamber. Many brass instruments are twisted or coiled, which lengthens the air chamber without making the instrument unmanageably long. As in wind instruments, larger air chambers create deeper sounds, and the pitch can be controlled by valves on the instrument. In addition, some brass instruments also control the pitch by the musician's mouth position on the mouthpiece. Common brass instruments include the French horn, trumpet, trombone, and tuba.

Table continued on next page

| Percussion Instruments | To play a percussion instrument, the musician hits or shakes the instrument. The sound is created from sound vibrations as a result of shaking or striking the instrument. Many materials, such as metal or wood, are used to create percussion instruments and different thicknesses or sizes of the material help control the sound. Thicker or heavier materials like drum membranes make deeper sounds, while thinner, metal materials (e.g., triangle) make higher-pitched sounds. Other common percussion instruments include the cymbals, tambourine, bells, xylophone, and wood block. |

Sample Test Questions and Rationale

Easy

1. The French horn, trumpet, trombone, and tuba are a part of which musical category?

    A. String Instruments

    B. Brass Instruments

    C. Percussion Instruments

    D. Wind Instruments

Answer: B – Brass Instruments

Rationale: Brass instruments are similar to wind instruments since music from brass instruments also results from air passing through an air chamber. They are called brass instruments, however, because they are made from metal or brass. Common brass instruments include the French horn, trumpet, trombone and tuba.

SKILL 28.2 Defining and applying common musical terms (e.g., pitch, tempo)

The resources available to man to make music have varied throughout the ages and have given the chance for a variety of musical styles or types to be created or invented. Social changes, cultural features, and historical purpose have all shared a part in giving birth to a multitude of different musical forms throughout the world.

Music can be traced to the people who created it by the instruments, melodies, rhythms, and records of performance (songs) that are composed in a community. From early musical developments, as far back as nomadic cave dwellers playing the flute and beating on hand drums, to the different electric instruments and recording technology of the modern music industry, the styles and types of music produced have been closely related to the people who chose it for their particular lifestyle and way of existence.

Western music, rising chiefly from the fusion of classical and folkloric forms, has always been the pocket of a large variety of instruments and music generating new techniques to fit the change in expression provided by the expansion of its possibilities. Instruments such as the piano and the organ; stringed instruments like the violin, viola, cello, guitar, and bass; wind instruments like the flute, saxophone, trumpet, trombone, tuba, and saxophone; and electronic instruments like the synthesizer and electric guitar have all provided for the invention of new styles and types of music created and used by different people at different times and in different places.

The rites of Christianity during the early middle ages were the focus of social and cultural aspiration and became a natural meeting place for communities to come together consistently for the purpose of experiencing God, through preaching and music. Composers and performers fulfilled their roles with sacred music through Gregorian chants and Oratorios. The art patron's court in the fifteenth and fourteenth centuries and the opera house of the nineteenth century satisfied the need of a nascent, progressive society looking to experience grander and more satisfying music. New forms were generated such as the concerto, symphony, sonata, and string quartet, which demonstrated a zeal and zest for creation typical of the burgeoning intellect at the end of the Middle Ages and the beginning of modern society.

Traditional types and styles of music in America, India, China, and throughout the Middle East and Africa, using a contrasting variety of stringed instruments and percussion to typical Western instruments, marked the beginning of an exciting merging of Western music with the music of colonialism. Western musical instruments were adopted to play the traditional musical styles of different cultures. Blues music, arising from the Southern Black community in the United States, would morph into Rock n' Roll and Hip Hop, alongside the progression of the traditional folk music of European settlers. Hispanic music arose from the use of Western musical instruments imbued with African rhythms from the Caribbean, resulting in Salsa, Merengue, Cumbia, and Son Cubano.

SKILL 28.3 Using basic scientific concepts to explain how music-related sound is produced, transmitted through air, and received by listeners

Variations in air pressure against the ear drum, and the resulting physical and neurological processing and interpretation, give the listener the experience called sound. Musical acoustics deal with the generation of sound by an instrument, transmitted to the listener through the air, ultimately received as the perception of musical sound.

The musical instrument vibrates and produces sound. The vibrations of a string or wire, a struck membrane, or a blown pipe of the instrument are the usual modes of vibration. Vibrations are motions that may range from the simple to-and-fro movement of a pendulum or the vibrations of a steel plate when struck with a hammer.

Most sound that people recognize as music is dominated by regular, periodic vibrations rather than nonperiodic ones, and we refer to the transmission of these vibrations as a sound wave. In a very simple case, the sound causes the air pressure to increase and decrease in a regular fashion and is heard as a tone that is distinguished as a musical sound rather than noise.

Most sound that people recognize as music is dominated by regular, periodic vibrations rather than nonperiodic ones, and we refer to the transmission of these vibrations as a sound wave.

SKILL 28.4 Relating characteristics of music (e.g., rhythm, beat) to musical effects produced

In music, a DIVISIVE RHYTHM is when a larger period of time is divided into smaller units. ADDITIVE RHYTHMS are when larger periods of time are made from smaller units of time added to a previous unit.

Any single strike or series of beats on a percussion instrument creates a rhythmic pattern, sometimes called a drum beat. Percussion instruments are sometimes referred to as nonpitched or untuned. This occurs when the sound of the percussion instrument has no pitch that can be heard by the ear. Examples of percussion instruments that are nonpitched are the snare drum, cymbals, and whistles.

The autoharp, or lyre, is a stringed instrument that has thirty to forty strings stretched across a flat soundboard and is usually plucked rather than strummed. In the acoustic version, the autoharp has no neck. Chord bars are attached to dampers that mute all the other strings except the desired chord. An autoharp is sometimes called a zither. The zither is mainly used in folk music, most common in German-speaking Alpine Europe.

DIVISIVE RHYTHYM: one in which a larger period of time is divided into smaller units

ADDITIVE RHYTHYM: one in which larger periods of time are made of smaller units of time added to a previous unit

Tone quality is the quality of a note or sound that distinguishes different types of musical instruments.

A keyboard instrument is any musical instrument played using a musical keyboard. The harpsichord and pipe organ was used in early European countries. The organ is the oldest, appearing in the third century BCE, and until the fourteenth century it was the only keyboard instrument. The harpsichord appeared at this time and was very common until the arrival of the piano in the eighteenth century.

The piano is popular because the player can vary the volume of the sound by varying the amount of intensity in which the keys are struck. Volume can also be adjusted with pedals that act as dampers. Other widely used keyboard instruments include electrictronic instruments, which are largely referred to as keyboard-style synthesizers. Significant developments in synthesizers occurred in the 1960s when digital synthesizers became more common.

Sample Test Questions and Rationale

Rigorous

1. **Most Western music is based on which type of rhythm?**

   A. additive

   B. divisive

   C. modern

   D. classical

Answer: B - divisive

Rationale: In music, a divisive rhythm is when a larger period of time is divided into smaller units. Additive rhythms are when larger periods of time are made from smaller units of time added to a previous unit. Most Western music is based on divisive rhythm, while non-Western music uses more additive rhythm.

SKILL 28.5 **Recognizing basic technical skills that musicians must develop to produce an aesthetically acceptable performance** *(e.g., manual dexterity, breathing techniques, knowledge of musical notation)*

A CAPPELLA: vocalization not accompanied by musical instruments

Vocal music is probably the oldest form of music, since it does not require any instrument besides the human voice. Unaccompanied music is referred to as A CAPPELLA. The human voice consists of sound made by using the vocal folds used for talking. The vocal folds, in combination with the lips, the tongue, the lower jaw, and the palate, are capable of producing highly intricate sound. The TONE of voice may be modified to suggest various emotions, such as happiness and sadness. Tone quality is the quality of a note or sound that distinguishes different types of musical instruments. Tone quality is what people use to distinguish the saxaphone from a trumpet, even when both instruments are playing notes at the same pitch.

> **TONE:** the pitch, intensity, and modulation of sound

The human voice is complex and vocalists use it as an instrument to create music. The vocal folds (vocal chords) can loosen, tighten, or change their thickness, transferring breath at various pressures. The position of the tongue and tightening of the muscles in the neck can result in changes of pitch and volume. Breath control, tone, and posture all require different techniques.

Breathing technique is very important for proper voice projection. To talk we use air from the top of the lungs and the muscles from the back of the throat. To properly project our voices, we pull air from the bottom of the lungs, and the diaphragm (or stomach area) is used to push it out. Finding ways to exercise and lift the diaphragm, such as singing musical scales can help singers reacher higher or lower notes. Stance is also important. It is recommended to stand up straight with your feet shoulder width apart and your foot slightly forward. This improves your balance as well as your breathing.

Sample Test Questions and Rationale

Average Rigor

1. **Which is probably the oldest form of music?**

   A. singing

   B. drum-playing

   C. harp-playing

   D. dancing

Answer: A – singing

Rationale: Vocal music is probably the oldest form of music, since it does not require any instrument besides the human voice. Unaccompanied music is referred to as a cappella. The human voice consists of sound made by using the vocal folds (vocal chords) used for talking. The vocal folds, in combination with the lips, the tongue, the lower jaw, and the palate, are capable of producing highly intricate sounds.

SKILL 28.6 Analyzing how different cultures have created music reflective of their histories and societies (e.g., call-and-response songs, ballads, work songs, folk songs)

CALL-AND-RESPONSE: a form of verbal and nonverbal interaction between a speaker and a listener

CALL-AND-RESPONSE songs are a form of verbal and nonverbal interaction between a speaker and a listener, in which statements by a speaker are responded to by a listener. In West African cultures, call-and-response songs were used in religious rituals and gatherings and are now used in other forms such as gospel, blues, and jazz as a form of musical expression. In certain Native American tribes, call-and-response songs are used to preserve and protect the tribe's cultural heritage and can be seen and heard at modern-day pow-wows. The men would begin the song as the speaker, with singing and drumming, and the women would respond with singing and dancing.

BALLAD: a song that contains a story

A BALLAD is a song that contains a story. Instrumental music forms a part of folk music, especially dance traditions. Much folk music is vocal, since the instrument (the voice) that makes such music is usually handy. As such, most folk music has lyrics and is descriptive about something. Any story form can be a ballad, such as fairy tales or historical accounts. It usually has simple repeating rhymes and often contains a refrain (or repeating sections) that are played or sung at regular intervals throughout. Ballads could be called hymns when they are based on religious themes. In the twentieth century, ballad took on the meaning of a popular song especially of a romantic or sentimental nature.

Folk music has endured and been passed down by oral tradition and emerges spontaneously from ordinary people. In early societies, it arose in areas that were not yet affected by mass communication. It was normally shared by the entire community and was transmitted by word of mouth. A folk song is usually seen as an expression of a way of life now, in the past, or that is about to disappear. In the 1960s, folk songs were sung as a way of protesting political themes.

The work song is typically sung a cappella by people working on a physical and often repetitive task. It was probably intended to reduce feelings of boredom. Rhythms of work songs also serve to synchronize physical movement such as when marching. Frequently, the verses of work songs are improvised and sung differently each time.

COMPETENCY 29

UNDERSTAND CONCEPTS, TECHNIQUES, AND MATERIALS RELATED TO THE THEATRE AND DANCE; ANALYZE WORKS OF DRAMA AND DANCE; AND UNDERSTAND THE CULTURAL DIMENSIONS AND CONTRIBUTIONS OF DRAMA AND DANCE

SKILL **Comparing dramatic and theatrical forms and their characteristics**
29.1 *(e.g., pantomime, improvisation)*

Students must be able to create, perform, and actively participate in theatre. Classes must be able to apply processes and skills involved in drama and theatre. From acting, designing, script writing, creating formal and informal theatre, and media productions there is a wide variety of skills that must encompass the theatre expression. Literature in the classroom opens many doors for learning. Reading and rehearsing stories with children allows them to explore the area of imagination and creative play. Students can take simple stories such as "The Three Little Pigs" and act out such tales. Acting allows students to experience newfound dramatic skills and to enhance their creative abilities. A school curriculum incorporating dramatic and theatrical forms should include the vocabulary for theatre and the development of a criterion for evaluation of dramatic events. Students must understand and appreciate a dramatic work.

A good drama curriculum should include:

- Acting: Acting involves the students' ability to skillfully communicate with an audience. It requires speaking, movement, sensory awareness, rhythm, and great oral communication skills.

- Improvisation: The actors must be able to respond to unexpected stimuli and be spontaneous and creative and they must adapt to any scene that may be unscripted.

- Drama: A reenactment of life and life situations for entertainment purposes.

- Theatre: Theatre involves a more formal presentation in front of an audience. Typically it involves a script, set, direction, and production.

- Production: This often includes arranging for the entire theatre performance and the production of the whole process.

- Direction: Coordinating and directing or guiding the onstage activities.

- Playmaking: This involves creating an original script and staging a performance without a set or formal audience.

- Pantomime: A form of communication by means of gesture and facial expressions. Telling a story without the use of words.

Various areas of art frameworks should be addressed, including, but not limited to:

- Directing of theatrical productions, auditions, analyzing scripts, demonstrating vision for a project as well as knowledge of communication skills, social group skills, and creativity

- Understanding the principles of production

- Applying scheduling, budget, planning, promotion, roles, and responsibilities of others and demonstrating knowledge of legal issues, such as copyright

- Selection of appropriate works

SKILL 29.2 **Relating types of dance** *(e.g., ballet, folk, modern)* **to their characteristic forms of movement, expressive qualities, and cultural origins**

There are seven primary styles of dance:

- Creative dance
- Modern dance
- Social dance
- Dance of other cultures
- Structured dance
- Ritual dance
- Ballet

Creative dance is the one that is most natural to a young child. Creative dance depicts feelings through movement. It is the initial reaction to sound and movement. The older elementary student will incorporate mood and expressiveness. Stories can be told to release the dancer into imagination.

Isadora Duncan is credited with being the mother of modern dance. Modern dance today refers to a concept of dance where the expressions of opposites are developed such as fast–slow, contract–release, vary height and level to fall and recover. Modern dance is based on four principles: substance, dynamism, met kinesis, and form.

Social dance refers to a cooperative form of dance with respect to one sharing the dance floor with others and to having respect for one's partner. Social dance may be in the form of marches, waltz, and the two-step. This style of dance requires a steadier capability that the previous levels. Changing partners frequently within the dance is something that is subtly important to maintain.

The upper level elementary student can learn dance in connection with social dances such as the minuet. The minuet was introduced to the court in Paris in 1650, and it dominated the ballroom until the end of the eighteenth century. The waltz was introduced around 1775 and was an occasion of fashion and courtship. The pomp and ceremony of it all makes for fun classroom experiences. Dance traditionally is central to many cultures and the interrelatedness of teaching history such as Native American dance or the Mexican hat dance; Japanese theatre incorporates theatre of both masks and dance. All are important exposures to dance and culture.

Structured dances are recognized by particular patterns, such as the tango or waltz, and were made popular in dance studios and gym classes alike.

Ritual dances are often of a religious nature that celebrate a significant life event, such as a harvest season or the rain season, glorifying the gods, asking for favors in hunting, and birth or death. Many of these themes are carried out in movies and theaters today but they have their roots in Africa where circle dances and chants summoned the gods and sometimes produced trance-like states where periods of divine contact convey the spiritual cleansing of the experience.

Dancing at weddings today is a prime example of ritual dance. The father dances with the bride. Then the husband dances with the bride. The two families then dance with each other.

In ballet a barre is used for balance to practice the five basic positions. Alignment is the way in which various parts of the dancer's body are in line with one another while the dancer is moving. It is a very precise dance form and executed with grace and form. The mood and expressions of the music are very important to ballet and form the canvas upon which the dance is performed.

Sample Test Questions and Rationale

Easy

1. **Which of the following are styles of dance?**

   A. Creative

   B. Modern

   C. Ritual

   D. All of the above

Answer: D – All of the above

Rationale: There are many styles of dance. Here are just a few:

- Creative dance
- Modern dance
- Social dance
- Dance of other cultures
- Structured dance
- Ritual dance
- Ballet

SKILL 29.3 Analyzing how technical aspects of performance (*e.g., costumes, props, lighting*) affect the message or overall impression created by a performance

Students must realize the effect that technical aspects of performance have regarding overall message and impression. Students should be able to recognize the basic tools, media, and techniques involved in a theatrical production. Students must use professional resources for theatre experiences. Students should be able to accomplish these tasks:

- Use of theatrical technology skills and facilities in creating the theatre experience
- Use of school and community resources, including library and media centers, museums, and theatre professionals as part of their production
- Visit local theatrical institutions and attend theatrical performances as an individual and as a group
- Understand the broad range of vocations/avocations in performing, producing, and promoting theatre

The student's mastery of skills will be evident when he or she can:

- Read and follow a lighting plot for a production, handling and focusing lighting instruments properly

- Read a script for a production, then complete pictorial research on the costuming and accessories of the time period before designing costumes

- Write a short review of a local community performance for publication in the school newspaper

- Create a publicity campaign for the high school production

- Create props that engage the audience as well as draw in performers to the actual scenery of the stage

SKILL 29.4 Recognizing how language, voice, gesture, and movement are used to develop character and create interaction among performers in theatrical productions

Students will create and perform theatre pieces as well as improvisational drama. They must understand and use the basic elements of theatre in their characterizations, improvisations, and play writing. Students will engage in individual and group theatrical and theatre-related tasks and will describe various roles and means for creating, performing, and producing engaging theatre through character and performances.

It is vital that students recognize these performance indicators:

- Use of creative drama to communicate feelings and ideas

- Imitation of experiences through pantomime, play making, dramatic play, story dramatization, story telling, and role playing

- Use of language, voice, expression, movement, and observation to express their experiences and communicate ideas and feelings

- Use of props, simple set pieces, and costume pieces to establish place, time, and character for participants

- Identify and use in individual and group experiences some of the roles, processes, and actions for performing and creating theatre skills and creating theatre pieces and improvisational drama

Other skills necessary for character development include:

- Recognizing the difference between real and pretend

- Definition of play space

- Recognition of appropriate dialogue in dramatic play

- Assuming roles of leader and follower

- Use of movement and voice to represent a feeling, animal, or action

- Different performance models such as storytelling, reader's theatre, puppets, choral speaking

- Expression of feelings both verbally and nonverbally

An example that early childhood or elementary teachers could include to ensure the mastery of these skills would be a circle time activity that requires students to demonstrate what they have learned. During circle time, the teacher shows students a picture of an animal (say a cat) or names an animal character from a familiar story. The teacher then asks students to help list common characteristics/behaviors of that animal. Using the list as a guide, students begin to act out these behaviors. The teacher can encourage movement, sounds, voice, and appropriate language for the activity.

> ### SKILL 29.5 Analyzing ways in which different cultures have used drama and dance (e.g., to teach moral lessons, to preserve cultural traditions, to affirm the sense of community, to entertain)

Greek History

The history of theatre dates back to early sixth century BCE in Greece. The Greek theatre was the earliest known theater experience. Drama was expressed in many Greek spiritual ceremonies. There are two main forms of dramatic forms that have both evolved in their own time.

- Tragedy: Typically conflict between characters
- Comedy: Typically paradoxical relationships between humans and the gods

Roman History

The history of theatre in Roman times dates to the third century BCE. These shows were also based on religious aspects of the lives of gods and goddesses. Drama wasn't able to withstand the fall of the Roman Empire in 476 BCE. By the end of the sixth century drama was nearly dead in Rome.

Medieval Drama

Medieval theatre was a new revelation of drama that appeared in around the tenth century CE. New religious rituals were introduced in many holiday services such as Christmas and Easter. Many theatre troupes toured churches presenting religious narratives and life stories with moral deeds. Over time, the once-small traveling groups grew into full sized productions, putting on plays, presentations, and elaborate passions. Performances became spectacles at outdoor theaters, marketplaces, and any place large audiences could gather. The main focus of these dramas was to glorify God and humanity and to celebrate local artisan trades.

Puritan Commonwealth

The Puritan Commonwealth, ruled by Oliver Cromwell, outlawed dramatic performances and that ban lasted for nearly twenty years. Following the Puritan era was the restoration of the English monarchy and new, more well-rounded plays became the focus of art. For the first time in history, women were allowed to participate.

Melodrama

Melodrama eventually took the stage, in which good always triumphed over the evil. This form of acting was usually pleasing to the audience, yet sometimes unrealistic.

Serious Drama

Serious Drama emerged late in the nineteenth and twentieth centuries following the movement of realism. Realism attempted to combine the dealings of nature with realistic and ordinary situations on stage.

Realism

Today, realism is the most common form of stage presentation. The techniques used today to stage drama combine many of the past histories and cultures of drama.

Sample Test Questions and Rationale

Average Rigor

1. **Drama was expressed in many Greek spiritual ceremonies. Name the two main forms of drama.**

   A. Comedy and Realism

   B. Tragedy and Comedy

   C. Realism and Drama

   D. Comedy and Drama

   Answer: B – Tragedy and Comedy

   Rationale: Drama was expressed in many Greek spiritual ceremonies. There are two main forms of dramatic forms that have both evolved in their own time:

   1. Tragedy, which was usually conflict between characters.

   2. Comedy, which was typically paradoxical relationships between humans and the gods. Comedies and tragedies were seldom mixed playwrights. Plays such as these were designed to entertain, contained little violence, and were based on knowledge and the teachings of Aristotle.

Rigorous

2. **The history of theatre can be dated back to:**

   A. late 6th century in Greece

   B. early 9th century in Italy

   C. early 6th century in Greece

   D. late 9th century in Italy

   Answer: C – early 6th century in Greece

   Rationale: The history of theatre can be dated back to the early sixth century BCE in Greece. The Greek theatre was the earliest known theater experience. Drama was expressed in many Greek spiritual ceremonies.

DOMAIN VI
HEALTH AND FITNESS

Enhanced features only available in our ebook edition:

 eStickynotes: allows you take digital notes anywhere in the ebook edition. It further allows you to aggregate and print all enotes for easy studying.

 eFlashcards: a digital representation of a card represented with words, numbers or symbols or any combination of each and briefly displayed as part of a learning drill. eFlashcards takes away the burden of carrying around traditional cards that could easily be disarranged, dropped, or soiled.

 More Sample Tests: more ways to assess how much you know and how much further you need to study. Ultimately, makes you more prepared and attain mastery in the skills and techniques of passing the test the FIRST TIME!

Visit www.XAMonline.com
and click on ebook.

PERSONALIZED STUDY PLAN

PAGE	COMPETENCY AND SKILL	KNOWN MATERIAL/ SKIP IT	BRIEFLY REVIEW eSTICKYNOTES	MAKE eFLASHCARDS	TAKE ADDITIONAL SAMPLE TESTS
363	**30: Basic principles of health and safety**	☐	☐	☐	☐
	30.1: Common health problems	☐	☐	☐	☐
	30.2: Positive health choices and behaviors	☐	☐	☐	☐
	30.3: Decision-making and problem-solving skills	☐	☐	☐	☐
	30.4: Principles of good nutrition	☐	☐	☐	☐
	30.5: Contemporary health-related issues	☐	☐	☐	☐
	30.6: Health-care information	☐	☐	☐	☐
	30.7: Impact of environmental conditions on health and safety	☐	☐	☐	☐
378	**31: Physical Education Concepts**	☐	☐	☐	☐
	31.1: Characteristics of physical development	☐	☐	☐	☐
	31.2: Development of motor skills and perceptual awareness	☐	☐	☐	☐
	31.3: Physical activity safety concepts and practices	☐	☐	☐	☐
	31.4: Successful participation in sports and activities	☐	☐	☐	☐
	31.5: Physical activities and the promotion of personal skills	☐	☐	☐	☐
386	**32: Health-related Physical fitness Concepts**	☐	☐	☐	☐
	32.1: Common disorders of major body systems	☐	☐	☐	☐
	32.2: Basic components of physical fitness	☐	☐	☐	☐
	32.3: Personal fitness plans and self-assessments	☐	☐	☐	☐
	32.4: Physical health and disease prevention	☐	☐	☐	☐
	32.5: Physical activities that reduce health risks	☐	☐	☐	☐

COMPETENCY 30

UNDERSTAND BASIC PRINCIPLES AND PRACTICES OF PERSONAL, INTERPERSONAL, AND COMMUNITY HEALTH AND SAFETY; AND APPLY RELATED KNOWLEDGE AND SKILLS (E.G., DECISION MAKING, PROBLEM SOLVING) TO PROMOTE PERSONAL WELL-BEING

SKILL Identifying common health problems and explaining how they can
30.1 be prevented, detected, and treated

Malfunctions of the Respiratory and Excretory Systems

EMPHYSEMA is a chronic obstructive pulmonary disease (COPD). These diseases make it difficult for a person to breathe. Partial obstruction of the bronchial tubes limits airflow, making breathing difficult. The primary cause of emphysema is smoking. People with a deficiency in alpha1-antitrypsin protein production have a greater risk of developing emphysema and at an earlier age. This protein helps protect the lungs from damage done by inflammation. This genetic deficiency is rare and doctors can test for it in individuals with a family history of the deficiency. There is no cure for emphysema, but there are treatments available. The best prevention against emphysema is to refrain from smoking.

> **EMPHYSEMA:** a chronic obstructive pulmonary disease (COPD)

NEPHRITIS usually occurs in children. Symptoms include hypertension, decreased renal function, hematuria, and edema. Glomerulonephritis (GN) is a more precise term to describe this disease. An antigen–antibody complex that causes inflammation and cell proliferation produces nephritis. Nephritis damages normal kidney tissue and, if left untreated, can lead to kidney failure and death.

> **NEPHRITIS:** an infection of the kidney

Malfunctions of the Circulatory System

Cardiovascular diseases are the leading cause of death in the United States. Cardiac disease usually results in either a heart attack or a stroke. A HEART ATTACK occurs when cardiac muscle tissue dies, usually from coronary artery blockage. A STROKE occurs when nervous tissue in the brain dies due to the blockage of arteries in the head.

> **HEART ATTACK:** occurs when cardiac muscle tissue dies, usually from coronary artery blockage

> **STROKE:** occurs when nervous tissue in the brain dies due to the blockage of arteries in the head

Atherosclerosis causes many heart attacks and strokes. Plaques form on the inner walls of arteries, narrowing the area in which blood can flow. Arteriosclerosis occurs when the arteries harden from the plaque accumulation. A healthy diet low in saturated fats and cholesterol and regular exercise can prevent atherosclerosis.

High blood pressure (hypertension) also promotes atherosclerosis. Diet, medication, and exercise can reduce high blood pressure and prevent atherosclerosis.

Malfunctions of the Immune System

The immune system attacks both microbes and cells that are foreign to the host. This is the problem with skin grafts, organ transplantations, and blood transfusions. Antibodies to foreign blood and tissue types already exist in the body. Antibodies will destroy the new blood cells in transfused blood that is not compatible with the host. There is a similar reaction with tissue and organ transplants.

The major histocompatibility complex (MHC) is responsible for the rejection of tissue and organ transplants. This complex is unique to each person. Cytotoxic T-cells recognize the MHC on the transplanted tissue or organ as foreign and destroy these tissues. Suppression of the immune system with various drugs can prevent this reaction. The complication with immune suppression is that the patient is more susceptible to infection.

AUTOIMMUNE DISEASE: when the body's own immune system destroys its own cells

AUTOIMMUNE DISEASE occurs when the body's own immune system destroys its own cells. Lupus, Grave's disease, and rheumatoid arthritis are examples of autoimmune diseases. There is no way to prevent autoimmune diseases. Immunodeficiency is a deficiency in either the humoral or cell-mediated immune defenses. HIV is an example of an immunodeficiency disease.

Malfunctions of the Digestive System

GASTRIC ULCERS: lesions in the stomach lining

GASTRIC ULCERS are lesions in the stomach lining. Bacteria are the main cause of ulcers, but pepsin and acid can exacerbate the problem if the ulcers do not heal quickly enough.

APPENDICITIS: inflammation of the appendix

APPENDICITIS is the inflammation of the appendix. The appendix has no known function, but is open to the intestine and hardened stool or swollen tissue can block it. The blocked appendix can cause bacterial infections and inflammation leading to appendicitis. The swelling cuts the blood supply, killing the organ tissue. If left untreated, this leads to rupture of the appendix allowing the stool and the infection to spill out into the abdomen. This condition is life threatening and requires immediate surgery. Symptoms of appendicitis include lower abdominal pain, nausea, loss of appetite, and fever.

DIABETES: a deficiency of insulin resulting in high blood glucose

Malfunctions of the Nervous and Endocrine Systems

DIABETES is the best-known endocrine disorder. A deficiency of insulin resulting in high blood glucose is the primary cause of diabetes. Type I diabetes is an autoimmune disorder. The immune system attacks the cells of the pancreas, ending the ability to produce insulin. Treatment for type I diabetes consists of daily insulin injections. Type II diabetes usually occurs with age and/or obesity. There is usually a reduced response in target cells due to changes in insulin receptors or a deficiency of insulin. Type II diabetics need to monitor their blood glucose levels. Treatment usually consists of dietary restrictions and exercise.

HYPERTHYROIDISM is another disorder of the endocrine system. Excessive secretion of thyroid hormones is the cause. Symptoms are weight loss, high blood pressure, and high body temperature. The opposite condition, HYPOTHYROIDISM, causes weight gain, lethargy, and intolerance to cold.

There are many nervous system disorders. The degeneration of the basal ganglia in the brain causes PARKINSON'S DISEASE. This degeneration causes a decrease in the motor impulses sent to the muscles. Symptoms include tremors, slow movement, and muscle rigidity. Progression of Parkinson's disease occurs in five stages: early, mild, moderate, advanced, and severe. In the severe stage, the person is confined to a bed or chair. There is no cure for Parkinson's disease. Private research with stem cells is currently underway to find a cure.

> **HYPERTHYRIODISM:** excessive secretion of thyroid hormones

> **HYPOTHYROIDISM:** inadequate secretion of thyroid hormones

> **PARKINSON'S DISEASE:** a degenerative disease of the central nervous system

SKILL 30.2 Recognizing the basic knowledge and skills necessary to support positive health choices and behaviors

Positive health choices and behavior must be supported by proper education, which includes fitness and health education. Obviously, without an understanding of the various choices available, and the ramifications of each choice, it is difficult to make a wise decision regarding personal and family health choices and behavior. This education should include an introduction to research skills, so that individuals have the freedom to inform themselves of pertinent information when new situations arise that call for them to make health decisions. Good venues for these personal research habits include the Internet, local libraries, and fitness and health-care professionals in the community.

Positive health choices and behavior will also require a layer of economic support, as healthy lifestyle choices will sometimes be more expensive than the less healthy alternative. It is also important for the environment to be conducive to positive choices and behavior regarding health. For example, the availability of resources (both educational and practical) and facilities (medical and fitness) in proximity to the individual can positively impact the decision-making process.

> ## SKILL 30.3 Applying decision-making and problem-solving skills and procedures in individual and group situations (e.g., situations related to personal wellbeing, self-esteem, and interpersonal relationships)

There is an important relationship to consider between physical activity and the development of personal identity and emotional and mental well-being, most notably the impact of positive body image and self-concept. Instructors can help children develop positive body image and self-concept by creating opportunities for the children to experience successes in physical activities and to develop a comfort level with their bodies. This is an important contributor to their personal and physical confidence.

Social Health

For most people, the development of social roles and appropriate social behaviors occurs during childhood. Physical play between parents and children, as well as between siblings and peers, serves as a strong regulator in the developmental process. Chasing games, roughhousing, wrestling, or practicing sport skills such as jumping, throwing, catching, and striking, are some examples of childhood play. These activities may be competitive or noncompetitive and are important for promoting social and moral development of both boys and girls. Unfortunately, fathers will often engage in this sort of activity more with their sons than their daughters. Regardless of the sex of the child, both boys and girls enjoy these types of activities.

Physical play during infancy and early childhood is central to the development of social and emotional competence. Research shows that children who engage in play that is more physical with their parents, particularly with parents who are sensitive and responsive to the child, exhibited greater enjoyment during the play sessions and were more popular with their peers. Likewise, these early interactions with parents, siblings, and peers are important in helping children become more aware of their emotions and to learn to monitor and regulate their own emotional responses. Children learn quickly through watching the responses of their parents which behaviors make their parents smile and laugh and which behaviors cause their parents to frown and disengage from the activity.

If children want the fun to continue, they engage in the behaviors that please others. As children near adolescence, they learn through rough-and-tumble play that there are limits to how far they can go before hurting someone (physically or emotionally), which results in termination of the activity or later rejection of the child by peers. These early interactions with parents and siblings are important in helping children learn appropriate behavior in the social situations of sport and physical activity.

Children learn to assess their SOCIAL COMPETENCE in sport through the feedback received from parents and coaches. Initially, authority figures teach children, "You can't do that because I said so." As children approach school age, parents begin the process of explaining why a behavior is right or wrong because children continuously ask, "Why?"

Similarly, when children engage in sports, they learn about taking turns with their teammates, sharing playing time, and valuing rules. They understand that rules are important for everyone and without these regulations, the game would become unfair. The learning of social competence is continuous as we expand our social arena and learn about different cultures. A constant in the learning process is the role of feedback as we assess the responses of others to our behaviors and comments.

In addition to the development of social competence, sport participation can help youth develop other forms of self-competence. Most important among these self-competencies is SELF-ESTEEM. Educators have suggested that one of the biggest barriers to success in the classroom today is low self-esteem.

Children develop self-esteem by evaluating abilities and by evaluating the responses of others. Children actively observe parents' and coaches' responses to their performances, looking for signs of approval or disapproval of their behavior. Children often interpret feedback and criticism as either a negative or a positive response to the behavior. In sports, research shows that the coach is a critical source of information that influences the self-esteem of children.

Little League baseball players whose coaches use a POSITIVE APPROACH to coaching (e.g., more frequent encouragement, positive reinforcement for effort and corrective, instructional feedback), had significantly higher self-esteem ratings over the course of a season than children whose coaches used these techniques less frequently. The most compelling evidence supporting the importance of coaches' feedback was found for those children who started the season with the lowest self-esteem ratings and increased considerably their self-assessment and self-worth. In addition to evaluating themselves more positively, low self-esteem children evaluated their coaches more positively than did children with higher self-esteem who played for coaches who used the positive approach. Moreover, studies show that 95 percent of children who played for coaches trained to use the positive approach signed up to play baseball the next year, compared with 75 percent of the youth who played for untrained adult coaches.

We cannot overlook the importance of enhanced self-esteem on future participation. A major part of the development of high self-esteem is the pride and joy that children experience as their physical skills improve. Children will feel good about themselves as long as their skills are improving. If children feel that their

SOCIAL COMPETENCE: ability to get along with and acceptance by peers, family members, teachers, and coaches

SELF-ESTEEM: how we judge our worth and indicates the extent to which an individual believes he or she is capable, significant, successful, and worthy

Educators have suggested that one of the biggest barriers to success in the classroom today is low self-esteem.

POSITIVE APPROACH: more frequent encouragement, positive reinforcement for effort and corrective, instructional feedback

performance during a game or practice is not as good as that of others, or as good as they think mom and dad would want, they often experience shame and disappointment.

Some children will view mistakes made during a game as a failure and will look for ways to avoid participating in the task if they receive no encouragement to continue. At this point, it is critical that adults (e.g., parents and coaches) intervene to help children to interpret the mistake or "failure." We must teach children that a mistake is not synonymous with failure. Rather, a mistake shows us that we need a new strategy, more practice, and/or greater effort to succeed at the task.

Physical education activities can promote positive social behaviors and traits in a number of different ways.

Physical education activities can promote positive social behaviors and traits in a number of different ways. Instructors can foster improved relations with adults and peers by making students active partners in the learning process and delegating responsibilities within the class environment to students. Giving students leadership positions (e.g., team captain) can give them a heightened understanding of the responsibilities and challenges facing educators.

Team-based physical activities such as team sports promote collaboration and cooperation. In such activities, students learn to work together, both pooling their talents and minimizing the weaknesses of different team members in order to achieve a common goal. The experience of functioning as a team can be very productive for development of loyalty between children, and seeing their peers in stressful situations that they can relate to can promote a more compassionate and considerate attitude among students. Similarly, the need to maximize the strengths of each student on a team (who can complement each other and compensate for weaknesses) is a powerful lesson about valuing and respecting diversity and individual differences. Varying students between leading and following positions in a team hierarchy are good ways to help students gain a comfort level being both followers and leaders.

Fair play, teamwork, and sportsmanship are all values that stem from proper practice of the spirit of physical education classes.

Fairness is another trait that physical activities, especially rules-based sports, can foster and strengthen. Children are by nature very rules-oriented and have a keen sense of what they believe is and isn't fair. Fair play, teamwork, and sportsmanship are all values that stem from proper practice of the spirit of physical education classes. Of course, a pleasurable physical education experience goes a long way toward promoting an understanding of the innate value of physical activity throughout the life cycle.

Finally, communication is another skill that improves enormously through participation in sports and games. Students will come to understand that skillful communication can contribute to a better all-around outcome, whether it be winning the game or successfully completing a team project. They will see that effective communication helps to develop and maintain healthy personal relationships, organize and convey information, and reduce or avoid conflict.

Group Processes and Problem Solving

Physical fitness activities incorporate group processes, group dynamics, and a wide range of cooperation and competition. Ranging from team sports (which are both competitive and cooperative in nature) to individual competitive sports (like racing), to cooperative team activities without a winner and loser (like a gymnastics team working together to create a human pyramid), there is a great deal of room for the development of mutual respect and support among the students, safe cooperative participation, and analytical, problem solving, teamwork, and leadership skills.

Physical fitness activities incorporate group processes, group dynamics, and a wide range of cooperation and competition.

Teamwork situations are beneficial to students because they create opportunities for them to see classmates with whom they might not generally socialize and with whom they may not even get along, in a new light. It also creates opportunities for students to develop reliance on each other and practice interdependence. Cooperation and competition can also offer opportunities for children to practice group work. These situations provide good opportunities to practice analytical thinking and problem solving in a practical setting.

The social skills and values gained from participation in physical activities are:

- The ability to make adjustments to both self and others by an integration of the individual to society and the environment

- The ability to make judgments in a group situation

- Learning to communicate with others and be cooperative

- The development of the social phases of personality, attitudes, and values in order to become a functioning member of society

- The development of a sense of belonging and acceptance by society

- The development of positive personality traits

- Learning for constructive use of leisure time

- A development of attitude that reflects good moral character

- Respect of school rules and property

Sample Test Questions and Rationale

Average rigor

1. Social skills and values developed by physical activity include all of the following except:

   A. winning at all costs

   B. making judgments in groups

   C. communicating and cooperating

   D. respecting rules and property

   Answer: A – Winning at all costs

   Rationale: Winning at all costs is not a desirable social skill. Instructors and coaches should emphasize fair play and effort over winning. Answers B, C, and D are all positive skills and values developed in physical activity settings.

Average rigor

1. Which type of physical education activity would be most likely to help students develop a sense of belonging?

   A. solitary activities

   B. teamwork activities

   C. competitive activities

   D. creative activities

   Answer: B – teamwork activities

   Rationale: The correct answer is teamwork activities. One of the benefits of participating in physical activities is that students often develop a sense of belonging. This most often occurs in team sports, where students feel a sense of belonging to the team. The relationships developed with others in the process can also create a larger sense of belonging, such as feeling like one belongs to the school community.

SKILL 30.4 Recognizing basic principles of good nutrition and using them to plan a diet that accommodates nutritional needs, activity level, and optimal weight

Nutrition and Weight Control

Students must identify these components of nutrition.

SIX COMPONENTS OF NUTRITION	
Carbohydrates	The main source of energy (glucose) in the human diet. The two types of carbohydrates are simple and complex. Complex carbohydrates have greater nutritional value because they take longer to digest, contain dietary fiber, and do not excessively elevate blood sugar levels. Common sources of carbohydrates are fruits, vegetables, grains, dairy products, and legumes.
Proteins	Necessary for growth, development, and cellular function. The body breaks down consumed protein into component amino acids for future use. Major sources of protein are meat, poultry, fish, eggs, dairy products, grains, and legumes.
Fats	A concentrated energy source and important component of the human body. The different types of fats are saturated, monounsaturated, and polyunsaturated. Polyunsaturated fats are the healthiest because they may lower cholesterol levels, while saturated fats increase cholesterol levels. Common sources of saturated fats include dairy products, meat, coconut oil, and palm oil. Common sources of unsaturated fats include nuts, most vegetable oils, and fish.
Vitamins and Minerals	Organic substances that the body requires in small quantities for proper functioning. People acquire vitamins and minerals in their diets and in supplements. Important vitamins include A, B, C, D, E, and K. Important minerals include calcium, phosphorus, magnesium, potassium, sodium, chlorine, and sulfur.
Water	Makes up 55 to 75% of the human body. Water is essential for most bodily functions and is attained through foods and liquids.

Students must determine the adequacy of diets in meeting the nutritional needs of students.

Nutritional requirements vary from person-to-person. General guidelines for meeting adequate nutritional needs are: no more than 30% total caloric intake from fats, no more than 15% total caloric intake from protein (complete), and at least 55% of caloric intake from carbohydrates (mainly complex carbohydrates).

Students must understand how exercise and diet helps maintain proper body weight by equalizing caloric intake and caloric output.

A healthy diet is essential for achieving and maintaining optimum mental and physical health. Making the decision to eat well is a powerful investment. Selecting foods that encompass a variety of healthy nutrients will help reduce your risk of developing common medical conditions and will boost your immune system while increasing your energy level.

Experts agree that the key to healthy eating is balance, variety, and moderation. Other tips include:

- Enjoy plenty of whole grains, fruits, and vegetables

- Maintain a healthy weight

- Eat moderate portions

- Eat regular meals

- Reduce but don't eliminate certain foods

- Balance your food choices over time

- Know your diet pitfalls

- Make changes gradually… remember, foods are not good or bad

Select foods based on your total eating patterns, not whether any individual food is "good" or "bad."

Sample Test Questions and Rationale

Rigorous

1. **Water makes up _____ of the human body.**

    A. 25–30%

    B. 55–75%

    C. 10–25%

    D. 75–88%

Answer: B – 55–75%

Rationale: Water makes up 55–75% of the human body. Water is essential for most bodily functions and is attained through foods and liquids.

SKILL 30.5 **Analyzing contemporary health-related issues** (e.g., HIV, teenage pregnancy, suicide, substance abuse) **in terms of their causes, effects, and significance for individuals, families, and society and evaluating strategies for their prevention**

Important contemporary health-related issues that significantly affect modern society include HIV, teenage pregnancy, suicide, and substance abuse.

HIV

The human immunodeficiency virus (HIV) can devastate both individuals and society. Advances in treatment options, namely pharmaceuticals, have greatly improved the prospects of those who contract the disease. However, due to the expense of treatment, many people, especially those in underdeveloped countries, do not have access to treatment. Thus, prevention is still of utmost importance.

HIV is a retrovirus that attacks the human immune system and causes AIDS (acquired immunodefiency syndrome). AIDS is a failure of the immune system that allows normally benign viruses and bacteria to infect the body, causing life-threatening conditions.

Humans acquire HIV through contact with bodily fluids of infected individuals. For example, transfer of blood, semen, vaginal fluid, and breast milk can cause HIV infection. The best means of prevention of HIV is sexual abstinence outside of marriage, practicing safe sex, and avoiding the use of injected drugs.

Because HIV is a sexually transmitted disease, it disproportionally affects people in the prime of their lives. Infected persons are often heads of households and families and key economic producers. Thus, the impact of HIV on society is particularly damaging. Not only are the costs of treatment great, but families often lose their mothers and fathers and communities lose their best producers and leaders. Society must find ways to fill these gaping voids.

Suicide

Suicide is a particularly troubling problem. Adolescent suicide is always devastating to families and communities. The main cause of adolescent suicide is mental disease, such as depression or anxiety. When untreated, such disorders can cause intense feelings of hopelessness and despair that can lead to suicide attempts. Suicides can tear families apart, often leaving behind feelings of guilt among friends and family members. The best means of suicide prevention is close monitoring of changing behaviors in adolescents. Parents, friends, and family members should watch for and never ignore signs of depression, withdrawal from friends and activities, talk of suicide, and signs of despair and hopelessness. Proper counseling, medication, and care from mental health professionals can often prevent suicide.

Teen Pregnancy

Teen pregnancy hurts the mothers, children, and society, by extension. Pregnancy disrupts the life of adolescent girls, often preventing them from finishing school, completing higher education, and finding quality employment. In addition, teenage girls are not emotionally or financially ready to care for children. Thus, the children of teen pregnancies may have a difficult start in life. Teen pregnancy also affects society because teenage parents often require government assistance and children of teen pregnancies often do not receive appropriate care and parenting. The best means of preventing teenage pregnancy is education about the importance of abstinence and contraception.

Substance Abuse

Substance abuse can lead to adverse behaviors and increased risk of injury and disease. Any substance affecting the normal functions of the body, illegal or not, is potentially dangerous and students and athletes should avoid them completely. Factors contributing to substance abuse include peer pressure, parental substance abuse, physical or psychological abuse, mental illness, and physical disability. Education, vigilance, and parental oversight are the best strategies for the prevention of substance abuse.

FOUR COMMONLY ABUSED SUBSTANCES	
Alcohol	This is a legal substance for adults but is very commonly abused. Moderate to excessive consumption can lead to an increased risk of cardiovascular disease, nutritional deficiencies, and dehydration. Alcohol also causes ill effects on various aspects of performance such as reaction time, coordination, accuracy, balance, and strength.
Nicotine	Another legal but often abused substance that can increase the risk of cardiovascular disease, pulmonary disease, and cancers of the mouth. Nicotine consumption through smoking severely hinders athletic performance by compromising lung function. Smoking especially affects performance in endurance activities.
Marijuana	This is the most commonly abused illegal substance. Adverse effects include a loss of focus and motivation, decreased coordination, and lack of concentration.
Cocaine	Another illegal and somewhat commonly abused substance. Effects include increased alertness and excitability. This drug can give the user a sense of overconfidence and invincibility, leading to a false sense of one's ability to perform certain activities. A high heart rate is associated with the use of cocaine, leading to an increased risk of heart attack, stroke, potentially deadly arrhythmias, and seizures.

Substance abuse—treatment and alternatives

Alternatives to substance use and abuse include regular participation in stress-relieving activities like meditation, exercise, and therapy, all of which can have a relaxing effect (a healthy habit is, for example, to train oneself to substitute exercise for a substance abuse problem). More important, the acquisition of longer-term coping strategies (for example, self-empowerment via practice of problem-solving techniques) is key to maintaining a commitment to alternatives to substance use and abuse.

Aspects of substance abuse treatment that we must consider include:

- the processes of physical and psychological withdrawal from the addictive substance

- acquisition of coping strategies and replacement techniques to fill the void left by the addictive substance

- limiting access to the addictive substance, acquiring self-control strategies

Withdrawal from an addictive substance has both psychological and physical symptoms. The psychological symptoms include depression, anxiety, and strong cravings for the substance. Physical withdrawal symptoms stem from the body, adapted to a steady intake of the addictive substance, adapting to accommodate the no-longer available substance. Depending on the substance, medical intervention may be necessary.

Coping strategies and replacement techniques, as discussed earlier, center around providing the individual with an effective alternative to the addictive substance as a solution to the situations that they would feel necessitate the substance.

Limiting access to the addictive substance (opportunities for use) is important, because the symptoms of withdrawal and the experiences associated with the substance can provide a strong impetus to return to using it. Finally, recovering addicts should learn strategies of self-control and self-discipline to help them stay off of the addictive substance.

SKILL 30.6 Interpreting advertising claims for health-care products and services and distinguishing between valid and invalid health information

There is generally a wide array of information available related to health, fitness and recreational activities, products, facilities, and services. It can be difficult for the untrained consumer to sort through it all to find information that is pertinent and accurate.

Exercise myths and gimmicks include:

- Drinking beer/alcoholic beverages is a good way to replenish loss of body fluids after exercising

- Women should not exercise while menstruating or pregnant

- Physically fit people will not die from heart disease

- You cannot be too flexible

- Spot reduction is possible

- Children are naturally active and do not need to exercise

- Muscle will turn into fat with the cessation of exercising

- Fat can turn into muscle

- You should exercise while sick regardless of how ill you are

- Exercise increases the appetite

- Exercise gets rid of sagging skin and wrinkles

- Yoga is a good way to develop endurance

- Losing cellulite requires special treatment

- Body wraps are a good way to lose weight

Advertising Trends

Current trends in media advertising and marketing practices related to fitness, recreational, and sports products and programs will typically display happy and fit individuals participating in the activity or making use of the advertised product. This trend has positive and negative ramifications for the work of physical educators.

On the positive side, the media advertising and marketing trend paints physical activity in a very positive light (as it should). The exposure that students have to the media today makes this a very helpful reinforcement of the messages that physical education professionals work to promote in the classroom and school gymnasium. On the negative side, these trends ignore the reality that the current national level of fitness is poor and obesity and heart disease are on the rise.

SKILL 30.7 Analyzing environmental conditions and their impact upon personal and community health and safety

The relative levels of pollution in a community can significantly affect family health. For example, proximity to industrial areas, which may be releasing carcinogenic emissions, can be dangerous. Similarly, a smoking habit within the home environment is highly detrimental, as it will negatively affect the respiratory and circulatory systems of all members of the household.

Pollution levels in the community can also affect public health by exposing the community as a whole to toxic and carcinogenic chemicals that negatively affect systems including (but not limited to) the circulatory and respiratory systems.

Healthy environmental conditions involve several areas of concern. These include:

- Drinking water

- Food safety

- Hazardous waste

- Housing

- Indoor air quality

- Land use and community design

- Occupational health

- Outdoor air quality

- Recreational water

- Solid waste and wastewater

- Vector-borne disease

It is the teacher's duty to be aware of these conditions, taking into account their impact on families and children. It is also important for a teacher to do all they can to improve environmental factors as much as is in their power to do so.

Studies have shown that low-income, racial, and ethnic minority individuals are much more likely to be exposed to toxic and hazardous wastes than affluent and white individuals. (Evans G, Kantrowitz E. *Socioeconomic Status and Health: The Potential Role of Environmental Risk Exposure. Annual Review of Public Health*, 2002; 23:303-331)

Though the teacher cannot effectively affect the socioeconomic, racial, or ethnic status of a student, it is important that he or she be aware of the possible impact of such factors on the student's health and the impact that would have on educational opportunities.

National standards relative to overcrowding in housing is considering any home where there is more than one person to a room as being overcrowded. For example, the common three-bedroom home with a living room, kitchen, and dining area, plus two bathrooms, can support only five family members without considered being overcrowded (seven if you count the bathrooms).

Lead is a very dangerous threat to the young school-aged child. The Centers for Disease Control and Prevention estimates that an estimated 4.1 million homes in

It is evident from all the many factors affecting personal and community health and safety that there is many chances for a student to be adversely affected by some aspect of their environment.

Lesson plans and resources for teaching about health issues:

http://www.teach-nology. com/teachers/lesson_ plans/health/

http://school. discoveryeducation.com/ lessonplans/health.html

http://www. theteacherscorner.net/ lesson-plans/health/

the United States (25% of U.S. homes with children aged <6 years) have a lead-based paint hazard and that racial minority and poor children are disproportionately affected. ("Interpreting and Managing Blood Lead Levels <10 µg/dL in Children and Reducing Childhood Exposures to Lead," Centers for Disease Control and Prevention. Accessed: July, 2002. http://www.cdc.gov/mmwr/preview/mmwrhtml/rr5608a1.htm#top)

COMPETENCY 31
UNDERSTAND PHYSICAL EDUCATION CONCEPTS AND PRACTICES RELATED TO THE DEVELOPMENT OF PERSONAL LIVING SKILLS

SKILL 31.1 Recognizing sequences and characteristics of physical development throughout the various developmental levels

Motor Learning Skills

The development of motor skills in children is a sequential process. We can classify motor skill competency into stages of development by observing children practicing physical skills. The sequence of development begins with simple reflexes and progresses to the learning of postural elements, locomotor skills, and, finally, fine motor skills. The stages of development consider both innate and learned behaviors.

STAGES OF MOTOR LEARNING SKILLS	
Stage 1	Children progress from simple reflexes to basic movements such as sitting, crawling, creeping, standing, and walking.
Stage 2	Children learn more complex motor patterns including running, climbing, jumping, balancing, catching, and throwing.
Stage 3	During late childhood, children learn more specific movement skills. In addition, the basic motor patterns learned in Stage 2 they become more fluid and automatic.
Stage 4	During adolescence, children continue to develop general and specific motor skills and master specialized movements. At this point, factors including practice, motivation, and talent begin to affect the level of further development.

Sequential development for locomotor skill acquisition	crawl, creep, walk, run, jump, hop, gallop, slide, leap, skip, step-hop
Sequential development for nonlocomotor skill acquisition	stretch, bend, sit, shake, turn, rock and sway, swing, twist, dodge, fall
Sequential development for manipulative skill acquisition	striking, throwing, kicking, ball rolling, volleying, bouncing, catching, trapping

Sample Test Questions and Rationale

Rigorous

1. **The sequential development of:** *stretching, bending, sitting, shaking, turning, rocking and swaying, swinging, twisting, dodging,* **and** *falling* **are representative of which acquisition?**

   A. nonlocomotor skill acquisition

   B. locomotor skill acquisition

   C. manipulative skill acquisition

   D. nonmanipulative skill acquisition

Answer: B – locomotor skill acquisition

Rationale: Sequential development for locomotor skill acquisition = crawl, creep, walk, run, jump, hop, gallop, slide, leap, skip, step-hop.

Sequential development for nonlocomotor skill acquisition = stretch, bend, sit, shake, turn, rock and sway, swing, twist, dodge, and fall.

Sequential development for manipulative skill acquisition = striking, throwing, kicking, ball rolling, volleying, bouncing, catching, and trapping.

> **SKILL 31.2** **Demonstrating knowledge of activities that promote the development of motor skills** *(e.g., locomotor, manipulative, body mechanics)* **and perceptual awareness skills** *(e.g., body awareness, spatial and directional awareness)*

Games like bean bag, parachute, hula hoop, gymnastics, and ball activities that instructors can modify and adapt to suit the particular needs of children are particularly helpful for building manipulative skills.

Motor skills are composed of locomotor skills, nonlocomotor skills, and manipulative and coordination skills. **Games like bean bag, parachute, hula hoop, gymnastics, and ball activities** that instructors can modify and adapt to suit the particular needs of children are particularly helpful. Physical activity should have the scope to adapt itself to suit an individual child's needs and goals. For an individual incapable of using his or her legs, an instructor can incorporate wheelchair races or activities that require the use of hands. For children in the grades 1 to 3, instructors should incorporate the concepts of movement and motor skills, allowing the child to perfect them.

Concepts of movements like spatial consciousness regarding location; level or height and direction; body awareness and recognition of how the body can be manipulated to perform an activity; effort required regarding time, flow and force; and the relationship to the various objects and to others, are developed through various activities.

A **five-year-old** is capable of walking backwards, using the heel and then the toe, and is able to easily climb up and down steps by alternating feet without any outside help. Five-year-olds can touch their toes without bending at the knee and balance on a beam. They may be able to do somersaults provided it is taught in a proper and safe manner. A five-year-old can ride a tricycle with speed and dexterity, make almost ten jumps or hops without losing balance and falling, and stand on one foot for about ten senconds.

Early **elementary school children** have already acquired many large motor and fine motor skills. Their movement is more accurate and with purpose, though some clumsiness may persist. An elementary student is always on the run and restless. A child older than five finds pleasure in more energetic and vigorous activities. He or she can jump, hop, and throw with relative accuracy and concentrate on an activity that sustains his or her interest. However, concentration on a single activity usually does not last long. Early elementary students enjoy challenges and can benefit greatly from them.

When proper and appropriate physical education is available, by the time a child finishes the fourth grade he is able to demonstrate well-developed locomotor movements. He is also capable of manipulative and nonlocomotor movement skills like kicking and catching. He is capable of living up to challenges like balancing a number of objects or controlling a variety of things simultaneously. Children at this developmental age begin to acquire specialized movement skills like dribbling. When a child has finished eighth grade, he is able to exhibit expertise in a variety of fine and modified movements (e.g., dance steps). Children begin to develop the necessary skills for competitive and strategic games. Despite a lack of competency in a game, they learn to enjoy the pleasure of physical activity. By the time the children finish the twelfth grade they can demonstrate competency of a number of complex and modified movements with relative ease (e.g., gymnastics, dual sports, dance). Students at this age display their interest in gaining a greater degree of competency at their favorite game or activity.

Perceptual Awareness Skills

PERCEPTUAL-MOTOR DEVELOPMENT refers to one's ability to receive, interpret, and respond successfully to sensory signals coming from the environment. Because many of the skills acquired in school rely on the child's knowledge of his body and its relationship to the surroundings, good motor development leads directly to perceptual skill development.

> **PERCEPTUAL-MOTOR DEVELOPMENT:** refers to one's ability to receive, interpret, and respond successfully to sensory signals coming from the environment

Development of gross motor skills lead to successful development of fine motor skills, which in turn help with learning, reading, and writing. Adolescents with perceptual-motor coordination problems are at risk for poor school performance, low self-esteem, and inadequate physical activity participation. Without a successful intervention, these adolescents are likely to continue avoiding physical activity and experience frustration and teasing from their peers.

Children with weak perceptual-motor skills may be easily distracted or have difficulty with tasks requiring coordination. They spend much of their energy trying to control their bodies, exhausting them so much that they physically cannot concentrate on a teacher-led lesson. Unfortunately, perceptual-motor coordination problems do not just go away and they don't self-repair. Practice and maturity are necessary for children to develop greater coordination and spatial awareness. Physical education lessons should emphasize activities that children enjoy doing, are sequential, and require seeing, hearing, and/or touching.

Discussing with students the actual steps involved in performing a fundamental skill is a great benefit. Activities and skills that can be broken down and taught in incremental steps include running, dribbling, catching or hitting a ball, making a basket in basketball, and setting a volleyball. Recommended strategies include introducing the skill, practicing in a variety of settings with an assortment of equipment, implementing lead-up games modified to ensure practice of the necessary skills, and incorporating students into an actual game situation.

Concept of Body Awareness Applied to Physical Education Activities

Body awareness is a person's understanding of his or her own body parts and their capability of movement.

Instructors can assess body awareness by playing and watching a game of "Simon Says" and asking the students to touch different body parts. You can also instruct students to make their bodies into various shapes, from straight to round to twisted, and varying sizes, to fit into different sized spaces.

In addition, you can instruct children to touch one part of their body to another and to use various body parts to stamp their feet, twist their neck, clap their hands, nod their heads, wiggle their noses, snap their fingers, open their mouths, shrug their shoulders, bend their knees, close their eyes, bend their elbows, or wiggle their toes.

Concept of Spatial Awareness Applied to Physical Education Activities

Spatial awareness is the ability to make decisions about an object's positional changes in space (i.e., awareness of three-dimensional space position changes).

Developing spatial awareness requires two sequential phases:

1. Identifying the location of objects in relation to one's own body in space

2. Locating more than one object in relation to each object and independent of one's own body

Plan activities using different size balls, boxes, or hoops and have children move toward and away; under and over; in front of and behind; and inside, outside, and beside the objects.

Concept of Effort Qualities Applied to Physical Education

Effort qualities are the qualities of movement that apply the mechanical principles of balance, time, and force).

- Balance: Activities for balance include having children move on their hands and feet, lean, move on lines, and balance and hold shapes while moving.

- Time: Activities using the concept of time can include having children move as fast as they can and as slow as they can in specified, timed movement patterns.

- Force: Activities using the concept of force can include having students use their bodies to produce enough force to move them through space. They can also paddle balls against walls and jump over objects of various heights.

Sample Test Questions and Rationale

Easy

1. Body awareness is a person's understanding of his or her own body parts and their capability of movement. Young children can gain the concept of body awareness through which of the following?

   A. nodding their heads

   B. wiggling their noses

   C. snapping their fingers

   D. all of the above

Answer: D – all of the above

Rationale: Teachers can assess body awareness by playing a game of "Simon Says" and asking the students to touch **different** body parts. Students can then perform the following activities: stamp their feet, twist their neck, clap their hands, nod their heads, wiggle their noses, snap their fingers, open their mouths, shrug their shoulders, bend their knees, close their eyes, bend their elbows, or wiggle their toes.

Average Rigor

2. Early childhood students are expected to be able to complete tasks using basic locomotor skills. Which of the following would <u>not</u> be included?

   A. walking

   B. galloping

   C. balancing

   D. jogging

Answer: D – jogging

Rationale: Early childhood students are only expected to complete basic motor skills at ages 3–5; such as: walking, running, jumping, hopping, and balancing.

Warm-up exercises and protective equipment are two key components of safety in physical activities. Instructors should be aware of the proper equipment for each sport or activity and ensure that students wear the appropriate safety equipment at all times.

Techniques and Benefits of Warming Up and Cooling Down

Warming up is a gradual 5 to 10 minute aerobic activity in which the participant uses the muscles needed in the activity to follow (similar movements at a lower activity). Warm-ups also include stretching of major muscle groups after the gradual warm-up.

The benefits of warming up are:

- Preparing the body for physical activity
- Reducing the risk of musculoskeletal injuries
- Releasing oxygen from myoglobin
- Warming the body's inner core
- Increasing the reaction of muscles
- Bringing the heart rate to an aerobic conditioning level

Cooling down is similar to warming up—a moderate to light tapering-off vigorous activity at the end of an exercise session.

The benefits of cooling down are:

- Redistributing circulation of the blood throughout the body to prevent pooling of blood
- Preventing dizziness
- Next-day recovery will be faster

SKILL 31.4 Understanding skills necessary for successful participation in given sports and activities (e.g., spatial orientation, eye-hand coordination, movement)

Skills necessary for successful participation in sports and fitness activities include proprioception, spatial orientation, hand-eye coordination, and movement skills.

SKILLS NECESSARY FOR SUCCESSFUL PARTICIPATION IN SPORTS	
Proprioception	The sense of the relative position of neighboring parts of the body. Unlike the six external senses (sight, taste, smell, touch, hearing, and balance) by which we perceive the outside world, proprioception is an internal sense that provides feedback solely on the status of the body internally. It is the sense that indicates whether the body is moving with required effort, as well as where the various parts of the body are located in relation to each other. We can improve proprioception by training.
Spatial Orientation	The process of aligning or positioning oneself with respect to a specific direction or reference system. Specifically, it is the relationship established between the body's self-oriented coordinate system and an external reference frame. This happens via the integration of sensory signals from the visual, vestibular, tactile, and proprioceptive systems.
Hand-eye Coordination	The ability of the visual perception system to coordinate the information received through the eyes to control, guide, and direct the hands in the accomplishment of a given task (examples include handwriting or catching a ball). Hand-eye coordination uses the eyes to direct attention and the hands to execute a task.
Movement Skills	The integration of balance and proprioceptive skills to produce movement that effectively manages the weight distribution of the body.

SKILL 31.5 Analyzing ways in which participation in individual or group sports or physical activities can promote personal living skills (e.g., self-discipline, respect for self and others, resource management) and interpersonal skills (e.g., cooperation, sportsmanship, leadership, teamwork, communication)

See also Skill 30.3

FOUR LEVELS OF CHILDREN'S SPORTS PROGRAMS			
Level I	**Level II**	**Level III**	**Level IV**
Stand-alone youth sports programs that are purely recreational and unassociated with any youth development agenda.	Sports participation deployed as a "hook" to attract youth at drop-in centers or other programs.	Sport is the centerpiece of a youth development program, but remains disconnected from the developmental or educational component, functioning merely as a lever to encourage program attendance/performance.	Sports become directly relevant to youth development. Elements of the sports experience are synthesized with character education, skills acquisition, academic subjects or other enrichment themes. (Baseball statistics are used to teach math skills; a Scuba Diving course incorporates the rudiments of marine biology/oceanography, etc.)

COMPETENCY 32

UNDERSTAND HEALTH-RELATED PHYSICAL FITNESS CONCEPTS AND PRACTICES

SKILL 32.1 Recognizing components, functions, and common disorders of the major body systems

See also Skill 30.1

Major systems of the human body consist of organs working together to perform important physiological tasks. In this section, we will discuss several major body systems including the musculoskeletal system, the cardiovascular system, the respiratory/excretory system, the nervous system, the endocrine system, the reproductive system, and the immune system. In addition, we will discuss how these systems adapt to physical activity, produce movement, and contribute to fitness.

Structures, Locations, and Functions of the Three Types of Muscular Tissue

The main function of the muscular system is movement. There are three types of muscle tissue: skeletal, cardiac, and smooth.

Skeletal muscle is voluntary. These muscles are attached to bones and are responsible for their movement. Skeletal muscle consists of long fibers and is striated due to the repeating patterns of the myofilaments (made of the proteins actin and myosin) that make up the fibers.

Cardiac muscle is found in the heart. Cardiac muscle is striated like skeletal muscle, but differs in that the plasma membrane of the cardiac muscle causes the muscle to beat even when away from the heart. The action potentials of cardiac and skeletal muscles also differ.

Smooth muscle is involuntary. It is found in organs and enables functions such as digestion and respiration. Unlike skeletal and cardiac muscle, smooth muscle is not striated. Smooth muscle has less myosin and does not generate as much tension as skeletal muscle.

Mechanism of Skeletal Muscle Contraction

A nerve impulse strikes a muscle fiber. This causes calcium ions to flood the sarcomere. Calcium ions allow ATP to expend energy. The myosin fibers creep along the actin, causing the muscle to contract. Once the nerve impulse has passed, calcium is pumped out and the contraction ends.

Movement of Body Joints

The axial skeleton consists of the bones of the skull and vertebrae. The appendicular skeleton consists of the bones of the legs, arms and tail, and shoulder girdle. Bone is a connective tissue. Parts of the bone include compact bone that gives strength, spongy bone that contains red marrow to make blood cells and yellow marrow in the center of long bones to store fat cells, and the periosteum that is the protective covering on the outside of the bone.

A joint is a place where two bones meet. Joints enable movement. Ligaments attach bone to bone. Tendons attach bone to muscle. Joints allow great flexibility in movement.

THREE TYPES OF JOINTS	
Ball and socket	Allows for rotational movement. An example is the joint between the shoulder and the humerus. Ball and socket joints allow humans to move their arms and legs in many different ways.
Hinge	Movement is restricted to a single plane. An example is the joint between the humerus and the ulna.
Pivot	Allows for the rotation of the forearm at the elbow and the hands at the wrist.

Human Nervous and Endocrine Systems

The central nervous system (CNS) consists of the brain and spinal cord. The CNS is responsible for the body's response to environmental stimuli. The spinal cord is located inside the spine. It sends out motor commands for movement in response to stimuli. The brain is where responses to more complex stimuli occur. The meninges are the connective tissues that protect the CNS. The CNS contains fluid filled spaces called ventricles. These ventricles are filled when cerebrospinal fluid which is formed in the brain. This fluid cushions the brain and circulates nutrients, white blood cells, and hormones. The CNS's response to stimuli is a reflex. A reflex is an unconscious, automatic response.

The peripheral nervous system (PNS) consists of the nerves that connect the CNS to the rest of the body. The sensory division brings information to the CNS from sensory receptors and the motor division sends signals from the CNS to effector cells. The motor division consists of somatic nervous system and the autonomic nervous system. The body consciously controls the somatic nervous system in response to external stimuli. The hypothalamus in the brain unconsciously controls the autonomic nervous system to regulate the internal environment. This system is responsible for the movement of smooth muscles, cardiac muscles, and the muscles of other organ systems.

> **HORMONES:** proteins that circulate in the bloodstream and stimulate actions when the interact with target tissue

The function of the endocrine system is to manufacture proteins called hormones. HORMONES circulate in the bloodstream and stimulate actions when they interact with target tissue. There are two classes of hormones. Steroid hormones come from cholesterol and include the sex hormones. Amino acids are the source of peptide hormones. Hormones are specific and fit receptors on the target tissue cell surface. The receptor activates an enzyme that converts ATP to cyclic AMP. Cyclic AMP (cAMP) is a second messenger from the cell membrane to the nucleus. The genes found in the nucleus turn on or off to cause a specific response.

Endocrine cells, which make up endocrine glands, secrete hormones.

MAJOR ENDOCRINE GLANDS AND THEIR HORMONES	
Hypothalamus	Located in the lower brain; signals the pituitary gland.
Pituitary gland	Located at the base of the hypothalamus; releases growth hormones and antidiuretic hormone (retention of water in kidneys).
Thyroid gland	Located on the trachea; lowers blood calcium levels (calcitonin) and maintains metabolic processes (thyroxine).
Gonads	Located in the testes of the male and the ovaries of the female; testes release androgens to support sperm formation and ovaries release estrogens to stimulate uterine lining growth and progesterone to promote uterine lining growth.
Pancreas	Secretes insulin to lower blood glucose levels and glucagon to raise blood glucose levels.

Role of Nerve Impulses and Neurons

The NEURON is the basic unit of the nervous system. It consists of an axon, which carries impulses away from the cell body to the tip of the neuron; the dendrite, which carries impulses toward the cell body; and the cell body, which contains the nucleus. Synapses are spaces between neurons. Chemicals called neurotransmitters are found close to the synapse. The myelin sheath, composed of Schwann cells, covers the neurons and provides insulation.

NEURON: basic unit of the nervous system, consisting of an axon, a dendrite, and the cell body

Nerve action depends on depolarization and an imbalance of electrical charges across the neuron. A polarized nerve has a positive charge outside the neuron. A depolarized nerve has a negative charge outside the neuron. Neurotransmitters turn off the sodium pump which results in depolarization of the membrane. This wave of depolarization (as it moves from neuron to neuron) carries an electrical impulse. This is actually a wave of opening and closing gates that allows for the flow of ions across the synapse. Nerves have an action potential. There is a threshold of the level of chemicals that must be met or exceeded in order for muscles to respond. This is the "all or nothing" response.

Structure and Function of the Skin

The skin consists of two distinct layers, the epidermis and the dermis. The epidermis is the thinner outer layer and the dermis is the thicker inner layer. Layers of tightly packed epithelial cells make up the epidermis. The tight packaging of the epithelial cells supports the skin's function as a protective barrier against infection.

The top layer of the epidermis consists of dead skin cells and contains keratin, a waterproofing protein. The dermis layer consists of connective tissue. It contains blood vessels, hair follicles, sweat glands, and sebaceous glands. The body releases an oily secretion called sebum, produced by the sebaceous gland, to the outer epidermis through the hair follicles. Sebum maintains the pH of the skin between 3 and 5, which inhibits most microorganism growth.

The skin also plays a role in thermoregulation. Increased body temperature causes skin blood vessels to dilate, causing heat to radiate from the skin's surface. Increased temperature also activates sweat glands, increasing evaporative cooling. Decreased body temperature causes skin blood vessels to constrict. This results in blood from the skin diverting to deeper tissues and reduces heat loss from the surface of the skin.

Human Respiratory and Excretory Systems

Surface area, volume, and function of the respiratory and excretory systems

The lungs are the respiratory surface of the human respiratory system. A dense net of capillaries contained just beneath the epithelium form the respiratory surface. The surface area of the epithelium is about $100m^2$ in humans. Based on the surface area, the volume of air inhaled and exhaled is the tidal volume. This is normally about 500mL in adults. Vital capacity is the maximum volume the lungs can inhale and exhale. This is usually around 3400mL.

The kidneys are the primary organ in the excretory system. Each of the two kidneys in humans is about 10cm long. Despite their small size, they receive about 20 percent of the blood pumped with each heartbeat. The function of the excretory system is to rid the body of nitrogenous wastes in the form of urea.

The respiratory system functions in the gas exchange of oxygen and carbon dioxide waste. The respiratory system delivers oxygen to the bloodstream and picks up carbon dioxide for release from the body. Air enters the mouth and nose, where it is warmed, moistened, and filtered of dust and particles. Cilia in the trachea trap and expel unwanted material in mucus. The trachea splits into two bronchial tubes and the bronchial tubes divide into smaller and smaller bronchioles in the lungs. The internal surface of the lung is composed of alveoli, which are thin walled air sacs. These allow for a large surface area for gas exchange. Capillaries line the alveoli. Oxygen diffuses into the bloodstream and carbon dioxide diffuses out of the capillaries and is exhaled from the lungs due to partial pressure. Hemoglobin, a protein containing iron, carries the oxygenated blood to the heart and all parts of the body.

The thoracic cavity holds the lungs. The diaphragm muscle below the lungs is an adaptation that makes inhalation possible. As the volume of the thoracic cavity increases, the diaphragm muscle flattens out and inhalation occurs. When the diaphragm relaxes, exhalation occurs.

Human Circulatory and Immune Systems

Structure, function, and regulation of the heart

The function of the closed circulatory system (cardiovascular system) is to carry oxygenated blood and nutrients to all cells of the body and return carbon dioxide waste to the lungs for expulsion. The heart, blood vessels, and blood make up the cardiovascular system. The diagram shows the structure of the heart:

Heart

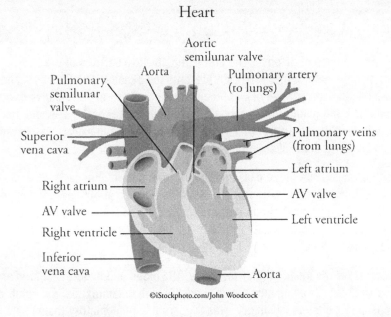

©iStockphoto.com/John Woodcock

The atria are the chambers that receive blood returning to the heart and the ventricles are the chambers that pump blood out of the heart. There are four valves, two atrioventricular (AV) valves and two semilunar valves. The AV valves are located between each atrium and ventricle. The contraction of the ventricles closes the AV valve to keep blood from flowing back into the atria. The semilunar valves are located where the aorta leaves the left ventricle and the pulmonary artery leaves the right ventricle. Ventricular contraction opens the semilunar valves, pumping blood out into the arteries, and ventricular relaxation closes the valves.

The cardiac output is the volume of blood per minute that the left ventricle pumps. This output depends on the heart rate and stroke volume. The heart rate is the number of times the heart beats per minute and the stroke volume is the amount of blood pumped by the left ventricle each time it contracts. Humans have an average cardiac output of about 5.25 L/min. Heavy exercise can increase cardiac output up to five times. Epinephrine and increased body temperature also increase heart rate and, thus, the cardiac output.

Cardiac muscle can contract without any signal from the nervous system. The sinoatrial node is the pacemaker of the heart. It is located on the wall of the right atrium and generates electrical impulses that make the cardiac muscle cells contract in unison. The atrioventricular node briefly delays the electrical impulse to ensure the atria empty before the ventricles contract.

Structure, function, and regulation of the immune system

The immune system is responsible for defending the body against foreign invaders.

TWO OF THE BODY'S DEFENSE MECHANISMS	
Nonspecific	This immune mechanism has two lines of defense. The first is the physical barriers of the body. These include the skin and mucous membranes. The skin prevents the penetration of bacteria and viruses as long as there are no abrasions on the skin. Mucous membranes form a protective barrier around the digestive, respiratory, and genitourinary tracts. In addition, the pH of the skin and mucous membranes inhibit the growth of many microbes. Mucous secretions (tears and saliva) wash away many microbes and contain lysozyme that kills microbes.
	The second line of defense includes white blood cells and the inflammatory response. Phagocytosis is the ingestion of foreign particles. Neutrophils make up about seventy percent of all white blood cells. Monocytes mature to become macrophages, which are the largest phagocytic cells. Eosinophils are also phagocytic. Natural killer cells destroy the body's own infected cells instead of the invading the microbe directly.
	The *other* second line of defense is the inflammatory response. The blood supply to the injured area increases, causing redness and heat. Swelling also typically occurs with inflammation. Basophils and mast cells release histamine in response to cell injury. This triggers the inflammatory response.
Specific	This immune mechanism recognizes specific foreign material and responds by destroying the invader. These mechanisms are specific and diverse. They are able to recognize individual pathogens. An antigen is any foreign particle that elicits an immune response. The body manufactures antibodies that recognize and latch onto antigens, hopefully destroying them. They also discriminate between foreign material versus self material. Memory of the invaders provides immunity upon further exposure.

IMMUNITY: the body's ability to recognize and destroy an antigen

IMMUNITY is the body's ability to recognize and destroy an antigen before it causes harm. Active immunity develops after recovery from an infectious disease (e.g., chicken pox) or after a vaccination (e.g., mumps, measles, rubella). Passive immunity may be passed from one individual to another and is not permanent. A good example is the immunities passed from mother to nursing child. A baby's immune system is not well developed and the passive immunity they receive through nursing keeps them healthier.

TWO PHYSICAL RESPONSES TO AN ANTIGEN	
Humoral response	Free antigens activate this response and B cells (lymphocytes from bone marrow) give rise to plasma cells that secrete antibodies and memory cells that will recognize future exposures to the same antigen. The antibodies defend against extracellular pathogens by binding to the antigen and making them an easy target for phagocytes to engulf and destroy. Antibodies are in a class of proteins called immunoglobulins. The five major classes of immunoglobulins (Ig) involved in the humoral response are: IgM, IgG, IgA, IgD, and IgE.
Cell mediated response	Infected cells activate T-cells (lymphocytes from the thymus). These activated T-cells defend against pathogens in the cells or cancer cells by binding to the infected cell and destroying them along with the antigen. T-cell receptors on the T helper cells recognize antigens bound to the body's own cells. T helper cells release IL-2, which stimulates other lymphocytes (cytotoxic T-cells and B cells). Cytotoxic T-cells kill infected host cells by recognizing specific antigens.

Vaccines are antigens given in very small amounts. They stimulate both humoral and cell mediated responses. After vaccination, memory cells recognize future exposure to the antigen so the body can produce antibodies much faster.

Human Digestive System

Roles of basic nutrients found in foods

The function of the digestive system is to break food down into nutrients, absorb them into the blood stream, and deliver them to all cells of the body for use in cellular respiration.

Essential nutrients are those nutrients that the body needs but cannot make. There are four groups of essential nutrients: essential amino acids, essential fatty acids, vitamins, and minerals.

There are about eight essential amino acids humans need. A lack of these amino acids results in protein deficiency. There are only a few essential fatty acids.

Vitamins are organic molecules essential for a nutritionally adequate diet. Scientists have identified thirteen vitamins essential to humans. There are two groups of vitamins: water-soluble (includes the vitamin B complex and vitamin C) and water insoluble (vitamins A, D and K). Vitamin deficiencies can cause severe problems.

Unlike vitamins, minerals are inorganic molecules. Calcium is important in bone construction and maintenance. Iron is important in cellular respiration and is a major component of hemoglobin.

Carbohydrates, fats, and proteins are fuel for the generation of ATP. Water is necessary to keep the body hydrated. We discussed the importance of water in previous sections.

Essential Amino Acids	Essential Vitamins
Arginine	Vitamin A
Histidine	Vitamin B complex (8 vitamins)
Isoleucine	Vitamin C
Leucine	Vitamin D
Lysine	Vitamin E
Methionine	Vitamin K
Phenylalanine	
Threonine	
Tryptophan	
Valine	

Mechanical and chemical digestion

The teeth and saliva begin digestion by breaking food down into smaller pieces and lubricating it to allow swallowing. The lips, cheeks, and tongue form a bolus or ball of food. The process of peristalsis (wave-like contractions) carries the food down the pharynx where it enters the stomach through the sphincter, which closes to keep food from going back up. In the stomach, pepsinogen and hydrochloric acid form pepsin, the enzyme that hydrolyzes proteins. This chemical action breaks the food down further and churns into a semifluid mass called acid chyme. The pyloric sphincter muscle opens to allow the food to enter the small intestine. Most nutrient absorption occurs in the small intestine. Its large surface area, resulting from its length and protrusions called villi and microvilli, allow for a great absorptive surface into the bloodstream. Neutralization of the chyme after arrival from the acidic stomach allows the local enzymes to function. Accessory organs function in the production of necessary enzymes and bile. The pancreas makes many enzymes to break down food in the small intestine. The liver makes bile, which breaks down and emulsifies fatty acids. Any food left after the trip through the small intestine enters the large intestine. The large intestine functions to reabsorb water and produce vitamin K. The feces, or remaining waste, pass out through the anus.

Human Reproductive System

Hormone control and development and function of male and female reproductive systems

Hormones regulate sexual maturation in humans. Humans cannot reproduce until puberty, about the age of 8-14 depending on the individual. The hypothalamus begins secreting hormones that help mature the reproductive system and develop the secondary sex characteristics. Reproductive maturity in girls occurs with their first menstruation and occurs in boys with the first ejaculation of viable sperm.

Hormones also regulate reproduction. In males, the primary sex hormones are the androgens, testosterone being the most important. The testes produce androgens that dictate the primary and secondary sex characteristics of the male. Female hormone patterns are cyclic and complex. Most women have a reproductive cycle length of about 28 days. The menstrual cycle is specific to the changes in the uterus. The ovarian cycle results in ovulation and occurs in parallel with the menstrual cycle. Hormones regulate this parallelism. Five hormones participate in this regulation, most notably estrogen and progesterone. Estrogen and progesterone play an important role in signaling to the uterus and the development and maintenance of the endometrium. Estrogens also dictate the secondary sex characteristics of females.

Gametogenesis, fertilization, and birth control

Gametogenesis is the production of the sperm and egg cells.

Spermatogenesis begins at puberty in the male. One spermatogonia, the diploid precursor of sperm, produces four sperm. The sperm mature in the seminiferous tubules located in the testes. Oogenesis, the production of egg cells (ova), is usually complete by the birth of a female. Females do not release egg cells until menstruation begins at puberty. Meiosis forms one ovum with all the cytoplasm and three polar bodies that the body reabsorbs. The ovaries store the ovum and release them each month from puberty to menopause.

Seminiferous tubules in the testes house sperm, where they mature. The epididymis, located on top of the testes, contains mature sperm. After ejaculation, the sperm travel up the vas deferens where they mix with semen made in the prostate and seminal vesicles and travel out the urethra.

Ovulation releases the egg into the fallopian tubes where cilia move the egg along the length of the tubes. Fertilization of the egg by the sperm normally occurs in the fallopian tube. If pregnancy does not occur, the egg passes through the uterus and is expelled through the vagina during menstruation. Levels of progesterone and estrogen stimulate menstruation. Implantation of a fertilized egg regulates the levels, stopping menstruation.

There are many methods of contraception (birth control) that affect different stages of fertilization. Chemical contraception (birth control pills) prevents ovulation by synthetic estrogen and progesterone. Several barrier methods of contraception are available. Male and female condoms block semen from contacting the egg. Sterilization is another method of birth control. Tubal ligation in women prevents eggs from entering the uterus. A vasectomy in men involves the cutting of the vas deferens, which prevents the sperm from entering the urethra. The most effective method of birth control is abstinence. Programs exist worldwide that promote abstinence, especially among teenagers.

> **SKILL Demonstrating knowledge of basic components of physical fitness**
> **32.2** *(e.g., strength, endurance, flexibility)* **and applying principles of training**

FIVE HEALTH RELATED COMPONENTS OF PHYSICAL FITNESS	
Cardiovascular endurance	The ability of the body to sustain aerobic activities (activities requiring oxygen utilization) for extended periods
Muscle strength	The ability of muscle groups to contract and support a given amount of weight
Muscle endurance	The ability of muscle groups to contract continually over a period of time and support a given amount of weight
Flexibility	The ability of muscle groups to stretch and bend
Body composition	An essential measure of health and fitness. The most important aspects of body composition are body fat percentage and ratio of body fat to muscle

Basic Training Principles

The Overload Principle is exercising at an above normal level to improve physical or physiological capacity (a higher than normal workload).

The Specificity Principle is overloading a particular fitness component. In order to improve a component of fitness, you must isolate and specifically work on a single component. Metabolic and physiological adaptations depend on the type of overload; hence, specific exercise produces specific adaptations, creating specific training effects.

The Progression Principle states that once the body adapts to the original load/stress, no further improvement of a component of fitness will occur without the addition of an additional load.

There is also a Reversibility-of-Training Principle in which all gains in fitness are lost with the discontinuance of a training program.

Modifications of Overload

We can modify overload by varying frequency, intensity, and time. Frequency is the number of times we implement a training program in a given period (e.g., three days per week). Intensity is the amount of effort put forth or the amount of stress placed on the body. Time is the duration of each training session.

PRINCIPLES OF OVERLOAD, PROGRESSION, AND SPECIFICITY APPLIED TO IMPROVEMENT OF HEALTH-RELATED COMPONENTS OF FITNESS		
OVERLOADING	**PROGRESSION**	**SPECIFICITY**
Cardio-Respiratory Fitness		
• **Frequency** = minimum of 3 days/week • **Intensity** = exercising in target heart-rate zone • **Time** = minimum of 15 minutes	• Begin at a frequency of 3 days/week and work up to no more than 6 days/week • Begin at an intensity near THR threshold and work up to 80% of THR • Begin at 15 minutes and work up to 60 minutes	• To develop cardiovascular fitness, you must perform aerobic (with oxygen) activities for at least fifteen minutes without developing an oxygen debt; aerobic activities include, but are not limited to brisk walking, jogging, bicycling, and swimming
Muscle Strength		
• **Frequency** = every other day • **Intensity** = 60% to 90% of assessed muscle strength • **Time** = 3 sets of 3 to 8 reps (high resistance with a low number of repetitions)	• Begin 3 days/week and work up to every other day • Begin near 60% of determined muscle strength and work up to no more than 90% of muscle strength • Begin with 1 set with 3 reps and work up to 3 sets with 8 reps	• To increase muscle strength for a specific part(s) of the body, you must target that/those part(s) of the body

Table continued on next page

Muscle Endurance		
• **Frequency** = every other day • **Intensity** = 30% to 60% of assessed muscle strength • **Time** = 3 sets of 12 to 20 reps (low resistance with a high number of repetitions)	• Begin 3 days/week and work up to every other day • Begin at 20% to 30% of muscle strength and work up to no more than 60% of muscle strength • Begin with 1 set with 12 reps and work up to 3 sets with 20 reps	• Same as muscle strength
Flexibility		
• **Frequency** = 3 to 7 days/week • **Intensity** = stretch muscle beyond its normal length • **Time** = 3 sets of 3 reps holding stretch 15 to 60 seconds	• Begin 3 days/week and work up to every day • Begin stretching with slow movement as far as possible without pain, holding at the end of the range of motion (ROM) and work up to stretching no more than 10% beyond the normal ROM • Begin with 1 set with 1 rep, holding stretches 15 seconds, and work up to 3 sets with 3 reps, holding stretches for 60 seconds	• ROM is joint specific
Body Composition		
• **Frequency** = daily aerobic exercise • **Intensity** = low • **Time** = approximately one hour	• Begin daily • Begin a low aerobic intensity and work up to a longer duration (see cardio-respiratory progression) • Begin low-intensity aerobic exercise for 30 minutes and work up to 60 minutes	• Increase aerobic exercise and decrease caloric intake

Sample Test Questions and Rationale

Rigorous

1. **The ability of muscle groups to contract and support a given amount of weight is called:**

   A. muscle strength

   B. muscle endurance

   C. cardiovascular strength

   D. flexibility

   Answer: A – muscle strength

   Rationale: There are five health related components of physical fitness: cardio-respiratory or cardiovascular endurance, muscle strength, muscle endurance, flexibility, and body composition.

   Cardiovascular endurance is **the** ability of the body to sustain aerobic activities (activities requiring oxygen utilization) for extended periods.

   Muscle strength is the ability of muscle groups to contract and support a given amount of weight.

   Muscle endurance is the **ability** of muscle groups to contract continually over a period of time and support a given amount of weight.

   Flexibility is the ability of muscle groups to stretch and bend.

   Body composition is an **essential** measure of health and fitness. The most important aspects of body composition are body fat percentage and ratio of body fat to **muscle**.

SKILL 32.3 **Applying strategies for developing a personal fitness plan based on self-assessment, goal setting, and an understanding of physiological changes that result from training**

The trend in physical education assessment is to move increasingly away from norm- and criterion-referenced evaluations (i.e., measuring a student's achievements against the achievements of a normative group or against criteria that are arbitrarily set by either the educator or the governing educational body), and toward performance-based, or "authentic" evaluations. This creates difficulty for physical educators because it eliminates preset reference points.

The advantage of performance-based evaluations is they are equally fair to individuals with diverse backgrounds, special needs, and disabilities. In all cases, the instructor evaluates students based on their personal performance.

Portfolio construction is one way of assessing the performance of a student. The student chooses the achievements to add to the portfolio. This creates a tool that assesses current abilities and serves as a benchmark against which the instructor can measure future performance (thus evaluating progress over time, and not just a localized achievement).

Student self-assessment is often an important part of portfolios. The instructor should ask children questions such as, "Where am I now? Where am I trying to go? What am I trying to achieve? How can I get from here to there?" This type of questioning involves the child more deeply in the learning process.

Goal Setting

Goal setting is an effective way of achieving progress. In order to preserve and/or increase self-confidence, you and your students must set goals that are frequently reachable. One such way of achieving this is to set several small, short-term goals to attain one long-term goal. Be realistic in goal setting to increase fitness levels gradually. As students reach their goals, set more in order to continue performance improvement. Keep in mind that maintaining a current fitness level is an adequate goal provided the individual is in a healthy state. Reward your students when they reach goals. Rewards serve as motivation to reach the next goal. Also, be sure to prepare for lapses. Try to get back on track as soon as possible.

PHYSIOLOGICAL BENEFITS OF EXERCISE	
Improved cardio-respiratory fitness	Reduced risk of musculoskeletal injuries
Improved muscle strength	Lower cholesterol levels
Improved muscle endurance	Increased bone mass
Improved flexibility	Cardiac hypertrophy and size and strength of blood vessels
More lean muscle mass and less body fat	Increased number of red cells
Quicker rate of recovery	Improved blood-sugar regulation

Table continued on next page

Improved ability of the body to utilize oxygen	Improved efficiency of thyroid gland
Lower resting heart rate	Improved energy regulation
Increased cardiac output	Increased life expectancy
Improved venous return and peripheral circulation	

SKILL 32.4 Analyzing the relationship between life-long physical activity and the prevention of illness, disease, and premature death

See also Skill 32.3

ROLE OF EXERCISE IN HEALTH MAINTENANCE	
cholesterol levels	early death
blood pressure	certain types of cancer
stress related disorders	musculoskeletal problems
heart diseases	mental health
weight and obesity disorders	susceptibility to infectious diseases

---

SKILL 32.5 Applying knowledge of principles and activities for developing and maintaining cardiorespiratory endurance, muscular strength, flexibility, and levels of body composition that promote good health

See also, Skill 32.2

Here is a list of physical activities that may reduce specific health risks, improve overall health, and develop skill-related components of physical activity.

Physical activity	Health-related components of fitness	Skill-related components of fitness
Aerobic Dance	cardio-respiratory, body composition	agility, coordination
Bicycling	cardio-respiratory, muscle	balance
Calisthenics	cardio-respiratory, muscle strength, muscle endurance, flexibility, body composition	agility
Circuit Training	cardio-respiratory, muscle strength, muscle endurance, body composition	power
Cross Country Skiing	cardio-respiratory, muscle strength, muscle endurance, body composition	agility, coordination, power
Jogging/Running	cardio-respiratory, body composition	
Rope Jumping	cardio-respiratory, body composition	agility, coordination, reaction time, speed
Rowing	cardio-respiratory, muscle strength, muscle endurance, body composition	agility, coordination, power
Skating	cardio-respiratory, body composition	agility, balance, coordination, speed
Swimming/Water Exercises	cardio-respiratory, muscle strength, muscle endurance, flexibility, body composition	agility, coordination
Brisk Walking	cardio-respiratory, body composition	

DOMAIN VII

FAMILY AND CONSUMER SCIENCE AND CAREER DEVELOPMENT

Enhanced features only available in our ebook edition:

 eStickynotes: allows you take digital notes anywhere in the ebook edition. It further allows you to aggregate and print all enotes for easy studying.

 eFlashcards: a digital representation of a card represented with words, numbers or symbols or any combination of each and briefly displayed as part of a learning drill. eFlashcards takes away the burden of carrying around traditional cards that could easily be disarranged, dropped, or soiled.

 More Sample Tests: more ways to assess how much you know and how much further you need to study. Ultimately, makes you more prepared and attain mastery in the skills and techniques of passing the test the FIRST TIME!

Visit www.XAMonline.com
and click on ebook.

PERSONALIZED STUDY PLAN

PAGE	COMPETENCY AND SKILL	KNOWN MATERIAL/ SKIP IT	BRIEFLY REVIEW eSTICKYNOTES	MAKE eFLASHCARDS	TAKE ADDITIONAL SAMPLE TESTS
405	**33: Child Development and Care**	☐	☐	☐	☐
	33.1: Stages and characteristics of child development	☐	☐	☐	☐
	33.2: Children's physical, dietary, and hygiene needs	☐	☐	☐	☐
	33.3: Common childhood accidents and emergencies	☐	☐	☐	☐
	33.4: Responsibilities of parenting	☐	☐	☐	☐
	33.5: Family structure and roles	☐	☐	☐	☐
	33.6: Interpersonal relationships	☐	☐	☐	☐
	33.7: Social and cultural influences on interpersonal relationships	☐	☐	☐	☐
417	**34: Child Development and Care**	☐	☐	☐	☐
	34.1: Consumer economics and personal resource management	☐	☐	☐	☐
	34.2: Recognizing and responding to consumer fraud	☐	☐	☐	☐
	34.3: Making major purchases	☐	☐	☐	☐
	34.4: Purchasing a home or motor vehicle; establishing credit	☐	☐	☐	☐
	34.5: Personal and family health resources	☐	☐	☐	☐
420	**35: Career Development**	☐	☐	☐	☐
	35.1: Evaluating work against personal needs and interests	☐	☐	☐	☐
	35.2: Conducting career research	☐	☐	☐	☐
	35.3: Factors affecting a job search	☐	☐	☐	☐
	35.4: Job interviews	☐	☐	☐	☐
	35.5: Effective work communication	☐	☐	☐	☐
	35.6: Employee rights	☐	☐	☐	☐

COMPETENCY 33

UNDERSTAND CONCEPTS AND PRACTICES RELATED TO CHILD DEVELOPMENT AND CARE AND APPLY KNOWLEDGE OF FAMILY AND INTERPERSONAL RELATIONSHIPS

SKILL 33.1 Recognizing stages and characteristics of physical, cognitive, social, and emotional development during infancy, childhood, and adolescence

FIVE AREAS OF CHILDREN'S DEVELOPMENT	
Physical Well-Being and (Gross and Fine) Motor Development	A child's health is connected to preparedness for school and performance in school. Optimal motor development is essential, from the large/gross motor movements that occur on the playground to the small/fine motor work required for holding a crayon or putting together puzzles.
Social and Emotional Development	Relationships give meaning to school experiences. Stable interactions in children's early lives provide a sense of well-being that enables children to participate positively in classroom activities. Emotional support and secure relationships help children acquire such characteristics as self-confidence and the ability to function as a member of a group.
Approaches Toward Learning	A child can be successful in school in many ways, and these approaches vary within and between cultures. By understanding the various styles that involve children in learning, adults can encourage and increase a child's engagement. Curiosity, creativity, independence, cooperation, and persistence are some of the approaches that enhance early learning and development.
Language Development	Language empowers children to participate in both the cognitive and affective parts of the educational program. Experience with written and oral language provides children with the tools to interact with others and to represent their thoughts, feelings, and experiences. Communicating effectively with adults and other children and having experiences with diverse forms of language are basic parts of this dimension.
Cognition and General Knowledge	Children need opportunities to interact with people and materials in their environment and to learn from their surroundings. Experiences in learning settings with skilled and appropriate adult interaction allow children to construct knowledge of patterns and relations, cause and effect, and ways of solving problems in everyday life.

The teacher of students in early childhood should have a broad knowledge and understanding of the phases of development that typically occur during this stage of life. And the teacher must be aware of how receptive children are to specific methods of instruction and learning during each period of development. A significant premise in the study of child development holds that all domains of development (physical, social, and academic) are integrated. Development in each dimension is influenced by the others. Equally important to the teacher's understanding of the process is the knowledge that developmental advances within the domains occur neither simultaneously nor parallel to one another, necessarily.

Physical Development

It is important for the teacher to be aware of the physical stages of development and how changes to the child's physical attributes affect the child's ability to learn.

It is important for the teacher to be aware of the physical stages of development and how changes to the child's physical attributes (which include internal developments, increased muscle capacity, improved coordination, and other attributes, as well as obvious growth) affect the child's ability to learn. Factors determined by the physical stage of development include: ability to sit and attend, the need for activity, the relationship between physical coordination and self-esteem, and the degree to which physical involvement in an activity (as opposed to being able to understand an abstract concept) affects learning and the child's sense of achievement.

Cognitive (Academic) Development

Children go through patterns of learning beginning with preoperational thought processes and move to concrete operational thoughts. Eventually, they begin to acquire the intellectual ability to contemplate and solve problems independently, when they mature enough to manipulate objects symbolically. Students in early childhood can use symbols such as words and numbers to represent objects and relations, but they need concrete reference points. Successful acquisition of the skills taught in early childhood, through the fourth grade, will progressively prepare the student for more advanced problem solving and abstract thinking in the later grades. The content of curriculum for younger students must be relevant for their stage of development (accessible and composed of acquirable skills), engaging, and meaningful to the students.

Social Development

PARALLEL ACTIVITIES: playing alongside their peers without directly interacting with one another

Children progress through a variety of social stages beginning with an awareness of self and self-concern. They soon develop an awareness of peers but demonstrate a lack of concern for their presence. For a time, young children engage in PARALLEL ACTIVITIES, playing alongside their peers without directly interacting with one another.

During the primary years, children develop an intense interest in peers. They establish productive, positive social and working relationships with one another. This area of social growth will continue to increase in significance throughout the child's academic career. The foundation for the students' successful development in this area is established through the efforts of the classroom teacher to plan and develop positive peer group relationships and to provide opportunities and support for cooperative small group projects that not only develop cognitive ability but promote peer interaction. The ability to work and relate effectively with peers contributes greatly to the child's sense of competence. In order to develop this sense of competence, children need to be successful in acquiring the information base and social skill sets that promote cooperative effort to achieve academic and social objectives.

High expectations for student achievement, which are age-appropriate and focused, provide the foundation for a teacher's positive relationship with young students and are consistent with effective instructional strategies. It is equally important to determine what is appropriate for specific individuals in the classroom and approach classroom groups and individual students with an understanding and respect for their emerging capabilities. Those who study childhood development recognize that young students grow and mature in common, recognizable patterns, but at different rates that cannot be effectively accelerated. This can result in variance in the academic performance of different children in the same classroom. With the establishment of inclusion as a standard in the classroom, it is necessary for all teachers to understand that variation in development among the student population is another aspect of diversity within the classroom. And this has implications for the ways in which instruction is planned and delivered and the ways in which students learn and are evaluated.

Sites for more detailed information about areas of childhood development:

http://www.occrra. org/core_knowledge/ CoreKnowledge.pdf

http://www. childdevelopmentweb. com/Development/

Sample Test Questions and Rationale

Rigorous

1. **Which of the following is a true statement?**

   A. Physical development does not influence social development.

   B. Social development does not influence physical development.

   C. Cognitive development does not influence social development.

   D. All domains of development (physical, social, and cognitive) are integrated and influence other domains

   Answer : D – All domains of development (physical, social ,and cognitive) are integrated and influence other domains.

   Rationale: All domains of development (physical, social and cognitive) are integrated and influence other domains

Rigorous

2. **Marcus is a first grade boy of good developmental attainment. His learning progress is good the first half of the year. He shows no indicators of emotional distress. After the holiday break, he returns much changed. He is quieter, sullen even, tending to play alone. He has moments of tearfulness, sometimes almost without cause. He avoids contact with adults as often as he can. Even play with his friends has become limited. He has episodes of wetting not seen before and often wants to sleep in school. What approach is appropriate for this sudden change in behavior?**

   A. Give him some time to adjust. The holiday break was probably too much fun to come back to school from.

   B. Report this change immediately to administration. Do not call the parents until administration decides a course of action.

   C. Document his daily behavior carefully as soon as you notice such a change; report to administration the next month or so in a meeting.

   D. Make a courtesy call to the parents to let them know he is not acting like himself, being sure to tell them he is not making trouble for others.

Answer: B – Report this change immediately to administration. Do not call the parents until administration decides a course of action.

Rationale: Anytime a child's disposition, attitude, or habits change significantly, teachers and parents need to seriously consider the existence of emotional difficulties. Emotional disturbances in childhood are not uncommon and take a variety of forms. Usually these problems show up in the form of uncharacteristic behaviors. Most of the time, children respond favorably to brief treatment programs of psychotherapy. At other times, disturbances may need more intensive therapy and are harder to resolve. All stressful behaviors need to be addressed, and any type of chronic antisocial behavior needs to be examined as a possible symptom of deep-seated emotional upset. In a case where the change is sudden and dramatic, administration needs to become involved.

SKILL 33.2 Demonstrating knowledge of children's physical, dietary, and hygienic needs (e.g., nutritional guidelines, dental care, proper washing procedures) and applying developmentally appropriate methods for promoting self-care during childhood

Classrooms are great places for children to learn responsibility and good citizenship. Teachers of young children can help students learn how to behave appropriately and take care of their surroundings by providing them with opportunities to practice ownership, chores, and leadership. First, teachers should arrange classrooms in ways that students can access materials.

However, materials should be arranged in ways that maintain cleanliness. Messy classrooms show students that teachers do not care enough to provide a clean, safe environment for students to learn in. It also presents a negative image to parents, principals, and other teachers.

Students should begin to understand the need for maintaining good personal hygiene and learn the proper way to care for themselves. As they begin to develop intellectually and mature, students will begin to understand the important role personal hygiene has in the classroom. It is important for teachers to stress that students take care of their own bathroom needs, reinforce hand-washing techniques, and learn basic manners such as covering their mouths when sneezing or coughing and using tissues for personal needs.

Another important area teachers need to focus on is dietary needs of young students. Teachers need to actively encourage students to make educated and responsible choices regarding their daily diet. Early education and preventative teaching will help ensure that children are on the right track to a healthy lifestyle that begins at an early age.

These skills are important for children to learn. They demonstrate to children how to keep their environments orderly and functional.

> *Teachers of young children can help students learn how to behave appropriately and take care of their surroundings by providing them with opportunities to practice ownership, chores, and leadership.*

> *Students should begin to understand the need for maintaining good personal hygiene and learn the proper way to care for themselves.*

> *Teachers need to actively encourage students to make educated and responsible choices regarding their daily diet.*

SKILL 33.3 Identifying causes of common childhood accidents and health care emergencies and applying physical care and safety guidelines for caregivers of infants, toddlers, and preschool and school-age children

Many childhood accidents are preventable. Proper precautions should be used to childproof the home and other spaces where developing children are present on a daily basis. In the school community, legal liabilities compel school personnel to

In the school community, legal liabilities compel school personnel to create safety arenas and preparedness for students.

create safety arenas and preparedness for students given that younger, elementary students experience common childhood accidents associated with coordination development and children's developmental levels. For younger children, the school playground presents a range of accidents waiting to happen for children trying to maneuver the required coordination of the jungle gym and the swing sets. As children begin formalized physical education programs, accidents are inherent within the physical demands and expectations of the programs. Toddlers, preschool, and school age children are still in a precarious development modality that may directly contribute to common childhood accidents.

The identification of common childhood accidents and health care emergencies are mostly attributed to falls or slips when, especially toddlers, are working to coordinate walking with stability of movements.

- Infants who are left alone for even a second can fall from changing tables to the floor simply because they are constantly working muscular developments of rolling and trying to hold themselves into positions for limited time periods. Infants who are left alone in larger areas can put foreign objects into their mouth and choke on these objects. Caregivers must provide areas for infants that are unobstructed and free of smaller objects that infants can automatically put into their tiny mouths. Along with keeping areas free of objects, caregivers must provide barriers that confine the infant into safety zones.

- For toddlers, who are curious and who have the ability to traverse larger distances, the common accidents include falls and grabbing unstable objects or furniture for their own stability, which contribute to bumps on the heads or more serious accidents if the object or furniture falls directly on the toddler. The caregiver must remember to never leave a toddler or any young child unattended during even the most minimal time period because the consequences of an accident increase with the lack of supervision and vigilant watchfulness of an adult.

- Preschool children and school-age children must be taught how to respond to adult commands of "Stop" and "No" when there is an inherent sense of danger and the adult can't respond or rescue quickly due to distance or the situation. School-age children who are seeking opportunities of independence must still be supervised and directed in safety issues that accompany their growing independence.

Caregivers must have safety guidelines in place to address any emergency that may happen in areas where groups of young children may gather.

Caregivers must have safety guidelines in place to address any emergency that may happen in areas where groups of young children may gather. Guidelines should include safety and emergency protocols that all caregivers have practiced and could implement in an instant in the event of an emergency. Proper emergency preparedness in handling the many accidents that could happen to a child from infant to school age should be visible and understood by all of the caregivers. The important thing to remember is that for a young child, an accident could be deadly, so having safety guidelines and procedures in place is crucial and could save a young life.

SKILL 33.4 Analyzing factors that affect decisions about whether and when to have children and recognizing ways to prepare for the responsibilities of parenthood

Parenthood is all about preparation and collaborative decision making between those who share responsibility for the upbringing of a child. The birth of a child is seen as a miraculous event, so the miracle must include proper planning to provide a nurturing family environment for the miracle child to develop and grow.

There are many factors that affect the decision making in whether to have children or not. The age and maturity of the parent(s) is a major decision that must be considered before engaging in child procreation. If potential parents possess the maturity to make daily decisions from conception to birth to the progressive development of the child through adulthood, then that parent or parent team might be ready to bring a child into the world.

What is not talked about before the birth of a child is the financial status of the expecting parents. With so many young teenagers giving birth to children, the financial expectation falls on the adult caregivers or grandparent(s) of the younger parent-to-be. In today's society, the financial burden and strain of raising a household of children is apparent in the single- and two-parent households where parents are working two to three jobs to meet the financial expectations of just providing the basics for children.

Preparing for the responsibilities of parenthood takes a conscious effort on the part of the parents, so maturity and financial acuity are essential in parent preparedness. Effective communication between two people wanting to parent a child must be on the forefront of the list of parent preparation. Parents must have their act together before conception so that children are provided the best possible family environment.

Preparing for the responsibilities of parenthood takes a conscious effort on the part of the parents, so maturity and financial acuity are essential in parent preparedness.

There is a diversity of support groups and extended families that can provide the necessary advice and support for those considering parenthood. For teenagers, school communities and neighborhood communities can provide counseling services and sometimes financial resources to help supplement the budgets required for parenting. Even for adults, the ability to calculate the financial budgets needed for the first year of a child's life can be astronomical if not attended to prior to the birth. The cost of baby supplies and food can create a major faction even in the best-laid plans, so communication and putting financial resources into a different fund source are crucial in making the first year and succeeding years less stressful and productive for parents and child.

The role of parent should not be taken lightly or engaged in on a whim to provide companionship to adults or to secure adult relationships. The education of the child begins before conception and the education of future parents begins with having a basket of knowledge about parenthood and a diversity of decision-making strategies that will create a strong and loving environment for any child.

> SKILL 33.5 **Demonstrating knowledge of family structure** (e.g., extended, blended, single parent, dual career)**, roles and responsibilities of family members, and the functions of families in society**

How the family functions is often defined by the identification of each family member within the family structure.

The role of the family structure provides a definitive identity of roles and responsibilities of each family member within the networking system. How the family functions is often defined by the identification of each family member within the family structure. From the first born to the last born, each position of birth in the family creates an expectation for that family member.

1. The first born in a family of siblings often takes on early responsibility and blame for the actions of younger siblings

2. The middle child can sometimes get lost in the dynamics between the older and younger siblings within the family structure

3. The youngest child is given the most attention due to developmental needs and the birth position

The expectations about the first born can be overwhelming for those children in that birth position and can create a sense of alienation or acting out in later years.

In today's society, the traditional family structure of two parents married for twenty years with orderly children has been traversed with divorced families regrouping into extended and blended families. The birth order in extended and blended families takes on a different persona for siblings in those positions. The family dynamics may supersede birth order predictions, because the psychological forging of families that are seeking to reestablish different relationships in an extended and blended manner must deal with the work and responsibility it takes to make a family community that is proactive and productive.

Single parents who are raising children are faced with sometimes daunting prospects if there are no extended family networks to count on for support. Many children raise themselves in single-parent households because the financial expectations required for basic sustenance may create impossible working hours for the parent that prevents a normal parenting timeframe for the child's needs. Both the child and the parent can lose if this type of parenting is not supplemented with the provision of other adult caregivers in the child's life to provide direction, instruction, and care for the child when the parent is not available.

Parents on the fast track with dual careers can create single-parent or no-parent households as well. Parents who are working hard to provide the financial resources for children can spend more time at work than at home, so both the child and parent can lose if additional adult caregivers or extended family support systems aren't in place to provide children with support or care.

The matriarchal or patriarchal family structures are typified in the history of American society and many societies that have the family lineages that are geographically and historically identified as providing societal role models for mainstream families. What is inherent with the typified families is the power and financial positioning associated with them. There is a juggling of maintaining privacy with normalcy in creating family structures that provide connections and support systems for families who have been in the limelight.

The family structure should be recognized as one of the most important mediums of interpersonal relationship building that creates groups of people engaged dynamically in creating histories because of blood lineages. The roles and functions of everyone in the family structure are designed to provide continued support and strength for each person's growth and development into adulthood and beyond.

SKILL 33.6 Recognizing the types and characteristics of interpersonal relationships and analyzing decision-making processes related to interpersonal relationships

Interpersonal relationships can be defined in relational contexts that comprise a diversity of interactions for communication and collaboration. There are researchers who have formulated theories around relational associations and developed decision-making matrixes that provide cooperative networking opportunities and competences for people. In general, the following types can categorize interpersonal relationships:

- Family: Relationships create patterns of communication and socialization that establishes sibling identity in the family structure. Dysfunctional patterns are also created within the interpersonal relationships between siblings and parent groups.

- Friends: The concept of choosing a group of people with whom to align one's beliefs and associations and who define an identity concept or perceived notion of self. Friendships are freely selected alliances that can be healthy ego promoters or provide negative dysfunction and negated self-esteem.

- Romantic association: The intimacy of how people align their passions and feelings of commitment provides another type of freely chosen interpersonal relationship. The longevity and monogamous nature of a societal-defined relationship between people in the form of a legal recognition of a coupling has provided a sense of stronger commitment and entitlement for some people contrasting with a sense of isolation within the relationship for others.

- Professional interactions: In the world of business, professional relationships are defined by the group interactions that are integral aspects of a dynamic organization. The business world in some ways demands a higher level of commitment and loyalty to a mission and vision that is ultimately defined by the group dynamics and productivity. People are interviewed and grouped into defined roles based on expertise and portfolios that provide categorizations as leaders or followers in organizations.

- Interpersonal competence: In the consulting world, a major business source has been built around the area of interpersonal competence. Consultants have created workshops amassing databases of organizational development models that govern the way that people in organizations are grouped and interact. In a work world, where the majority of people spend the most waking moments of the day at work, the ability to interact and develop professional relationships that create promotional opportunities and feelings of contribution to an organization are crucial and emotionally healthy. The personal delivery of communication within an organization creates a networking linkage of communication that either is perceived as effective and dynamic or as a crucial divide within an organization. Crucial divides of interpersonal relationship building in any organization can equal a perception of lack of commitment or dedication to an organization. Any types of conflict within relationships are often assessed as a performance issue of incompetence and seen as detrimental to the healthy core of an organization.

- Communication competence: Defined leaders in organizations are effective communicators who are able to ascertain the core of issues and concerns among the stakeholders and develop appropriate avenues of creating a diversity of communication techniques to deal with core issues.

SKILL 33.7 Examining social and cultural influences on interpersonal communication and analyzing factors affecting the formation of positive relationships in the family, workplace, and community

The student's capacity and potential for academic success within the overall educational experience are products of her or his total environment: classroom and school system; home and family; neighborhood; and community in general. All of these segments are interrelated and can be supportive or divisive, one against the other. As a matter of course, the teacher will become familiar with all aspects of the system, the school, and the classroom pertinent to the students' educational experience. This would include not only process and protocols but also the availability of resources provided to meet the academic, health, and welfare needs of students. But it is incumbent upon the teacher to look beyond the boundaries of the school system to identify additional resources as well as issues and situations that will effect (directly or indirectly) a student's ability to succeed in the classroom.

Examples of resources:

- Libraries, museums, zoos, or planetariums.

- Departments of social services operating within the local community. These can provide background and program information relevant to social issues that may be impacting individual students. And this can be a resource for classroom instruction regarding life skills, at-risk behaviors, etc.

- Clubs, societies, and civic organizations, community outreach programs of private businesses and corporations and of government agencies. These can provide a variety of materials and media as well as possible speakers and presenters.

Initial contacts for resources outside of the school system will usually come from within the system itself: from administration, teacher organizations, department heads, and other colleagues.

Examples of issues/situations:

- Students from multicultural backgrounds: Curriculum objectives and instructional strategies may be inappropriate and unsuccessful when presented in a single format that relies on the student's understanding and acceptance of the values and common attributes of a specific culture that is not his or her own

- Parental/family influences: Attitude, resources, and encouragement available in the home environment may be attributes for success or failure

Families with higher incomes are able to provide increased opportunities for students. Students from lower-income families will need to depend on the resources available from the school system and the community. This should be orchestrated by the classroom teacher in cooperation with school administrators and educational advocates in the community.

Family members with higher levels of education often serve as models for students and have high expectations for academic success. And families with specific aspirations for children (often regardless of their own educational background) encourage students to achieve academic success, and are most often active participants in the process.

A family in crisis (caused by economic difficulties, divorce, substance abuse, physical abuse, etc.) creates a negative environment that may profoundly impact all aspects of a student's life, particularly his or her ability to function academically. The situation may require professional intervention. It is often the classroom teacher who will recognize a family in a crisis situation and instigate an intervention by reporting on this to school or civil authorities.

Link with information about ensuring equity in education:

http://www.nwrel.org/cnorse/booklets/training/KeyComponents.html

Regardless of the positive or negative impacts on the students' education from outside sources, it is the teacher's responsibility to ensure that all students in the classroom have an equal opportunity for academic success. This begins with the teacher's statement of high expectations for every student and develops through planning, delivery, and evaluation of instruction which provides for inclusion and ensures that all students have equal access to the resources necessary for successful acquisition of the academic skills being taught and measured in the classroom.

COMPETENCY 34

UNDERSTAND SKILLS AND PROCEDURES RELATED TO CONSUMER ECONOMICS AND PERSONAL RESOURCE MANAGEMENT

SKILL 34.1 **Recognizing rights and responsibilities of consumers in various purchasing situations** *(e.g., rights in relation to product and service warranties and guarantees)*

For an overview of consumer rights, see this Web site:

http://en.wikipedia.org/wiki/Consumer protection

For a more specific overview of federal regulations, see this Web site:

http://www.fdic.gov/consumers/consumer/rights/index.html

For information specific to the state of New York, see this Web site:

http://www.consumer.state.ny.us/

SKILL 34.2 **Demonstrating knowledge of types and characteristics of consumer fraud and applying procedures for seeking redress and registering consumer complaints**

This Web site contains general information about registering consumer complaints:

http://longisland.about.com/od/governement/f/cons_complaint.htm

Although this Web site is relevant only to one particular city—as many consumer laws are—it gives a good preview of what one might find in other cities:

http://www.nyc.gov/html/dca/html/home/home.shtml

This final Web site contains an enormous amount of information regarding fraud:

http://www.nclnet.org/publications/

SKILL 34.3 Applying knowledge of procedures for making major purchases
(e.g., comparison shopping, negotiation, interpreting labels or contract terminology)

These Web sites contain articles with tips on bargain shopping:

http://www.mommysavers.com/money-saving-ideas/bargain-shopping-tips.shtml

http://nd.essortment.com/bargainshopping_rezl.htm

http://www.associatedcontent.com/article/52951/discount_shopping_tips_and_tricks_the.html

This Web site provides a good overview of how to read nutrition labels:

http://www.kidshealth.org/parent/nutrition_fit/nutrition/food_labels.html

SKILL 34.4 Analyzing considerations involved in selecting and maintaining housing and motor vehicles, obtaining credit and insurance, and making investments

This Web site provides a compendium of sites with information on purchasing a home:

http://homebuying.about.com/od/howtobuyahome/

This Web site contains an article with advice on purchasing automobile insurance:

http://auto.consumerguide.com/articles/index.cfm/act/expertadvice/article/EAA_Lease_or_Buy.html

This Web site contains an article on managing credit:

http://ezinearticles.com/?Tips-For-Managing-Credit&id=284066

This Web site contains an article on the basics of investing:

http://www.moneyinstructor.com/art/investingprinciples.asp

SKILL 34.5 Examining steps and considerations involved in planning and maintaining a personal or family budget and applying money management guidelines appropriate for various situations

These Web sites contain basic articles on family budgeting:

http://www.moneyinstructor.com/art/familybudget.asp

http://www.simplejoe.com/article-chemain-evans-setting-up-budget.htm

This Web site contains good advice on spending money wisely:

http://novella.mhhe.com/sites/0079876543/student_view0/freshman_year-999/your_finances3/money_management.html

This Web site contains a sample household budget spreadsheet:

http://financialplan.about.com/cs/budgeting/l/blbudget.htm

SKILL 34.6 Demonstrating knowledge of personal and family resources (*e.g., time, skills, energy*) and applying decision-making and goal-setting procedures for managing personal and family resources in various situations

These Web sites provide general advice on decision making:

http://www.time-management-guide.com/decision-making-skills.html

http://www.mindtools.com/dectree.html

http://www.possibilities.nu/betterdecisions.htm

These Web sites provide general time-management advice:

http://www.dartmouth.edu/~acskills/success/time.html

http://en.wikipedia.org/wiki/Time_management

COMPETENCY 35

UNDERSTAND BASIC PRINCIPLES OF CAREER DEVELOPMENT; APPLY PROCESSES AND SKILLS FOR SEEKING AND MAINTAINING EMPLOYMENT; AND DEMONSTRAGE KNOWLEDGE OF WORKPLACE SKILLS, BEHAVIORS, AND RESPONSIBILITIES

SKILL 35.1 Demonstrating knowledge of the relationship of personal interests, skills, and abilities to successful employment and recognizing the relationship between the changing nature of work and educational requirements

These Web sites provide good advice on selecting the right career. Some contain quizzes and other links:

http://www.selfgrowth.com/articles/Banaszak1.htmlTH

http://money.cnn.com/2005/10/10/news/economy/annie/fortune_annie101005/index.htm

http://featuredreports.monster.com/career-direction/path1/TH

This Web site provides interesting information on how work is changing in the twenty-first century and how employees can prepare for the changes:

http://www.siop.org/tip/backissues/TIPDec95/may.aspxTH

SKILL 35.2 Recognizing factors to consider when evaluating careers and applying procedures for conducting career research

These Web sites provide detailed advice on selecting appropriate careers:

http://interview.monster.com/articles/researching/TH

http://www.muhlenberg.edu/careercenter/mules/research.htmlTH

SKILL 35.3 Demonstrating knowledge of steps involved in searching for a job and recognizing factors affecting the success of a job search *(e.g., writing an effective letter of application, résumé preparation)*

These Web sites provide general tips on job searches:

http://jobsearch.about.com/cs/jobsearchhelp/a/jobtips.htm

http://www.bls.gov/oco/oco20042.htm

http://www.bls.gov/oco/oco20043.htm

These Web sites provide advice on writing resumes:

http://www.how-to-write-a-resume.org/resume_writing_tips.htm

http://www.soyouwanna.com/site/syws/resume/resume.htmlTH

These Web sites provide advice on writing cover letters:

http://www.soyouwanna.com/site/syws/coverletter/coverletter.htmlTH

http://www.how-to-write-a-resume.org/cover_letter_tips.htm

This Web site provides a good overview on how to evaluate a job offer:

http://www.bls.gov/oco/oco20046.htm

SKILL 35.4 Applying skills and procedures for job interviews *(e.g., personal appearance and demeanor, communicating effectively during an interview)*

These Web sites provide tips for interviewing:

http://www.bls.gov/oco/oco20045.htm

http://www.quintcareers.com/interview_mistakes.htmlTH

http://www.job-interview.net/interviewguide.htm

SKILL 35.5 Applying knowledge of effective communication principles, work etiquette, interpersonal skills, and techniques for handling stress or conflict in the workplace

These Web sites provide workplace etiquette advice:

http://www.sideroad.com/Business_Etiquette/workplace-etiquette.htmlTH

http://www.umich.edu/~urecord/9596/Jun11_96/artcl17.htm

This Web site provides advice on interpersonal communication skills for the workplace:

http://www.allbusiness.com/human-resources/careers-career-development/11134-1.htmlTH

SKILL 35.6 Recognizing rights and responsibilities in relation to employment *(e.g., protection from harassment and discrimination, employer's performance expectations)*

This Web site provides a number of links that provide specific information on various employment laws:

http://www.managementhelp.org/legal/emp_law/emp_law.htm#anchor193091TH

This Web site provides a good overview of employee rights in the workplace:

http://www.mypersonnelfile.com/TH

SAMPLE TEST

Reading, Language & Literature

(Average Rigor) (Skill 1.1)

1. **Which of the following indicates that a student is a fluent reader?**

   A. reads texts with expression or prosody

   B. reads word-to-word and haltingly

   C. must intentionally decode a majority of the words

   D. in a writing assignment, sentences are poorly-organized structurally

(Easy) (Skill 1.1)

2. **All of the following are true about phonological awareness EXCEPT:**

   A. It may involve print.

   B. It is a prerequisite for spelling and phonics.

   C. Activities can be done by the children with their eyes closed.

   D. It starts before letter recognition is taught.

(Average Rigor) (Skill 1.1)

3. **Which of the following theories was spearheaded by Noam Chomsky in the 1950s?**

   A. learning approach

   B. linguistic approach

   C. cognitive approach

   D. montessori approach

(Average Rigor) (Skill 1.5)

4. **The arrangement and relationship of words in sentences or sentence structure best describes:**

   A. style

   B. discourse

   C. thesis

   D. syntax

(Rigorous) (Skill 1.5)

5. **To decode is to:**

   A. use a special code to decipher a message

   B. sound out a printed sequence of letters

   C. change communication signals into messages

   D. change a message into symbols

(Rigorous) (Skill 1.5)

6. **To encode means that you:**

   A. change a message into symbols

   B. construct meaning from a code

   C. change communication signals into messages

   D. sound out a printed sequence of letters

(Rigorous) (Skill 2.4)

7. **Which of the following is NOT a reading comprehension strategy?**

   A. K-W-L chart

   B. note-taking

   C. standardized test

   D. Venn diagram

(Average Rigor) (Skill 2.4)

8. **A K-W-L chart is which of the following?**

A. graphic organizer

B. abbreviations chart

C. word list

D. Venn diagram

(Average Rigor) (Skill 2.4)

9. **K-W-L charts are useful for which of the following?**

A. comprehension of expository text

B. format for note taking

C. report writing

D. all of the above

(Rigorous) (3.5)

10. **Behavioral learning theory suggests that people:**

A. learn socially

B. learn through stimulation

C. learn through repetition

D. all of the above

(Rigorous) (Skill 3.5)

11. **Most educators believe that children learn:**

A. cognitively

B. behaviorally

C. physically

D. emotionally

(Easy) (Skill 4.1)

12. **Which of the following is not a technique of prewriting?**

A. clustering

B. listing

C. brainstorming

D. proofreading

(Rigorous) (Skill 4.4)

13. **Which of the following is a complex sentence?**

A. Anna and Margaret read a total of fifty-four books during summer vacation.

B. The youngest boy on the team had the best earned run average, which mystified the coaching staff.

C. Earl decided to attend Princeton; his twin brother Roy, who aced the ASVAB test, will be going to Annapolis.

D. "Easy come, easy go," Marcia moaned.

(Average Rigor) (Skill 5.1)

14. **Which of the following is NOT an approach to keep students ever conscious of the need to write for audience appeal?**

A. pairing students during the writing process

B. reading all rough drafts before the students write the final copies

C. having students compose stories or articles for publication in school literary magazines or newspapers

D. writing letters to friends or relatives

(Easy) (Skill 5.4)

15. **Writing that is intended to change the reader's mind is called:**

    A. narration

    B. expository

    C. persuasion

    D. description

(Average Rigor) (Skill 6.2)

16. **Which of the following is NOT an effective listening skill for students?**

    A. follows complex directions

    B. orally retells stories

    C. watches body language

    D. takes notes

(Average rigor) (Skill 7.1)

17. **The elements of plot, characters, settings, themes, interpretations, opinions, theories, and research can be found in what type of literature?**

    A. nonfiction

    B. fairy tale

    C. fiction

    D. folktales

(Rigorous) (Skill 7.2)

18. **At what point does exposition occur within a story?**

    A. after the rising action

    B. after the denouement

    C. before the rising action

    D. before the setting

(Average Rigor) (Skill 7.2)

19. **Which is an untrue statement about a theme in literature?**

    A. The theme is always stated directly somewhere in the text.

    B. The theme is the central idea in a literary work.

    C. All parts of the work (plot, setting, mood, etc.) should contribute to the theme in some way.

    D. By analyzing the various elements of the work, the reader should be able to arrive at an indirectly stated theme.

(Rigorous) (Skill 7.3)

20. **Plot is the series of events in a story. Typically, plot moves in the following sequence:**

    A. rising action, exposition, climax, denouement, falling action

    B. exposition, rising action, climax, falling action, denouement

    C. denouement, rising action, climax, falling action, exposition

    D. rising action, exposition, denouement, climax, falling action

(Easy) (Skill 7.4)

21. **Texts that present information to readers in a quick and efficient manner are called:**

    A. essays

    B. memoirs

    C. journals

    D. newspaper articles

(Average Rigor) (Skill 7.5)

22. Which is NOT a true statement concerning an author's literary tone?

A. Tone is partly revealed through the selection of details.

B. Tone is the expression of the author's attitude toward his or her subject.

C. Tone in literature is usually satiric or angry.

D. Tone in literature corresponds to the tone of voice a speaker uses.

(Easy) (Skill 7.6)

23. The examples "Nate never knows" and "People who pen poetry" are representative of what form of poetry?

A. assonance

B. slant rhyme

C. alliteration

D. onomatopoeia

(Rigorous) (Skill 8.5)

24. Which of the following is a ballad?

A. "The Knight's Tale"

B. *Julius Caesar*

C. *Paradise Lost*

D. "The Rime of the Ancient Mariner"

(Rigorous) (Skill 8.5)

25. Which of the following is an epic?

A. *On the Choice of Books*

B. *The Faerie Queene*

C. *Northanger Abbey*

D. *A Doll's House*

Math

(Rigorous) (Skill 9.1)

26. If $4x - (3 - x) = 7(x - 3) + 10$, Then:

A. $x = 8$

B. $x = -8$

C. $x = 4$

D. $x = -4$

(Average Rigor) (Skill 10.1)

27. Which words in a test problem would indicate that an addition operation is needed?

A. each

B. recreased by

C. in each group

D. increased by

(Easy) (Skill 11.2)

28. The _____ property states that you can change the order of the terms or factors.

A. commutative

B. associative

C. identity

D. distributive

(Average Rigor) (Skill 11.5)

29. A sofa sells for $520. If the retailer makes a 30% profit, what was the wholesale price?

A. $400

B. $676

C. $490

D. $364

(Rigorous) (Skill 11.5)

30. An item that sells for $375 is put on sale at $120. What is the percent of decrease?

A. 25%

B. 28%

C. 68%

D. 34%

(Easy) (Skill 12.3)

31. Each (x,y) relationship between a pair of values is called the _____ and can be plotted on a graph.

A. coordinate pair

B. parallel value

C. symbolic rule

D. proportional function

(Rigorous) (Skill 13.2)

32. If the radius of a right circular cylinder is doubled, how does its volume change?

A. no change

B. also is doubled

C. four times the original

D. pi times the original

(Average Rigor) (Skill 13.3)

33. In similar polygons, if the perimeters are in a ratio of $x: y$, the sides are in a ratio of:

A. $x: y$

B. $x^2: y^2$

C. $2x: y$

D. $\frac{1}{2} x: y$

(Average Rigor) (Skill 13.6)

34. Kindergarten students are doing a butterfly art project. They fold paper in half. On one half, they paint a design. Then they fold the paper closed and reopen. The resulting picture is a butterfly with matching sides. What math principle does this demonstrate?

A. slide

B. rotate

C. symmetry

D. transformation

(Easy) (Skill 14.2)

35. What measure could be used to report the distance traveled in walking around a track?

A. degrees

B. square meters

C. kilometers

D. cubic feet

(Average Rigor) (Skill 14.2)

36. The mass of a cookie is closest to:

A. 0.5 kg

B. 0.5 g

C. 15 g

D. 1.5 g

(Rigorous) (Skill 14.3)

37. 3 km is equivalent to:

A. 300 cm

B. 300 m

C. 3000 cm

D. 3000 m

(Rigorous) (Skill 14.4)

38. What is the area of a square whose side is 13 feet?

   A. 169 feet

   B. 169 square feet

   C. 52 feet

   D. 52 square feet

(Rigorous) (Skill 14.5)

39. Given the formula $d = rt$, (where d = distance, r = rate, and t = time), calculate the time required for a vehicle to travel 585 miles at a rate of 65 miles per hour.

   A. 8.5 hours

   B. 6.5 hours

   C. 9.5 hours

   D. 9 hours

(Average Rigor) (Skill 14.5)

40. $(\frac{-4}{9}) + (\frac{-7}{10}) =$

   A. $\frac{23}{90}$

   B. $\frac{-23}{90}$

   C. $\frac{103}{90}$

   D. $\frac{-103}{90}$

(Average Rigor) (Skill 15.1)

41. Corporate salaries are listed for several employees. Which would be the best measure of central tendency?

| $24,000 | $24,000 | $26,000 |
| $28,000 | $30,000 | $120,000 |

   A. mean

   B. median

   C. mode

   D. no difference

(Easy) (Skill 15.3)

42. The following chart shows the yearly average number of international tourists visiting Palm Beach for 1990–1994. How many more international tourists visited Palm Beach in 1994 than in 1991?

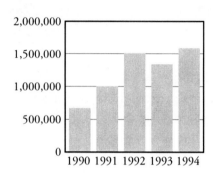

   A. 100,000

   B. 600,000

   C. 1,600,000

   D. 8,000,000

(Average rigor) (Skill 15. 3)

43. Which type of graph uses symbols to represent quantities?

   A. bar graph

   B. line graph

   C. pictograph

   D. circle graph

(Rigorous) (Skill 15.4)

44. Given a drawer with 5 black socks, 3 blue socks, and 2 red socks, what is the probability that you will draw two black socks in two draws in a dark room?

   A. $\frac{2}{9}$

   B. $\frac{1}{4}$

   C. $\frac{17}{18}$

   D. $\frac{1}{18}$

(Rigorous) (Skill 15.7)

45. What is the probability of drawing 2 consecutive aces from a standard deck of cards?

A. $\frac{3}{51}$

B. $\frac{1}{221}$

C. $\frac{2}{104}$

D. $\frac{2}{52}$

Science

(Rigorous) (Skill 16.1)

46. In an experiment measuring the growth of bacteria at different temperatures, what is the independent variable?

A. number of bacteria

B. growth rate of bacteria

C. temperature

D. size of bacteria

(Average rigor) (Skill 16. 1)

47. Which is the correct order of methodology?
1. collecting data
2. planning a controlled experiment
3. drawing a conclusion
4. hypothesizing a result
5. revisiting a hypothesis to answer a question

A. 1, 2, 3, 4, 5

B. 4, 2, 1, 3, 5

C. 4, 5, 1, 3, 2

D. 1, 3, 4, 5, 2

(Average rigor) (Skill 16. 6)

48. Accepted procedures for preparing solutions should be made with _____ .

A. alcohol

B. hydrochloric acid

C. distilled water

D. tap water

(Easy) (Skill 16.6)

49. Chemicals should be stored:

A. in the principal's office

B. in a dark room

C. according to their reactivity with other substances

D. in a double locked room

(Average rigor) (Skill 17. 5)

50. The measure of the pull of the earth's gravity on an object is called _____ .

A. mass number

B. atomic number

C. mass

D. weight

(Rigorous) (Skill 17.6)

51. Which parts of an atom are located inside the nucleus?

A. electrons and neutrons

B. protons and neutrons

C. protons only

D. neutrons only

(Rigorous) (Skill 18.4)

52. **Which of the following is a biome?**

A. a set of surroundings within which members of a species normally live

B. a large area of land with characteristic climate, soil, and mixture of plants and animals

C. a community (of any size) consisting of a physical environment and the organisms that live within it

D. none of the above

(Average Rigor) (Skill 18.4)

53. **A condition in which two organisms of different species are able to live in the same environment over an extended period of time without harming one another is called:**

A. symbiosis

B. biodiversity

C. habitat

D. ecosystem

(Rigorous) (Skill 19.3)

54. **In an experiment measuring the growth of bacteria at different temperatures, what is the independent variable?**

A. number of bacteria

B. growth rate of bacteria

C. temperature

D. size of bacteria

(Easy) (Skill 19.4)

55. **An ecosystem is defined by its _____ .**

A. climate

B. indigenous plants and animals

C. location to the equator

D. answers A and B

(Average Rigor) (Skill 19.6)

56. **An appropriate method for graphically representing data to the scientific community would be _____ .**

A. computer-linked probes

B. graphing calculators

C. both A and B

D. neither A nor B

(Easy)(Skill 20.1)

57. **Which of the following scientists proposed the relative theory of $E = mc^2$?**

A. Albert Einstein

B. Sir Isaac Newton

C. Thomas Edison

D. Charles Darwin

History and Social Science

(Easy)(Skill 21.1)

58. **The end of the feudal manorial system was caused by:**

A. the Civil War

B. the Black Death

C. the Christian Riots

D. westward expansion

(Rigorous) (Skill 21.1)

59. **In 1957 the formation of the Southern Christian Leadership Conference was started by:**

A. Martin Luther King, Jr

B. Rev. T. J. Jemison

C. Ella Baker

D. all of the above

(Average Rigor)) (Skill 21.3)

60. **This country is considered by some historians to be the oldest uninterrupted civilization in the world.**

    A. Japan

    B. China

    C. Canada

    D. Mexico

(Rigorous) (Skill 21.4)

61. **The practice of dividing time into a number of discrete periods or blocks of time is called:**

    A. eras

    B. chronological time

    C. periodization

    D. years

(Average Rigor)) (Skill 21.5)

62. **New York was initially inhabited by what two native peoples?**

    A. Sioux and Pawnee

    B. Micmac and Wampanoag

    C. Iroquois and Algonquin

    D. Nez Perce and Cherokee

(Easy) (Skill 21.6)

63. **What was the name of the cultural revival after the Civil War that took place in New York?**

    A. The Revolutionary War

    B. The Second Great Awakening

    C. Th. .rlem Renaissance

    D.   .ge

(Average Rigor) (Skill 22.2)

64. **The term spatial organization refers to:**

    A. latitude and longitude lines

    B. the alignment of the stars

    C. how things are grouped in a given space

    D. the space between point A and point B

(Rigorous) (Skill 22.5)

65. **Vital statistics, social trends, and crude rates are all apart of a branch of science of statistics which is concerned with the social well being of people. What is the name of this branch?**

    A. cartography

    B. sociology

    C. demography

    D. psychology

(Average Rigor)) (Skill 23.5)

66. **_____ is the belief that one's own culture is the central and the superior culture.**

    A. Ethnocentrism

    B. Egocentrism

    C. Prejudice

    D. Superiority

(Rigorous) (Skill 24.1)

67. **Economics is defined as a study of:**

    A. how scarce resources are allocated to satisfy unlimited wants

    B. anything that is manufactured to be used in the production process

    C. anyone who sells his ability to produce goods and services

    D. decisions of buyers that are equal to the selling decisions of seller

(Rigorous) (Skill 24.3)

68. Laissez-faire capitalism is based on:

A. government ownership of the means of production

B. custom and usually exists in less developed countries

C. the premise of no government intervention in the economy

D. none of the above

(Average Rigor) (Skill 25.1)

69. The ability of the president to veto an act of Congress is an example of:

A. separation of powers

B. checks and balances

C. judicial review

D. presidential prerogative

(Average Rigor)) (Skill 25.6)

70. Jim Crow laws dealt with:

A. minority rights

B. animal control

C. segregation

D. adoption

(Rigorous) (Skill 26.2)

71. The process of putting the features of the Earth onto a flat surface is called:

A. distortion

B. projection

C. cartography

D. illustration

(Easy) (Skill 26.4)

72. The name for one who makes maps is:

A. haberdasher

B. geographer

C. cartographer

D. demographer

Visual Art

(Average Rigor) (Skill 27.1)

73. Which of the following is a universal theme in art, music, theatre, and dance?

A. Man vs. Society

B. Man vs. Himself

C. Good vs. Evil

D. all of the above

(Rigorous) (Skill 27.1)

74. Which time period of arts do the themes of Roman mythology, Humanism, and Ancient legends reflect?

A. Renaissance Arts

B. Baroque Arts

C. Mesopotamian Arts

D. Middle Ages Arts

(Average Rigor) (Skill 27.5)

75. Aesthetic art principles vary from culture to culture. Which of the following is NOT an element of Eastern art?

A. more universal in nature

B. portray the human figure with symbolic meanings

C. convey a concise, detailed, and complicated view

D. use arbitrary choices of color

(Easy) (Skill 28.1)

76. The French horn, trumpet, trombone, and tuba are a part of which musical category?

A. string instruments

B. brass instruments

C. percussion instruments

D. wind instruments

(Rigorous) (Skill 28.4)

77. Most Western music is based on which type of rhythm?

A. additive

B. divisive

C. modern

D. classical

(Average Rigor) (Skill 28.5)

78. Which is probably the oldest form of music?

A. singing

B. drum-playing

C. harp-playing

D. dancing

(Easy)(Skill 29.2)

79. Which of the following is a style of dance?

A. creative

B. modern

C. ritual

D. all of the above

(Average Rigor) (Skill 29.5)

80. Drama was expressed in many Greek spiritual ceremonies. Name the two main forms of drama.

A. comedy and realism

B. tragedy and comedy

C. realism and drama

D. comedy and drama

(Rigorous) (Skill 29.5)

81. The history of theatre can be dated back to:

A. late sixth century in Greece.

B. early ninth century in Italy

C. early sixth century in Greece

D. late ninth century in Italy

Health, Fitness, and Consumer Science

(Average rigor) (Skill 30.3)

82. Social skills and values developed by physical activity include all of the following EXCEPT:

A. winning at all costs

B. making judgments in groups

C. communicating and cooperating

D. respecting rules and property

(Average rigor) (Skill 30.3)

83. Which type of physical education activity would most likely help students develop a sense of belonging?

A. solitary activities

B. teamwork activities

C. competitive activities

D. creative activities

(Rigorous) (Skill 30.4)

84. Water makes up _____ of the human body.

A. 25–30%

B. 55–75%

C. 10–25%

D. 75–88%

(Rigorous) (Skill 31.1)

85. The sequential development of: *stretching, bending, sitting, shaking, turning, rocking and swaying, swinging, twisting, dodging,* and *falling* is representative of which acquisition?

A. nonlocomotor skill acquisition

B. locomotor skill acquisition

C. manipulative skill acquisition

D. nonmanipulative skill acquisition

(Easy) (Skill 31.2)

86. Body awareness is a person's understanding of his or her own body parts and their capability of movement. Young children can gain the concept of body awareness through which of the following?

A. nodding their heads

B. wiggling their noses

C. snapping their fingers

D. all of the above

(Average Rigor) (Skill 31.2)

87. Early childhood students are expected to be able to complete tasks using basic locomotor skills. Which of the following would NOT be included?

A. walking

B. galloping

C. balancing

D. jogging

(Rigorous) (Skill 32.2)

88. The ability of muscle groups to contract and support a given amount of weight is called:

A. muscle strength

B. muscle endurance

C. cardiovascular strength

D. flexibility

(Rigorous) (Skill 33.1)

89. **Which of the following is a true statement?**

   A. Physical development does not influence social development.

   B. Social development does not influence physical development.

   C. Cognitive development does not influence social development.

   D. All domains of development (physical, social, and cognitive) are integrated and influence other domains.

(Rigorous) (Skill 33.1)

90. **Marcus is a first grade boy of good developmental attainment. His learning progress is good the first half of the year. He shows no indicators of emotional distress. After the holiday break, he returns much changed. He is quieter, sullen even, tending to play alone. He has moments of tearfulness, sometimes almost without cause. He avoids contact with adults as often as he can. Even play with his friends has become limited. He has episodes of wetting not seen before, and often wants to sleep in school. What approach is appropriate for this sudden change in behavior?**

   A. Give him some time to adjust. The holiday break was probably too much fun to come back to school from.

   B. Report this change immediately to administration. Do not call the parents until administration decides a course of action.

   C. Document his daily behavior carefully as soon as you notice such a change, and report to administration within the next month or so in a meeting.

   D. Make a courtesy call to the parents to let them know he is not acting like himself, being sure to tell them he is not making trouble for others.

ANSWER KEY

1. A	11. A	21. D	31. A	41. B	51. B	61. C	71. B	81. C
2. A	12. D	22. C	32. C	42. B	52. B	62. C	72. C	82. A
3. B	13. B	23. C	33. A	43. C	53. A	63. C	73. D	83. B
4. D	14. B	24. D	34. C	44. A	54. C	64. C	74. A	84. B
5. C	15. C	25. B	35. C	45. B	55. D	65. C	75. C	85. B
6. A	16. C	26. C	36. C	46. C	56. C	66. A	76. B	86. D
7. C	17. A	27. D	37. D	47. B	57. A	67. A	77. B	87. D
8. A	18. C	28. A	38. B	48. C	58. B	68. C	78. A	88. A
9. D	19. A	29. A	39. D	49. C	59. D	69. B	79. D	89. D
10. D	20. B	30. C	40. D	50. D	60. B	70. C	80. B	90. B

RIGOR TABLE

Rigor level	Questions
Easy 20%	2, 12, 15, 21, 23, 28, 31, 35, 42, 49, 55, 57, 58, 63, 72,76, 79,86
Average Rigor 40%	1, 3, 4, 8, 9, 14, 16, 17, 19, 22, 27, 29, 33, 34, 36, 40, 41, 43, 47, 48, 50, 53, 56, 60, 62, 64, 66, 69, 70, 73, 75, 78, 80, 82, 83, 87
Rigorous 40%	5, 6, 7, 10, 11, 13, 18, 20, 24, 25, 26, 30, 32, 37, 38, 39, 44, 45, 46, 51, 52, 54, 59, 61, 65, 67, 68, 71, 74, 77, 81, 84, 85, 88, 89, 90

Constructed Response Sample Question

Directions: In the next few pages, you will need to prepare a short essay. Write a response of about 300 words on the assigned topic. Your score will be based on these following factors:

- **Purpose:** You will be assessed on the extent to which you answer the question on each prompt. You must write your response so that it directly addresses what the prompt asks you to do.

- **Subject matter knowledge:** You will be assessed on the extent to which you demonstrate content knowledge.

- **Support:** You will be assessed on the extent to which you provide a coherent, fully supported response. Your response should provide evidence for any assertions you make.

Even though your writing ability will not be directly assessed, please take care to write an essay that is as free of grammatical errors as possible.

Reading, Language & Literature

The Writing Process

Using your knowledge of teaching English Composition at the middle school level, write a response in which you:

- Instruct students as to effective strategies for selecting an appropriate topic for a 400-word essay; and

- Relate this to three stages of composition: prewriting, drafting, and revision

Sample Strong Response

For this assignment my first question to students is: What is an experience, person, value, or interest in your life so important to you that you want others to know about it? This question dovetails with the writer's commandment: write about what you know. Of course I will emphasize this but I will also try to inspire students by insisting that writing can be more than an academic exercise. It is also a part of self-expression.

Before choosing a topic, however, one must tailor it to the length requirement of the assignment. For a 400-word personal experience essay, the general rule is: the more narrowly focused the topic, the better. This sounds quite vague, which is why the rule will be backed up with readings of brief personal essays appearing in our course textbook. In particular, essays that cover only a very short period of time will be read. Furthermore, students will be asked to judge the likely appropriateness of sample titles that indicate how much time an essay covers: "My Year as an Exchange Student in Germany" vs. "My Most Memorable Day in Berlin" are but two possible examples intended to drive home the point: in a 400-word essay, less is more.

In-class discussions and brief written assignments will follow from this, thereby giving students the opportunity to study how topics are introduced and developed by experienced writers. When techniques, structures, and strategies are recognized and subsequently described, students will be encouraged to imitate them—in their own words.

Much has been made, and rightly so, about the process of writing—especially regarding the stages of prewriting, drafting, and revision. Textbook material related to this will be introduced and thoroughly explained in class. However, I must take care to avoid making these processes seem too iron-clad or programmatic; indeed, "going too far" on this point can make writing seem terribly mechanical and boring. If a student wishes to stand on her head, speak into a tape recorder, transcribe the words, then turn them into a clear, concise, and grammatically correct essay, this would be—as far as I'm concerned—perfectly acceptable. Sometimes even revision isn't necessary, if only rarely. What counts is the final product.

CPSIA information can be obtained at www.ICGtesting.com
Printed in the USA
BVOW040120170113

310677BV00007B/6/P

9 781607 871569